NEWS

THE POLITICS OF ILLUSION

SIXTH EDITION

W. LANCE BENNETT
University of Washington

with Foreword by

DORIS GRABER
University of Illinois–Chicago

PEARSON
Longman

New York   San Francisco   Boston
London   Toronto   Sydney   Tokyo   Singapore   Madrid
Mexico City   Munich   Paris   Cape Town   Hong Kong   Montreal

Vice President and Publisher: Priscilla McGeehon
Executive Editor: Eric Stano
Senior Marketing Manager: Elizabeth Fogarty
Production Manager: Charles Annis
Supplements Editor: Kristi Olson
Project Coordination, Text Design, and Electronic Page Makeup: Shepherd, Inc.
Cover Designer/Manager: Wendy Ann Fredericks
Cover Photos: left: Steve Allen/Brand X Pictures/Getty Images, Inc., and right: AP/WideWorld Photos
Senior Manufacturing Buyer: Dennis J. Para
Printer and Binder: Phoenix Color Corp.
Cover Printer: Phoenix Color Corp.

Library of Congress Cataloging-in-Publication Data

Bennett, W. Lance.
   News : the politics of illusion / W. Lance Bennett ; with a foreword by Doris Graber.—
6th ed.
       p. cm. — (Longman classics in political science)
   Includes bibliographical references and index.
   ISBN 0-321-22466-3
   1. Journalism—Political aspects—United States. I. Title. II. Series.

   PN4888.P6B46 2005
   302.23'0973—dc22   2004050353

Please visit our website at http://www.ablongman.com/bennett

ISBN 0-321-22466-3

1 2 3 4 5 6 7 8 9 10—PBT—07 06 05 04

Contents

Foreword by Doris Graber   vii

Preface   xiv

Acknowledgments   xxv

CHAPTER 1   **THE NEWS ABOUT DEMOCRACY: AN INTRODUCTION
TO GOVERNING THE AMERICAN POLITICAL SYSTEM**   1

News and Democracy   *3*
Gatekeeping: Who and What Makes the News   *3*
News as a Democratic Information System   *5*
Politicians, Press, and the People   *6*
A Definition of News   *9*
The New Gatekeeping   *10*
How Mediated Government Works   *11*
   Case Study: *Governing with the News: Terror Comes
   to America*   *13*
The Fragile Link Between News and Democracy   *20*
Why Free Speech Cannot Guarantee Good Information   *20*
Soft News and the Turn Away from Politics   *22*
Myths About News Bias   *25*
What Kind of News Would Better Serve Democracy?   *30*
Notes   *31*

CHAPTER 2   **NEWS CONTENT: FOUR INFORMATION BIASES THAT MATTER**   36

A Different Kind of Bias   *37*
Four Information Biases That Matter: An Overview   *39*
Personalization   *40*
Dramatization   *40*
Fragmentation   *42*
The Authority-Disorder Bias   *42*
How Competing Journalists Write Such Similar Stories   *44*
   Case Study: *How George W. Bush Got His Swagger*   *47*
Four Information Biases in the News: An In-Depth Look   *51*
Bias as Part of the Political Information System   *67*
News Bias and Discouraged Citizens   *68*
Reform Anyone?   *69*
Notes   *70*

CHAPTER 3   **THE POLITICAL ECONOMY OF NEWS**   74

Corporate Profit Logic and News Content   *76*
   Case Study: *All the News That Fits (the Audience
      Demographics)*   *78*
The Political Economy of News   *82*
Economics Versus Democracy: Inside the News Business   *83*
The Media Monopoly: Arguments For and Against   *86*
The Telecommunications Act of 1996   *87*
Effects of the Media Monopoly: Five Information Trends   *89*
How Does Corporate Influence Operate?   *100*
News on the Internet: Perfecting the Commercialization of
   Information?   *101*
Commercialized Information and Citizen Confidence   *102*
Megatrends: Technology, Economics, and Social Change   *103*
Personalized Information and the Future of Democracy   *105*
Whither the Public Sphere?   *107*
Notes   *108*

CHAPTER 4   **HOW POLITICIANS MAKE THE NEWS**   113

The Politics of Illusion   *114*
The Sources of Political News   *116*
   Case Study: *Selling the Iraq War*   *119*
News Images as Strategic Political Communication   *122*

News Bias and Press-Government Relations   *124*
The Goals of Strategic Political Communication   *125*
Symbolic Politics and the Techniques of Image Making   *128*
News Management: From Staging to Damage Control   *131*
News Management Styles and the Modern Presidency   *136*
Press Relations: Feeding the Beast   *142*
Government and the Politics of Newsmaking   *145*
Notes   *147*

CHAPTER 5   HOW JOURNALISTS REPORT THE NEWS   151

Work Routines and Professional Norms   *153*
When Routines Produce High-Quality Reporting   *154*
    Case Study: *Top Ten Reasons the Press Took a Pass
    on the Iraq War   156*
How Reporting Practices Contribute to News Bias   *161*
Reporters and Officials: Cooperation and Control   *162*
The Insider Syndrome   *163*
Reporters as Members of News Organizations: Pressures to
    Standardize   *165*
Reporters as a Pack: Pressures to Agree   *168*
Feeding Frenzy: When the Pack Attacks   *170*
The Paradox of Organizational Routines   *173*
When Journalism Works   *174*
Democracy With or Without Citizens?   *176*
Notes   *177*

**CHAPTER 6   INSIDE THE PROFESSION: OBJECTIVITY AND POLITICAL
AUTHORITY   180**

Journalists and Their Profession   *181*
The Paradox of Objective Reporting   *181*
Defining Objectivity: Fairness, Balance, and Truth   *182*
The Origins of Professional Journalism Standards   *184*
    Case Study: *The Curious Origins of Objective Journalism   185*
Professional Practices and News Bias   *188*
The Adversarial Role of the Press   *188*
Standards of Decency and Good Taste   *193*
Documentary Reporting Practices   *196*
The Use of Stories as Standardized News Formats   *197*
Reporters as Generalists   *199*
The Practice of Editorial Review   *201*

Objectivity Reconsidered   *202*
Notes   *204*

CHAPTER 7   **THE NEWS AUDIENCE: INFORMATION PROCESSING AND PUBLIC OPINION**   208

News, Citizen Information, and Public Opinion   *210*
The Citizen's Dilemma: Who and What to Believe   *210*
Internet Versus Mass Media: Why Mainstream News
   Still Matters   *211*
Processing the News   *211*
Why People Prefer TV: Audio and Visual Information   *213*
News Frames and Political Learning   *213*
   Case Study: *National Attention Deficit Disorder?*   *214*
News and Personal Experience: What Gets Through   *217*
Uses and Gratifications: Other Reasons People Follow
   the News   *222*
The Future: Citizens, Information, and Politics   *232*
Notes   *233*

CHAPTER 8   **ALL THE NEWS THAT FITS DEMOCRACY: SOLUTIONS FOR CITIZENS, POLITICIANS, AND JOURNALISTS**   236

The News About the Private Media System   *237*
The News About Public Broadcasting   *238*
The News About Objective Journalism   *239*
News and Power in America: Ideal Versus Reality   *239*
Why the Myth of a Free Press Persists   *241*
Proposals for Citizens, Journalists, and Politicians   *243*
   Case Study: *Citizen Input from Interactive News to Desktop
      Democracy*   *254*
The Perils of Virtual Democracy   *259*
Corporate Social Responsibility: A Place to Start   *260*
Notes   *261*

Index   *263*

Foreword

Doris A. Graber, University of Illinois-Chicago

There is an old saying that "there's nothing new under the sun." Like most gems of folk wisdom, it holds true to a large extent for many realms of knowledge, including the study of politics. For instance, it is an old truth that communication is the glue that holds political communities together. Aristotle knew it and wrote extensively about it in 350 B.C. in Rhetoric where he discussed how verbal messages can spur public support for various political causes. Machiavelli knew it as well when he wrote *The Prince* many centuries later, in A.D. 1513, to instruct his sovereign in the art of using political messages to advance his policy objectives. The list goes on and on, studded with names of renowned thinkers from many countries and many periods in history.

To discuss what is, to plan what should be, and to carry out these plans collectively requires formulating comprehensible messages and transmitting them to others. Although scholars and lay people have known and used the power of communication for political purposes throughout human history, academicians have frequently ignored it in their analyses of how political systems function.

A New Approach to News/Politics Studies

Not so Professor W. Lance Bennett. He cast the spotlight on the major role played by news in the conduct of politics. He did it at a time when the study of news media impact had reached a particularly low ebb. This is why his book which you are about to read—*News: The Politics of Illusion*—was a milestone work when it was first published in 1983.

The study of mass media impact on politics had withered in the decades following World War II when several narrowly focused research projects suggested that media had little impact on voting behavior. The crowning blow to the desire to study media impact on politics was a book by sociologist Joseph Klapper. Based on a massive overview of an array of studies drawn from various social sciences, Klapper argued in *The Effects of Mass-Communication* (1960) that mass media impact was minimal. The message to social scientists was clear. There was no point in wasting their talents on researching a trivial phenomenon.

In 1980, I had defied the then prevalent wisdom by publishing a text on *Mass Media and American Politics.* The book was based on my belief that the finding that mass media effects were minimal was obviously proven wrong when one observed American politics in action. Researchers in the preceding decades had failed to detect news effects because they had focused on a very narrow realm of political phenomena—mainly changes in individuals' voting behavior. Other effects, such as learning new information, or becoming disgusted with politicians were ignored, as were mass media effects on the behavior of larger social units, such as interest groups or the national government. My book was designed to give political science students an overview of the many aspects of politics where news stories about politics had made an impact on political situations.

Three years later, in *News: The Politics of Illusion,* Lance Bennett took a different approach to cover virgin intellectual territory. Starting with the same premise that had guided my work—namely that news *about* politics does influence politics, Bennett's book focused on what this means for democratic governance in the United States. Rather than outlining how news affects all phases of government, including the formation of public opinion, Bennett asked a number of basic questions designed to evaluate the role of news media from a particular perspective. He wanted to know how well the news serves the needs of America's democracy. To find out, he asked questions such as, What determines which stories get published and which are ignored? He inquired whether news choices enhance or diminish the quality of grassroots and elite discourse about politics; and he gathered data to discover whose interests were served by what is published and whose interests were harmed.

His concerns led Bennett to explore aspects of news production and consumption that had hitherto received relatively little scholarly attention from the small corps of scholars interested in political communication research. For instance, Bennett focused on the human sources from whom journalists draw their information when they construct the news, rather than concentrating solely on how journalists select news topics and how they cover them.

For students of political news, looking at its sources means more than reporting what politicians do and what they advocate. It means scrutinizing the substance, format, and presentation styles used by politicians for messages about their activities. Message studies are crucial because most political news stories are based on what individual politicians disclose to journalists who interview them. In an age when the handling of media relations has moved from being an art, influenced primarily by the practitioners' native talents, to becoming a science practiced by well-trained professionals, scholars must examine how politicians frame political images. They must also study how politicians manage to get them published when so many competing individuals and groups try to get their messages into the news.

Here is where the book's subtitle—*The Politics of Illusion*—comes into play. Bennett demonstrates that political images reported in news stories are artfully constructed visions of a reality that may have very little relation to what an unbiased observer might see. As in the fable *The Emperor's New Clothes,* messages about a reality that benefits a particular politician's objectives often conceal the cynical, possibly ugly, reality that would debase these policies and actions.

Bennett has definite views about the issues that he raises. That forces you, the reader, to be more critical than would be necessary when faced with a more descriptive account. Instead of merely asking whether the facts that he reports are accurate, you also must assess whether the conclusions that he draws from these facts are warranted. You must consider his underlying assumptions carefully and determine whether or not you share them. That is a challenging task. I happen to agree with most of Professor Bennett's interpretations, but recognize, as does he, that different interpretations are possible.

To give just one example: Bennett believes that the news should educate the public about the most important political problems facing the nation. He judges media performance based on that assumption. But is public education really the media's mission? In the United States, news media are private business enterprises whose owners can claim that it is their prerogative to decide their business's mission within the limits set by public laws. There are no laws that command that the news must educate the public. In fact, the Constitution explicitly prohibits Congress from making laws about what news media may report. Even television stations, which are subject to licensing regulations, are only required to "serve the public interest, convenience, and necessity." Education is not mentioned.

Bennett also acknowledges that the likes and dislikes of news audiences play an important role in the news production system. Many Americans avoid programs designed to educate them about major political issues. They prefer light, entertaining news that allows them to relax, rather than news that forces them to think and likely worry about the affairs of the nation. Pursuing leisure in their off-hours is their right, of course.

If that is what media audiences want, shouldn't the news media be free to cater to their desires, rather than determining what audiences must learn to perform their civic duties and attempt to force such information down their throats? Besides, it is questionable that people will allow themselves to be force-fed "spinach news"—stories that are good for their civic health but only rarely palatable. When people have many other options for occupying their spare time, they are unlikely to attend to news that they find irrelevant or unpleasant.

Wrestling with questions about what information news stories ought to feature is difficult because it requires dealing with clashing values that most people hold. In this case, it is the shared desire of news professionals and their audiences to be free to choose the kind of information that they wish to publish or consume, and the shared belief that democratic government requires a well-informed citizenry capable of judging the soundness of public policies. The news media are the only institution that can supply most of the public with readily available information about evolving political events.

The Search for New Theories

Bennett's contributions to the study of politics go much further than pioneering a critical approach to the media/politics interplay. *News: The Politics of Illusion,* in its various editions, has been a showcase for a number of theories developed and tested by Professor Bennett. Again, one example must suffice. It is the theory of indexing. Not satisfied with merely reporting what kinds of subjects are covered or ignored by the news media and how stories are framed to feature the news from particular perspectives, Bennett has steadfastly explored the all-important "Why" questions. Why are particular stories selected and not others? Why are particular frames chosen? Why, for instance, are the government's foreign policy decisions reported uncritically much of the time, and why are controversies about the wisdom of these policies featured at other times? It took painstaking research and analysis of the circumstances surrounding each type of coverage to suggest indexing theories.

Bennett found that featuring controversy could not be attributed to deliberate or capricious choices by media personnel. Rather, journalists take their cues from the political environment. If credible spokespersons, such as members of Congress or established community leaders, challenge the policies, the news media will report their views. Absent such challenges, most news stories merely report the official version of the events, as told by spokespersons of the incumbent administration. This theory—that the reporting of conflicting views about public policies and events is indexed to the surfacing of conflict by widely-known, credible sources—has been tested repeatedly by Bennett as well as by many other scholars. So far, it has stood firm so that, like all theories supported by solid evidence, it can be used as a guide to predict what is likely to happen.

A Recipe for Scholarly Excellence

What goes into the making of a pioneering scholar like Lance Bennett? First, one needs to be exceptionally curious about one's world. Next, one needs to fall in love with the scholarly discipline that is most likely to provide answers to one's burning questions. Lance Bennett fell in love with the world of politics and how it is shaped by communication.

Bennett earned bachelors, master's and doctoral degrees from the University of California at Irvine and from Yale University. In each case, he received high honors for his work. The pattern of producing work of exceptional quality has continued ever since. Following his formal education, Bennett immediately embarked on a research and teaching career, most of it spent at the University of Washington.

By the time he wrote *News: The Politics of Illusion,* Bennett had already published numerous articles in scholarly journals as well as three important book-length studies dealing with the way people form their opinions about politics. An interest in public opinion leads quite naturally to an interest in the stream of information that people use to form their political views. Hence the publication of *News: The Politics of Illusion,* along with other articles that deal with media impact on diverse phases of politics.

Subsequently, Bennett focused his research and writing on elections, the showcase of democratic politics. In *The Governing Crisis: Media, Money and Marketing in American Elections* he analyzed the impact of news coverage, political spinning, and money on elections. His judgment, as the title indicates, is that the American system of governance is in bad shape due to flaws in the election message process. In fact, the political system is in crisis. Bennett's clarion call for election communication reform was followed by another ground-breaking work, *Democracy and the Marketplace of Ideas,* a comparison of political communication in Sweden and in the United States. Erik Åsard is the coauthor. The book points to major flaws in the message systems that link governments and people in modern democracies. The authors' detailed analysis of political malaise sparks numerous ideas about ways in which the marketplace of ideas that is such an essential part of democracies can be reinvigorated in the United States and elsewhere.

The Making of a Classic

After making so many contributions to the political communication field and receiving multiple prestigious professional awards, many scholars would be tempted to rest on their laurels and merely embellish their pioneering works. Not so Lance Bennett. He has resisted the temptation to ride on his well-earned reputation, and media/politics scholarship has benefited tremendously. *News: The Politics of Illusion,* now in its sixth edition, is testimony to the fact that it takes persistent scholarly efforts over many years to produce a masterpiece that is widely acknowledged as a classic—a work of exceptional excellence. The interplay of news and politics represents a moving target for analysts. Assessments of the status quo, therefore, must be updated frequently. Lance Bennett has risen to that challenge repeatedly in *News: The Politics of Illusion* and in other works.

Over the brief span of twenty-two years that separates the first and the sixth edition, much has remained stable in the interactions between the news and politics, but there have also been major changes. Technological advances have moved American society from the age of broadcasting to the age of narrow-casting. News producing and disseminating institutions and audiences for particular news offerings are vastly different from what they were in the 1980s. The Internet has become the giant gorilla that looms over the new political communication landscape, forcing many adjustments. A host of newly popular terms like *surfing* the Web and *digital divide* are obvious markers of the ever-changing media environment.

News: The Politics of Illusion is popular with students for many reasons, foremost among them are its realism and clear writing style. In each new edition, Bennett reports his own latest research of the shifting political communication scene as well as the findings of other scholars. Bennett always tells it like it is—news/politics dynamics are complex, messy, full of surprises, and contradictions. The many brief case studies interspersed throughout the book make it clear that Bennett's descriptions and analyses are based on events in the real world, rather than ideologically driven philosophizing. The author's conclusions are firm but never dogmatic.

News: The Politics of Illusion is written in smoothly flowing prose, free from the jargon that obscures so much social science writing. Bennett is critical but never carping, praising the news system for what he considers its many strengths and condemning it for what he perceives to be its shortcomings. Unlike many other critiques of the American media system, this is not a depressing book that leaves readers wishing they could escape because our political communication system is a hopeless mess that must be endured because there are no cures. Not surprisingly, when students tell me which of their textbooks they intend to sell at the end of a course and which they intend to keep, Bennett's book is invariably in the keep category.

Some Questions to Ponder

I am ending this foreword with a small sample of the kinds of fundamental questions that are worth pondering while you study this stimulating book. Such questions deserve your attention because they concern basic issues about what kind of media system will best serve the United States at this point in history.

1. Most scholars agree that media can and often do perform an important watchdog role when public officials misbehave or policies misfire. Should journalists' judgments about the merits of policies be given greater weight than the judgments of politicians on the assumption that journalists are wiser and more honest than politicians?

2. Can journalists who have never been elected by the public validly claim to be the voice of public opinion? Do they enjoy the kind of legitimacy that politicians have because they were chosen by citizens to represent them? Do politicians forfeit the right to speak for the public if they are self-seeking and deaf to the voices of their constituents?

3. Are average Americans profoundly disinterested in politics so that the spike in attention to news that routinely occurs during political crises is merely a fluke? Could it be that they are disinterested only when the substance of much of the news is not relevant to their lives because it is, indeed, trivial or because its relevance had been obscured by the pedantic way in which many political stories are told?

4. Are American journalists focusing their stories primarily on situations about which average citizens can do nothing while neglecting situations that provide opportunities for citizen participation? Unrest in Sri Lanka may have larger consequences for the lives of Southeast Asian people than the problems that Chicagoans face from arbitrary police arrest tactics in Chicago. Should one argue, therefore, that it is more important for Chicagoans to forego news from abroad so that they can learn about their local police problems when that information may arouse them to pressure effectively for reforms?

5. Journalists organize their work by identifying the places—called beats—where they expect to collect news routinely. In practice, this has led to a preponderance of news from selected government sources. Is such heavy emphasis on official sources sound? Would you change it if you could? If so, why and how?

6. In periods of history when people distrust politicians because of numerous well-publicized scandals, should they distrust the news that features politicians' pronouncements? If so, should journalists act as a buffer and scrutinize and interpret politicians' pronouncements, rather than leaving it to citizens to examine politicians' words and draw their own conclusions?

Such problem-laden questions deserve your attention, thought, and judgment because a dysfunctional news system harms all citizens since it cannot serve the functions that are essential for democratic governance. Bennett points out that the three pillars on which our current media system rests include the public on a par with politicians and journalists. Thus far the public's voice has been mostly inaudible and, therefore, far less influential than it might be. You and your fellow citizens of all ages can change that. Learning about how the news system really operates is the first step.

The following are leads to a few books whose authors have important things to say about our current news system and how it might be reformed. Read and ponder them as you delve more deeply into the mysteries of political communication in our time.

SUGGESTED READINGS

Alger, Dean. *Megamedia: How Giant Corporations Dominate Mass Media, Distort Competition, and Endanger Democracy.* Lanham, MD: Rowman and Littlefield, 1998.

Compaine, Benjamin, and Douglas Gomery. *Who Owns the Media: Competition and Concentration in the Media Industry,* 3rd ed. Mahwah, NJ: Erlbaum, 2000.

Cook, Timothy E. *Governing with the News: The News Media as a Political Institution.* Chicago: University of Chicago Press, 1998.

Glasser, Theodore L. ed. *The Idea of Public Journalism.* New York: Guilford Press, 1999.

Graber, Doris A. *Processing Politics: Learning from Television in the Internet Age.* Chicago: University of Chicago Press, 2001.

Norris, Pippa. *A Virtuous Circle: Political Communications in Postindustrial Societies.* Cambridge, U.K.: Cambridge University Press, 2000.

Page, Benjamin. *Who Deliberates? Mass Media in Modern Democracy?* Chicago: University of Chicago Press, 1996.

Patterson, Thomas E. *Out of Order.* New York: Alfred A. Knopf, 1993.

Schudson, Michael. *The Power of News.* Cambridge, MA: Harvard University Press, 1995.

Tillinghast, Charles H. *American Broadcast Regulation and the First Amendment.* Ames: Iowa State University Press, 2000.

Wilhoit, G. Cleveland, and David H. Weaver. *The American Journalist in the 1990's: U.S. News People at the End of an Era.* Mahwah, NJ: Lawrence Erlbaum, 1996.

Preface

This is a book about the importance of news for governing the American democracy. It is written from a citizen's perspective. When I began thinking about the political importance of the news media for the first edition of this book more than twenty years ago, I was able to draw on the great legacy of journalists and scholars from Walter Lippmann to Murray Edelman, among others, who recognized how the news links citizens to government and to the larger world of politics. Today, most scholars and journalists understand the importance of news in the political process. They also recognize the underlying problems with sensationalism, negativity, and citizen dissatisfaction that haunt our government, media, and politics. It may not be an exaggeration to say that the American news system today is approaching a crisis of confidence on the part of citizens. It may also be approaching a period of historic choices for journalists who recognize that many of their core professional practices are becoming hard to defend even within the profession.

It is hard to argue with the ideals of balance, fairness, and truth. These legacies of a century-old tradition of objective reporting continue to define what journalists do even as the term *objectivity* is being retired from the professional vocabulary as too hard to defend against shrill attacks of political bias. The irony is that the more reporters strive to achieve a neutral point of view on the public record, the more that record itself is constructed by political image consultants bent on using the news as a partisan publicity tool. The resulting sameness of the daily news, combined with the self-imposed inability of news organizations to report the larger context of many stories, frustrates journalists and publics alike. Add to this the economic squeeze of corporations draining the profits and, some would say, the civic vitality out of news organizations, and the argument for addressing the crisis of journalism becomes even more compelling. In short, this seems a good time to raise the question: What sort of news and public communication best suits democracy today? This question presents the challenge for the Sixth Edition of *News: The Politics of Illusion*.

With the crisis of confidence in journalism and politics as a backdrop, this edition of *News* continues to explore the book's enduring focus on the close relationship between the press and government. Since the early days of the last century, with the rise of modern public relations, many influential politicians and intellectuals have regarded news management as an essential means of engineering the public consent they believe necessary to govern in a democracy. Others continue to believe that the news should act as a people's forum and a watchdog that checks the power of the governors. Both views establish the centrality of news to governing, but one limits the role of the public in government and the other puts citizens at the center. This historic controversy about the ideals of public information in democracy is alive in every chapter of the sixth edition, illustrated with timely examples from the 2004 election and the war in Iraq.

THE POLITICS OF ILLUSION

Filled with growing volumes of political spin, sensation, and insider buzz, the daily news sometimes provides, but increasingly does not offer, citizens a solid basis for critical thinking or effective action. At least this is what a good deal of evidence presented in this book suggests. Perhaps it would be a happier prospect if the news were merely an entertainment medium—a sort of theater of the daily absurd hosted by friendly media personalities. Such a political information system would not be so worrisome if it did not have real effects on government decisions and people's lives. For example, was there a link between Iraq and the terrorist strikes of 9/11? The president and his chief advisors said so repeatedly in their news campaign in the fall of 2002 and winter of 2003 to go to war against Iraq. A majority of the American people believed them. The news media reported those administration claims largely for the record without challenging them. Today, many journalists lament that there were many areas on which the evidence (or lack of evidence) for those claims could have been challenged when it might have made a difference. Would Americans have gone to war just because Saddam Hussein was a very bad guy that the world was better off without? We can't know the answer to that question now, but we can imagine that it would have been a different kind of national decision—one that would have raised fewer doubts afterward. Why was it so difficult for major news organizations to raise such crucial questions prominently before the war? What was the effect on public confidence in the press and government of raising them after the war, when it was too late to take back a fateful decision? This edition of *News* explores these questions and offers a general perspective for understanding this recurring dilemma in the relationship between the press and the government.

Before going further, I should note that there are also many cases of good investigative reporting that continue to put the spotlight on serious issues, pressuring government and citizens to address them. For example, during the week in which I wrote this preface, the *New York Times Magazine* published a compelling report on the international sex trade in children. The investigation combined harrowing stories of children who survived their brutal ordeals and offered overviews of the magnitude of the problem, how the crime syndicates work, why this situation often slips under the radar of law enforcement agencies, and what governments can do about it. The trouble is that such reports are relatively few in number compared to daily formula news that depends overwhelmingly on government officials to define and solve problems. This book is concerned primarily with the daily flow of politics—the routine communication between public officials, reporters, and citizens on which the quality of government and democracy depend.

Despite (or perhaps because of) their simplicity and familiarity, news images of the political world can be tragically self-fulfilling. Scary images of distant enemies can promote war or military interventions that in retrospect seem dubious (Vietnam, for example, and Iraq, perhaps). Failure to report the full extent of real-life atrocities can delay timely actions. For example, underplaying news of the extent of Nazi genocide and death camps may have delayed the United States entry in World War II. Nearly a decade of reporting AIDS in the 1980s as primarily a disease affecting the gay community distracted public attention and delayed government policy. Dominant political images, when acted upon, can create a world in their own image—even when such a world did not exist to begin with. A media crime wave in the 1990s occurred while most categories of violent crimes were actually declining. Yet politicians sold tougher crime policies to frightened citizens. Thus the illusions of news become translated into political realities.

The pressing desire of news organizations to find dramatic twists to keep big stories going can blur the connection between news and underlying political realities. We see this in the feeding frenzies that swirl around sex and political scandal. This tendency applies to nearly everything that becomes big news. All too often, the issues that cannot be dramatized may not become news at all. Few news stories were more dramatic than those coming from inside tanks hurtling toward Baghdad as told by reporters who were embedded with the military they were covering. Is this how the press should cover a war—"embed" with the military? Many journalists initially hailed their invitation to join the invasion forces as really getting inside a big story. Later, many regretted having lost perspective on what was really happening on the larger scale.

Today, as the crisis of citizen confidence in news and government deepens, many journalists are beginning to raise questions about their own somewhat captive relationship—caught between corporate owners who demand more profitable content, and politicians who offer little that is not packaged for public consumption. This bind permits journalists to introduce little of their own material into news beyond setting an unhelpful tone of negativity and cynicism. Journalism critic Steven Brill summarized the growing conventional wisdom among many journalists in his list of the factors that increasingly force news organizations to substitute sensation for substance in political reporting:

- The speed of a twenty-four-hour "all news all the time" news cycle that never rests, and that continually demands fresh information and new angles on stories for those viewers who tune in sporadically for updates.
- The conflict between economizing in news production and satisfying the demand for more material is resolved by substituting controversy for reporting. Commentary programs draw audiences to rehash this impoverished news fare by substituting screaming for analysis.

- The proliferation of news options on cable and the Internet leave traditional organizations such as the original three television networks increasingly desperate as they watch their market shares shrink. Such competition pushes once-serious news organizations toward sensationalism.
- Reduced journalistic and audience attention spans leave little patience for lulls in stories, whether they be about sex or war.
- All of these trends are changing the journalistic standards for sourcing, with unattributed sources, rumor, and innuendo now carrying many stories. This, in turn, directly foists journalists themselves into the news, as they first provoke and then judge the significance of story developments.

WARNING: THE NEWS HAS NO DEMOCRATIC WARRANTY

It can be unsettling to take the news down from its democratic pedestal and see it as an often disjointed social, economic, and political production. Recognizing that there is no guarantee that the news will suit the needs of democracy raises a disturbing question: Why is there so little focused public (and formal government) debate aimed at defining and improving this most important product to better supply the information needs of democracy?

What little public debate there is may be focused on precisely the wrong issues: the alleged political biases of reporters and the call for more balanced or objective reporting. As noted in the first chapter of this book, there is no acceptable solution for the bias problem because different individuals expect the news to conform to their own political views. As noted earlier, the added irony is that ideological bias is one of the few information characteristics that people are generally aware of and able to correct on their own.

There is a ray of hope in the continuing signs that most people are disillusioned with both politics and the media these days. People clamor for more representation from government, for less filtered information, and for the right to have more say in political life. The big question—given the nature of the current information system and the personalization of demands from politics—is whether the public is truly capable of more direct democracy and whether they would like the results.

DEMOCRACY WITHOUT CITIZENS?

The case for more direct citizen control of government (even though digital technologies make it feasible, as noted in Chapter 8) is challenged by the low levels of information displayed by citizens on most issues. Many media scholars argue that an uninformed citizenry is hardly surprising given the fact that citizens are seldom portrayed as actively involved in the majority of issues in the news. The marginal roles for the public in media politics constitute what political communication scholar Robert Entman has called a "democracy without citizens." The marginalization of the public in the logic of political communication extends throughout all levels of government, at least down to the state level. Susan Herbst's interviews with journalists and political players (activists and legislative staffers) in the Illinois state capital revealed that the communication process was largely for the benefit of these inside players themselves and that they had only a dim sense of the existence of a larger public or what their information needs might be.

Why are citizens and their information needs often afterthoughts for politicians, journalists, and political insiders alike? There are many explanations, and we will examine them throughout the book. However, the overarching reason may be, as Thomas Patterson suggests, that journalists lack clearly defined political or democratic norms to help them decide how to cover the increasingly contrived and managed news performances of entrepreneurial politicians in an age in which political parties have less control over the ideas, electoral appeals, and general public performances of their members.

The fuzziness of news organizations' democratic responsibilities generally results in an emphasis on conflict over consensus during crucial stages of policy making, followed by an often cynical recap of policy results that emphasizes winners and losers, insider deals, and political calculations. The overall result, as indicated in research by Joseph Cappella and Kathleen Jamieson, is that disillusioned citizens end up tuning out large amounts of what they experience as political deception and negativity. In short, it may not be possible to govern without the news, but the evolution of the current news system may make such government less authoritative, less trusted, and less legitimate. For all their dysfunctional aspects, the news media—and the ways in which political actors and citizens use them—retain a major role in the American political system.

An irony of this information system that generally fails to inform is that the rise of the digital age makes it possible to imagine vibrant national discussions with direct communication to the centers of power, right from our desktops. The potential for computer voting seems far brighter than the antiquated procedures that plunged the 2000 Florida presidential contest into weeks of uncertainty, clouding the results of the national election in the minds of many citizens. Beyond national deliberations and electronic voting, the digital communication age offers possibilities for startling changes in citizen involvement. The truly revolutionary idea of trusting people with the responsibility for their own government has waited in the wings of American politics since Thomas Jefferson proposed it over 200 years ago. Now, with the advent of home computers, interactive video systems, and satellite-link technology, we have the capability to put direct democracy to a serious test. As noted in the concluding chapter of the book, however, this technology cannot simply be switched on with the expectation that people will use it wisely or that changes for the better will automatically follow. To the contrary, the dangers of extreme political fragmentation, individual isolation, and even more sophisticated political marketing urge us to think seriously about how we should use political information in the digital age.

Meaningful change requires people to better understand some of the underlying defects in the current communication system. In particular, change requires thinking more critically about how to inform people in ways that bring them together around programs of political action that might actually solve problems both in private life and in society. We will return to consider the possibilities for electronic democracy and, more generally, for better political communication, at the close of the book. If such active reforms are possible, however, it is important to build a basis for thinking sensibly about how to implement them. Above all, a better understanding of how the communication system operates might enable journalism schools, news organizations, government representatives, and citizens themselves to convert disillusionment into constructive responses. All of which returns us to the central concern of this book: understanding the continual interplay of news and politics.

A NOTE TO THE READER

- Why is a society that is so rich in information populated with people who are so confused about and alienated from politics?
- Is it possible or even desirable for journalism to be objective as it is practiced in America?
- Is the news mainly a propaganda forum for organized partisan factions? Is it mainly a profitable product for the companies that sell it? Or is it a valuable citizen resource?

These are just a few of the questions you will encounter in this book. In the final analysis, it is up to you to draw conclusions. The goal of this book is to challenge comfortable myths by introducing evidence that invites new ways of thinking about our political information system. In order to stimulate your thinking, the book provides a perspective that is critical of the news—a perspective intended to provoke thought and reaction. I have chosen to present a broad, alternative point of view for a simple reason: There would be little gained by going over the story of the free press in America for yet another time. As an American citizen, you already know by heart the saga of a free press and a free people. True, you may have forgotten a few characters or some of the episodes. Nevertheless, memorizing those missing facts once again would not change the plot about how the enduring struggle for freedom of speech and information has created the foundation for democracy in America. Because you know this story already, you should use it in thinking about the argument in this book. Don't feel that you must accept either the story of the free press or the perspective in this book in its entirety. Use the two perspectives to challenge each other and to help you draw your own conclusions. After all, the capacity to think independently, without fear or insecurity, is the foundation on which our political freedom rests.

CHAPTER OVERVIEW AND NEW FEATURES

The thing that makes each edition of this book such a pleasure to write is that society, media, and democracy are in continual change. Thinking about these changes and how they affect our political affairs offers the motivation to continue this project and to bring new ideas to these pages. In keeping with the spirit that unites all the editions of *News,* this sixth edition continues to follow the evolution of news, both as a social and economic product and as a key to understanding the American political process. The core organizing theme of how the press, public, and politicians interact in a (not always functional) political system is developed and integrated even more fully than in the past. Like the previous one, this edition also represents a sweeping revision, reflecting the important changes that have redefined the news business, news audiences, and the turbulence of public life in recent years. The topical organization of the book remains close to the previous edition, with several chapters gaining new features and perspectives.

Chapter 1 introduces the American political information system and suggests that news is a constantly changing and evolving social construction built daily through the interactions of journalists, politicians, and citizen-consumers. The first chapter in this edition provides an even better taste of the entire book. I have continued to clarify and expand the simple model of why the institution of the press, despite coming under fire from publics and politicians, remains a key to understanding politics and governance in the United States. In addition, there is a new opening discussion of why different political actors, from presidents and members of Congress to interest groups and activists, often regard making and managing the news as central to their political success. The case study on government-press relations following the events of September 11, 2001 now continues through the fall and capture of Saddam Hussein in the Iraq War, offering some vivid examples of how news, and the struggle to define it, set the tone for democracy as we know it. The opening chapter also introduces a number of basic press-politics concepts, such as gatekeeping, and explores how they work in the context of changing media and political environments.

Chapter 2 examines the underlying information biases of this news system from the standpoint of citizens interested in participating in the political process. This edition offers an even sharper explanation of why the popular belief in the ideological bias of news reporting is off the mark. This conventional wisdom about a liberal press distracts attention from other, more serious information biases in the news system that frustrate effective citizen engagement in political life. The chapter explains these biases with contemporary illustrations aimed at providing students with examples that they can use in class discussions and analyses of their own.

Chapter 3 on the political economy of news was added two editions ago to better explain the business and economic underpinnings of news as a commercial product. The goal of this chapter is to explain the economic, political, social, and technological forces that affect the production and consumption of news. The emphasis is on the business practices that create the information biases described in Chapter 2. This edition continues to track the merger mania of recent years and explores how the quest for profits has undermined the social responsibility of news organizations.

The middle chapters of the book take an in-depth look at the press-politics interactions that produce the news. Chapter 4, 5, and 6 continue to dissect the ways in which politicians and the press alternately cooperate and compete in the odd symbiotic relationship that produces the daily news.

Chapter 4 shows how political actors attempt to control news content. The focus here, as in past editions is to show how news management strategies work, and how they can go awry. Those loyal adopters of the book who continue to use the "textbook case" of Reagan administration news management in their teaching can now find that material incorporated in the discussion of the Reagan presidential news style. A new case study of George W. Bush's Iraq War news management looks at the Hollywood production behind his iconic "Top Gun" landing on the aircraft carrier *Abraham Lincoln*.

Chapter 5 explains how the everyday organizational routines and practices of journalism contribute to the information biases of the news. This look inside news organizations retains much of its familiar focus on the basic operations of American journalism, with new material on digital media and the impact of corporate pressures in the newsroom. A new case study has been added to this chapter explaining why mainstream press reporting on the buildup to the Iraq War raised so few questions about the administration case for the invasion.

Chapter 6 deepens our understanding of the press system by examining how the journalism profession has evolved in the United States with fragile connections to the needs of democracy. A close look at the professional norm of objectivity (as defined by fairness, accuracy, balance, and detached, fact-based reporting) shows how this seemingly noble standard, as it is applied, actually contributes to the information problems with the news. Since Chapter 6 is largely historical in nature, the discussion of the origins of professional journalism norms and practices has not been changed much from the last edition. I have, however, expanded the discussion of the strains on journalism norms and values created by sensationalism and the emphasis on sex, violence, and mayhem in the news.

Chapter 7 addresses the question of how citizens process the political information that comes at them through the news media. Our analysis of citizen information processing looks at how people react to the news produced by the press-politics system detailed in Chapters 3 through 6. This edition maintains the emphasis on features of news reports that either enhance or inhibit citizen engagement. New material has been added to help explain why more people are disconnecting from news and public life in America. The problems of youth engagement continue to be featured prominently in this edition, along with ideas about how digital interactive media might be used to transmit news and political action pathways that might bring young citizens back into political life. Updates have been added to features on global issue activism and the uses (and implications) of Web information channels that bypass traditional news. A new case study in this chapter explores the "national attention deficit disorder" with a review of research on how people follow politics and what they learn from sources as diverse as Comedy Central's *The Daily Show* and *The News Hour* on PBS.

Chapter 8 concludes the book with a discussion of how politicians, press, and citizens can each act to improve the quality of our public communication. Core concepts from the book are combined to show how citizens can better "decode" the news that they consume in order to get more useful perspectives from it. This edition expands the discussion of what journalists can do to work more effectively within the constraints of profit-driven news organizations to report news that is more useful to citizens. I also have expanded the discussion of government policies that can increase the diversity and depth of the political communication that travels over the public airwaves. I have also expanded the case study on new communication technologies that hold promise for greater citizen engagement. The conclusion takes a new look at the growing social movement for corporate media responsibility in providing communication that addresses citizens and enhances public life.

KEY ORGANIZING THEMES

Several broad themes are woven throughout the book to address important issues in the relations among press, political actors, and the people. New examples are included throughout to illustrate these themes, along with new developments in the field of political communication.

How strategic communication works (and why it is essential for governing today). Political messages are increasingly defined by communication professionals to shape news images. The book explains political market research techniques that are used to target audiences and to design and deliver messages to them. Instead of richer political debate supported by powerful communication technologies, the trend is to fit images to prevailing moods and conventional wisdoms. Policy debates within political institutions typically echo the rhetoric of these issue campaigns, making the news an echo chamber for partisan information campaigns more than a perspective on the underlying issues.

How the press works. In order to understand why news organizations report so much packaged communication, it is essential to get inside the profession. This book does that with a view to understanding why the norms adopted by professional journalists often prevent them from reporting what they know or suspect about the stories behind the stories.

The limits of media manipulation. It is important to recognize the limits on the degree to which the news and public opinion can be manipulated. Communication campaigns may run into forces in the media and society that make effective news management difficult. For example, the scandal *royal* involving Bill Clinton and Monica Lewinsky (culminating in the impeachment trial of 1999) illustrates the ability of the public to reach impressively independent judgments about important issues—despite the news making efforts of a special prosecutor and a majority opposition party in Congress. People may be less swayed by the news when particular issues invade daily life experience. Subjects such as sexual morals, abortion, racial discrimination, sexual harassment, environmental crises, and AIDS have all become the subjects of movies, talk shows, and conversations with friends. These personal experience issues may break down the traditional news gatekeeping process and provide other foundations for public opinion.

How the news defines citizenship. News images offer implicit definitions of who participates in American politics and who counts in society. This construction of citizenship is crucial for understanding popular attitudes about government and politics today, as well as levels of citizen engagement and information.

Youth civic disengagement and information habits. The book explores new perspectives on the fragmentation of the public from an information standpoint, with continuing emphasis on why young citizens increasingly reject mainstream news sources and the politics they portray. Chapter 7 expands the focus on political information processing to examine the problems of young people disconnecting from the information process altogether. This chapter examines how the news fails to address younger audiences, while pointing to positive developments in interactive media that may help with these problems.

Political information processing and new information technologies. It is important to recognize that new technologies contain the potential to address some of the problems with citizen disengagement and political disconnection. We need to understand what the information processing capabilities of people are and what motivates them to acquire and apply new ideas and information. While the Internet is clearly attractive to young citizens as a primary information source, the fragmentation of audiences into small communication networks and virtual communities presents challenges to forming larger publics and joining together in broad public action.

Corporate profit imperatives in the news room. It was hard to imagine that profit pressures could continue to grow and dominate journalistic decisions beyond the levels documented in the last edition. Yet the profit ride of the 1990s has been compounded by the economic recession of the new millennium, creating a dynamic that further threatens news quality. This edition continues to trace the effects of this corporate-side profit logic through the news industry and details how the news itself is being redefined by it.

The fragmentation of the news audience. With the proliferation of cable, Internet information providers, and the marketing of newspapers and periodicals to more specific demographic niches, the traditional conceptions of mass communication have diminishing capacity to describe the distribution of information and the ways people engage with politics. Perhaps the most fascinating and ironic aspect of these changes is that the proliferation of information outlets does not mean that political information itself has become richer or more diverse. In many respects, similar political information continues to flow through most of these increasingly personalized communication channels. Explanations for the proliferation of channels and standardization of information range from the consolidation of the media and information markets described in Chapter 3 to the rise of professional media consultants and communication strategists.

The greater play given to these ideas in this edition and the last should help the reader understand why this exhilarating time of change in technologies and markets does not automatically result in more meaningful citizen information choices or in much greater diversity of the political content being communicated.

The future of news. Throughout the book, I also examine the responses of journalists and news organizations to the loss of audiences and diminished public confidence in the news itself. Important debates about, and experiments with, civic journalism and other news formats are examined here. The closing case study in Chapter 8 also looks at new interactive news formats that bring citizens, journalists, and politicians into more direct communication about important issues. The recent emergence of a citizen's movement for media reform is an interesting development. The prospects for citizen-driven information systems are both intriguing and unsettling in their implication for political communication as we currently know it.

The sixth edition continues to track the often-dizzying pace of change in media and political communication with a number of the following special features.

SPECIFIC FEATURES DESIGNED TO HELP UNDERSTAND THE CHANGING COMMUNICATIONS ENVIRONMENT

- Why news is essential for governing. Even stronger emphasis throughout on how political actors use the news and why they must.
- Focus citizen: What is the citizen's role in democracy today? How is citizenship defined by news images and political communication trategies?
- 9/11 and the Iraq War: A case study and extensive examples of the press-politics of terrorism. The discussion has been expanded to follow developments through the Iraq War.
- The new gatekeeping: A discussion of how news content is selected and how the rules have changed.
- How high-quality news can succeed with audiences and corporate owners.

- A richly illustrated political economy of the news business, including:
  - Overview of mergers and global media corporations
  - Importance of the Telecommunications Act of 1996 and the general climate of deregulation
  - Examples of how these trends affect news content and audience engagement
  - How tabloid journalism has entered more mainstream news organizations, with related trends in infotainment, soft news, news magazines, and reality TV
- How technologies of news production and transmission shape program content, including:
  - Importance of the twenty-four-hour news cycle
  - How breaking news on the Internet can pressure mainstream organizations to report more rumor and fewer reliably sourced stories
- Updates in the popular chapter on news biases, including a detailed analysis of George W. Bush's "Top Gun" aircraft carrier landing.
- Assessing the current national news culture:
  - How core norms of the journalism profession (such as the commitment to objectivity) have adjusted to declining public trust and increased levels of cynicism about politics
  - Shifting patterns of political coverage and content
  - Changing audience habits and interests
- Attention to positive signs of change:
  - Evaluation of efforts by journalists to counter audience erosion and declining public confidence
  - Civic journalism projects
  - Experiments by some local TV stations to balance, and in some cases replace, mayhem with more serious news
- Citizen information habits:
  - New research on citizen engagement (and disengagement) with the news
  - New coverage of interactive information formats using digital media
- Focus on the Internet:
  - Evaluation of information sources on the Internet
  - Explanation of generational differences in the use of Internet vs. other media
  - The author's Web sites located at **www.ablongman.com/bennett** (or at **www.faculty.washington.edu/bennett/**) and **www.engagedcitizen.org** provide access to many news organizations, professional journalism and political communication associations, liberal and conservative news criticism sites, government information databases, and discussions of new technologies that are putting citizens at the center of the news picture.

Acknowledgments

Each edition of *News* reminds me that this is still a work in progress. The focus on press, citizens, public officials, and democracy keeps me mindful of historic changes and contemporary events. Each time I do a revision, I also realize that I have learned new things about citizenship, democracy, and the importance of communication in the governing process. I owe much of my continuing engagement with these topics to the many colleagues with whom I have discussed these subjects over the years. Not all of those who have commented and reacted to the ideas in this book agree with my views and interpretations, but their lively engagement has stimulated my thinking and helped me reach new insights about a rich and complex subject.

It is not possible to acknowledge all the people who have influenced my thinking, but I am particularly indebted to Regina Lawrence, Tim Cook, Marie Danziger, B. J. Bullert, Doris Graber, Bruce Bimber, William Gamson, Jay Blumler, Steve Livingston, Jerry Manheim, Bruce Williams, Ann Crigler, Marion Just, Michael Delli Carpini, Susan Herbst, Bob McChesney, Valerie Hunt, John Zaller, Marvin Kalb, Jerry Baldasty, David Domke, Michael McCann, Bill Haltom, Phil Noble, Bob Entman, Michael Schudson, Dan Hallin, Kathleen Jamieson, David Altheide, Henry Kenski, Lloyd Jansen, Adam Simon, Thomas Patterson, Shanto Iyengar, and Sabine Lang. I am also grateful to the students who work with me and keep my thinking fresh. The enduring influence of Murray Edelman lives on in these pages.

I also thank the anonymous reviewers who once again struck the right balance between preserving the spirit of the book and suggesting how to keep it current with the rapidly changing worlds of media and politics. Their names, revealed to me only now, are Theresa Capelos, State University of New York, Stony Brook; Jason Barabas, Southern Illinois State University; and Frauke Schnell, West Chester University. The reviews were both supportive and most helpful.

The continuing interest of Longman through the years of corporate mergers that have redefined today's media business is also appreciated. Eric Stano has my gratitude for recognizing this book in its last edition as one of Longman's greatest hits. And his involvement in this edition was all that a writer could ask: reading chapters, asking good questions, and encouraging me to tell it like it is.

This book is dedicated to my father who taught me to work hard and think independently: Walter D. Bennett (1920–2003).

Chapter 1

The News About Democracy: An Introduction to Governing the American Political System

. . . a journalist's job is to sift the facts from the allegations, and to provide citizens with accurate and reliable information upon which they can self govern. That process is at risk. . . . People are already drifting away from journalism as it has moved increasingly toward being a forum for conflict. . . . This kind of journalism appeals to extremes, but it is a less reliable, less efficient way for citizens to learn and navigate their world.
Tom Rosenstiel and Bill Kovach

Does the news matter? Consider the case of the Iraq War. Somehow it all began with 9/11, when airliners full of passengers were hijacked and flown into the World Trade Center towers and the Pentagon. But what was the connection? Long after the war failed its advertised image of an easy victory with an open-armed welcome from liberated Iraqi citizens, Americans retained only dim understandings about what happened and why. How was it, for example, that the invasion and occupation of Iraq became part of the war on terror? There were early news reports that the Central Intelligence Agency (CIA) had found no clear link between Saddam Hussein and the al Qaeda network that orchestrated the events of 9/11. To the contrary, Osama bin Laden had branded Saddam's secular regime a threat to Islamic fundamentalism. Far more evidence linked al Qaeda with backers in Saudi Arabia.[1] But the war was on, and the news was filled with breathless battlefield accounts by reporters embedded in military units. Images of Saddam's statue being toppled in Baghdad overshadowed reports that the Bush administration had distorted the facts in making its case to the American people.

The few news stories that challenged Saddam's connection to the terrorist attacks of 9/11 and questioned claims that he was trying to obtain nuclear weapons could not compete for public attention with the daily administration spin. On May 1, 2003, President George W. Bush made his dramatic tailhook landing on the aircraft carrier *Abraham Lincoln.* That "top gun" moment was a media event supreme—designed to capture huge news audiences for the president's ringing sound bite: "The battle of Iraq is one victory in a war on terror that began on September 11, 2001 and still goes on."[2]

Months later, the battle was still going on in Iraq. The triumphal media images became threatened by a guerilla war that soon took more American lives than the invasion itself. In response, the administration stepped up its news management operation. Vice President Dick Cheney dismissed charges that the administration had distorted the facts as "second guessing" by critics. He renewed the claim that "Iraq has become the central front on the war against terror."[3] Whatever the facts or the justification for the war, one thing had become clear afterward: the battle for control of news images was the most important factor in shaping public support both for the war and for the Bush administration's capacity to govern effectively.

Who and what were the American people to believe? Thanks to administration domination of the news, a majority of 57 percent of Americans continued to believe—long after facts to the contrary had come out—that Iraq had something to do with the events of 9/11, either through direct involvement by Saddam Hussein or through indirect assistance to al Qaeda terrorists.[4] Fully 69 percent felt that an Iraq connection to 9/11 was at least somewhat likely. And close to a majority (47 percent) substantially overestimated levels of European public support for the U.S. invasion. In fact, popular support among all major U.S. allies was extremely low—even in Britain, which participated in the invasion and occupation. Fully 24 percent of those polled in the fall of 2003 believed that weapons of mass destruction had been found in Iraq (they hadn't).

The case study in Chapter 5 explains why the administration was able to dominate the news and put its spin on so many of the facts and issues that were important to deciding and supporting a critical decision to go to war. The case study in Chapter 7 explores how news is consumed by citizens with low political attention levels. When news matters little, from the citizen's point of view, little effort may be made to critically evaluate it. Factual misperceptions also reflect the news sources that people rely on for their information. For example, 80 percent of the viewers of FOX news had one or more of the above misperceptions about the war, while only 23 percent of Public Broadcasting Service (PBS) and National Public Radio (NPR) audiences were similarly mistaken. Other mainstream news sources misinformed people at rates closer to FOX than NPR, with CBS at 71 percent, ABC at 61 percent, NBC at 55 percent, CNN at 55 percent, and the average of print news sources had a reader misperception rate of 47 percent.[5] One view of this picture is that even the best news sources left large numbers of people misinformed. Another interpretation is that the more mainstream or popular the news source, the greater the audience illusion about what the government was doing. The point here is not that journalists were making up facts, but that most news organizations were simply more likely to report what came from administration sources over available accounts to the contrary. This book explores how this news process works and why it matters.

NEWS AND DEMOCRACY

As the opening quote in this chapter indicates, there are reasons to be dissatisfied with the news these days. Yet news remains the primary source of information about society, politics, and government. Information is so basic to democratic government that it is easy to take for granted. Yet without a free flow of accurate, timely, and useful information, people cannot participate effectively. Think of some of the ways in which public information affects the quality of government and our public lives:

- Information about what government and interest groups are doing affects citizen understanding and involvement.
- Government policies are generally more effective and legitimate when based on informed public debate.
- Most government officials and interest groups have strategies aimed at shaping public debate in the news.
- Campaigning in the news for public support goes on during elections and in governing after elected officials take office.
- Our sense of where we fit into society and politics comes from seeing how people like us are represented in the news.

In addition to the importance of reliable information for everyday politics, the quality of information is also essential to our safety and peace of mind during times of crisis. For example, following the terrible events of 9/11, Americans followed the news for information about future threats, and for reports on the progress of wars in Afghanistan and Iraq. The case study later in this chapter illustrates how the press and government clashed in shaping that information.

With the growing popularity of the Internet and World Wide Web, there are new ways for people to create and exchange information. This so-called information revolution may well change how people learn about and engage with politics. For now, the communication format that remains most common for understanding what is happening in the world is NEWS. The core question explored in this book is: *How well does the news, as the core of the national political information system, serve the needs of democracy?* In exploring this question, we examine how various political actors—from presidents and members of Congress to interest organizations and citizen-activists—try to get their messages into the news. Understanding how politics and government work requires understanding who makes the news, who does not, and how that news affects public opinion and the resolution of issues and events.

GATEKEEPING: WHO AND WHAT MAKES THE NEWS

Evaluating the impact of news on the quality of democracy is challenging because both democracy and news are ever-changing. However, one thing remains constant: each news story contains only some of the voices, facts, and organizing ideas that could have been included. *Gatekeeping* is a term often used to refer to *whose voices and what messages get into the news.* Journalists and, more importantly, their news organizations make choices about what to cover and how to report it. Some stories feature statements by ordinary citizen-activists and interest organizations, while other news reports leave most of the talking to government officials. Gatekeeping decisions are made in part by individual journalists, but they are also shaped by editors and executives in news organizations. Those organizations, in turn, are influenced by economic pressures, audience reactions, and a host of other considerations that all go into the construction of the daily news.

In an ideal world, journalists would recognize only the most important trends and developments and find the sources who represent the most insightful and diverse points of view. The ideal news sources would try to engage their opponents in convincing debate aimed at helping the public decide what is the best course of action. And the ideal public would want to take the time to learn about different approaches to important social issues. In the real world, many factors work against these ideals of democracy, from business pressures in news organizations, to lazy citizens, to deceptive politicians.

For all of its flaws, the American information system can produce impressive levels of good information and public deliberation, leading publics and policymakers to fairly sensitive understandings about some complex social problems.[6] The news system can also produce virtual blackouts of information about important social problems and public policies or cover them from a very narrow range of viewpoints. Issues that tend to be covered in depth and detail tend to be personal matters over which there is considerable public conflict. Sociologist William Gamson cites abortion as an issue that has attained impressive levels of information quality and diversity of public viewpoints, resulting in sophisticated public opinion responses to complex policy questions.[7] Abortion is also one of those political issues that has spilled outside the bounds of news, becoming the subject of movies and television programs, church sermons, talk shows, and conversations among friends. On many other issues, however, the public is often in the dark. Gamson cites a continuum of other issues that tend to be less personally engaging than abortion. Part of what makes the difference between high- and low-citizen involvement for Gamson is whether the news reports grassroots citizen action where it actually exists in society, a factor that encourages other citizens to get involved by seeing an issue from the standpoint of ordinary people who are concerned about it.[8]

The presence or absence of citizen voices depends largely on whether journalists find influential government officials or established interest groups who already endorse those grassroots views. I have used the term *indexing* to refer to the journalistic practice of opening or closing the news gates to citizen-activists (and more generally, a broader range of views) according to levels of conflict among public officials and established interests involved in making decisions about an issue. When open conflict breaks out among key decision makers (e.g., Congress and the president on energy policy), the news gates will open to broader social voices, from grassroots activists to interest organizations.[9]

However, when breaking events, crises, or dramatic scandals occur, more fluid news patterns can develop. For example, in the days immediately following 9/11, the news replayed the images of a plane hitting the World Trade Center, the towers collapsing, brave rescue workers trying to save lives, and a nation grieving. In such rare moments, the news becomes a collective screen on which grand images of fear, loss, grief, patriotism, and hope are projected. News organizations produced dramatic stories of a people under siege, responding bravely, and rising from the ashes to deal with the terrorist challenge. Within days, however, the government began to act decisively in waging war and passing new domestic security laws, and the news returned to its familiar focus on government. Whether setting the tone for routine politics or for crisis, the news is the core of our political information system. This book explores how that system works.

NEWS AS A DEMOCRATIC INFORMATION SYSTEM

Political communication scholar Bruce Bimber makes a bold assertion about power in American politics: "I claim that democratic power in the U.S. tends to be biased toward those with the best command of political information."[10] Bimber follows this claim by tracing the development of American democracy from *The Federalist* to the present day in terms of information regimes. The first great expansion of democratic participation came with the rise of a national mail system, perhaps making the U.S. Post Office the most important institution for expanding democracy in the early American republic. What did the post office have to do with public information, much less with news? Consider one fact: the post office carried more newspapers than personal correspondence in its early years (the 1830s), making it possible for ordinary people to share information about the important issues facing the nation and enabling the rise of a Populist majority on the frontier who rallied around Andrew Jackson.[11]

More recently (since the 1930s), American democracy has evolved through the information regime of the mass media, which is now in its late stages. Technologies such as broadcast television and satellite communication enabled Americans to share common experiences that affected the entire nation. Politicians in the mass media age became experts at "going public" by using the media to deliver messages directly to large audiences.[12] In the prime of this information regime, from roughly 1950–1970, American democracy was characterized by strong parties, loyal citizens, relatively high levels of voting, and a capacity to handle great social strains, such as the civil rights upheavals and the Vietnam War (generally), within the bounds of stable political institutions.

Toward the end of the mass media information regime (a time we are living in at present), American democracy has become less associated with broadly supported political parties and civic-minded citizens and has been perceived often as a media game for well-financed politicians and organized interests serving up the daily political spin of hired communication professionals. Many observers now worry about civic disengagement (particularly among young citizens) and growing cynicism about government and the reliability of political information.

As the mass media information regime begins to erode, we are at the dawn of an Internet age (more broadly, a digital, multichannel age) in which people are far less likely than in the past to watch the same news programs or to buy a newspaper for its political content instead of lifestyle features such as movies and fashion. Like the information regimes that came before, the digital age presents new challenges and possibilities for the future of democracy. Observers of the current scene worry that there are now so many media channels that individuals may become informed about just the issues and the perspectives that suit their personal lifestyles. Can a public with so many exclusive, personalized media niches share a common purpose?[13] Of course, threats and fears may bring people together, as happened after the attacks of 9/11. But fateful decisions such as going to war and rewriting civil liberty protections were then promoted to a fearful public with little critical examination in the news, as explained in the case studies in Chapters 4 and 5.

A period of great change, such as the one we are currently experiencing, contains many new developments. For example, reliance on Internet information channels boomed following the terrorist attacks of 9/11, with an average of 11.7 million Americans visiting online information services each day during the week following the tragedy, compared with 6 million per day during the previous week.[14] In the 2004 presidential contest, Democratic candidate Howard Dean learned how to use the Internet to communicate with grassroots supporters and raise record contributions online. This ability to open digital communication channels through *micro media* (e.g., e-mail) and *middle media* (e.g., Web logs such as **http://www.blogforamerica.com** and automated meeting sites such as **http://www.meetup.com**) took the Dean campaign from obscurity to a leading position that also commanded the lead in mass media news coverage. Unfortunately, the Dean campaign failed to manage the press as effectively as its direct communications with supporters, and died as quickly as it emerged.

As the rise and fall of Howard Dean indicates, the mass media age may be nearing its end, but it is far from over. Most Americans also returned to traditional media such as the television networks following the attacks on America in September of 2001, and those networks devoted more time to live event coverage than at any time in their histories. All of this suggests that as much as the news and democracy are changing, there is much that remains familiar from the past. The challenge of this book is to explain how information and democracy work today, with a grasp of the past and an eye to the future.

POLITICIANS, PRESS, AND THE PEOPLE

In order to think about how the news system affects the performance of democracy, we will take a behind-the-scenes tour of communication in American politics, from the newsroom, to the war room, to the living room. From the start, we find that the three major actors in the news process—politicians, journalists, and the public—occupy quite different positions in both the political system and the communication system. Despite the vast differences in these actors' political worlds, each world contributes important elements to the construction of what we call news. Consider, briefly, the news politics of politicians, journalists, and the public.

Politicians and Other Political Actors

From the standpoint of politicians and the businesses and interest organizations that largely define politics in America, it has long been clear that power and influence depend on the control and strategic use of information. Despite growing public skepticism, news-making continues to be the most important way to get issues on the public agenda. The idea of *agenda setting* involves using the news to influence what the public regards as important for them to think about in society and politics.[15] Because of the importance of newsmaking for public relations, politicians from presidents and members of Congress to abortion activists, environmentalists, and antitax groups, all have learned to *go public* by finding ways to take their political messages into the news.[16] An irony of mediated politics is that being well informed about the issues on the public agenda often means taking cues from familiar sources using the news to *frame* stories around their partisan viewpoints.[17] When this influence process works, the news not only tells people what to think about, it can also tell them what to think.[18]

The digital age may challenge these familiar mass media–governing patterns because people can more easily avoid common news channels and find personal sources on the issues that matter to them. This makes it more difficult for politicians to reach people with their messages, suggesting both greater information independence and greater difficulties for governing. When political actors have trouble reaching the public with their messages, they typically hire communication professionals, who often drive up the costs of democracy by designing sophisticated strategies for reaching ever more elusive segments of the public.[19] Democratic theorist Robert Dahl points to the growing control of information by elites as the single greatest obstacle to the continued development of democratic citizen participation in the policy process.[20]

The Press: Journalists and News Organizations

As mass media news organizations are driven by profit pressures from the megacorporations that now own most of them, the tendency is to seek the most convenient and attention-grabbing stories. Serious political reporting (so-called hard news) is being replaced by cheap lifestyle features and *news you can use* (health, consumer, weather, fashion, and travel information). The news industry becomes more receptive to the packaged information and news events produced by official spokespersons and communication consultants. These trends are all discussed in detail in Chapter 3.

Citizen information can, of course, be improved greatly by those rare moments of investigative reporting and watchdog journalism in which crusading reporters expose lies, gross deceptions, and corruption on issues that really matter. However, such news content is directly limited by business values that favor profit over civic responsibility. As a result, what often passes for independence from politicians are the scandals and feeding frenzies that further magnify the public's love-hate relationship with the news media.

The great preponderance of news is the product of routine journalism: reporters patrolling their regular beats and assignments; gathering the daily handouts, briefings, and statements of newsmakers; and passing them along to audiences. For the rest, news directors pray for (and politicians pray for escape from) juicy scandals that can fill the "news hole" for weeks or for months on end. In their defense, editors and news directors often claim that their market research shows little consumer interest in more serious news (unless it is of a spectacular sort such as airliners ramming into tall buildings). However, this response begs the question of why something as important as the news should be allowed to follow the course of least consumer resistance. If serious news does not engage people (a claim we will examine more critically), should the people be blamed or should ways of doing journalism be examined?

If political information is becoming less centrally organized as we move from the mass media into the digital age, journalists may lose even more of their once hallowed gatekeeping power to screen the quality and sources of information. More information is streamed from dubious sources on the Internet and increasingly finds its way into the news. For example, the Monica Lewinsky–Bill Clinton sex scandal was a communication landmark as the first major political news story served up from poorly documented Internet sources to the mass media and then followed by large numbers of people through a mix of traditional and digital online media—a pattern that may be changing the normal pathways through which information is screened by journalists and received by publics.

The People: Attentive Publics and Lifestyle Consumers

Politically managed information and a profit-driven passive press do not brighten the prospects for an enlightened citizenry. This does not mean that people are brainwashed or turned into unthinking zombies by their exposure to the daily news. Far from it! As we will see in Chapter 7, most people actively draw their own interpretations from news stories. The problem is that few stories contain much information beyond that provided by politicians and prominent interest organizations, raising questions about how often the news is likely to stimulate learning or useful democratic deliberation. Recall that news deliberation on important problems occurs mainly when two evenly matched sides are in conflict and keep a story advancing over a substantial period of time. Since these long-running media battles occur on only a small percentage of issues, the typical news day is filled with choppy and disconnected episodes from various halls of government, a scattering of crises and disasters, and profiles of public figures, business leaders, and celebrities. The result is typically a general public with low levels of attention and information on most issues.[21]

In fairness to the press, we should note that surveys of news consumers, as well as audience ratings of actual program content (discussed in Chapter 3), confirm that serious news about world affairs is not very popular. The most popular news subjects reflect topics that affect people and their lifestyles: crime, celebrities, health, consumer features, and entertainment. Political news and international affairs rank the lowest in news-interest surveys (except when international crises develop, as happened after the terrorist attacks in September 2001). These trends are even more exaggerated if we look at different age groups. Political and world news is of great interest to slightly more than 20 percent of people over the age of 50 but to a bare 10 percent of 18- to 29-year-olds. Crime news, by contrast, is interesting to upwards of 40 percent of all age groups surveyed.[22]

The important question, of course, is what accounts for these seemingly unimpressive audience tastes? Communication scholar Doris Graber argues that the generational problem is largely the result of the failure of news organizations to present information in the visually rich, interactive modes that are attractive to "cyber-age" citizens.[23] Consistent with Graber's analysis is research presented in Chapter 3 showing that when television news spends the money and allows journalists the time to report creatively, the resulting serious, high-quality news does compete effectively in the marketplace of public attention. In the process, however, news organizations must sacrifice some of their fat profit margins when they invest in quality news.

As we move from a mass media era into a digital media age, it is important to recognize that the Internet lowers the costs of political communication for citizens who cannot get their messages into the news. Many activists have learned how to use the Internet to communicate with others in cheap, fast, and effective ways. And supporters of long-shot 2004 presidential candidate Howard Dean used the Internet to spread his anti-war message when the mass media largely ignored him. Communities of environmentalists, pro- and antiabortion advocates, fair labor and fair trade campaigners, human rights workers, and computer privacy groups have mastered communicating with each other and with larger audiences on the Internet. Campaigns against the World Trade Organization that made news from Seattle to Sydney were organized in important ways through e-mail and activist sites on the World Wide Web (see, for example, **www.indymedia.org**), as were successful news campaigns alleging environmental, human rights, labor, or consumer choice abuses by such prominent corporations as McDonald's, Nike, Monsanto, and Microsoft, among others. A key question about the coming digital age is whether the balance of power in democracy and the definition of news will be changed. For now, most Americans who still follow the news tune to mass media sources such as television, newspapers, news magazines, and radio. What do they find there?

A DEFINITION OF NEWS

How do the often chaotic interactions among political actors, publics, and the press affect the way we define the news? As a starting point, it makes sense to adopt a simple definition of political news as:

- what newsmakers (politicians and other political actors) promote as timely, important, or interesting
- from which news organizations select, narrate, and package for transmission (via communication technologies)
- to people who consume it at a given time in history.

Doris Graber suggests that news is not just any information, or even the most important information about the world; rather, the news tends to contain information that is *timely*, often *sensational* (scandals, violence, and human drama frequently dominate the news), and *familiar* (stories often drawing on familiar people or life experiences that give even distant events a close-to-home feeling).[24] In this view, the news is constructed through the constantly changing interactions of journalists, politicians, and people seeking ends that are sometimes similar and sometimes very different. The key question about this somewhat chaotic information form is how well it serves the needs of democracy.

THE NEW GATEKEEPING

As noted earlier, the press plays the crucial role of gatekeeper in the media-based American political system, opening the news gate to admit certain voices and ideas into public view and closing it to others. For all of its flaws, mainstream news remains an important communication link between the people and their leaders. The trends toward sensationalism, the growth of personal digital information channels, and the fragmentation of the mass media audience all affect the press gatekeeping system. It has become more complex and, perhaps, less able to set the national agenda of politics and keep that agenda on a serious course—particularly on the big stories and scandals that increasingly fill the news hole on the so-called 24/7 cable channels.

Sensational stories may spill beyond the news and into entertainment programming in ways that seem to further diminish the traditional capacity of the press to screen and select perspectives on what is important and why it matters. Communication scholars Michael Delli Carpini and Bruce Williams note the rise of big political stories that have less to do with issues and government than with seamy human melodrama such as the Bill Clinton–Monica Lewinsky sex scandal. The preoccupation with such stories may place news as a secondary political information source behind TV docudramas or late-night comedy monologues. Delli Carpini and Williams go so far as to suggest that the once-hallowed gatekeeping function of the news may be dissolving as politics spills outside the bounds of news and throughout other media formats that are better suited to telling dramatic and entertaining stories.[25]

The embrace of dramatic political stories by popular culture media is indicated in the topics and frequencies of jokes told by late-night comedians such as Jay Leno or Bill Maher. For example, the number of jokes about Bill Clinton told by the four most popular late-night comedians more than doubled during the year of the Lewinsky scandal (1,712 jokes in 1998) compared to the year before (810 jokes in 1997).[26] As more Americans gain perspective from late night comedy such as *The Tonight Show with Jay Leno* or the *Daily Show with John Stewart,* there may be reason to think that the news is losing its capacity to focus public attention on the aspects of issues that may be most important. Yet people who suspect that news is already heavily constructed by politicians and journalists may look to entertainment for help in deconstructing it. As Jay Leno noted, so much of the political information in the news is produced by spin doctors that people look to comedians like him for "anti-spin."

In the aftermath of the terrible events of 9/11, networks such as FOX and CNN competed to brand their programming with dramatic titles such as *America Strikes Back.* Jon Stewart's *The Daily Show* on *Comedy Central* offered an antidote to the news melodrama with its own long-running segment titled *America Freaks Out!* And when the war in Iraq began to slip the grasp of administration spin, *Daily Show* coverage was tagged *Mess O'Potamia.* Stewart appeared on the cover of *Newsweek's* WHO'S NEXT issue that launched 2004. The feature story credited him with providing political perspective on big stories and making election coverage interesting, while drawing a younger audience that has largely tuned out conventional news.[27] *The Daily Show* won a Peabody Award for its *Indecision 2000* coverage of the Bush-Gore contest.

Political scientist Matthew Baum argues that the so-called "inattentive public" may actually get more useful information about world developments from entertainment programs such as *E!* or *The Daily Show* than from conventional news sources.[28] Before we declare the news irrelevant, however, or Peter Jennings less important an information source than Jay Leno, we should remember that the same issues that make the entertainment circuits first reach frenzied proportions in the news. Comedians and television scriptwriters often draw their cues from actual news content in the first place. More importantly, beyond a few huge stories, the vast majority of political issues never appear in the media outside the context of the news or public affairs programs, meaning that most available information about the political world still comes through the news.

There are, however, important senses in which the gatekeeping role of news is changing. As news executives fear public boredom with many routine policy stories, big stories and scandals occupy more of the news, and a strange sort of gatekeeping develops. Scandals and dramatic stories are given longer play than they may deserve on the basis of their political consequence. When faced with no new developments in such a story, journalists may be forced to write the next chapter by creating their own issues and recycling past developments. In the past, reporters were supposed to just report the news; now they often admit each other through the gates as sources.[29]

Even in election coverage, journalists now occupy more airtime than the candidates they are covering. In a startling study of election 2000, the Center for Media and Public Affairs found that 74 percent of the TV election stories in the last two months of campaign coverage consisted of statements by journalists, and just 12 percent of the coverage reported what the candidates actually said. Thomas Patterson offers this interpretation:

> In broadcast network coverage of the 2000 presidential campaign . . . reporters who were covering the candidates spoke six minutes for every minute the candidates' words could be heard on the air. Reporters now regularly pass sweeping judgments about what politicians are saying and doing. Their statements are constrained by a norm of partisan neutrality, but there is no norm that limits negativity.[30]

These confusions of the gatekeeping process may undermine the credibility of news for many citizens. Yet for all of these problems, the news remains central to governing in contemporary America. How can this be?

HOW MEDIATED GOVERNMENT WORKS

For all its flaws, as Timothy Cook has argued, it may be impossible to govern today without the news.[31] How do we explain this? Consider the possibility that much of political communication in this system may be aimed less at the general public than at other political insiders who create the "media buzz" about which politicians and political ideas are up and which ones are down. In many ways the media and politicians have circled the wagons against a public that does not appreciate or understand them, creating a somewhat insulated reality based on strategic communication, spin control, and attempts to damage the images of opponents while avoiding the appearance of damage in return. Surrounding this daily flow of political communication is the insider political buzz created by the incessant press analysis of these skirmishes. Even when general audiences are annoyed by this pretentious insiderism, the small but powerful audience of Washington insiders and the corporate leaders who finance politics may be influenced by mediated realities that are primarily about them.

In the view of CNN pollster and pundit William Schneider, Washington is increasingly a town of individual political entrepreneurs who rely less on parties for their political support than on their own media images. Those images can be boosted or lowered as they are associated with the popularity of other visible politicians, like the president, or with popular developments such as economic booms or successful wars.[32] When the president appears to be a loser, other politicians do not want to be associated with him or his programs. Journalists report on such political damage, opinion polls often reflect (and validate) those reports, and the real power of the presidency goes down. When the president appears to be a winner in the news, everyone wants a piece of the media action, and the real power of everyone who jumped into the television spotlight—most of all the president—goes up.

The public enters this mediated reality at select moments, when targeted audience segments are rallied to vote, to participate in polls, or to send e-mail barrages to Congress. More often, the public is addressed at the end of the policy process, when results need to be "sold" through news images. Governing with the news is thus also about controlling what gets to the public, as explained in the following case study of how the Bush administration became rather heavy-handed with press reporting of the War on Terror.

Journalist Marvin Kalb describes these perverse democratic developments as an age of "press-politics," in which political actors simply cannot ignore the importance of the news media in responding to political events:[33]

> . . . there isn't a single major and sometimes minor decision reached at the White House, reached up on the Hill, reached at the State Department or the Pentagon, that does not have the press in mind. The way in which this is going to be sold to the American people is a function of the way in which the press first understands it, and then accepts it, and then is prepared to propagate a certain vision to the American people.[34]

In some big stories, the public (generally in the form of polls taken by and reported in the press) often plays the role of a Greek chorus. In the Clinton–Lewinsky sex scandal, the chorus registered its independent disdain for the spectacle in Washington, while refusing to join the insider consensus that Clinton's presidency was surely over. Also like the Greek chorus, the broad public disapproval of Clinton's impeachment had little impact on the vote by the House to impeach the president. The Republican leaders of the impeachment drive in the House of Representatives were playing far more to their local districts than to the national audience, although they tried valiantly to persuade that national audience that they were doing the right thing. Whether the public is broadly united or narrowly divided, the battle for public opinion remains a key feature of politics and government. In some cases, the battle for public support becomes so important for governing that the news itself is the prime political target, as explained in the following case study.

Case Study: *Governing with the News: Terror Comes to America*

On the morning of September 11, 2001, millions of Americans witnessed an event that would forever change their sense of personal security and national destiny. Airplanes filled with passengers were hijacked and flown into the World Trade Center and the Pentagon, grand symbols of national, economic, and political strength. Such vivid images can be thought of as *news icons* that can change the ways people think about themselves, their problems, and possible solutions.[35] For example, the picture of an American ally assassinating a man on a Saigon street raised profound questions about the ideals motivating U.S. involvement in the Vietnam War. The TV spectacle of the spacecraft *Challenger* exploding after launch raised questions that shook the entire U.S. space program.

The battle for control of the news was engaged from the moment the World Trade Center towers collapsed, and Air Force One was routed from one air base to another amid rumors that it and the White House had been targeted by another hijacked airliner that was not accounted for. Where was the president? ABC anchor Peter Jennings wondered how Mr. Bush would address the American people in this time of distress, noting that "The country looks to the president on occasions like this to be reassuring to the nation. Some presidents do it well, some don't." Conservative political radio commentator Rush Limbaugh misreported this statement to his large national audience by charging that Jennings had linked the president's delayed return to Washington with an inability to rise to the occasion in leading the people. ABC switchboards lit up with calls from enraged Limbaugh fans, angry that the liberal media was undermining the president in a time of crisis.[36]

With the terrifying images of a plane hitting a World Trade Center tower and the towers collapsing in flames replaying endlessly on the news, President Bush announced that the country was at war against terrorism. Other nations of the world were told they must either support that war or declare themselves on the side of the enemy. The principal enemy was identified as Osama bin Laden and his al Qaeda network of Islamic extremists, along with the Taliban government of Afghanistan and any other government that supported their activities.

Soon atop the international agenda was a bombing campaign in Afghanistan and the coordination of secret operations and military actions on the ground aimed at finding bin Laden and toppling the Taliban government. Atop the domestic agenda was legislation freeing law enforcement agencies to gather personal information about large numbers of citizens and visitors to the country, prompting many critics, from libertarians to liberals, to worry about a serious undermining of civil liberties.

War presents one of the most serious challenges to democracy, and the news media ultimately decide how well democracy survives that challenge. On one side of the struggle is the government's interest in controlling the flow of information to maintain popular support (and suppress criticism) of its policies. On the other side is the freedom of the press and, in turn, the public to inspect and criticize those policies to make sure they are sound enough to merit support and sacrifice. From the standpoint of governments, serious public questions may make them appear weak or lacking in popular support, particularly in the eyes of enemies who may not grasp the subtleties of democratic culture. Yet from the standpoint of citizens, government secrecy and information censorship can protect bad decisions that citizens end up paying for in bloody military operations abroad or the loss of civil liberties at home.

In the aftermath of 9/11, news reports that ran too far outside official administration views quickly ran into a broad set of political efforts to control the media. The players in this news control operation included members of the administration and its allies in Congress, but also a vocal contingent of conservative journalists, commentators, and media organizations, including Limbaugh, FOX *News*, the *Drudge Report*, the *New York Post* editorial page, and various conservative columnists. These "press police" drew support for their charges against various journalists, news organizations, and public figures from the Media Research Council, a conservative media watchdog organization dedicated to gathering facts to prove left wing media bias. As one news executive who felt the sting of this operation put it, "Any misstep and you can get into trouble with these guys and have the Patriotism Police hunt you down. These are hard jobs. Just getting the facts straight is monumentally difficult. We don't want to have to wonder if we are saluting properly. Was I supposed to use the three-fingered salute today?"[37]

Journalists were not the only targets of the censorship campaign. As noted earlier, the "new gatekeeping" involves more attention to big stories by the entertainment media. Following 9/11, entertainers and cultural figures who discussed the war on terrorism in terms deemed politically incorrect were also attacked by "Patriotism Police." Among the casualties was talk show host Bill Maher whose ABC program was aptly titled *Politically Incorrect*. Maher had the misfortune of aiming one of his politically incorrect comments at the stereotypes that everyone seemed obliged to apply to the terrorists. One of the conservative guests on his program began the exchange by saying that whatever they were, people willing to die for their cause were not cowards. Maher followed up with the comment that "We have been the cowards lobbing cruise missiles from 2,000 miles away. That's cowardly."[38] With this statement, Maher suddenly took politically incorrect to a new level. His remark was met with a public lecture from White House press secretary Ari Fleischer, who denounced Maher personally and offered a more general warning: "The reminder is to all Americans that they need to watch what they say, and watch what they do, and that this is not a time for remarks like that."[39] Maher's program was dropped by nineteen ABC network affiliates and two major sponsors, Federal Express and Sears. Some of the affiliates were later persuaded to come back, but the sponsors stayed away, not wanting their brands associated with a program branded as unpatriotic by such a high authority.

A few public voices took up Maher's defense. *The New York Times* columnist Maureen Dowd argued that it was insulting for any loyal-but-thinking American to be told how to think. Moreover, she suspected that the real root of the White House censorship campaign was to make George W. Bush appear larger than life, echoing the puzzlement of a Republican communication consultant who remarked that "They're overselling a product that's selling itself." Dowd's general point was that "At a time when Americans are willing to vest extraordinary power in the president, to trust him with life-and-death decisions, to give him considerable leeway in curbing civil liberties and spending billions, this is a time when questions and debate are what patriotism demands. Even the most high minded government is not infallible."[40]

Maher was not the only American thinking incorrect thoughts. Author Susan Sontag wrote a brief comment on 9/11 in a collection of reactions by literary figures in *The New Yorker.* Her point was similar to Maher's: that public discussion of the incident should strive to understand who our enemy really is, rather than burying possible understanding with stereotypes like "cowards." Her plea was simple: "Let's by all means grieve together. But let's not be stupid together."[41] This point was immediately blasted with heavy fire from conservative columnists in leading newspapers, including William Safire in *The New York Times* and Charles Krauthammer in *The Washington Post,* who assured readers that the terrorists were indeed cowards, and that Americans need not stoop to understand their motives in order to bring them to justice.

Following the Peter Jennings and Bill Maher incidents, ABC continued to receive a disproportionate share of public condemnation. David Westin, president of ABC News responded to a question from the audience at a journalism forum at Columbia University, saying that as an objective journalist it was not his place to judge whether the Pentagon was a legitimate military target. The stream of criticism from Limbaugh and others soon wrung a public apology from Westin, who later qualified it by suggesting he was less sure that he was wrong than that the controversy was distracting him from reporting the biggest story of the new century.[42] But the critics were not through with ABC. Next, the Media Research Council reported that *World News Tonight with Peter Jennings* reported far more often on civilian casualties in the bombing campaign than the other networks. The Council issued a report containing strong language implying that ABC was aiding the enemy with such coverage: "ABC knows that the despotic Taliban are using both real and phony instances of U.S. errors to undermine our war against terror. But at least so far, its correspondents have reserved most of their skepticism for America."[43]

Beyond the stereotypes of liberal press bias, questions about the effectiveness of a bombing campaign reflect the traditional press function of providing citizens with information they need to evaluate government policy. As *Los Angeles Times* bureau chief Doyle McManus said, the suppression of information and condemnation of reporters' questions could have grave effects on the flow of democratic information in the long run ". . . as we try to evaluate how this war is going, whether after a succession of different kinds of military operations, the strategy is working."[44]

But the patriotism campaign went on. When Joe Biden, as chair of the Senate Foreign Relations Committee also raised concerns about the bombing (in a speech to the Council on Foreign Relations), he linked the issue to the stability of the military regime in neighboring Pakistan. Pakistan had been pressed into an unsteady support role for the U.S. war in Afghanistan. Pakistani army factions had strong ties to the Taliban, and many ordinary citizens saw U.S. policy as an attack on Islamic fundamentalism. Biden quickly discovered that he, too, had entered the realm of the politically incorrect. Speaker of the House Dennis Hastert came close to accusing Biden of treason, calling Biden's remarks "completely irresponsible" and explaining that "The American people want us to bring these terrorists to justice. They do not want comments that bring comfort to our enemies."[45]

As explained earlier, the news is unlikely to introduce alternative points of view or go out of the way to investigate government information claims when there are few government officials willing to challenge a dominant administration line. Journalists tend to index the range of competing viewpoints to the degree of opposition among powerful officials. Silencing someone like the Chair of the Senate Foreign Relations Committee also indirectly silences the press by closing the news gates.

It was not until President Bush delivered a poorly received sound bite during his State of the Union Address in 2002 that a storm of negative world opinion offered leading Democrats an opening to again question the direction of the terrorism campaign. Mr. Bush had referred to Iran, Iraq, and North Korea as an "axis of evil," raising questions about his understandings of those nations and the meaning of the term *axis,* while threatening a fragile political reform movement in Iran and the delicate warming of relations between North and South Korea. Many world leaders and international commentators challenged the remark, and a presidential trip to Asia was marked by reporters raising the issue at nearly every stop. Against this backdrop, Democratic leaders Tom Daschle, Robert Byrd, and Joe Biden all questioned the future plans for the war on terrorism. Their questions were met with familiar innuendos of treason by Republicans like Trent Lott, who said: "How dare Senator Daschle criticize President Bush while we are fighting our war on terrorism, especially when we have troops in the field? He should not be trying to divide our country while we are united."[46] House Republican Whip Tom DeLay characterized the remarks as "Disgusting."[47] And so the battle for public speech went on.

When political opposition is suppressed, news organizations are particularly vulnerable to censorship and official news management. Consider the dilemma of CNN. As the American news organization with the best international news team and resources on the ground in the region, CNN was singled out for particularly harsh scrutiny. Early on, CNN was accused of aiding the enemy with its broadcasts of Osama bin Laden tapes that were first aired on Al Jazeera, an Arabic satellite news channel. What CNN had regarded as a mark of its journalistic quality was challenged by an imposing a pair of figures: National Security Advisor Condaleeza Rice and Secretary of State Colin Powell. They branded the bin Laden broadcasts as subversive, and even suggested that they might be a platform for bin Laden to send coded signals to his operatives in the United States (Al Jazeera was already available on U.S. satellite dish systems as part of an Arabic programming subscription package).

While CNN was being hit with administration charges of aiding the enemy, the Media Research Council and conservative journalists and commentators challenged CNN reports on civilian casualties of the bombing. In an effort to defuse the building criticism, CNN adopted a policy of "balancing" its reports of civilian casualties in Afghanistan with reminders of the American civilian death toll on 9/11. This policy finally received the seal of approval from FOX news anchor Brit Hume, who rationalized suppressing critical information in the news media this way: "Look, neutrality as a general principle is an appropriate concept for journalists who are covering situations of some comparable quality. This is a conflict between the United States and murdering barbarians."[48]

Former CNN war correspondent Peter Arnett (whose patriotism was challenged for his broadcasts from Baghdad, including an interview with Saddam Hussein, during the Gulf War in 1991) asked whether it was in the interests of the public for the government to try to suppress the flow of democratic information: "Should the American public get everything reported from the other side of the story and be given the chance to evaluate it sensibly?"[49] He concluded that the administration had answered that question for the public with a decisive "no." In such an environment, with fear and patriotism stirred to unprecedented levels, the public can easily be convinced to endorse its own censorship.

Arnett also observed that the government pressure played into internal conflicts within news organizations pitting journalists against owners and managers who favored ratings-grabbing content over expensive and perhaps more controversial investigative reporting. CNN, like most of the news industry, had already begun to sacrifice serious news as a succession of corporate owners demanded higher profits and reduced expenses. First, Time Warner bought the original CNN parent, Turner Broadcasting, and then AOL bought Time Warner. Arnett remarked, "The change in CNN under new management is most instructive. The company developed much more interest in soft news, scandal and gossip than in the hard reality of the world. The management became much more sensitive to viewer opinions." In this context, the dynamics of official condemnation and viewer reaction hit home, closing CNN's news gates to airing much in the way of controversial information. Arnet concluded, "Consequently in this War on Terrorism CNN is tending to follow the U.S. government line with much more enthusiasm than I think is necessary."[50]

Americans by the tens of millions were glued to their TV sets, seeking the latest information on the situation in Afghanistan. FOX, CNN, and MSNBC wrapped their screens in bunting and flags, developed theme music, and branded their logos with riveting program titles such as *America's New War*, *Tracking the Terrorists*, and *America Strikes Back*. The CNN audience had declined to alarming levels over the decade of the 1990s since the heyday of the Gulf War in 1991, in part due to increased competition from other cable news operations. Just before the events of 9/11, in August 2001, the CNN average daily audience was 330,000, barely ahead of FOX's 311,000 and MSNBC's 229,000. In the period between September 11–14 before the censorship campaign focused on CNN, the network's old brand image as the place to go for live event coverage was still able to deliver viewers. The CNN audience hit a peak of over 4 million daily viewers, and averaged 1.8 million over the next month, far ahead of FOX's rating average of 1.1 million, and MSNBC at 900,000.[51]

The value of brand-building was acknowledged by CNN's corporate owners. The chief financial officer for AOL Time Warner, J. Michael Kelly, described the sudden, if temporary, reversal of budget cutting at CNN: "We're going to spend whatever we need to spend to cover the story appropriately. That's how you build brands in this business, by being renowned by your editorial coverage of these kinds of stories."[52]

However, CNN did not anticipate the degree of censorship it would soon face. Nor did it anticipate the degree to which its chief competitor FOX would trade on patriotic support for the government to build its own brand. FOX news anchors were encouraged by management to personalize the war and insert their own feelings into their reports. Thus, FOX personnel referred on the air to Osama bin Laden as "a dirtbag" and a "monster."[53] FOX ratings soon went up more than 40 percent over the previous year. FOX news chairman Roger Ailes explained the conscious departure from the norms of objective or morally neutral reporting in this way: "Look, we understand the enemy—they've made themselves clear: they want to murder us. We don't sit around and get all gooey and wonder if these people have been misunderstood in their childhood. . . . I don't believe that democracy and terrorism are relative things you can talk about, and I don't think there's any moral equivalence in those two positions. If that makes me a bad guy, tough luck. I'm still getting the ratings"[54]

In short, the FOX decision to mirror public emotions rather than balance them with information about the enemy was clearly good for ratings and brand identification. But the combination of news as patriotic drama and as branding process—all with a censorship campaign in the background—left little room to report information that might help the American people form independent opinions about the enemy, the war, or the domestic restrictions on civil liberties. *The point here is not whether various war-related policies were right or wrong, but whether people were given the information required to think independently about those questions.*

The pressure on the press continued as the Iraq War replaced the Afghanistan War as the focus of national attention. When the initial victory in Iraq was replaced by a guerilla conflict that put American troops in the uncomfortable role of an occupation force, some soldiers decided to speak out. A group of soldiers from the Third Infantry Division told an ABC correspondent that they felt misled about the war, and one remarked that "If Donald Rumsfeld was here, I'd ask him for his resignation." The Defense Department and the White House were understandably outraged by this report. The White House press office went so far as to research the background of the reporter and leak information to Internet gossip columnist Matt Drudge, who ran the smear headline: ABC NEWS REPORTER WHO FILED TROOP COMPLAINTS STORY—OPENLY GAY CANADIAN.[55] Questioning both the sexual orientation and the patriotism of a journalist suggests the willingness of the administration to play hardball with the press. Shortly after this incident, a number of high administration officials visited Iraq, including Donald Rumsfeld, Paul Wolfowitz, and eventually, the president went on a secret Thanksgiving mission. Their message to the people—conveyed dutifully through the press—was that things here in Iraq are better than they seem in the press. The administration spin was much the same from 9/11 through the Iraq War: the liberal press biases the reality that is presented to the American people.

Indeed, the entire censorship campaign preyed on the implicit popular belief in the liberal bias of the press. When political criticism comes wrapped in patriotism and surrounded by a fearful public, it is difficult for anyone, journalist or comedian, to defend themselves against charges of bias by saying that they were just doing their democratic duty.

What do you think? Where is the proper balance between government control of the press and the free flow of information and ideas? Why were conservative journalists and politicians not widely charged with conservative bias? What do you choose to believe about the wars on terrorism, Afghanistan, and Iraq? On what basis do you believe it?

THE FRAGILE LINK BETWEEN NEWS AND DEMOCRACY

Why is something as important as public information left to be defined by a poorly understood and often turbulent mix of business profit imperatives, political spin techniques, and consumer tastes? This puzzle would be less intriguing if the news was not so important. Yet few things are as much a part of our lives as the news. Although it is tempting to assume that the news is somehow geared to the information needs of citizens, a more disturbing possibility exists. There is no institutional check or monitoring system to guarantee that the news, as it has evolved, will serve the needs of American democracy. To the contrary, substantial evidence indicates that the news is largely a freewheeling entity shaped by a combination of commercial forces in the news business, technologies of communication perfected by politicians and their media consultants, and the tastes and personal entertainment habits of citizens. More than in any other advanced democracy, political information in the United States is manufactured and sold with few of the quality controls that even far less important household products have.

The forces acting on the news operate with little concerted regard for some larger public interest. There is a good deal of complacency about this information system. Consider, for example, the lack of much deliberate public debate and even less governmental inquiry about what kind of information the nation and its citizens need in order to best decide their political course. Despite (or perhaps because of) the faith in the free press system in the United States, Americans have paid far less attention than other societies to the quality of democracy's most important product: political information.

WHY FREE SPEECH CANNOT GUARANTEE GOOD INFORMATION

Consider the most shocking example of good news gone bad: local TV news. Paul Klite (who died several years ago) was one of the most prominent critics of the "if it bleeds, it leads" editorial philosophy that guides most local news. Klite was a former radio talk show host and founder of Rocky Mountain Media Watch. The Media Watch, based in Denver, often made news in high quality outlets with its "mayhem index" that measured the degree to which local news is filled with scary images of crime, accidents, fires, drugs, gangs, child molesting, and other forms of abuse, and the general breakdown of society. The local news mayhem index rose until Media

Watch decided to file a petition in 1998 with the Federal Communications Commission (FCC) to deny licenses to four Denver stations on grounds that their local news was "toxic" to citizens. One Denver station (KMGH, the ABC affiliate) scored a stunning 60 percent of its editorial content in the mayhem category. Unfortunately, Denver is fairly typical of national trends. Media Watch asserts that local news across the nation is "severely unbalanced, with excessive coverage of violent topics and trivial events," creating "a public health issue" that "goes beyond bad journalism."[56]

The Media Watch allegations touched on embarrassing but financially successful nationwide industry practices. The FCC is normally reluctant to intrude upon programming practices, but the timing of the Media Watch complaint was particularly unlikely to catch the FCC in a regulatory mood. Just prior to this case, media companies had been given the green light by Congress and the president to pursue business interests over social responsibility with passage of the landmark Telecommunications Act of 1996 (stay tuned to find out why this legislation mattered in Chapter 3). The FCC soundly rejected the Media Watch petition, wrapping itself, its ruling, and the entire broadcast industry in the hallowed language of free speech: "Journalistic or editorial discretion in the presentation of news and public information is the core concept of the First Amendment's free press guarantee."[57] National broadcaster groups and the Denver stations heralded this formulaic pronouncement as an important victory for free speech—a triumph over censorship and the intrusion of government in the newsroom. Many media and law scholars worry about using the Constitution to defend publicly licensed communication content that is produced with little political or social purpose beyond making money.[58] Media Watch argued that such high-minded defenses of bad news are part of the reason that we end up with news that "covers schoolyard shootings but not schools, train wrecks but not transportation, bloopers by local politicians but not local elections, and the latest murder but not dropping crime rates."[59]

The point here is not to weaken the First Amendment, but to identify communication practices that may be weakening it. Indeed one of the toughest questions for democracy is how far its guarantees of freedoms should go—particularly to protect behaviors that may undermine democracy itself. It is important to acknowledge that the hallowed standing of free speech protects us from the threat of concerted government control of news—and this is a supremely important protection. Other important reasons for keeping constitutional protections strong include protecting a journalist's confidential sources. The lamentable fact is that there is so little reporting these days that so threatens the powers that be that news organizations often need to use the First Amendment for protection.

We may have built a national information fortress with just one wall, protecting the press from formal censorship, yet leaving the information system vulnerable to degradation at the hands of little-controlled business interests. Such interests, as any beginning economics student learns, have no intrinsic reason to embrace social responsibility beyond returning profits to their private investors. In the next section, we examine where these free market forces are taking news content and consider some of the implications for politics.

SOFT NEWS AND THE TURN AWAY FROM POLITICS

Whether we ever think about the quality of information the way we think about air or water quality, there are many indicators that impoverished and demoralizing news content is spreading beyond local TV and into nearly all the mainstream national media. In thinking about such news trends, it is helpful to first make the distinction between "hard news" and "soft news." A common journalistic hard news standard is what an informed person in society should know. This standard applies to many government activities, the positions of candidates in election campaigns, international developments that may affect us, policies that may change our lives, emerging social problems, environmental hazards, and historic events, among other things. By contrast, soft news is emotional and immediate. It requires no justification beyond grabbing the attention of an audience and, ideally, getting them talking the next day about what they saw on NBC or FOX last night. Soft news stories have little social significance beyond the drama or sensational images that stir emotions in audiences. Soft news is not based on the journalistic ideal of what citizens or members of society should know; it is largely meant to be entertaining. Soft news is often constructed according to marketing guidelines aimed at grabbing the attention of the audience demographics that a program is trying to deliver to advertisers.

Drawing these distinctions between hard and soft news requires some practice. For example, a crime report might count as hard news even if it begins with a nasty crime story but then moves to an analysis of trends, causes, and possible solutions. However, a crime story is soft if the report does little more than detail the gory incident, paint a tearful portrait of the victim, and interview grief-stricken family and friends. Other crime stories may fall closer to the line between hard and soft news, as when a serial killer is stalking a particular type of victim and using particular methods. Putting the focus on information that is useful for protecting personal safety tilts the balance toward hard news. On the other hand, the breathless, nonstop media coverage of the dramatic death of celebrity fashion designer Gianni Versace at the hands of a deranged spree killer was soft news. The vast majority of crime stories fall in the soft news category—not because they have to, but because that is how news organizations market them.

Thomas Patterson defines hard news as news that contains some public policy content or other useful public information:

> Hard news refers to coverage of breaking events involving top leaders, major issues, or significant disruptions in the routines of daily life, such as an earthquake or airline disaster. Information about these events is presumably important to citizens' ability to understand and respond to the world of public affairs.[60]

In his study of over 5,000 news stories between 1980 and 1999 on television, newspapers, and news magazines, stories without public policy content increased from 35 percent of all news to nearly half of all news. The areas of biggest soft news increase were sensationalism in general (e.g., scandals), up from just over 20 percent to nearly 40 percent of all news; human interest, which rose from just over 10 percent to over 25 percent; and crime and disaster, which rose from 8 percent to 14 percent of all stories, across the local, national, print, and broadcast news media.[61]

The time period between roughly 1980 and the end of the century is important because it spans the period of greatest corporate media mergers and ownership consolidation in American history. Whether we look at what happened during this period nationally or locally, or in magazines, newspaper, radio, or TV, the information-to-infotainment trends are clear. There is less hard news and more soft news, and there is less reporting about government and politics and more about social chaos and personal drama. Consider just a few of these trends:

- Network TV newscasts between 1990 and 1998 more than doubled the time devoted to entertainment, disasters, accidents, and crime while reducing the coverage of environment, government activities, and international affairs to make the room.[62]
- International news on network TV declined from 45 percent of stories in the 1970s to 13.5 percent of stories in 1995.[63]
- Newspapers reduced international news coverage from over 10 percent of non-advertising space in the early 1970s to 6 percent in the early 1980s to less than 3 percent in the 1990s.[64]
- Among the national news weeklies, between 1985 and 1995, international news declined from 24 percent to 14 percent in *Time,* from 22 percent to 12 percent in *Newsweek,* and from 20 percent to 14 percent in *U.S. News & World Report.*[65] (Entertainment, celebrity stories, recreation, lifestyle, and sports filled the editorial space).
- In 1987, *Time* ran eleven covers that focused on international news. Only one cover in 1997 was about an international story.[66]
- Overall, the network news, the cover stories of news magazines, and the front pages of major newspapers saw an increase from 15 percent to 43 percent between 1977 and 1997 in celebrity, scandal, gossip, and human-interest stories.[67]

What did *Time* put on its cover at century's end? Ellen DeGeneres, Steven Spielberg, Jewel, Bill Cosby, "What's Cool This Summer," "How Mood Drugs Work," and "The Most Fascinating People in America." When *Time* and *Newsweek* each ran covers on Princess Diana two weeks in a row following her death, they both had the biggest newsstand sales in their histories.[68]

Patterson concludes that these news trends help explain why the public is tuning out politics. The first step may be tuning out the news itself. When questioned about what kind of news they want, people picked examples of hard news by a margin of 2 to 1.[69] Later in the book, we learn that news executives maintain that what people say and what they watch are two different things. The fact remains, however, that news audiences are shrinking. Moreover, as noted previously, and explained in Chapter 3, news programs emphasizing quality hard news formats compete profitably at the top of their markets. The dilemma is that hard news costs far more to gather and to report creatively than soft news; thus, news organizations can make *greater* profits—even with shrinking audiences—with soft news than with hard. The most profitable period in the modern history of newspapers was the 1990s. This was a time when most papers switched to soft news and watched their audiences decline. The tradeoff was accepted because the cheap news formulas helped profits grow.

Has the soft news deluge become toxic to community values and democracy? Here are some trends. You decide:

- A national study of local news by the Center for Media and Public Affairs found that crime dominated most programs and that after removing the combination of crime, weather, accidents, disasters, other soft news, and sports, only 5 minutes and 40 seconds remained out of the 24 minutes and 20 seconds of noncommercial news time for coverage of government, health, foreign affairs, education, science, and the environment.[70] Hard news got less time than commercials.

- The trends in increased violent-crime news cannot be explained as reflections of actual rates of crime in society. To the contrary, the trends in crime news have been going up as actual crime has declined. In the period from 1990 through 1998, for example, the number of crime stories broadcast annually on the NBC, CBS, and ABC evening news programs rose from 542 to 1,392, during a time in which the actual levels of most violent crimes dropped significantly in society.[71] If we look just at news about murder on the national networks, the number of murder stories increased by 700 percent between 1993 and 1996, a period in which the murder rate in society actually declined by 20 percent.[72]

- According to a national survey, nearly two-thirds of people get most of their views about crime from television, compared to just 20 percent from newspapers, 7 percent from radio, and less than 10 percent from friends, neighbors, co-workers, or personal experience.[73]

Does any of this matter? People who watch more news and "reality programs" (such as the cop shows discussed in Chapter 3) are significantly more likely to misjudge the seriousness of the crime problem and their own chances of being victims.[74] Fewer people felt safe in their neighborhoods (29 percent) in the late 1990s than in the early 1980s (44 percent), even though objective crime conditions warrant just the opposite feelings.[75] Media critic Daniel Lazare summed up this tendency of news to grab the emotions of targeted audiences rather than focus broadly on public life:

> Consumers grow picky about what they read and watch. Thus, for example, reporting about grim conditions in the inner cities, though perhaps only a few miles away from many readers and viewers, is hard to sell because middle class consumers who pick and choose their reality much as they choose their fashions can't relate to it; because poor people are a turn-off for advertisers and retailers; because a consumerist approach to the news means giving the consumer what he wants, not what he needs.[76]

To return to the issue that opened this section: How can one of the freest press systems in the world produce news that so often misses the political mark? It is hard for most Americans to imagine that freedom and competition do not automatically guarantee the best results. As a result of this deep cultural faith in unrestricted political communication, there is stunningly little public discussion about how to design a news and information system that might better suit the needs of democratic politics and citizen involvement. A goal of this book is to contribute to such a discussion by explaining how the current news system has evolved: how news is produced and sold, how it is shaped by political actors, how it is reported by journalists and news organizations, and how it is used by citizens. When this larger news picture is considered, problems such as the fabled ideological bias of reporters become the least of the information problems facing citizens.

MYTHS ABOUT NEWS BIAS

There is much that remains useful about contemporary news. However, concerns about the deterioration in the general quality of coverage of politics and government are getting increasing public and journalistic attention. Even in time of war, branding and drama may overshadow efforts to expand the diversity of content. Because of these developments, many journalists and scholars echo concerns such as those expressed by Rosenstiel and Kovach at the opening of the chapter.[77] How have news and politics become entwined in the spiral of negativity that has dragged both of them down in the esteem of most Americans? And what makes it so hard to fix the problems in our primary political information system? These turn out to be challenging questions that will guide us on an inside tour of news organizations, politicians' war rooms, and citizens' lives in the remainder of this book.

One thing that will not help us understand the evolving relations between news and government is to blame the information defects on journalists as individuals. Yet the most common complaints from both the public and politicians are aimed at journalists and news organizations as being politically biased. Recall these attacks from our case study of the War on Terror. Polls show that growing majorities of people believe that reporters introduce their own political views into the news and generally do not even get the facts straight. According to polls taken by the Pew Research Center for the People & the Press, vast changes occurred in public regard for the press over the last two decades. Even though public confidence in the press began its steep decline by the mid-1980s, a majority (55 percent) still felt that news organizations at least got their facts straight most of the time. This figure dropped to 37 percent in the late 1990s. Meanwhile perceptions of press fairness—the belief that news organizations generally deal fairly with all sides in news accounts—plunged to a stunning low of 27 percent toward century's end.[78]

The news has changed in important ways in recent years, but the reasons for our contemporary news troubles are not as simple as journalists twisting the news to fit their political or personal biases. However, the popular stereotype of a liberal press contains the proverbial "grain of truth:" survey results show that many journalists are more liberal than the general population.[79] Where conventional wisdom breaks down, however, is with the assumption that the personal politics of reporters translate into the political content of their journalism. Think about how you would judge CBS News anchor Dan Rather based on two bits of information about him. In one incident Rather gave a speech at a Democratic Party fund-raising event at which his daughter was a host. After receiving criticism for this partisan act, Rather claimed that when he accepted the invitation he did not know the event was a fund-raiser, and after he found out, he could not disappoint his daughter to whom he had made the commitment. This situation was cited by conservatives to support the claim that Rather was a biased liberal. Yet the same Dan Rather appeared on the David Letterman show following the terrorist attacks of 9/11. He discussed his emotional reaction to the attacks, as well as to the discovery that his office had been targeted with anthrax delivered in the mail and an assistant had tested positive for exposure to the bacteria. He broke down and cried on the program, pledging his allegiance to President George W. Bush by saying, "He wants me to line up, just tell me where." Rather later clarified what he meant by elaborating: "George Bush is the commander in chief. If he asks me to line up in uniform, to clean latrines, to KP duty or carry a rifle, he has only to tell me where to line up and I'm there."[80]

Even if reporters like Rather are liberals in their private lives, it is not clear how this translates into the news. In an experimental study in which journalists were asked to imagine how they personally would cover hypothetical stories, the ideology of reporters had only a small effect on their professional judgments.[81] In reality, journalists do not work in hypothetical situations in which they have free reign over how to cover a story. The vast majority of individual journalists would have trouble getting consistent ideological slants past editors and owners throughout the entire news industry. The next section explains how the common perception of political bias in the news flies in the face of deeper realities in the news business.

Putting Journalistic Bias in Perspective

Consider a few of the realities that must be ignored in order to link overall news content with the private political beliefs or biases of reporters. First, both liberal and conservative reporters tend to behave as a "pack" (for reasons explained in Chapter 5). The press pack ends up with similar, and most often politically centrist, stories on most issues and events. Even the swings in emphasis that may occur over the course of a big story make little sense as political favoritism. Such swings generally occur as journalists perceive power shifts among players in a political conflict; this is the indexing aspect of gatekeeping described earlier in the chapter. The overall tendency is for reporting that aims toward the political middle.

A second problem with the ideological bias thesis is that the political leanings of reporters often run against the tone of their own news accounts of the politicians they cover. In cases where the press seems to bend for or against a particular politician, the reasons generally have more to do with the news-management skills of the politician's media consultants than with the political favoritism of reporters. As discussed later in the book, most observers regard news coverage of the Reagan presidency (1981–1988) as generally favorable to Reagan and his "Republican revolution." Even when journalists attempted to take critical stances, they were often diffused by skillful White House press management and by Reagan's media-friendly personal charm—earning Reagan titles such as "The Great Communicator" and "The Teflon President."

By contrast, the Clinton Democratic years (1993–2000) witnessed some of the most stormy and combative press relations and news coverage of the modern era. Despite generally favorable coverage during his election campaign (thanks largely to creative media events such as bus tours, MTV, and late night, shades-wearing, sax-playing talk show appearances), the press soon challenged the policies and probity of the new administration. As discussed in Chapter 4, Clinton press relations contrasted sharply with those of the Reagan administration, both in terms of failing to develop daily coordinated communication strategies, and in excluding reporters from the everyday work routines and social life of the White House. Not long after Clinton's first election, a national press corps that probably voted heavily for him anointed conservative Republican leader Newt Gingrich "the most exciting politician" in a generation. The same press pack later turned on Gingrich.

George W. Bush enjoyed the highest recorded levels of public approval following his triumphant Top Gun jet landing on the aircraft carrier Abraham Lincoln, and his declaration of an end to major combat in Iraq. As explained at the opening of this chapter and in the case studies in Chapters 4 and 5, the press faithfully reported most of the administration's spin on the war long after there were plenty of questions to be raised about its justification and progress. Yet all that stood between Mr. Bush and the shift to popularity-damaging news coverage was a news hook on which to hang the story of a weakened president: the emergence of political opposition among Democrats in Congress, a scandal or rift within the administration, a military catastrophe in Iraq, or a new economic tailspin.

The habit of the press to build up today's news heroes only to turn them into tomorrow's fools may not win special favor among politicians or the public. However, these familiar news cycles suggest that what drives press coverage has little to do with the political biases of journalists and far more to do with shifting power struggles inside government, the spin and political communication strategies of newsmakers, and the economic imperative compelling news organizations to find new dramatic stories to tell to fickle audiences who watch TV with the remote control in hand.

A third reason not to get too worked up over the ideological biases of journalists is that reporters share a code of professional ethics that emphasizes impartiality as a core value. This code may be fraying in some areas due to the economic pressures favoring sensationalism in the news business, but it still holds strong in the area of politically balanced reporting. When reporters lose their perspective, there are editors to correct them. In order to find ideological bias in the news, we would have to assume that the procedures in news organizations designed to edit bias out of stories are either ineffective, or worse, they are part of a clever liberal media conspiracy to let bias through.

Fourth, and finally, even if some consistent political bias survived these screening mechanisms, the business managers for mainstream news organizations would surely root it out. There are some exceptions to this rule, such as FOX News (discussed in

Chapter 3), in which an ideological tint (conservative in this case) is used as a marketing strategy. For the most part, most reporters are small cogs in large business organizations that have a vested interest in producing a marketable, neutral, product. As journalism scholar Everette Dennis put it:

> . . . profits are central to the media; the news is more and more driven by market forces and market segmentation. Deliberately or even innocently alienating a portion of the audience through unfair and biased coverage of candidates and causes would be self-destructive. More important, it would be absolutely unacceptable to publishers, broadcast executives, and owners, who, last time I checked, were still running the show.[82]

What accounts then for the popular perception that members of the press introduce a liberal bias into the news? Above all, when it comes to politics and its emotional core of values, bias is largely in the eye of the beholder. Both conservatives and liberals tend to be upset with the press, but in the modern era, conservatives have raised charges of liberal bias more effectively as a tool of governing. More than thirty years ago, Richard Nixon charged the press with favoring liberal intellectuals and leftist activists in covering the War in Vietnam, and failing to report the views of the great "silent majority" of Americans who favored his policies. Because the right has waged its press bias campaign so effectively, relatively few voices from the left actually get into the mainstream media. For example, media scholars such as Edward Herman and Noam Chomsky tend to be heard only in alternative press outlets. Their view is that on important national interest issues of economics, military, and foreign policy, the press is more conservative than liberal, following the political cues of corporate interests, Wall Street, and the government.[83]

How could news reports possibly satisfy the conflicting public beliefs about politicians and political issues? Despite the impossibility of achieving perfect news neutrality (assuming that this is even desirable), both left and right continue to muster plenty of evidence for their charges of bias. The reader might be interested in comparing the news criticism of the leading conservative organization, Accuracy in Media (AIM), with that of the leading liberal one, Fairness and Accuracy in Reporting (FAIR). The AIM Web address is **www.aim.org**. The FAIR Web site is located at **www.fair.org**. In addition, more general access to news organizations, professional journalism associations, public opinion about the press and politics, and other political communication resources can be found on the author's Web site: **faculty.washington.edu/bennett**.

To be sure, fluctuations in the political content of the news do exist, but they tend not to be systematic (i.e., they are not all liberal or conservative). The political content fluctuations that do show up in studies can almost always be explained by factors outside of the ideological thinking of individual journalists.[84] Everette Dennis has summed up the endless debate over ideological bias in the press as "pointless and repetitive," concluding that "The media, alas, are centrist, determinedly so."[85]

What's Wrong with Press Bias and Political Partisanship?

Even if the contradictory perceptions of press bias were somehow true, they should not cause so much concern. We might even welcome an avowedly partisan press of the sort that thrived before the rise of commercial newspapers in the nineteenth century. The point of this discussion is simply to suggest that much of the popular thinking on the press today actually gets in the way of understanding more important information problems with the news about politics. It is unrealistic to think that the news could somehow report the truth in a way that everyone would see. This common fantasy about political reporting overlooks the fact that emotionally charged value clashes and contradictory information are at the core of politics.

The role for the press that the founders of this country imagined was far removed from the fantasies harbored by many people today. Thomas Jefferson imagined that communities would have many partisan news sources—not that any individual would achieve balance by reading them all. The path to public understanding in a society rich with competing partisan information was described in the famous Hutchins commission report on the American press over a half century ago:

> Nor was it supposed that many citizens would subscribe to all the local journals. It was more likely that each would take the one which would reinforce his prejudices. But in each village and town, with its relatively simple social structure and its wealth of social contacts, various opinions might encounter each other in face-to-face meetings; the truth, it was hoped, would be sorted out by competition in the local marketplace.[86]

As the Hutchins report made clear, we no longer live in such a world. Even fifty years ago, it was clear that competing partisan news sources were not commonly available, and that people did not live in communities where they would deliberate until reaching higher understandings of situations. For better or worse, the news has become distilled into highly uniform reports that present themselves as neutral, and from which people are expected to draw their own personal conclusions—generally without confronting fellow citizens with whom they disagree. The Hutchins Commission noted that this change from the democratic model of the press on which the nation was founded places important responsibilities on the contemporary press. In particular, news organizations should attempt to challenge dominant points of view that dominate simply because they are better publicized by government or interests. Those news organizations also need to go out of their way to bring into their reporting the perspectives of diverse voices from communities who have little opportunity for face-to-face deliberation. Unfortunately, news organizations fail to shoulder these responsibilities much of the time. The result is that citizens lack the perspective and deliberation necessary to reach confident personal understandings, much less public consensus, about many important issues.

A simple response to frustration about being unable to reach confident understandings or to reconcile our differences of opinion is to blame the press for bias. There may be press bias at work in the failure to translate the Jeffersonian role of the press into the modern mediated society. But the belief in liberal press bias surely distracts our attention from more troublesome information problems. Chapter 2 explores these more fundamental news biases, which include fragmentation (the lack of context surrounding emergent issues and problems), the personalization of stories around the most emotional aspects (rather than emphasizing broader social conditions and issues), the dramatization of often trivial aspects of events (and the search for sensational stories rather than representative ones), and a preoccupation with questions of authority and social order at the expense of analyzing underlying social problems and issues.

Beyond Truth and Objectivity

Beyond the understandable, but impossible, demand for truth or objectivity in the news lie the more serious information problems documented in this book. As outlined previously, the news is often too fragmentary and superficial in its focus on crises, scandals, human melodramas, and political authorities and their power games to be of much use to citizens. According to this view, the public receives a too timid and politically limited picture of events, along with little motivation to support critical political thought and action.[87]

The general preoccupation with finding the best story, rather than the best understanding of a situation, produces little information diversity in mainstream news reporting. For example a comparative study of journalists in five nations found that American journalists may be the freest in the world—at least they cited fewer limits on their reporting than their counterparts in other democracies. American reporters, however, also made the narrowest range of choices about how they would cover various hypothetical news situations.[88]

It may be true, as we will learn later in the book, that most people are lazy in their information-gathering habits. Yet rather than exploring ways to stimulate more active and informed citizens, neither news organizations nor political actors seem committed to creating an information environment that would stimulate critical public deliberation and high levels of attention and interest in most political issues.[89] Many issues, from abortion rights to taxes, generate rich news coverage and sophisticated public understandings. However, those issues are often driven by intense citizen activism in the first place. By contrast, important issues such as military spending, energy policy, and even decisions to go to war may receive little critical media scrutiny until crisis or scandal prompt dramatic, after-the-fact stories, such as What happened to California's energy supply? or Why did the war and the rebuilding of Iraq not go according to plan?

Understanding our national information system and considering what to do about its problems are the subjects of this book. The first step is to look beneath the surface of the news to see how images of society and politics are produced and distributed. After that, we can evaluate how those images either help or hinder people in thinking and acting effectively in their lives.

WHAT KIND OF NEWS WOULD BETTER SERVE DEMOCRACY?

If we allow ourselves to imagine a different kind of news, there are a number of features that might be desirable from a democratic standpoint:

- Independent issue agendas developed by each news organization would provide a more diverse information environment.

- Diverse voices and viewpoints aimed at reducing the gap that ordina often feel separating them from the politicians and political insiders inate news content.
- More analysis of how politics operates behind the scenes of news events would help people understand how political decisions are reached and how they might become involved.
- More historical context would help establish the origins of problems in the news and limit the ability of politicians to reinvent history to suit their purposes.
- More coverage of citizen political activists would help ordinary people evaluate official spin more critically.
- More positive images of active citizens might encourage more people to become involved in the political conflicts they witness in the news.
- Better use of interactive technologies could link news audiences to each other and to civic organizations to learn more about issues and take effective action.

Many interesting experiments are underway that may reinvent the news and more generally improve how citizens communicate with each other and with their leaders. We will explore some of them in later chapters. The development of digital technologies is already enabling citizen activists to create their own information channels and to organize effective political actions. In the case study in Chapter 8, we will see how a news organization as venerable as the British Broadcasting Corporation (BBC) is pioneering an interactive system involving *micro media* e-mail news alerts that draw people to *middle media* Web sites where they can communicate with each other and even shape the stories covered on BBC *mass media* news. Going beyond its charter to inform citizens, the BBC is reinventing its very mission by adding the goal of helping citizens to organize and act effectively. While such experiments may not be good news for the spin doctors, they may reinvigorate democracy from the citizen standpoint.

NOTES

1. For investigative reports that were generally not followed up by the mainstream press, see Seymour Hersh, "King's Ransom," *New Yorker,* October 22, 2002, 35–44, and "Selective Intelligence," *New Yorker,* May 12, 2003, 44–51. For an explanation of why, see Robert M. Entman, *Projections of Power: Framing News, Public Opinion, and U.S. Foreign Policy* (Chicago: University of Chicago Press, 2004).
2. For more detailed analysis of this, see the case study in Chapter 5 of this book. Also, W. Lance Bennett, "Operation Perfect Storm: The Press and the Iraq War," *Political Communication Report,* International Communication Association and American Political Science Association, 13, no. 3. (Fall 2003).
3. David Stout, "U.S. Ignores Saddams at Its Peril, Cheney Says," *International Herald Tribune,* Saturday–Sunday, October 11–12, 2003, 4.
4. Based on national polls of 3,334 respondents taken from June–September 2003 and reported in Steven Kull, "Misperceptions, the Media, and the Iraq War," report of the Program on International Policy Attitudes, University of Maryland, October 2, 2003.
5. Ibid.

6. See Benjamin I. Page, *Who Deliberates?* (Chicago: University of Chicago Press, 1996).

7. William A. Gamson, "Promoting Political Engagement," in ed. W. Lance Bennett and Robert M. Entman, *Mediated Politics: Communication in the Future of Democracy,* (New York: Cambridge University Press, 2001), 56–74. See also Myra M. Feree, William A. Gamson, Jurgen Gerhards, and Dieter Rucht, *Shaping Abortion Discourse: Democracy and the Public Sphere in Germany and the United States* (New York: Cambridge University Press, 2002).

8. These issues range from industrial collapse and the dislocation of workers on the low end of citizen engagement images in news coverage to the controversy over nuclear power on the higher end. See Gamson, "Promoting Political Engagement."

9. See W. Lance Bennett, "Toward a Theory of Press-State Relations in the United States," *Journal of Communication* 40 (Spring 1990): 103–27.

10. Bruce Bimber, *Information and American Democracy from the Federalist to the Internet* (New York: Cambridge University Press, 2003). The quote is from Chapter 1, based on a prepublication draft of the manuscript.

11. See also, Richard R. John, *Spreading the News: The American Postal System from Franklin to Morse* (Cambridge, MA: Harvard University Press, 1995), and Timothy E. Cook, *Governing with the News: The News Media as a Political Institution* (Chicago: University of Chicago Press, 1998).

12. Samuel Kernell, *Going Public: New Strategies of Presidential Leadership,* 3rd ed. (Washington, DC: Congressional Quarterly Press, 1997).

13. See various perspectives on this in Bennett and Entman, eds., *Mediated Politics.*

14. Source: Politics Online *Politicker,* November 17, 2001, **http://www.PoliticsOnline.com**.

15. Shanto Iyengar and Donald R. Kinder, *News That Matters* (Chicago: University of Chicago Press, 1987).

16. Kernell, *Going Public.*

17. John Zaller, *Nature and Origins of Mass Opinion* (New York: Cambridge University Press, 1992).

18. Shanto Iyenger, *Is Anyone Responsible?* (Chicago: University of Chicago Press, 1991).

19. For further discussion and illustration of this point, see W. Lance Bennett and Jarol B. Manheim, "The Big Spin: Strategic Communication and the Transformation of Pluralist Democracy," in *Mediated Politics: Communication in the Future of Democracy,* ed. W. Lance Bennett and Robert M. Entman (New York: Cambridge University Press, 2001), 279–98.

20. Robert Dahl, *Democracy and Its Critics* (New Haven, CT: Yale University Press, 1989).

21. See Michael X. Delli Carpini and Scott Keeter, *What Americans Know About Politics and Why It Matters* (New Haven, CT: Yale University Press, 1996).

22. Based on Pew Research Center surveys. **http://www.people-press.org/agerept.htm**.

23. Doris Graber, "Adapting Political News to the Needs of Twenty-First Century Americans," in *Mediated Politics,* ed. Bennett and Entman, 433–52.

24. Doris Graber, *Mass Media and American Politics,* 3rd ed. (Washington, DC: Congressional Quarterly Press, 1989).

25. Michael X. Delli Carpini and Bruce A. Williams, "Let Us Infotain You: Politics in the New Media Environment," in *Mediated Politics,* ed. Bennett and Entman, 160–81.

26. Number of jokes told by Jay Leno, David Letterman, Conan O'Brien, and Bill Maher based on research by the Center for Media and Public Affairs reported in *Brill's Content,* "Ticker," (July/August 1999): 143.

27. Marc Peyser, "Jon Stewart: Seriously Funny," *Newsweek,* January 5, 2004: 70–77.

28. Matthew Baum, "Sex, Lies, and War: How Soft News Brings Foreign Policy to the Inattentive Public," *American Political Science Review* 96, no. 2 (2002): 91–109.

29. See, for example, Kevin G. Barnhurst and Diana Mutz, "American Journalism and the Decline of Event-Centered Reporting," *Journal of Communication* 47, no. 4 (Autumn 1997): 27–53.

30. Thomas E. Patterson, "Doing Well and Doing Good: How Soft News and Critical Journalism Are Shrinking the News Audience and Weakening Democracy—And What News Outlets Can

Do About It," (Published by Joan Shorenstein Center on the Press, Politics, and Public Policy, Kennedy School of Government, Harvard University, 2000), 14.

31. Timothy Cook, *Governing with the News: The News Media as a Political Institution* (Chicago: University of Chicago Press, 1998).

32. William Schneider, remarks delivered at the conference on "The Clinton Presidency: Campaigning, Governing and the Psychology of Leadership," held at the Graduate Center, City University of New York, November 18–19, 1993. (A video of Schneider's talk is available from the university's Ph.D. program in political science; attn: Stanley Renshon.)

33. Marvin Kalb, "Press-Politics and Improving the Public Dialogue," *Political Communication Report* 3 (June 1992): 1–3.

34. Ibid., 1.

35. See W. Lance Bennett and Regina Lawrence, "News Icons and the Mainstreaming of Social Change," *Journal of Communication* 45, no. 3 (Summer 1995): 20–39.

36. Jim Rutenberg and Bill Carter, "Network Coverage a Target of Fire from Conservatives," *New York Times,* (November 7, 2001), B2.

37. Ibid.

38. For a detailed account of the comment and its aftermath, see the syndicated column by Arianna Huffington on September 24, 2001. **http://www.ariannaonline.com/columns/files/092401.html**.

39. Maureen Dowd, "We Love the Liberties They Hate," *New York Times,* September 30, 2001, "Week in Review", 13.

40. Ibid.

41. Susan Sontag, comment, *New Yorker,* September 24, 2001, 32.

42. Ibid.

43. Ibid.

44. Felicity Barringer, "Reporters Want More Access, but Are Careful to Ask Nicely," *New York Times,* October 22, 2001, B3.

45. Biden and Hastert quotes are from Seymour M. Hersh, "Watching the Warheads," *New Yorker,* November 5, 2001, 50.

46. Todd S. Purdom, "Democrats Are Questioning Bush on the Future Conduct of the War," *New York Times,* March 1, 2002, A1.

47. Ibid.

48. Rutenberg and Carter, "Network Coverage a Target of Fire from Conservatives," B2.

49. Peter Arnet's remarks are from a speech titled " A Crtitical Test for the World's Media: Does It Help or Hinder the War Against Terrorism?" (delivered at the Renaissance Theater in Berlin, Germany, November 18, 2001).

50. Ibid.

51. Jim Rutenberg, "Hearts, Minds, and Satellites," *New York Times,* October 15, 2001, C11.

52. Seth Schiesel and Felicity Barringer, "News Media Risk Big Losses to Cover War," *New York Times,* October 22, 2001, C1.

53. Jim Rutenberg, "Fox Portrays a War of Good and Evil, and Many Applaud," *New York Times,* December 3, 2001, C1.

54. Ibid., C5.

55. Maureen Dowd, "It's Ugly When Control Freaks Lose Control," *International Herald Tribune,* July 22, 2003, 8.

56. Lawrence K. Grossman, "Does Local TV News Need a Nanny?" *Columbia Journalism Review* (May/June 1998), 33.

57. Quoted in James Brooke, "The F.C.C. Supports TV News as Free Speech," *New York Times,* May 3, 1998, 27.

58. Robert McChesney, *Rich Media, Poor Democracy: Communication Politics in Dubious Times* (Urbana: University of Illinois Press, 1999).

59. Lawrence K. Grossman, "Does Local TV News Need a Nanny?" 33.

60. Thomas E. Patterson, "Doing Well and Doing Good: How Soft News and Critical Journalism Are Shrinking the News Audience and Weakening Democracy—And What News Outlets Can Do About It," (Harvard University: Joan Shorenstein Center on Press, Politics, and Public Policy, 2000), 3.

61. Ibid., 4.

62. Center for Media and Public Affairs study. **http://www.cmpa.com/factoid/prevyrs.htm**.

63. James F. Hoge, Jr., "Foreign News: Who Gives a Damn?" *Columbia Journalism Review* (November/December 1997): 49.

64. Ibid.

65. Neil Hickey, "Money Lust: How Pressure for Profit Is Perverting Journalism," *Columbia Journalism Review* (July/August 1998): 32.

66. Ibid.

67. Ibid., 33.

68. Ibid., 32.

69. Ibid., 7.

70. Grossman, "Does Local TV News Need a Nanny?" 33.

71. *Brill's Content,* "Ticker." July/August, 1999, p. 143.

72. Center for Media and Public Affairs study reported in Richard Morin, "An Airwave of Crime: While TV News Coverage of Murders Has Soared—Feeding Public Fears—Crime Is Actually Down," *Washington Post National Weekly Edition,* August 18, 1997, 34.

73. Ibid.

74. See Mark Fishman and Grey Cavender, eds., *Entertaining Crime: Television Reality Programs* (New York: Aldine de Gruyter), 1998.

75. Richard Morin, "An Airwave of Crime," *Washington Post National Weekly Edition,* August 18, 1997, 34.

76. Daniel Lazare, "The Upside to a Downturn," *Columbia Journalism Review* (May/June 1991), 56.

77. Tom Rosenstiel and Bill Kovach, "Don't Facts Matter Anymore? We Are Descending into an Era of Journalism by Assertion Rather Than Verification," *Washington Post National Weekly Edition,* March 8, 1999, 21. At the time of this statement, Rosenstiel was director of the Pew Project for Excellence in Journalism, and Kovach was curator of Harvard's Nieman Foundation for Journalism. An expanded version of this argument appears in their book, *Warp Speed: America in the Age of Mixed Media* (New York: The Century Foundation Press, 1999).

78. Based on Pew Research Center polls taken in 1985 and 1997. Located on the Internet at **http://www.people-press.org/97medrpt.htm**.

79. This finding is reported, for example, in David Weaver and G. Cleveland Wilhoit, *The American Journalist: U.S. News People at the End of an Era* (Mahwah, NJ: Lawrence Erlbaum, 1996). A 1996 Freedom Forum/Roper survey of 139 Washington news people indicated that those with a left-of-center leaning outnumbered those leaning right-of-center by a margin of 61 percent to 9 percent. See Neil Hickey, "Is Fox News Fair?" *Columbia Journalism Review* (March/April 1998): 31.

80. Quoted in Jim Rutenberg, "Making News Instead of Broadcasting It," *New York Times,* October 19, 2001, B6.

81. Thomas Patterson and Wolfgang Donsbach note a slight but significant difference in how liberal and conservative journalists approach hypothetical stories. However, it is not clear whether even such small differences persist when hypothetical stories are replaced by real ones and subjected to editing processes within news organizations. See Thomas E. Patterson and Wolfgang Donsbach, "News Decisions: Journalists as Partisan Actors," *Political Communication* 13 (October-December 1996): 455–68.

82. Everette E. Dennis, "How 'Liberal' Are the Media, Anyway? The Continuing Conflict of Professionalism and Partisanship," *Press/Politics* 2 (Fall 1997): 116.

83. Edward S. Herman and Noam Chomsky, *Manufacturing Consent: The Political Economy of the Mass Media* (New York: Pantheon, 1988).

84. See, for example, Bennett, "Toward a Theory of Press-State Relations in the United States."

85. Dennis, "How 'Liberal' Are the Media, Anyway?" 119.

86. From Robert D. Leigh, ed., *A Free and Responsible Press* (Chicago: University of Chicago Press, 1947), 15. Report of the Hutchins Commission on Freedom of the Press.

87. See, for example, Iyenger, *Is Anyone Responsible?*

88. Thomas E. Patterson, "Irony of the Free Press: Professional Journalism and News Diversity," paper presented at the annual meeting of the American Political Science Association, Chicago, September 3–6, 1992, 2.

89. Robert Entman has asserted that the contemporary information system virtually excludes citizen-engagement values in constructing most political messages. See Robert M. Entman, *Democracy Without Citizens: The Media and the Decay of American Politics* (New York: Oxford University Press, 1989). According to another scholar, this communication system leaves people with little useful understanding of the issues that affect their lives. See Jarol B. Manheim, *All of the People, All the Time: Strategic Communication and American Politics* (Armonk, NY: M.E. Sharpe, 1991).

Chapter 2

News Content: Four Information Biases That Matter

It is a writer's obligation to impose narrative. Everyone does this. Every time you take a lump of material and turn it into something you are imposing a narrative. It's a writer's obligation to do this. And, by the same token, it is apparently a journalist's obligation to pretend that he never does anything of the sort. The journalist claims to believe that the narrative emerges from the lump of material, rises up and smacks you in the face like marsh gas.

Nora Ephron

Here is how *The Washington Post* described President Bush's dramatic landing on the aircraft carrier *Abraham Lincoln*—the news event that set the stage for his speech announcing that the military phase of the War in Iraq was over:

> When the Viking carrying Bush made its tailhook landing on the aircraft carrier *USS Abraham Lincoln* off California yesterday, the scene brought presidential imagery to a whole new level. Bush emerged from the cockpit in a full olive flight suit and combat boots, his helmet tucked jauntily under his left arm. As he exchanged salutes with the sailors, his ejection harness, hugging him tightly between the legs, gave him the bowlegged swagger of a top gun.[1]

This image was replayed time and again on television news shows. It was proclaimed as the mother of all photo-ops, a publicity event that would establish Mr. Bush as a world leader, and a supremely confident commander in chief. Many journalists anticipated that this news image would also help secure an easy victory over any imaginable Democratic candidate who might emerge to challenge Mr. Bush in the 2004 election. Consider how MSNBC's Keith Olberman introduced the live coverage on his program *Countdown* and then discussed it with his guest Chris Matthews, the anchor of another MSNBC program *Hardball:*

> **OLBERMAN:** Good evening. Franklin Delano Roosevelt was the first serving president to fly in an airplane, Theodore Roosevelt was the first to take the still risky ride in an automobile, and White House historians disagree about whether it was James K. Polk or John Tyler, who in the 1840s was the first to, as his contemporaries feared, risk his immortal soul by being photographed. Today George W. Bush skipped the safer route of declaring combat over from the White House to instead become the first president to make an arrested landing on an Air Force carrier. The president's speech is live here on MSNBC in 58 minutes. . . .

> **OLBERMANN:** This was victory lap day. I mean, we're seeing the sign aboard the Lincoln right now that reads "Mission Accomplished." And we. . . .

> **MATTHEWS:** More than that, Keith, it's a statement. It's saying to the Democratic Party or anyone else who wants to challenge this man for a full eight-year presidency, Try to do this. Look at me. Do you really think you've got a guy in your casting studio, your casting director can come up with, who can match what I did today? Imagine Joe Lieberman in this costume, or even John Kerry. Nobody looks right in the role Bush has set for the presidency—commander-in-chief, medium height, medium build, looks good in a jet pilot's costume—or uniform, rather—has a certain swagger, not too literary, certainly not too verbal, but a guy who speaks plainly and wins wars. I think that job definition is hard to match for the Dems.[2]

Whether the story is told by the venerable *Washington Post,* or in breathless cable talk show chatter, the terms are much the same. The emphasis is on how the news story plays as an entertainment drama. Does the flight suit look good? Does the swagger seem natural? Does Mr. Bush look right for the part? Can the opposition cast anyone more convincing for the role of president? But what about the relationship between such news images and more substantial leadership qualities or the progress of the war itself? These questions will be addressed more fully in the case study later in this chapter, which uses tools developed in the chapter to analyze George W. Bush's news image.

A DIFFERENT KIND OF BIAS

The general focus of this chapter is on a deeper but less obvious sort of news bias—one that favors *dramatic* and *personalized* aspects of events over more complex—and potentially more engaging—underlying political realities. The result of focusing on individual actors and the dramas swirling around them is to make many political situations seem fragmented and confusing. Audiences are often left hanging, waiting for daily story updates about disorder and the restoration of authority, normalcy, and control, rather than installments on news narratives that reveal the politics behind the events.

Consider some of the other choices that news organizations had in framing the aircraft carrier landing story. *Framing involves choosing a broad organizing theme for selecting, emphasizing, and linking the elements of a story. Frames are thematic categories that integrate and give meaning to the scene, the characters, their actions, and supporting documentation.*[3] For example, the carrier landing story could have been framed as a publicity stunt. The story also could have been framed around challenges to the administration link between Iraq and the War on Terror. The path of least resistance was to fill the news frame with a well-staged White House dramatic production starring the president. This near universal news framing decision left the underlying situation fragmented: obscuring the link between terrorism and Iraq and endowing a formerly weak foreign policy leader with a Hollywood swagger. The Hollywood moment also made for a nice chapter ending in the authority-disorder narrative: a promise of return to normalcy—"Mission Accomplished."

Yet the long-term news frames offered by the administration did not comfortably contain disturbing reports of U.S. battle casualties and civil chaos in Iraq. Journalists who shifted the framing of the conflict away from White House communication strategies on their own were accused of liberal bias, or being unpatriotic, as explained in the case study in Chapter 1. The Democrats failed to offer much of an opportunity to open the news gates, as they were too busy attacking each other in the presidential primaries to agree on a party position that might shift the framing to a more substantive drama involving a clash between the president and political opponents. As a result, only 34 of 414 stories told by ABC, NBC, and CBS on the buildup to and rationale for the Iraq War from September 2002 through February 2003 originated outside the White House.[4]

What were people to think? The polls reported at the opening of Chapter 1 show that most people tried to accept what they saw on the news and generally supported administration framing even months after the situation in Iraq deteriorated. One factor in this public response was a poor factual grasp of the situation. New events or political developments would eventually lead news organizations to reframe the story, but the risk of such sudden frame shifts is that people feel deceived and even less sure what to believe. This is how the biases in the U.S. communication system contribute to a public that is increasingly cynical and disillusioned with politics and government.[5]

The paradox is that journalists complain about the scripted and staged events they cover, but they seem unable to find other ways to write stories or to replace the cynical tone with perspectives that might help citizens become more engaged. As a result of these and other factors, large numbers of people actively avoid politics, while watching the media spectacle with a mixture of disbelief and disapproval. Meanwhile, more people escape from public affairs and political participation into ever more personalized media worlds that one observer has likened to the gated communities and suburban enclaves into which many people have physically migrated in society.[6]

The point here is not to place the blame for civic disengagement on the news media. Journalists complained frequently that events that are so heavily managed by professional communication consultants give them little to work with. This begs the question: Why was there so little innovative coverage that might stimulate citizen engagement with events as they are happening? This chapter takes a close look at news content. The concern is with information biases that make news hard to use as a guide to citizen action because they obscure the big picture in which daily events take place. In addition, they often convey a negative or cynical tone about politics that undermines citizen motivation for digging deeper to learn more or to become engaged.

As explained in Chapter 1, most debates about journalistic bias are concerned with the question of ideology. For example, does the news have a liberal or conservative, a Democratic or Republican, drift? To briefly review the argument from the last chapter, some variation in news content or political emphasis does occur, but it can seldom be explained as the result of journalists routinely injecting their partisan views into the news. The avoidance of political partisanship by journalists is reinforced, among other means, by the professional ethics codes of journalists, by the editors who monitor their work, and by the business values of the companies they work for.

Another important point to recall is that people who see a consistent ideological press bias are seeing it with the help of their own ideology. This generalization is supported by opinion research showing that people in the middle see the press as generally neutral, whereas those on the left complain that the news is too conservative, and those on the right think the news has a left-leaning bias.[7] If neutrality or objectivity could be achieved, citizens with strong views on particular issues would not recognize it. Moreover, even if the news contained strong ideological biases, people with a point of view are most able to detect and to defend themselves against them. Indeed, many nations favor a partisan press system as the best way to conduct public debates and to explore issues, a matter to which we will return in later chapters.

While many Americans are caught up in dead-end debates about one kind of news bias that is less dangerous than commonly assumed, few are noticing other information bias that really are worth worrying about. A more sensible approach to news bias is to look for those universal information problems that hinder the efforts of citizens, whatever their ideology, to take part in political life. The task for the remainder of this book is to understand the U.S. public information system at a deeper level. Fortunately, most of the pieces to the news puzzle are right in front of us. For all of its defects, the news continues to be largely a public production, with government press offices, media organizations, and popular tastes all available for inspection. The openness of the system may be its saving grace when we turn to questions of reform later in the book.

FOUR INFORMATION BIASES THAT MATTER: AN OVERVIEW

Our expectations about the quality of public information are rather high. Most of us grew up with history books full of journalistic heroism exercised in the name of truth and free speech. We learned that the American Revolution was inspired by the political rhetoric of the underground press and by printers' effective opposition to the British Stamp Act. The lesson from the trial of Peter Zenger has endured through time: *the truth is not libelous.* The goal of the history book journalists was as unswerving as it was noble: to guarantee for the American people the most accurate, critical, coherent, illuminating, and independent reporting of political events. Yet Peter Zenger would probably not recognize, much less feel comfortable working in, a modern news organization.

Like it or not, the news has become a mass-produced consumer product, bearing little resemblance to history book images. Communication technologies, beginning with the wire services and progressing to satellite feeds and digital video, interact with corporate profit motives to create generic, "lowest-common-denominator" information formats. In particular, there are four characteristics of news that stand out as reasons why public information in the United States does not always advance the cause of democracy: *personalization, dramatization, fragmentation,* and the *authority-disorder bias.*

PERSONALIZATION

If there is a single most important flaw in the American news style, it is the overwhelming tendency to downplay the big social, economic, or political picture in favor of the human trials, tragedies, and triumphs that sit at the surface of events. For example, instead of focusing on power and process, the media concentrate on the people engaged in political combat over the issues. The reasons for this are numerous, from the journalist's fear that probing analysis will turn off audiences to the relative ease of telling the human-interest side of a story as opposed to explaining deeper causes and effects.

When people are invited to take the news personally, they can find a wide range of private, emotional meanings in it. However, the meanings inspired by personalized news may not add up to the shared critical understandings on which healthy citizen involvement thrives. The focus on personalities encourages a passive spectator attitude among the public. Whether the focus is on sympathetic heroes and victims or hateful scoundrels and culprits, the media preference for personalized human-interest news creates a "can't-see-the-forest-for-the-trees" information bias that makes it difficult to see the big (institutional) picture that lies beyond the many actors crowding center stage who are caught in the eye of the news camera.

The tendency to personalize the news would be less worrisome if human-interest angles were used to hook audiences into more serious analysis of issues and problems. Almost all great literature and theater, from the Greek dramas to the modern day, uses strong characters to promote audience identifications and reactions in order to draw people into thinking about larger moral and social issues. American news often stops at the character development stage, however, and leaves the larger lessons and social significance, if there is any, to the imagination of the audience. As a result, the main problem with personalized news is that the focus on personal concerns is seldom linked to more in-depth analysis. What often passes for analysis are opaque news formulas such as "he/she was a reflection of us," a line that was used in the media frenzies that followed the deaths of Britain's Princess Diana and America's John Kennedy, Jr. Even when large portions of the public reject personalized news formulas, as during the frenzied journalistic and prosecutorial preoccupation with President Clinton's personal sexual behavior, the personalization never stops. This systematic tendency to personalize situations is one of the defining biases of news.

DRAMATIZATION

Compounding the information bias of personalization is a second news property in which the aspects of events that are reported tend to be the ones most easily dramatized in simple "stories." As previously noted, American journalism has settled overwhelmingly on the reporting form of stories or narratives, as contrasted, for example, to analytical essays, political polemics, or more scientific-style problem reports. Stories invite dramatization, particularly with sharply drawn actors at their center.

News dramas emphasize crisis over continuity, the present over the past or future, and the personalities at their center. News dramas downplay complex policy information, the workings of government institutions, and the bases of power behind the central characters. Lost in the news drama (*melodrama* is often the more appropriate term) are sustained analyses of persistent problems such as inequality, hunger, resource depletion, population pressures, environmental collapse, toxic waste, and political oppression. Serious though such human problems are, they just are not dramatic enough on a day-to-day level to make the news until they produce crises that trigger the authority-disorder narrative.

Crises are the perfect news material because they fit neatly into the dramatization bias. The "crisis cycle" portrayed in the news is classic dramatic fare, with rising action, falling action, sharply drawn characters, and of course, plot resolutions. By its very definition, a crisis is something that will reach dramatic closure through cleanup efforts or humanitarian relief operations. Unfortunately, the crisis cycles in the news only reinforce the popular impression that high levels of human difficulty are inevitable and therefore acceptable.[8] Crises in the news are often resolved when situations return to "manageable" levels of difficulty, yet underlying problems often continuing to grow. The news is certainly not the cause of these problems, but it could become part of the solution if it substituted illumination of causes for dramatic coverage of symptoms.

As in the case of personalization, dramatization would not be a problem if it were used mainly as an attention-focusing device to introduce more background and context surrounding events. Drama can help us engage with the great forces of history, science, politics, or human relations. When drama is used to bring analysis to mind, it is a good thing. When drama is employed as a cheap emotional device to focus on human conflict and travail, or farce and frailty, the larger significance of events becomes easily lost in waves of immediate emotion. The potential advantages of drama to enlighten and explain are sacrificed to the lesser tendencies of melodrama to excite, anger, and further personalize events. Thus the news often resembles real-life soap operas, only with far more important consequences.

One of the things that makes the news dramatic—indeed, that may even drive news drama—is the use of visuals: photos, graphics, and live-action video. These elements of stories not only make the distant world seem more real, they make the news more believable. In many ways, particularly for television, the pictures may help editors and reporters decide which stories to tell and how to tell them. Again, there is nothing inherently wrong with emphasizing visuals in news production. In fact one might argue that thinking visually is the best way to engage the senses in communicating about society and politics. There is often, however, a tension between not reporting important stories that are hard to picture and reporting possibly unimportant stories simply because they offer great visual images. The discussion in Chapter 3 explains the economics of editorial decisions to start with the pictures and then add the words. The selection of news stories primarily because they offer dramatic images is one of several important reasons why the news is often so fragmented or disconnected from larger political or economic contexts that would provide other ways to tell the story.

FRAGMENTATION

The emphasis on personal and dramatic qualities of events feeds into a third information characteristic of the news: the isolation of stories from each other and from their larger contexts so that information in the news becomes fragmented and hard to assemble into a big picture. The fragmentation of information begins by emphasizing individual actors over the political contexts in which they operate. Fragmentation is then heightened by the use of dramatic formats that turn events into self-contained, isolated happenings. The fragmentation of information is further exaggerated by the severe space limits nearly all media impose for fear of boring readers and viewers with too much information.

As a result, the news comes to us in sketchy dramatic capsules that make it difficult to see the causes of problems, their historical significance, or the connections across issues. It can even be difficult to follow the development of a particular issue over time as stories rise and fall more in response to the actions and reactions of prominent public figures than to independent reporting based on investigation of events. In addition, because it is difficult to bring historical background into the news, the impression is created of a world of chaotic events and crises that appear and disappear because the news picture offers little explanation of their origins.

THE AUTHORITY-DISORDER BIAS

Whether the world is returned to a safe, normal place, or whether the very idea of a normal world is called into question, the news is preoccupied with order, along with related questions of whether authorities are capable of establishing or restoring it. It is easy to see why these generic plot elements are so central to news: They are versatile and tireless themes that can be combined endlessly within personalized, dramatized, and fragmented news episodes. When the dramatic restoration of normalcy is not a plausible frame for an event, the news may quickly challenge authority itself, perhaps by publicizing the latest scandal charge against a leader or by opening the news gates to one politician willing to attack another.

In the past, it could be argued (as earlier editions of this book did) that the news more often resolved the authority-order balance in favor of official pronouncements aimed at "normalizing" conflicted situations by creating the appearance of order and control. A classic scenario of politics, according to political scientist Murray Edelman, is for authorities to take center stage to respond to crises (sometimes after having stirred them up in the first place) with emotionally reassuring promises that they will be handled effectively.[9] Today's authorities still play out their parts, but the news increasingly finds ways to challenge the pronouncements of officials and the presumption of order in society. In short, the biggest change in portrayals of authority and order in the news since earlier editions of this book is that the news balance has shifted away from trusted authorities providing reassuring promises to restore chaotic situations to a state of order or normalcy. Normalizing stories continue to appear, of course, but a growing news trend is to portray unsympathetic, scheming politicians who often fail to solve problems, leaving disorder in their wake. Local news has streamlined the plot even further to report simple mayhem.

What is the evidence for the proposition that news is more negative and less likely to paint reassuring pictures of the return to normalcy following dramatic crises and scandals? Recall the research discussed in the last chapter suggesting that, for reasons having more to do with the news business than with external realities, the following changes have been charted in news content in recent years:[10]

- Increased levels of mayhem (crime, violence, accidents, health threats, freeway chases, and other images of social chaos)
- Greater volume of criticism of government, politicians, and their policies, and less focus on the substance of policies
- Higher journalistic tone of cynicism and negativity

In an industry competing for fickle and shrinking audiences, images of disorder can be amplified through subtle emphases in news writing. For example, is the traditional American family *threatened* by the increase in single-parent and two-working-parent households, or is the family in America simply *changing* in these ways as part of the normal course of social change?

As news organizations take greater dramatic license with news plots, the elements of authority and disorder are often mixed to achieve the greatest dramatic effect. A typical example comes from a local newscast in Orlando, Florida, where Channel 6 announced an "exclusive" and promised a report from their "live truck" at the scene. The newscast opened with the anchor describing "A shocking scene in a Lake Mary neighborhood tonight. A home surrounded by crime-scene tape. A death police are calling 'suspicious.' " As the anchor spoke, the screen flashed the words "Neighborhood Shocker." Cut to the reporter live from the scene who further dramatized the death of a 66-year-old woman by saying that police did not know what happened. As if to document this claim, the reporter interviewed a police officer who said that there were no signs of violence, forced entry, or robbery. Although this statement could easily have supported either an order or a disorder plot for the story, the local news format clearly favored playing the murder mystery/shocker plot. The reporter announced that the police planned an autopsy the next day and did not know what they would find. The live feed ended with the reporter saying that, in the meantime, they "want to keep a very tight lid on what happened. . . . Live in Lake Mary, Nicole Smith, Channel 6 News." The next day, it turned out that the woman had died naturally of a heart attack. So much for the "Neighborhood Shocker." As one observer noted, "Journalism Shocker" would have been a more appropriate on-screen warning.[11]

The political poster story of the 1990s was about wasteful government spending. Many news organizations, both local and national, have run prominent features on "How government is wasting your tax dollars." The lure of such dramatic accounts over more representative news descriptions is illustrated in a *Los Angeles Times* investigative series on government spending on computers in different agencies. Even though the investigation turned up many positive examples of taxpayer dollars well spent, here is how the story opened:

> WASHINGTON—After pumping $300 billion into computer systems in the last two decades, the federal government has compiled a record of failure that has jeopardized the nation's welfare, eroded public safety and squandered untold billions of dollars.[12]

Whether or not most events fit the authority-disorder plot, it is easy enough to make them fit. A news show with a regular feature on government waste will, of course, find some alleged example of waste every time the feature is scheduled. Also, since there are few features on good things the government is doing, examples of government thrift (other than those forced by budget cuts) are less likely to be news.

HOW COMPETING JOURNALISTS WRITE SUCH SIMILAR STORIES

How does the news become so standardized despite competition among journalists for fresh angles? Let's begin with three propositions.

- First, journalists write stories. These narratives organize complex events into familiar, easy-to-grasp communication packages.
- Second, because they seek to avoid ideology or political bias, journalists represent those stories as neutral or impartial (codes for "objective") renderings of political reality.
- Third, because many stories continue into the future, journalists face the constant prospect of how to advance a story even when there may be nothing new coming from the principal actors to report.

On the face of it, there is nothing inherently wrong with the narrative form. People grasp stories intuitively and generally find them more engaging than dry analyses. One may learn more about a period in history from reading great novels than standard academic works—or from reading academic works presented as dramatic narratives. In practice, however, the narrative style of American journalism often translates into a strange combination of (1) uncritical reporting of staged political dramas crafted by professional consultants for the purpose of being reported as objective political happenings, (2) followed by scathing press criticism of the very same politicians later on when the supply of new plot developments is not coming fast enough from the spin doctors, or when opponents go on the attack and provide more personalized and dramatic material.

This dynamic produces a steady supply of news even when there is little of substance to report. This explains how journalists can compete often ruthlessly for the next detail in a story and all end up sticking to much the same daily story line. And, if one news organization drifts away into new plot territory (unless it is on the trail of a bombshell tip), the implicit principle of objectivity leads the editors to ask their journalists how come they didn't get the story right (i.e., the same as the other leading organizations). Finally, when challenged as to why the news so often takes on a numbing sameness, journalists can cite the code of neutrality (objectivity) that forces them to cover what they are offered by politicians even if it seems contrived or tedious. In an acerbic look at how so many competing reporters manage to converge on such unhelpful information formats, Joan Didion describes the code of Washington reporting:

> The genuflection toward "fairness" is a familiar newsroom piety. In practice the excuse for a good deal of autopilot reporting and lazy thinking but in theory a benign ideal. In Washington, however, a community in which the management of the news has become the single overriding preoccupation of the core industry, what "fairness" has often come to mean is a scrupulous passivity, an agreement to cover the story not as it is occurring but as it is presented, which is to say, as it is manufactured.[13]

These simple reporting codes explain a great deal about the information system that the American people live with. Cut into this system where you will, each player—whether political actor, journalist, or citizen—has a different view of it. Yet the result is a remarkably standardized information system that has a set of clearly recognizable biases, which we shall explore in greater depth in the remainder of this chapter. The system produced by this core code is competitive, adversarial, and fully captivating for those insiders (politicians and the press) who are caught up in it. It is equally off-putting for those members of the public who often see themselves as outsiders. In a poll taken after the unpleasant coverage of the Clinton-Lewinsky sex scandal, fully 72 percent of the public felt that the press was driving the story rather than just reporting the facts.[14] The main point is that we can begin to understand how journalistic choices are made and how the information biases described in this chapter become inscribed in so much of the news. For example, we can understand why most journalists who told and retold the story of the Clinton–Lewinsky sex scandal covered the tawdry details and not the political motives or the questionable links among those who served up those details to the press. In his review of Didion's book, prominent journalist Joseph Lelyveld summarizes Didion's criticism of Michael Isikoff, a reporter who brought much of the scandal to light:

> Isikoff—the *Newsweek* reporter who brought Linda Tripp and Lucianne Goldberg and, through them, Monica Lewinsky into all our lives is taken to task for precisely this: for following the trail as it was being laid out for him to the Oval Office, without dwelling on why those particular breadcrumbs were being dropped before him and who was dropping them. For him what mattered was the promise of an exclusive.[15]

Yet journalists cannot see it this way. As Lelyveld notes, most Washington insiders—both politicians and journalists—would see this account as "wickedly" off target:

> Far from belonging to a permanent class that conspires to shape a common "narrative," the insiders would argue, they are at one another's throats: the journalists

are seeking to find out what is really going on, to avoid being deflected by "the spin," while their adversaries, the politicians and their spinners, battle to get their story out without filters. Why have campaign days become so inanely repetitive? Because the politicians are afraid to say anything spontaneous on which reporters—and thereafter their opponents—may seize. . . . Why in the end do journalists retail what is manufactured for them? It is not merely on account of laziness or obstruction, they can't get their mitts on anything else.[16]

The complaint that there is little really original news to report in most news events may explain the persistence of one of the oldest political story lines in journalism: the election horse race. Every year, news organizations persist in telling us who is in front, who is trailing, and who is coming up from behind, until someone crosses the finish line on election day. Journalists stick with these narrative choices in the face of clear voter disinterest. In the 2000 election, for example, the horserace dominated the news—and there was a continuing lack of interest in the election. A majority of Americans became interested in the 2000 contest only after election day, when they discovered that there was no clear winner.[17] Even in the crucial final weeks of the contest, stories with standardized dramatized framings, such as the *horse race,* the *war room,* and other military metaphors outnumbered stories on all the issues in the race, combined, by a wide margin. For example, a study of *The Washington Post* and *The New York Times* in the final two weeks of the campaign showed that dramatized framings of the race or the strategic conflict outnumbered all policy issue stories by a margin of 69 to 45 in the *Post,* while the *Times'* melodrama-to-issue gap was even greater at 93 to 63.[18] *Consider the possibility that the choices of such narrative framings of politics contain information biases that are far more serious and at the same time more difficult for the average person to detect than the kinds of ideological biases discussed in the last chapter.*

Communication scholar Shanto Iyengar summarizes these information biases by saying that most news is episodic rather than thematic. *Episodic news* parachutes the journalist and the audience into the middle of an already developed situation and puts the focus on the people who are in trouble or in conflict. By contrast, *thematic news* looks beyond the immediate human drama to explore the origins of problems and the larger social, economic, or political contexts in which the immediate news story has developed. Iyengar's research shows that episodic news, which is the most commonly encountered form of reporting, particularly on television, leaves people with shallow understandings of the world around them. For example, viewers of episodic coverage tend to hold the people at the center of news stories responsible for the problems and conflicts that surround them, rather than see more fundamental social, political, or economic causes at work.[19]

Iyengar's work suggests that the news is an important link in a chain of poor reasoning about social problems. If individuals, alone, are held responsible for problems ranging from poverty and crime on the domestic scene to population explosions and wars on the world stage, then politicians and voters are unlikely to find workable solutions to these problems through their public communication process. The key problem with most news, in this view, is that when personal and dramatic elements isolate or fragment a story from larger social, historical, or political context, the news fails to offer a basis for learning and generalizing. It is often in such cases, in fact, that some variation on the authority-disorder plot comes into play as a substitute for a larger point to a story.

If personal or emotionally dramatic elements are used to introduce audiences to more abstract ideas or to link stories to each other or to broader ideas, theories, or insights, then they are useful. It is also important to recognize here that *it is not the stories that create information problems with the news, it is how those stories are told.* The conclusion of this book returns to look at how stories might be told differently and with more positive effect on citizen engagement. The following case study shows how to use these biases to analyze news stories, after which we will return for a more detailed look at the four information biases.

Case Study: *How George W. Bush Got His Swagger*

Let's return to the passage from *The Washington Post's* coverage of President Bush's dramatic aircraft carrier landing that opened this chapter:

> When the Viking carrying Bush made its tailhook landing on the aircraft carrier USS Abraham Lincoln off California yesterday, the scene brought presidential imagery to a whole new level. Bush emerged from the cockpit in full olive flight suit and combat boots, his helmet tucked jauntily under his left arm. As he exchanged salutes with the sailors, his ejection harness, hugging him tightly between the legs, gave him the bowlegged swagger of a top gun.[20]

This news event was covered around the world and replayed time and again in the American media. It was hailed by journalists, politicians, and public relations professionals as one of the great publicity events of all time. A news source for communication consultants reviewed the coverage and cited journalists' lavish praise for the event as: "the mother of all photo opportunities," the greatest photo-op of all time," and "the kind of attention that other politicians can only dream of," among other accolades.[21] "It has a huge visual impact," said an admiring Michael Deaver, who created such images for Ronald Reagan, including the Gipper's famous Normandy speech. "This is a powerful, powerful visual, not only of Bush as commander in chief, but of his strength as a world leader."[22]

What was the connection between the Top Gun image of the president and his qualities as a leader? How did that iconic military moment sit with Mr. Bush's own military record? And how would the dramatic claim that major fighting was over in Iraq play out as the war turned into a continuing guerilla conflict? The short answer to these questions is that well-crafted news images often stand on their own, disconnected from more complex realities. A more provocative answer is that the Bush Top Gun moment was not just about the war in Iraq. It was also the culmination of a long running campaign to shape Mr. Bush's leadership image—a campaign that can be traced to his first weeks in office. It was also about the image of the president that the White House communication staff planned to project in the 2004 election. The author of the *The Washington Post* story saw all of this at the time: "Bush aides are planning to make his war leadership the focus of his 2004 reelection campaign, and yesterday's images are crucial in burning that impression into the national cornea."[23]

A *New York Times* feature article also viewed the carrier landing in the context of the larger news management operation of the Bush White House:

> Pres[ident] Bush's "Top Gun" landing on the deck of [the] carrier Abraham Lincoln is only [the] latest example of how his administration is using [the] powers of television and technology to promote [the] presidency like never before; officials of past Democratic and Republican administrations marvel at how this White House never misses [an] opportunity to showcase Bush in dramatic and perfectly lighted settings; in fact, [the] White House has stocked its communications operation with people from network television who have expertise in lighting, camera angles and [the] importance of backdrops; White House efforts are ambitious—and costly; they include renting the kind of lights used to illuminate sports stadiums and rock concerts and creating scenic backdrops for every Bush speech and appearance.[24]

This acknowledgment by the reporter illustrates our earlier point that journalists usually recognize what they are covering, yet they still complete the political image-making process by reporting stories much as they have been designed for publicity purposes. As a result, the Bush Top Gun moment was generally reported as designed by the Bush communication team, with few distracting references to larger, well known, realities that would have diminished its dramatic impact.

Picking up the White House spin, reporters soon generated a common script and an image vocabulary that would echo through their stories well into the future. The word that burned the Bush image into hundreds of news reports was *swagger*, which spread through news accounts like a contagion. Papers large and small reported how the president swaggered like a top gun after he deplaned and greeted the cheering sailors on the carrier deck. Television news replayed images that were as well-produced as a music video. Cable news talk shows echoed the Bush swagger effect for months afterward. A Google search on the terms *Bush and swagger* produced more than eight thousand hits, revealing that the term became "sticky" in descriptions of Mr. Bush by admirers and critics alike.

Mr. Bush was even proclaimed a "hottie" by a columnist in the usually austere ed-itorial page of the *The Wall Street Journal*. *The New York Times* columnist Maureen Dowd offered this comment on the Journal's bout of swagger-mania: "Lisa Schiffren, a Quayle speechwriter . . . gushed Friday in a *The Wall Street Journal* piece titled "Hey, Flyboy" that President Bush in a flight suit was "really hot . . . as in virile, sexy and powerful." She polled her soccer-mom girlfriends in Manhattan and got the same reaction. "He's a hottie," said one. "Hot? SO HOT!!!!! THAT UNIFORM!" said an-other. A third panted: "That swagger. George Bush in a pair of jeans is a treat to watch." (If it gets any hotter, Wal-Mart may have to ban *The Journal*.)"[25]

It turns out that journalists did not spontaneously come to the term *swagger;* they were led to it from early on in the administration. The Bush communication team faced major image challenges with a newly elected president who took of-fice with an electoral victory decided by a Supreme Court vote. In his early months as president, Mr. Bush seemed unsure of himself, and news photos often captured him with a deer-in-the-headlights look. One of the first image break-throughs was a *People* magazine piece appearing the month of the Bush inau-gural in which Laura Bush described the family style as being comfortable in jeans. *The Washington Post* soon ran an article in its style section contrasting Mr. Bush's stiff appearance in suits with " . . . a relaxed swagger in his faded jeans."[26] By August, swagger had spun out over the Associated Press wires, hitting papers across the land: "With campaign swagger, President Bush told a crowd in Harry Truman's hometown Tuesday that the federal budget has enough money for his massive tax cut and bolstering the military, Social Security and Medicare."[27] With *swagger* already on the tongues of journalists, Mr. Bush rode to historic levels of popularity as news events built upon one another, culminating with the landing on the *Abraham Lincoln.*

Like so many news events, the carrier landing story displayed all of the elements of news bias—not because journalists were particularly lax in their reporting, but because they picked up on precisely what makes for a good news story by today's journalism standards. First and foremost, the staging of the landing was *dramatic:* a president in full flight suit—doing a tailhook landing—on an aircraft carrier at sea—to the cheers of its crew just back from the war—and a national news audience ready to celebrate an American victory. It doesn't get more dramatic than that. Even better, the war could be *personalized* through this news event: the president as leader and commander-in-chief had made the fateful decision to go to war, and he now announced proudly that the military phase of the mission was accomplished. What could be easier for Americans to relate to on a personal level, whether they get their news from *The New York Times* or *The Daily Show?*

The very elements that made for a great personalized and dramatic news story, however, also contributed for its *fragmentation:* its disconnection from underlying factors that might have been important to helping citizens engage with the situation in a realistic way. Some of these disconnections from reality might be excused as innocent sacrifices for sake of a good story. For example, the full-blown image of Mr. Bush as a navy pilot needed to be disconnected from his own military past in order to invite positive personal associations from the audience. The landing on the carrier needed to be disconnected from the carrier's actual situation in order to make the drama credible rather than laughable or even scandalous.

Among the few U.S. news sources to put these contextual realities back in the news picture were a columnist for the Cox newspaper group and an editorial writer for a small South Carolina paper who noted the following, among other things:

1. An initial press briefing told reporters that the president had to fly in on a jet because the ship was hundreds of miles off shore beyond helicopter range and the president did not want to delay the sailors who had been away from home so long. Actually, the ship was just thirty miles offshore at the time of the landing, and the reunion of the sailors with their families was delayed an extra day as the ship made lazy circles just over the horizon to avoid distracting shots of the San Diego skyline in news images of the landing and the speech.
2. The pilot suit with George W. Bush inscribed on the chest obscured the president's own military career, which involved avoiding service in Vietnam with a checkered stint in the air national guard that included not showing up for duty after he was transferred from Texas to Alabama and being discharged eight months early so that he could go to business school.
3. Using an aircraft carrier as a prop and its crew as extras might be a questionable appropriation of public resources for what was at the time planned as an election campaign ad.[28]

Surely the major disconnection created by the news event was its dubious relationship to the war itself. Consistent with the administration's earlier campaign to generate public support for the invasion, the president's speech called the liberation of Iraq a major victory in the War on Terror. Here is a passage from *The New York Times:*

> He spoke in emotional terms not only about the troops who toppled Mr. Hussein, but also about the Sept. 11 attacks, melding the battle against terrorism with the battle against Iraq. "We have not forgotten the victims of September 11th, the last phone calls, the murder of children, the searches in the rubble," he said. "With those attacks, the terrorists declared war on the United States. And war is what they got."[29]

Although the *Times* noted for the record that the link between Iraq and al Qaeda had not been well established, such slight journalistic allusions to reality were no match for the drama of the moment. Recall the polls from Chapter 1 showing large majorities believing that there was some connection between Iraq and the events of

9/11. That connection was supported by near universal journalistic framing of more than a year of news reports in terms favored by the administration.

After more than a year of war and terrorism alerts, it is not surprising that the news had become preoccupied with issues of *authority and order.* Was the world safer? Was the dictator toppled? Did America win? Is the president in control? Such preoccupations of the disorder-authority bias are better addressed by simple, personalized, and fragmentary news dramas than by exploring complex realities. Both the president's speech and his swagger were aimed at conveying the image that order had been restored at least for a time as Mr. Bush declared "one victory in a war on terror that began on September 11, 2001, and still goes on."[30]

Let's close this case by returning to the question of why the press reported the administration framing of events so faithfully. Recall our discussion of what leads independent reporters to write stories around blatantly manufactured images, even when they recognize the manipulation that is happening in front of them. The explanation typically offered by journalists is that they have nothing else to report other than what newsmakers offer them. This begs several questions, including why more investigative reporting is not used to balance staged events, or why the known gaps between the staging and other versions of events are not the main focus of the reporting. Let's add to this explanation our point from Chapter 1 about the centrality of news to governing: journalists understand that the real game of politics is about image shaping, and so they tend to pass those images on when they are done well—even if they are actively completing the image formation process in the bargain. It is hard to resist a good story.

FOUR INFORMATION BIASES IN THE NEWS: AN IN-DEPTH LOOK

It is important to be able to recognize each of the basic news biases in action. This section explores more familiar examples of the four biases, with an eye to why news organizations are inclined to pursue stories that fit these information patterns.

Personalized News Revisited

Following the previous overview, *personalized news* can be defined as the journalistic bias that gives preference to individual actors and human-interest angles in events over larger institutional, social, and political contexts. The news is further personalized by creating a brand identity relationship between the consumer and the news product. TV anchors model their delivery styles and even their looks based on the results of market research, and newspapers key in on the lifestyles of readers. This trend toward personalized packaging was pioneered by news consultants, or news doctors, like Philip McHugh: "There has to be an emphasis on human interest and human beings.

You have to have an anchorman who can establish rapport with the audience. . . . It takes a very special kind of personality."[31]

The media (led by television, the major news source for most Americans) have settled on a formula that is profitable, cheap, and easy to produce, but just not terribly helpful to the citizens who consume this news. So important is this private, emotional bias in the news that it is understood as formal policy in most organizations. Here is an excerpt from a memo by an executive producer of ABC News to his staff:

> The Evening News, as you know, works on elimination. We can't include everything. As criteria for what we do include, I suggest the following for a satisfied viewer: (1) "Is my world, nation, and city safe?" (2) "Is my home and family safe?" (3) "If they are safe, then what has happened in the past 24 hours to help make that world better?" (4) "What has happened in the past 24 hours to help us cope better?"[32]

One interesting feature of this news maxim is that it has not changed much in the decades since it was written. Consider what Jonathan Wald, producer of NBC's *Today* said after 9/11: "People want to know when they wake up if their world is safe. They look to us for reassurance that things are OK or not."[33] In today's more sinister news world, the answers to the personalized question of "Is my world safe?" may not be as reassuring, but the personal bias ("my world") remains as dominant as ever.

Examples of personalized news coverage can be found in virtually any newspaper, magazine, or broadcast. Consider, for instance, the personalization of a familiar political issue, welfare reform, followed by the personalization of an important branch of government, the presidency.

Personalizing an Issue: Welfare Reform   News coverage of welfare has been intensive over the past twenty years. The modern era of welfare politics began with Ronald Reagan's Republican revolution in the early 1980s, a time of fierce political battles over cutting welfare benefits to the poor and chronically unemployed. By the late 1990s, Bill Clinton had stolen the Republican thunder and welcomed sweeping cutbacks of government benefits. A common feature of the news over the two decades of policy change was the focus on personal stories, from Reagan's demonized cheaters and "welfare Cadillac" owners, to the hardships experienced by people whose support was cut, to the later success stories of people leaving the support rolls to take productive jobs in society.

Consider, for example, an early *Wall Street Journal* report on an early Reagan era decision to terminate a large-scale public employment program. Despite the numerous big-picture social, political, and economic themes that could have been used to frame the report, this was the opening paragraph of the story:

> SAN FRANCISCO—As the chill, first light breaks on a Haight-Ashbury curbside, a street sweeper stops to gather the gutter's yield of leaves, litter, and dog waste. "This job's the best thing ever happened to a poor man," he says. "It's

feeding babies. When it's over, I'll be putting cardboard in my little girl's shoes, like my mama did me."[34]

Although there is a journalistic convention that stories should be organized with the most important information first and the least important facts last, the article did not mention the large-scale social, political, or economic implications of the program cuts until paragraphs eight, nine, and ten. After these brief passages, the article returned to the heart-rending story of the street sweeper's fate.

As Clinton-era reforms of the late 1990s swept through the land, journalists swarmed welfare offices and job-training programs in search of other personal stories to tell. Reflecting the bipartisan consensus behind the reforms, the tone of these stories was positive and authority affirming: The government had done something right for a change. In the process, hundreds if not thousands of poor people got their fifteen minutes of media fame. Indeed, the personalization of their stories was so intense that the news often became part of the plot rather than an invisible recorder of personal experiences. When a German film crew asked how a Milwaukee, Wisconsin, training program had helped a young woman, she did not talk about finding a job or getting her degree. Instead, she announced that "It really helped me with the interview for *Dateline NBC*," adding that her social worker had coached her on press interview techniques. Another newly placed job holder had worked out a polished sound bite about welfare from FDR to a new beginning of hope. One woman's story cycled from *The New York Times* to ABC, giving her enough news exposure to generate fan mail. In a later *The New York Times* interview, she told a reporter that one of her proudest moments in the transition from welfare to work was when her 11-year-old son declared, "Mama, you're going to be on the news."[35]

Personalizing the Presidency   Personalized treatments are not just reserved for complex policies or obscure events that people would otherwise have trouble relating to. Even the coverage of government institutions puts personal themes atop the list of reporting priorities. As a result, we learn more about the powerful and glamorous personalities in government than about how government works. As Paletz and Entman observed, "Prime news generally involves prominent, powerful people in action, or, more desirable from the media's point of view, in conflict."[36]

A textbook case of personalizing the presidency is press coverage of Ronald Reagan's years in office. From the outset of his presidency, Reagan initiated many domestic and foreign policies of great national and international importance. However, the news formula that quickly emerged in most of the stories about those historic actions was the theme of whether Reagan was personally "winning" or "losing" in his battles with Congress, the bureaucracy, business leaders, and foreign governments. This theme reduced momentous political issues to engrossing but trivial questions about Reagan's personal power, his political "scorecard," and his risks of public embarrassment. The personal focus on Reagan so dominated the news that he was able to manipulate and enhance his news coverage simply by emphasizing his personal stake in policy decisions.

Reagan's success was not just due to his personal charm and communication abilities. As the case of George W. Bush's carrier landing demonstrated, on-screen political actors rely on professional communications staff to construct media events and communication strategies to take advantage of the predictable biases of the American reporting style. David Gergen was among the first communication strategists who understood the tendency of the press to personalize Washington politics. Before he worked for Bill Clinton, Gergen was one of the media managers who helped Reagan earn the nickname "the Great Communicator" from the national press corps. As Gergen saw it, politicians live or die depending on whether they appear to be personally weak or powerful in news accounts. His strategy was a media version of "the best defense is a good offense" in which his boss was at the center of events carefully orchestrated by the White House. The goal was to create images of confident control that drove out competing suggestions of presidential failure. (The details of this news-management approach are explained in Chapter 4.)

This view of power in the media age has become part of the thinking of Washington insiders. As a result of personal scandals, policy conflicts, and the failure to properly utilize Gergen's talents, Bill Clinton's public approval ratings hovered under 50 percent during many of his major policy initiatives. As a member of his own administration told a reporter: "Any time you have a 48 percent [approval] president, every major vote is a death struggle. You are dealing with members [of Congress] who don't know whether to embrace him or run from him."[37] Shortly after Gergen was shuffled out of the Clinton White House, a major crime bill that Clinton supported was voted down in a procedural maneuver in the House of Representatives. Although a slightly revised version of the bill passed two weeks later, every major news organization played the original vote as a huge personal defeat for Clinton. ABC correspondent and National Public Radio (NPR) analyst Cokie Roberts put it this way in an NPR interview the morning after the defeat: "[For Mr. Clinton, it was] not a good day. I could hear reporters in the [press] gallery hammering out 'Stunning Defeat,' 'Staggering Defeat.' I like your [NPR's] 'Stinging Defeat.' "[38] NPR further personalized its coverage by adding that the president appeared "visibly shaken" as he addressed reporters afterward.[39] Clinton eventually righted his press strategy just in time to help him weather the impeachment storm during his second term in office. So Clinton, like all modern politicians, learned the often painful lesson that the success of his political agenda depended as much on his media image as on the sheer force of his ideas or the strength of his institutional politics.

Perhaps the most personalized arenas of presidential politics are the election campaigns, which also settle into a set of personalized and dramatized news plots that typically relegate issues to a minor place in the media scheme. For example, the 2000 presidential campaign had not even officially begun before the news was brimming with personal problems allegedly plaguing the most visible candidate, Democratic Vice President Al Gore. Gore was dogged by impossible-to-refute charges that his personality was too stiff, that he exaggerated his accomplishments, and that he could not connect with voters. One interviewer noted how personable Gore was in the interview but concluded that the stereotype of woodenness would stick because that was the dominant story in the media.[40]

The Political Costs of Personalized News   The focus on winners and losers and on personalities and their personal conflicts gives the news audience a distorted view of power and its political consequences. As Paletz and Entman have concluded, "Power seems to be understood in a limited sense by the media. . . . Stories emphasize the surface appearances, the furious sounds and fiery sights of battle, the well-known or colorful personalities involved—whatever is dramatic. Underlying causes and actual impacts are little noted nor long remembered."[41] Without a grasp of power structures, it is virtually impossible to understand how the political system really works. As a result, the political world becomes a mystical realm populated by actors who either have the political "force" on their side or do not.

In addition, direct emotional projection onto distant news figures can result in highly egocentric and ethnocentric views of the world. The news gives people a me-first view of the world in which "my" well-being, "my" group, and "my" country are emphasized over social realities that differ from one's own. Even the two-sided format used in most reporting provides few intellectual tools for resolving the differences between the sides. To the contrary, the sides are often portrayed as in stark conflict. As a result, the path to easy understanding is to pick the reality that most closely resembles one's own beliefs and prejudices. The next best alternative is to remain confused about how to decide who is right or what is really happening.

Dramatized News Revisited

It is no secret that reporters and editors search for events with dramatic properties and then emphasize those properties in their reporting. Consider the conscious emphasis on news drama in the following policy memo from the executive news producer of a major television network to his editors and reporters:

> Every news story should, without any sacrifice of probity or responsibility, display the attributes of fiction, of drama. It should have structure and conflict, problem and denouement, rising action and falling action, a beginning, a middle, and an end. These are not only the essentials of drama; they are the essentials of narrative.[42]

The weight of such evidence led Paletz and Entman to conclude that "drama is a defining characteristic of news. An event is particularly newsworthy if it has some elements of a dramatic narrative. . . . American officials held hostage in the far-off but journalistically accessible land of Iran provide a particularly strident example."[43] Indeed, the hostage crisis that dragged down the Carter presidency offered 444 days of sustained news coverage because it contained so many dramatic angles, almost all of which involved personalized themes and plots: What happened in the story today? How are the hostages? Is the president doing anything to bring them home safely? And, of course, there was the overriding dramatic question that kept people tuning in each day: How will it end?

Dramatized news fits neatly with the personalization bias. Drama, after all, is the quintessential medium for representing human conflict. Promising psychological release and resolution, drama satisfies emotional concerns aroused in the development of characters and plots. Although there are occasional walk-on roles for ordinary people, the majority of news plots revolve around a cast of familiar officials who play standard roles in news dramas. There are also the rich, the famous, the powerful, and the glamorous, along with plenty of bad guys threatening the lives of decent people.

Among the most familiar bad guys are terrorists. Yet who are they? How do they become cast as terrorists in news dramas? There is no universal standard that defines them because our terrorists are almost always someone else's heroes and freedom fighters. A fascinating study by Steven Livingston shows that in nearly all cases, acts of political violence wait for definition in the news until they are labeled (as terrorist, accidental, or heroic) by government officials who have political reasons for designating some groups bad and others good.[44]

In general, the main principle guiding the casting of newsmakers in their nightly roles has more to do with their potential as dramatic actors than with any natural preeminence they may have in the political scheme of things. For example, in the U.S. government, the three branches share equal power, both under the Constitution and, for the most part, in actual practice. Yet the president is the dramatic news actor par excellence: There is only one of him, he is easy to keep track of, he can be typecast (e.g., as a national father figure, as a staunch defender of freedom against an enemy, or as a flawed character who somehow maintains his public support), and he is easy to bring onto the scene on almost any political pretext. It is also helpful that presidents are usually willing to feed journalists as many dramatic "moments" as the latter are willing to broadcast and print.

By contrast, the justices of the Supreme Court make poor dramatic material, largely because they are reluctant to walk on stage and play for the audience. The small number of articulate, often eccentric, justices would otherwise make wonderful dramatic characters. Also, there is no shortage of available information about court proceedings—it is just that the business of the Court, while important, doesn't fit the news bias toward personalized, dramatic coverage. If the media adopted another information format, the Court might share the front pages with the president—a place more in keeping with its constitutional role.

Congress is another political institution with equal standing under the Constitution but with grossly unequal coverage in the media. A handful of glamorous members of the Senate receive the lion's share of coverage, while the House remains largely a jumbled assembly of nameless seatholders. Washington press observer Stephen Hess has noted the following:

> The Senate has the constitutional right to reject a president's treaties and a president's nominees, appealing prospects to a press corps that loves controversy. The Senate is also the incubator of presidential candidates who are then automatically newsworthy. But most important, there are almost four-and-a-half times as many House members as there are senators. As philosopher David Sidorsky notes, the goal of journalists is to transpose "an inherently ambiguous and complex event into a short narrative that can be simply told, have a central plot, and retain the interest of the reader or viewer." It is easier and faster to build a coherent story with a smaller cast of characters. The House of Representatives is too much like *War and Peace;* the Senate is more on the scale of *Crime and Punishment.*[45]

Because of this news bias, members of Congress have learned to play the media game. As Timothy Cook has shown, members of the once obscure House increasingly rely on news management to bring attention to legislation and put the spotlight on political careers.[46]

When Journalists Write the Script   Robert Darnton told of his early problems as a journalist before he had learned to parse the dramatic highlights from the dull details of most stories. On one of his early assignments on the city desk of a Newark, New Jersey, paper, he wrote a story of a bicycle stolen from a paperboy. The story was rejected by his editor. A colleague suggested a much more dramatic version involving the boy's love for the bike, his trauma following the theft, and his Horatio Alger-like scheme to pay for a new one. Upon checking this more dramatic new plot against the facts, Darnton decided that reality was close enough to the dramatized version to write the story—a story that was published in his paper.[47]

Lewis Lapham, the editor of *Harper's,* tells of similar experiences in his early days as a reporter. He notes how he marveled at the ease with which the senior reporter in the city room "wrote the accounts of routine catastrophe."[48] Finally, the old reporter's secret came out:

> In the drawer, with a bottle of bourbon and the manuscript of the epic poem he had been writing for twenty years, he kept a looseleaf notebook filled with stock versions of maybe fifty or sixty common newspaper texts. These were arranged in alphabetical order (fires, homicides, ship collisions, etc.) and then further divided into subcategories (fires—one-, two-, and three-alarm; warehouse; apartment building; etc.). The reporter had left blank spaces for the relevant names, deaths, numbers, and street addresses. As follows: "A ———— alarm fire swept through ———— at ———— St. yesterday afternoon, killing ———— people and causing ———— in property damage."[49]

Dramatized news as largely a journalistic creation has progressed to its wildest extremes on local TV. Beyond the focus on mayhem, the delivery and visual formats are painstakingly stylized with the help of news doctors who have developed the so-called action-news format. Nearly all major media markets now have news programs called *Action News* or *Eyewitness News*. Action formats set the pace, delivery, scenery, and casting of the program. The action focus also directly affects the story content and presentation. Consider, for example, the multitude of ways in which a routine event like a murder can be covered. At one extreme, a murder can be reported analytically or, in Iyengar's terms, "thematically," in order to show how various aspects of the crime reflect social problems known to be linked with violent crime (e.g., poverty, family violence, unemployment, alcoholism, social instability, or prison system failures). Such reporting angles are seldom used in action-news programs because they contradict the action philosophy of the news doctors. TV and radio stations in competitive media markets tend to follow the costly advice of news consultants like the pioneering Frank Magid, who reportedly endorsed building a murder story around the dramatic effects of the camera retracing the route of the killer as he stalked his victim. Such reporting, according to Magid, has the virtue of making you feel "as if you were really there."[50]

As the preoccupation with action news has grown to dominate the business, dramatization has become routine—to the point of using the events in the story as mere foils for sensationalism. For example, local stations have purchased expensive helicopters, airplanes, and remote transmission equipment to enhance their action-news image. Such equipment usually becomes a visible feature of the station's news coverage, both to justify its expense and to ensure that the news program lives up to its action-news advertising. As a result of this built-in bias in favor of action reporting, a new breed of news stories has begun to appear: stories that have less to do with the importance or meaning of an event than with the capacity to use costly equipment and to convey images of drama and action in covering the event.[51] TV journalists talk to us from high-tech choppers and sleek vans while rushing to news scenes where they may become the most animated actors present. Routine stories are enhanced by cutting live to a reporter sitting in the newsroom somewhere beyond the anchor desk.

Dramatized news is more melodrama than serious theater, more soap opera than Shakespeare. One does not leave the theater after watching *Hamlet* with the feeling that poor Hamlet was a real loser. If journalists pursued more serious dramatic techniques, the results might be less objectionable. It would not require the talents of a Shakespeare to make big changes in the way the news selects and represents reality. In legitimate drama, including many movies and popular novels, one is made aware of the role played by history, institutions, power, conflict, hidden interests, and accident in human affairs. These factors are usually missing in news melodrama.

The Political Costs of Dramatized News   The most obvious effect of dramatization is to trivialize news content. In place of unswerving attention to major events and problems, there is an increasing tendency to substitute manufactured drama. Even when the drama may reflect an actual feature of the situation, as in the case of a congressional vote, the preoccupation with drama often distracts attention from any broad or enduring political significance the event may have had. The action imperative feeds on events that have some rapidly developing action to report. One result, as Gaye Tuchman has observed so cogently, is that chronic social problems and long-standing political issues often go unreported because they develop too slowly.[52] In these respects, dramatization compounds many of the same effects of personalization.

Its unique blend of emotionalism and dramaturgy sets American journalism apart from other news systems, while setting Americans apart from the world they live in. Fiction writer Don DeLillo has captured these aspects of foreign affairs coverage:

> I think it's only in a crisis that Americans see other people. It has to be an American crisis, of course. If two countries fight that do not supply the Americans with some precious commodity, then the education of the public does not take place. But when the dictator falls, when the oil is threatened, then you turn on the television and they tell you where the country is, what the language is, how to pronounce the names of the leaders, what the religion is all about, and maybe you can cut out recipes in the newspaper of Persian dishes. I will tell you. The whole world takes an interest in this curious way Americans educate them-

selves. TV. Look, this is Iran, this is Iraq. Let us pronounce the word correctly. E-ron. E-ronians. This is a Sunni, this is a Shi-ite. Very good. Next year we do the Philippine Islands, okay?[53]

Dramatized news also creates another information dilemma: the temptation for news organizations to look for the most extreme cases rather than the most representative examples of a subject. The preoccupation with drama makes it hard to draw the line between journalists as reporters of fact and as creators of fiction. After noting that drama is a requirement for a major news story, Paletz and Entman observed that some stories deficient in their own "high drama" may "have drama grafted on." "Journalists have been known to highlight if not concoct conflict and to find characters to symbolize its different sides. One reason: to attract an audience that is thought to have little patience for the abstract, the technical, the ambiguous, the uncontroversial."[54]

Because dramas are simple, easy to grasp, and offer a semblance of insight into the individual motives behind an action, they may give people a misguided sense of understanding the politics of a situation. People may think they understand an issue when, in fact, their understanding is based on a mixture of fantasy, fiction, and myth. Under these circumstances, according to Lapham, the political world becomes sheer abstraction, and "we exhaust ourselves in passionate arguments about things that few of us have ever seen. We talk about the third world as if it were a real place rather than a convenient symbol, about the gears of the national economy as if it were as intelligible as the gears on a bicycle."[55] This, ultimately, is what is wrong with the false sense of understanding conveyed by melodramatic news: It leaves people unprepared to deal effectively with serious social problems. The human capacity for planning, compromise, and sensitive analysis dissolves in the face of crisis, confrontation, and simplistic images.

We shall see later on that the public is not as simpleminded as the news experts assume, but this is beside the point. Nowhere in journalism texts is news defined as "whatever the audience wants, no matter how contrived or irrelevant." News, at least in theory, is supposed to inform people, not merely entertain them. The trend toward ever more dramatic and entertaining news may mean that a new form of communication is emerging. This evolving communication form may still go by the term *news,* but it would be a serious mistake to assume that the traditional meanings of that term still apply. As noted in Chapter 1, for example, large numbers of people regard cop shows and other dramatized reality programs as news.

In a world where political events are already far removed from the immediate experience of the average person, news dramas may push political consciousness permanently into the realm of fiction. This principle applies equally to coverage of foreign affairs and to issues seemingly much closer to home, like crime. For example, a big-city television station produced an expensive and much-advertised documentary special on violent crime. The newspaper and television ads were dominated by the horror movie use of the word *fear,* which seared the page and dripped from the TV screen. True to its advertising, the program presented numerous examples of particularly violent crimes and showed how local people reacted to them. When the news adopts the images of popular drama and literature, it is little wonder that people begin to confuse reality and fantasy. As the following personal statement of a newspaper columnist indicates, our own lives become dramatized:

> Is it possible for a woman to walk along, footsteps echoing through the night city, without feeling as if she's performing in a Brian DePalma movie? I can't. I've been conditioned into DePalma-style reflexes: twitches and eye rolls, in response to any unlikely sight or sound. What is that shape moving shadowlike in the alley? Is that a garbage bag or a man hunkered down in the service doorway? If I venture out alone after midnight, I enter an atmosphere as different from the everyday world as if I've gone under water. I can hear my own breathing, the hammering of my heart, the clickety-clack of my heels on the pavement. Unescorted, I am accompanied by fear, chaperoned by phantoms of my own imagination. Why has that man changed direction, just as I've turned the corner? Is that he now walking behind me?[56]

There is no doubt that being a victim of a crime is a fearful prospect, but so are things like lung cancer, poverty, hunger, unemployment, homelessness, war, AIDS, and many other social "disasters." The news audience is exposed to more fearful images of some of these issues than others—not because they are inherently more or less fearful, but because the conditions conducive to media melodrama come together more coherently around some issues than others. Crime is an issue tailor-made for hyperdramatism. Almost everyone agrees it is a problem and should be eliminated; almost everyone agrees that criminals are bad and have no excuse for their behavior; politicians get a lot of mileage from talking about an issue that is guaranteed to produce a supportive response from a scared public; and the media appear to be performing a useful public service by running cautionary stories on the issue. The result, however, is that the popular fear of crime is way out of proportion to the chances of ever being affected by it, and tax dollars may be thrown at emotionally satisfying solutions that have little real impact on the problem.

Here, then, is the sequence of political effects flowing from dramatized news: (1) distraction from potentially important causes of problems, (2) creation of a false sense of understanding rooted in individualistic explanations, and (3) the political promotion of dramatically satisfying but practically unworkable solutions. As Murray Edelman has argued so persuasively, many of the chronic problems that diminish the quality of life both nationally and on the world stage are surely worsened by the way they are represented in the news. The news has become a means of turning problems into political spectacles that drown out serious debate, while creating an appetite for quick dramatic resolutions on the part of audiences.[57]

Fragmented News Revisited

Lifting actors out of political context and surrounding their actions with titillating but irrelevant fantasy themes make it very hard to put together a coherent picture of the world.[58] News fragments exist in self-contained dramatic capsules, isolated from each other in time and space. The impression given by the news is of a jigsaw puzzle that is out of focus and missing many pieces. When focus is provided, it is on the individual pieces, not on how they fit into the overall picture. When information is delivered in such fragments, people are invited all the more to project their own interpretations onto the world. In place of new information about situations, information is either cast adrift or assimilated into old plot formulas. In either case, the world is reduced time and again to myriad encapsulated happenings, each with its own emotional coherence but isolated from the others. The world appears fragmented and confusing, even though each of its parts is coherent and dramatically whole. With respect to information fragmentation, the news defies the old adage that the whole is greater than the sum of its parts. In news reality, the whole is decidedly less than the sum of its parts. Columnist Russell Baker once parodied the typical newscast in the following terms:

> Meanwhile, in Washington, the . . . Administration was reported today as firemen still sifted through the ruins of a six-alarm blaze in Brooklyn that left two Congressmen, who were said to have accepted cash contributions from Korean agents, despite their fifth defeat in a row at the hands of the Boston Celtics. . . .
>
> Seventeen were dead and scores injured by the testimony that two Senators, whom he declined to name, rioted in the streets of Cairo following her son's expulsion from school for shooting a teacher who had referred to him in the easy-going style of the . . . White House, as exemplified by the dispute over the B–1 bomber.[59]

Lacking real guidelines for analysis and criticism, media efforts to be analytical or critical can border on nonsense. Edwin Diamond tells the story of a network news producer who visited a seminar at MIT devoted to television news. The producer proudly showed a videotape of a recent "analytical" report on the economy. Diamond describes the report and his students' reaction:

> There was the anchor wishing us good evening; cut to the Washington reporter with the latest inflation bad news; then quickly three consumer reports from around the country; then a U.S. map with graphics showing cost-of-living rates; back to the anchor and then the Washington reporter, followed by tape and sound "bites"—15-second quotes—from congressional leaders and cabinet officers. Finally, a Wall Street reaction . . . and then break for commercial. In all, no more than three minutes had elapsed.
>
> As the various tape, sound, and graphics parts in the economics package gave way to each other, the producer snapped her fingers and whispered "hit it . . . " right in time with each element. She was proud of the network handiwork, but students in the classroom shot up their hands. What was that all about? What did it mean? What were you trying to tell us about the economy? . . . When we all watched the videotape once again from the point of view of the audience—people who know little about the effort that goes into the smooth mingling of tape and sound videofonts and slides, and care even less—we had to admit that it was difficult to grasp, sort out and understand the news somewhere underneath all the production.[60]

As this example illustrates, action news often tries to imitate analysis by trading in the story format for news collages, called "clusters" in radio and television, which contain many images with few coherent connections.[61] Similar fragmentation effects are achieved in newspapers, which jump back and forth between interviews, actors, scenes, factual information, and plots. Recall, for example, how the newspaper article on the elimination of the government job program required the reader to make the leap from the isolated personal case of a San Francisco street sweeper to the broad economic implications involved.

Long-term trends and historical patterns are seldom made part of the news because it is hard to tell them as simple stories. Events spring full-blown, from out of nowhere, into the headlines. In place of seeing a coherent world anchored in clear historical, economic, and political tendencies, the public is exposed to a world made chaotic by seemingly arbitrary and mysterious forces.

Fragmented news has a life and a reality of its own. Story plots are self-contained and incorporate broader social context only at the peril of overloading the simple melodrama of the moment. A shred of credibility is added to the mix by documenting that at least most of what is reported actually happened. Never mind that much more of what actually happened went unreported.

The Political Costs of Fragmentation   There are, of course, numerous "good reasons" for such reporting. Journalism's hallowed prohibitions against commentary and interpretation seem to justify the representation of events as isolated, no matter how interrelated they may be. Moreover, press releases from official news sources seldom take pains to point out inconsistencies, complex relations, or other big-picture aspects of events. These strategies of propagandists are rewarded by the journalistic preoccupation with daily news, which means that the news slate is often wiped clean each day. Update sections are relegated to the backs of newspapers, and analysis pieces are saved for slow news days in radio and television broadcasts.

The imperatives for drama and action further separate stories from one another. Because dramatic formats contain their own plots and resolutions, linkages between these news capsules can reduce their impact and confuse their plots. In fact, connections between news stories can raise the unsettling idea that nothing should be taken at face value and that behind every story there is a still larger story.[62] An unfortunate byproduct of using the story as the basic unit of news reporting is that linkages among stories tend to complicate simple, if isolated, realities. By contrast, other forms of presenting information such as ideologies or theories use connections among issues and events to simplify explanations and enhance meaning.

Consider, for example, how personalization and dramatization also invited fragmentation in the great health care debate of the 1990s, which drew attention to the plight of some forty million Americans who lacked medical insurance for illness or accident. Instead of putting the focus on how everyone could be accommodated under some new health plan, news reporting generally settled on a more dramatic and personal plot involving the paralyzing issue of whether people already receiving health coverage would have to face change and uncertainty. Doctors, insurance associations, and other opponents of the Clinton plan fed so many fearful images into the media that they quickly drove the story into the fragmentary exchange of scary emotional charges and countercharges.

According to communication scholar Kathleen Jamieson, the coverage quickly strayed from the ways in which a workable policy might be achieved. Audiences were treated, instead, to a mix of fearful threats about loss of existing coverage and to a series of personalized battles between the president and Congress. Individual members of Congress became personally identified with a confusing list of alternative proposals as the attacks on the president's plan multiplied. Even Hillary Clinton came under heavy fire for her role in organizing policy groups to work out details of a plan. Above all, the leadership and authority of the president became the focal issue in the news.

In the end, the entire episode was framed as a political game in which the president's authority was a primary issue, and the capacity of the national government to conduct orderly business was implicitly questioned. The president was described as losing his biggest policy battle to date, and doubts were raised about the ability of government to accomplish major national goals.

Instead of cutting off connections to surrounding political contexts, the news could have put the focus on many larger questions about the propriety of the health industry's role in defeating health reform or about the trails of campaign contributions from that industry to members of Congress who suddenly emerged as opponents to reform. These issues were raised but never became dominant frames for the story. Once again, news biases conveniently capsulized events at the expense of broader understandings. What happened to public understanding of the issues after such intensive news coverage? A disturbing study by the Times Mirror (now Pew) Center for the People & the Press found that fewer Americans understood key aspects of the Clinton administration health care plan after three months of intense news coverage than at the time the plan was first announced.[63]

It is no wonder that public opinion studies show that a majority of people have trouble thinking in abstract, logically integrated ways about political issues. An inventory of findings from public opinion research sounds like a list of the effects of news fragmentation: The average person has trouble stating clear positions on issues; most people tend to remember few facts about important issues; the majority of people see few connections between issues; and many people change their opinions easily about issues. John Zaller's research on a number of foreign policy situations from Vietnam to the Gulf War suggests that the more "informed" people are about a situation, the more they simply take their cues from the party leaders and political elites who dominate the news.[64]

Mort Rosenblum, a respected foreign correspondent for the Associated Press, wrote a passionate book about why the world depicted in the American news always seems on the verge of chaos. The book's title is provocative: *Who Stole the News? Why We Can't Keep Up with What Happens in the World and What We Can Do About It.*[65] His comparison of the BBC *News Desk* and the *CBS Evening News* suggests that the difference between British and American coverage patterns and priorities is so vast that they might as well be broadcasting from two different planets! In an interview with Rosenblum, *CBS News* anchor and managing editor Dan Rather seemed helpless to explain why his newscast led with the story of a Maryland man who was shot in an attempt to steal an FBI car—on a day in which the siege of Sarajevo had reached a crisis point and the Peruvian government captured that nation's most notorious revolutionary leader. As journalist Mark Hertsgaard concluded about Rosenblum's critical look at American news:

The unfortunate truth is that, for many Americans, the rest of the world does not really exist. It's more an abstraction than a real place where real people catch the bus to work, read newspapers, raise children, live lives. Our consciousness can be pierced if outsiders start making trouble for us—if swarthy, bearded "fanatics" take Americans hostage or cut off our oil supplies—but by the time we start paying attention, it's often too late; events have taken on their own momentum and there is little choice but to live with the consequences.[66]

The Authority-Disorder Bias Revisited

It is no wonder that details of policy debates often escape the public, even when issues receive considerable news coverage. As several of our examples indicate, intense news coverage can undermine understanding of a situation at the same time that people become more concerned and emotionally involved in it. Part of this disorientation is a result of the biases in many news stories that put disproportionate emphasis on what authorities are doing (taking charge, losing control, winning, losing, or in partisan conflict), and whether the situation in question seems to be moving in a more orderly and reassuring or disorderly and disturbing direction.

Authority plots and order-disorder images provide easy material when larger contexts surrounding events are cut off. Writing dramatic endings for fragmented stories often becomes the highest imperative in the newsroom. Sometimes authorities save the day, and order is restored to some corner of society. Sometimes authorities fight valiantly, but the forces of evil are simply overwhelming, and disorder seems to prevail. In other cases, such as health reform, authorities appear to be weak or deceitful or too preoccupied with their personal squabbles to get anything done, and both authority and order are challenged in the news. The point here is not that news accounts are fictional. Most news stories document aspects of the actual events being reported, but they are often selective in their documentation and tangential in their focus on what is important about a story. The point is that since the biases favoring dramatized, personalized, and fragmented news also favor writing images of authority and order into scripts in the first place, news organizations also have considerable dramatic license as to whether these authorities appear to be solving problems or restoring order in society.

Perhaps the greatest dilemma facing news decision makers is how to resolve this built-in tension between choosing the most dramatic endings for news accounts and the most representative or accurate ones. For reasons discussed in Chapter 3, journalistic misrepresentations find their way into many serious and sensitive areas of social life. For example, Robert Entman shows that news coverage of affirmative action (the policy of providing educational and employment opportunities to minorities) in the 1990s vastly distorted actual public opinion on the subject. Even though polls at the time showed upwards of 70 percent of Americans favoring some sort of affirmative action in society, news stories portrayed society as racially divided, hopelessly in conflict, and unable to solve this paralyzing problem. In what Entman calls a process of "manufacturing discord," the media told of a "tide of white anger," "backlash in the white community," and "deep despair among blacks."[67] Entman argues that in reality, the media represented the views of the most extreme politicians and news commentators as typical of the entire society. He suggests that the story could easily and more accurately have been told as one involving broad support among Americans on a difficult issue that a few extremists had attempted (but failed) to make politically disruptive and racially divisive. The only trouble with that sort of news, of course, is that it is not nearly as dramatic. Manufactured disorder is far more dramatic.

Of course, there may also be genuine crises of authority or challenges to social order in the news. It is important to be able to distinguish between the politically genuine and the journalistically contrived. In the modern era, grand news stories such as Vietnam and Watergate are obvious examples of serious challenges to authority and order that were far bigger (e.g., more enduring, triggering more citizen activism, engaging more news makers, and touching on more issues) than could be easily created and contained with dramatically enhanced news writing. Wrenching national experiences such as Watergate or Vietnam are often regarded by historians and political scientists as exceptional historical events. Many journalists also regard them as exceptional in marking the beginnings of trends toward more critical watchdog (critics would say scandal-oriented) journalism.[68] For our purposes, there is an important distinction between these landmark conflicts in history and routine journalistic dramatizations of authority and disorder:

- The authority-disorder bias clearly operates by isolating (fragmenting) a particular story from surrounding social or historical trends and dramatizing it in terms of far more one-dimensional plot formulas (e.g., as political game, leadership challenge, sign of social breakdown) than would be warranted by examining it in broader historical, political, or factual context.
- By contrast, grand historic moments generally emerge in the news by breaking down the plot formulas of routine stories and following trails of documentary information into society or institutions. In these cases, issues of authority or order are not used to wall off news episodes from surrounding contexts but to open up questions about the meaning of events and widely shared social experiences.

In the 1960s, for example, with millions of antiwar protesters in the streets and a national civil rights movement in full swing, one could argue that authority was palpably challenged by large numbers of people and that society was in some disorder. In the case of Watergate, the authority of the presidency was used to carry out and then cover up a long list of illegal activities. The news became a forum for debates about abuses of power and grounds for impeachment. Recent years have witnessed few incidents that plausibly qualify as constitutional crises, and there have been no riotous social movements challenging the legitimacy of the system itself. One important exception has been the ability of the Religious Right to make effective use of the media to amplify its claims that moral order is threatened in contemporary American life. Some social movements such as the antiabortionists and neo-Nazis have taken the law into their own hands. In general, however, authority-disorder stories are grafted onto the news by news organizations' application of formulas.

The more disturbing these news treatments become, the more likely they are to score hits as "talker" or "water cooler" stories (what people talk about at work the next day) that news directors press their staffs to create. For example, it has become common to hear people talking about abuse of the legal system to win large settlements on ridiculous liability claims. A classic story of the 1990s was the McDonald's lawsuit in which a woman won a huge settlement from the fast-food company because she was burned by hot coffee. As political scientists William Haltom and Michael McCann have demonstrated, however, the woman's claim was far more reasonable than it was portrayed in the news. Moreover, the numbers of frivolous lawsuits and extreme settlements have actually decreased, not increased, as implied in the steady stream of disturbing news accounts.[69]

The Political Costs of the Authority-Disorder Bias   Among the most common story lines used by journalists is one that goes like this: "Something has gone awry in the world today, but officials are hopeful that the situation will return to normal soon. And now, for a report from the scene, we go to. . . ." The plot thickens when different officials disagree about what measures are appropriate to the restoration of normalcy, or, failing that, when journalists stir up the story by asking an authority-challenging question designed to get a reaction that can be reported as a new development. There are generally two dramatic outcomes or resolutions possible for these authority dramas. One standard ending for the news drama is that some official action wins out, the day is saved, and the story ends with a return to "normal." Alternatively, a course of action fails, or is challenged by another player, and authority and social order are left in doubt. The problem is that either of these dramatic endings is likely to put the focus on pseudoissues rather than on the underlying politics of the situation. In more routine cases of everyday news, whether the balance is struck on the side of authority and order or on the side of mistrust and disorder, this central news bias displaces other possible ways of representing events. Even worse, with the balance tipping more in the direction of negative and disturbing news, the authority-disorder bias can become distorted to the point of seriously misrepresenting society and politics. We have already discussed coverage of crime and affirmative action as important examples of this problem.

It can be argued that crime and racial opportunity are, at least, real problems even if they are distorted in the news. Many other stories come dangerously close to being made up, at least in the sense that extreme and unrepresentative cases are offered as though they are typical or commonplace occurrences. As discussed in Chapter 3, for example, news magazines have turned distorted and misleading reporting into a formula: "Scare them and they will watch." Grainy hidden-camera videos and dramatic editing and writing create the impression of a sinister world in which a host of threats and dangers lurk behind the orderly facades of the supermarket or the doctor's office.

A prominent journalism review investigated a fairly typical hidden camera exposé on ABC's *PrimeTime* several years after the segment won two journalism awards. The piece was on how medical laboratories often worked too quickly and missed many early warning signs of cancer in women's Pap smears. The show sent producers in disguise into a lab in Arizona and had another producer pose as a new customer who needed a large number of Pap smears read over a weekend (a tactic designed to overwork the lab technicians and create errors in reading the Paps). Sure enough, the lab was reported as having a number of warning signs on the tests. However, according to the journalism review's evaluation of the piece, what the news magazine never reported was that the lab's results were well within normal industry standards for what turns out to be an imperfect and hard-to-read test. Instead, the story created the appearance of sinister lab operators routinely endangering women's health. The overall result was that the lab in the report went out of business, ABC News won two awards, and the audience may have been needlessly scared, not to mention selectively misinformed, about a number of aspects of cancer detection.[70] Perhaps information is beside the point with scare TV.

Whether it arbitrarily emphasizes the good or the bad, this sort of daily news falls short of its ideal function of presenting representative accounts of social and political life so that people can draw informed conclusions from them. It is closer to the mark to conclude that the news helps people confirm their favorite political stereotypes because those dramatic distortions fit better with the implicit guidelines for selecting and writing news stories. As one critic observed, both the public and journalists are involved more in a process of creating convenient fictions than discovering convincing facts: "We are all engaged in the same enterprise, all of us caught up in the making of analogies and metaphors, all of us seeking evocations and representations of what we can recognize as appropriately human. Stories move from truths to fact, not the other way around."[71]

BIAS AS PART OF THE POLITICAL INFORMATION SYSTEM

Consider the picture so far: Each day news consumers are bombarded by dozens of compartmentalized, unrelated dramatic capsules. Some emotional satisfaction can be derived from forming strong identifications with or against the actors who star in these minidramas. But what about facts? What about knowledge and practical information? Unless the consumer has an existing interest or perspective on the subject, recalling facts from the news resembles a trivia game played alone. Most people cannot remember three-fourths of the stories in a TV news broadcast immediately after watching it, and information recall about the remembered quarter is sketchy at best.[72]

There is now a sizable literature that reads like an inventory of these problems.[73] The tendencies toward personalization, dramatization, and fragmentation have all been remarkably enduring over time, although they may have become more exaggerated with the economic pressures of the business explained in the last chapter. While the focus on authority and order is also an enduring defining feature of the news, the shifting balance from order to mayhem and the unreflectively negative tone toward officials has left many observers puzzled and concerned. Indeed, many politicians say they have left government because of the relentlessly negative media scrutiny, while others have surrounded themselves by legions of media consultants and handlers. At the same time that many journalists criticize their own product in these terms, they confess being helpless to change it under the current system of profit- and ratings-driven business values.

NEWS BIAS AND DISCOURAGED CITIZENS

The general perspective developed in this book is that each aspect of the political information system described here is influenced by the others. For example, the weakness of journalism norms and cultural values for educating citizens may result in citizens who are easily discouraged from thinking seriously about serious issues. This, in
turn, may encourage political actors to employ superficial and emotional public relations techniques in their presentation of partisan political issues and policy choices.
Sensing little public interest in hard news and having few resources for investigative
reporting, the press passes off these strategically crafted political messages as the substance of the story of the day, perhaps overlaid with cynical commentary about the political games being played by politicians. This core of daily political news is interspersed with scandals and personal dramas justified by ratings reports suggesting that,
despite their protests to the contrary, many people really do follow these spectacles.

Whether people follow scandals and mayhem as guilty pleasures or with anger
and disgust, the convenient claim by media executives—that this is really what people
want—misses at least two important points. First, many people are tuning out political
news and homing in on more personal information about health, sports, celebrities,
fashion, travel, and lifestyles. As explained in later chapters, these trends are occurring despite the abundance of available news topics and the ease of becoming informed. Perhaps most distressing for the future of political participation is that
younger generations are most likely to tune out hard news. Second, according to research by communication scholars Joseph Cappella and Kathleen Hall Jamieson, even
the people who consume news often become discouraged about politics and public
life by cynical, negative news.[74]

So the public information cycle goes, one element of the press-politician-public
news triangle affecting another in a dysfunctional manner until nearly everyone is dissatisfied. However, few citizens possess enough understanding of the overall system
to recommend convincing solutions. Rather than thinking about the information system as a rational process in which objectivity is the highest and most desirable outcome, it makes more sense to think of this system as a game in which the different
players are not all playing for the same goals or even by the same rules, but in which
each uses the others to achieve particular ends:

- Politicians play for public support and favorable insider buzz by using news
  management and public relations techniques intended to put their political
  bias (or "spin") on news content.
- The press competes for ratings, sales, and "scoops" (being first to break a
  story), and perhaps most importantly, to avoid being "beaten" on a story by
  other news organizations. Business-driven news formulas dictate manufacturing the most dramatic audience-grabbing stories for the least cost and with a
  minimum of attention-distracting complexity. At the end of the day, stories often end up looking much the same from one news outlet to another, but the
  competition for audiences and the aggression toward politicians create the illusion of independence.

- The people occasionally enter the game as voters or as members of organized interests, searching the news for information that helps them decide what to do politically. Sometimes they find useful information, particularly when they are motivated by interest in a particular issue. Often they turn away, confused or discouraged. For the most part, however, they are the spectators. Political scientist Murray Edelman describes the focus of the daily news as political spectacle, attracting attention for its entertainment value even if it often fails to provide much information that is useful to citizens.[75]

REFORM ANYONE?

These trends offer little promise that, despite tremendous gains in communication technology and the vast potential of the Internet, the news of the future will come any closer than we are today to meeting the information needs of democracy—unless, that is, people such as the readers of this book begin to understand how this information system works and think about how to fix what is wrong with it. In place of thinking seriously about the problems of information in this information age, many people have simply withdrawn from politics and joined the chorus of those who hurl easy criticisms at politicians and press alike. Public disapproval alone has not produced an improvement in the quality of information on which the health of democracy depends. While criticisms of the news are legion, relatively few of those critics offer much in the way of solid proposals for change. Press reform is the subject of the final chapter in this book, but a brief look at one model of more useful news reporting is in order now.

The most recent attempt to create an information system with more of the qualities outlined above is a now-fading movement for *public* or *civic* journalism. Although there is no single approach to this effort at news reform, it generally involves local news organizations inviting citizen participation in shaping news coverage that "encourages civic engagement—especially in elections—and supports communities in solving problems."[76] This movement grew impressively in the late 1990s. By 1998, the Pew Center for Civic Journalism had funded sixty-two projects, each involving more than one news organization in coordinating agendas of issue and election coverage through opinion polls and citizen forums in communities.[77]

The irony is that this movement has drawn harsh criticism from prominent journalists and news organizations. For example, editors at the *New York Times* and the *Washington Post* have condemned the loss of journalistic independence that comes from letting citizens help decide what is important to cover. Many journalists feel that keeping the focus on a set of issues that may not be the ones government is currently addressing risks crossing the line from objective reporting to issue advocacy. A 1997 survey of media executives sponsored by the Associated Press found little in the way of broad support for the civic journalism movement in the industry. For example, only 14 percent of media executives felt that reporting was improved by news organizations listening to input from "citizens' juries" or "citizens' forums." Fully 33 percent felt that establishing such direct communication links between citizens and news organizations was a bad idea. The executives were evenly divided (35 percent to 34 percent) on the question of whether crossing the line between reporting and advocacy would further undermine journalism credibility. Perhaps the most damning charge against civic journalism is that it is little more than boosterism, a marketing ploy, or a "gimmick to make publishers feel better about themselves." A plurality of 41 percent of media executives strongly agreed with these charges, while only 33 percent strongly disagreed.[78]

The closing chapter of the book examines ways in which citizens and a grassroots media reform movement are trying to move beyond these obstacles to reform. For now, we continue to explore why the news has become so stuck in patterns that seem to satisfy none of its public stakeholders: politicians, journalists, or publics. The next chapter examines news as a political and economic construction with the focus on the economics of the news business. Because the greatest changes in recent times have occurred in the economic conditions affecting news organizations and the shifting social habits of the audiences for news itself, these topics are addressed in the greatest detail. In the process, we will learn a few eye-opening things about the ways in which information is constructed, not with citizens in mind, but for the consumer audiences on which the profits of the media depend. Following this discussion of the social and economic foundations of news, the next four chapters show how the different interests of politicians, the press, and the public converge to actively produce this system of political information that we know as the daily news. The goal is to understand the kind of information that reaches the average citizen and to assess its impact on the quality of public life in the American democracy.

NOTES

1. Dana Milbank, "The Military Is the Message: Triumphant President Casts Strong Image for '04 Election." *Washington Post,* May 2, 2003, A24.
2. *Countdown,* May 1, 2003. MSNBC. Based on transcript from a Lexis-Nexis search (thanks to Steve Livingston).
3. See Robert Entman, "Framing: Toward Clarification of a Fractured Paradigm," *Journal of Communication* 43 (1993), no. 4: 51–58.
4. Brent Cunningham, "Re-thinking Objectivity," *Columbia Journalism Review* 4, (July/August 2003). **cjr.org/issues/2003/4/objective_cunningham.asp**.
5. See Joseph Cappella and Kathleen Hall Jamieson, *Spiral of Cynicism: The Press and the Public Good* (New York: Oxford University Press, 1997).
6. Joseph Turow, *Breaking Up America: Advertisers and the New Media World* (Chicago: University of Chicago Press, 1997).
7. Gallup-Times Mirror, *The People and the Press* (Los Angeles: Times Mirror, 1986), 28–29; see also Robert P. Vallone, Lee Ross, and Mark R. Lepper, "The Hostile Media Phenomenon: Biased Perceptions and Perceptions of Media Bias in Coverage of the Beirut Massacre," *Journal of Personality and Social Psychology* 49, no. 3 (1985): 577–85.
8. Murray Edelman, *The Symbolic Uses of Politics* (Urbana, IL: University of Illinois Press, 1964).
9. Ibid.
10. Recall from Chapter 1, for example, the Media Watch mayhem index and the broad evidence that soft news is displacing hard news at all levels of media. Also recall the discussion of increases in press criticism of government and politicians by Thomas Patterson in *Out of Order* (New York: Knopf, 1993). See also the analysis of rising cynicism and news negativity by Joseph Cappella and Kathleen Hall Jamieson in *Spiral of Cynicism* (New York: Oxford University Press, 1997).

11. Michael Winerip, "Looking for an Eleven O'Clock Fix," *New York Times Magazine,* January 11, 1998, 54.
12. Ralph Vartabedian, "Federal Computers: Is the System Haywire?" *Los Angeles Times,* December 8, 1996, 1.
13. Joan Didion, *Political Fictions* (New York: Alfred A. Knopf, 2001). The quote is from Joseph Lelyveld, "Another Country," *New York Review of Books,* December 20, 2001, 10.
14. Andrew Kohut, "Public Support for the Watchdog Is Fading," *Columbia Journalism Review* (May/June 2001): 46.
15. Lelyveld, "Another Country," 10.
16. Ibid.
17. Thomas E. Patterson, *The Vanishing Voter: Public Involvement in an Age of Uncertainty* (New York: Afred A. Knopf, 2002).
18. Christina Alsina, Philip John Davies, and Bruce E. Gronbeck, "Preference Poll Stories in the Last Two Weeks of Campaign 2000." *American Behavioral Scientist* 44 (August 2001): 2288–305.
19. See Shanto Iyengar, *Is Anyone Responsible? How Television Frames Political Issues* (Chicago: University of Chicago Press, 1992).
20. Milbank, "The Military Is the Message," A24.
21. Hugh Clifton, "President's Aircraft Carrier Appearance Hailed as Brilliant PR," *PR Week,* May 19, 2003, 10.
22. Milbank, "The Military Is the Message."
23. Ibid.
24. Elisabeth Bumiller, "Keepers of Bush Image Lift Stagecraft to New Heights," *New York Times,* May 16, 2003, 1A.
25. Maureen Dowd, "Look Good, Act Cool," *New York Times,* May 11, 2003, 13, sec. 4.
26. "Upholding the Dignity of the Office—With Starch." *Washington Post,* January 26, 2001, C2.
27. Associated Press, August 11, 2001.
28. James Werrell, "Was This Photo-Op Really Necessary?" *Rock Hill Herald,* May 9, 2002, 6A.
29. David E. Sanger, "Bush Declares 'One Victory in a War on Terror,'" *New York Times,* May 2, 2003, 1A.
30. Ibid.
31. Quoted in Edward W. Barrett, "Folksy TV News," *Columbia Journalism Review* (November/December 1973), 19.
32. Reported in David L. Paletz and Robert M. Entman, *Media Power Politics* (New York: Free Press, 1981), 17.
33. Howard Kurtz, "Since September 11 Attacks, TV Morning Shows Rediscover World News," *Seattle Times,* November 25, 2001, A2.
34. *Wall Street Journal,* June 17, 1981, 1.
35. Jason DeParle, "From the Welfare Rolls to the Starring Roles: TV Offers Recipients Brushes with Fame," *New York Times,* June 25, 1999), A10.
36. Paletz and Entman, *Media Power Politics,* 16–17.
37. Quoted in Ann Devroy and Don Balz, "The White House Wins Again, but Was the Victory Pyrrhic?" *The Washington Post National Weekly Edition,* November 22–28, 1993, 12.
38. National Public Radio, *Morning Edition,* August 12, 1994.
39. Ibid.
40. Joe Klein, "Learning to Run," *New Yorker,* December 8, 1997, 53–59.
41. Paletz and Entman, *Media Power Politics,* 17.
42. Reported in Edward Jay Epstein, *News from Nowhere* (New York: Random House, 1973), 4–5. Such a conscious statement of a defining characteristic of news is all the more remarkable considering that most journalists have difficulty in clearly defining their professional product.
43. Paletz and Entman, *Media Power Politics,* 17.

44. See, Steven Livingston, *The Terrorism Spectacle* (Boulder, CO: Westview Press, 1994).
45. Stephen Hess, "Covering the Senate: Where Power Gets the Play," *Washington Journalism Review* (June 1986), 41–42.
46. Timothy E. Cook, *Making News and Making Laws: Media Strategies in the U.S. House of Representatives* (Washington, DC: Brookings Institution, 1989).
47. Robert Darnton, "Writing News and Telling Stories," *Daedalus* 104 (Spring 1975): 190.
48. Lewis H. Lapham, "Gilding the News," *Harper's* (July 1981): 34.
49. Ibid.
50. Reported in Barrett, "Folksy TV News," 19.
51. I am indebted to Liz McHale for bringing this phenomenon to my attention.
52. Gaye Tuchman, *Making News: A Study in the Construction of Reality* (New York: Free Press, 1978).
53. Don DeLillo, *The Names* (New York: Vintage, 1982), 58.
54. Paletz and Entman, *Media Power Politics,* 16.
55. Lapham, "Gilding the News," 35.
56. Opening paragraph of a column by Laura Cunningham, *New York Times,* September 3, 1981, Home section, 16.
57. Murray Edelman, *Constructing the Political Spectacle* (Chicago: University of Chicago Press, 1988).
58. Dan Nimmo and James E. Coombs, *Mediated Political Realities* (New York: Longman, 1983).
59. Russell Baker, "Meanwhile, in Zanzibar. . . ," *New York Times Magazine,* February 6, 1977, 12.
60. Edwin Diamond, "Disco News," in *Watching American Politics,* ed. Dan Nimmo and William L. Rivers, (New York: Longman, 1981), 250.
61. Paletz and Entman, *Media Power Politics,* 23.
62. See, for example, Edward Jay Epstein's fascinating suggestion that there may have been a much larger scandal behind Watergate than the one revealed in *All the President's Men* by Carl Bernstein and Bob Woodward (New York: Warner Books, 1979). The dramatic plot confined the story to the White House. Moreover, any suggestion of larger conspiracies would have overburdened the already complex plot and undermined the credibility of the neatly contained White House story. See Epstein, "The Grand Coverup," *Wall Street Journal,* April 19, 1976, 10.
63. Reported in Stuart Schear, "Covering Health Care: Politics or People?" *Columbia Journalism Review* (May/June 1994), 36–37.
64. See John Zaller, *The Nature and Origins of Mass Opinion* (New York: Cambridge University Press, 1992). See also, Zaller, "Elite Leadership of Mass Opinion: New Evidence from the Gulf War," in *Taken by Storm,* W. Lance Bennett and David L. Paletz, eds. Chicago: University of Chicago Press, 1994, 186–209.
65. Mort Rosenblum, *Who Stole the News?* (New York: John Wiley, 1993).
66. Mark Hertsgaard, "Isolated by the Media," *Washington Post National Weekly Edition,* November 22–28, 1993, 35.
67. Robert Entman, "Manufacturing Discord: Media in the Affirmative Action Debate," *Press/Politics* 2 (Fall 1997): 32–51.
68. See, for example, Bob Woodward, *Shadow: Five Presidents and the Legacy of Watergate* (New York: Simon and Schuster, 1999).
69. William Haltom and Michael McCann, "Law and Lore: Media Production of Legal Knowledge and Tort Reform" (paper presented at the annual meeting of the American Political Science Association, Boston, 1998).
70. D. M. Osborne, "Lab Scam," *Brill's Content* (February 1999): 100–103.
71. Lapham, "Gilding the News," 33.
72. David H. Weaver and Judith M. Buddenbaum, *Newspapers and Television: A Review of Research on Uses and Effects* (Washington, DC: American Newspaper Publishers Association Research

Center, Report No. 19, 1979); John Stauffer, Richard Frost, and William Rybolt, "The Attention Factor in Recalling Network Television News," *Journal of Communication* (Winter 1983): 29–37.

73. See, for example: David L. Altheide, *Media Power* (Beverly Hills, CA: Sage, 1985); Michael Parenti, *Inventing Reality: The Politics of the Mass Media* (New York: St. Martin's Press, 1986); Epstein, *News from Nowhere;* Herbert Gans, *Deciding What's News* (New York: Vintage, 1979); Timothy Crouse, *The Boys on the Bus* (New York: Free Press, 1978); Robert Darnton, "Writing News and Telling Stories," *Daedalus* 104 (Spring 1975): 175–97; Mark Fishman, *Manufacturing the News* (Austin: University of Texas Press, 1980); Todd Gitlin, *The Whole World Is Watching* (Berkeley: University of California Press, 1980); Harvey Molotch and Marilyn Lester, "News as Purposive Behavior," *American Sociological Review* 39 (1974): 101–12; Harvey Molotch and Marilyn Lester, "Accidental News: The Great Oil Spill," *American Journal of Sociology* 81 (1975): 235–60; Leon V. Sigal, *Reporters and Officials: The Organization and Politics of Newsmaking* (Lexington, MA: Heath, 1973); Paletz and Entman, *Media Power Politics;* Robert M. Entman, *Democracy Without Citizens: Media and the Decay of American Politics* (New York: Oxford University Press, 1989); and Iyengar, *Is Anyone Responsible?*
74. See Capella and Hall Jamieson, *Spiral of Cynicism.*
75. For an exploration of the news as popular spectacle, see Murray Edelman, *Constructing the Political Spectacle* (Chicago: University of Chicago Press, 1988).
76. Charlotte Grimes, "Whither the Civic Journalism Bandwagon?" (discussion paper Joan Shorenstein Center, Harvard University, February 1999), 3.
77. Ibid.
78. Ibid.

Chapter 3

The Political Economy of News

They've got us putting more and more fuzz and wuzz on the air, cop-shop stuff, so as to compete not with other news programs but with entertainment programs, including those posing as news programs, for dead bodies, mayhem, and lurid tales.

Dan Rather

If a story needs a real investment of time and money, we don't do it anymore. In assignment meetings, we dream up "talker" stories, stuff that will attract attention and get us talked about, tidbits for busy folks who clip items from the paper and stick them on the fridge. Who the hell cares about corruption in city government, anyway, much less dying Bosnians?

Reporter on an Illinois Daily Paper

Neither TV anchor Dan Rather nor the middle-America newspaper reporter were happy about their observations from the newsroom. High-profile media personalities like Rather must endure corporate executives defending the glitz and gore as ways of saving dinosaur network-news organizations from extinction as the media climate around them changes. Rank-and-file reporters in newsrooms across the land are similarly forced to recognize that trends toward "lite" news and features have turned newspapers from a dying breed into profitable businesses.[1]

Enormously profitable times for all the traditional branches of the media—television, print, and radio—were celebrated throughout the 1980s and 1990s on Wall Street as well as by the studios and producers of game shows, TV sitcoms, drama series, reality programs, movies, and news. The conventional wisdom among the chieftans of giant media corporations was *bigger is better,* as expressed in the mantra of *synergy*. The common goals were (1) to become large enough to own the production, marketing, and distribution of media content; (2) to have enough channels and publications to dominate advertising markets, while using free internal advertising to draw audiences from one channel or publication to others in the media empire; and (3) to recycle both talent and old *prime-time* programming within the system to reduce the costs of filling the schedules of multiplying cable and broadcast outlets.

The unprecedented growth surge in media empires that closed the twentieth century came at a price: the serious deterioration of news. Consider the example of the newspaper. The media merger mania of the 1980s saw the near extinction of independently owned and competing papers in American cities. It is important to understand that having independent and competing papers, alone, did not mean that the second or third papers in a town offered citizens higher information quality. To the contrary, weaker papers were often put out of business by higher quality competitors, leading some analysts to argue that the consolidation actually raised news quality in many cities.[2] Why bemoan the consolidation of the newspaper industry? Two decades of industry restructuring resulted in the social and economic reengineering of the newspaper.

The economic story in the newspaper industry is also a story about what happened to the content. The 1990s dawned brightly: the average profit margin was a healthy 14.8 percent for companies in the newspaper industry. The prospects of even greater profits stimulated an even larger wave of mergers and buyouts in the 1990s. The megamedia companies squeezed a whopping 21.5 percent average profit from their expanding newspaper holdings by the end of the decade.[3] Such stunning profit margins were achieved through the three-step industry formula of (1) cheapening the content, (2) marketing content directly to the audiences that were most attractive to advertisers, and (3) allowing the less profitable audiences to wither away, producing a net savings of printing and distribution costs. (Newspaper circulation actually fell during this period of historic profitability).

Just when the new formulas were working smoothly, the dot com boom shook newspapers with fears that people would flock to online information sites that offered free features (movie reviews, weather, sports, fashion, and even political news), drawing audiences and precious advertising dollars away from papers. The bad news about the rise of electronic information media was delivered by computer guru (and former CEO of Intel) Andrew Grove to the Association of Newspaper Editors. Grove cheerily remarked that "Nothing sharpens the awareness of a situation like the sight of a gallows."[4] The dotcoms went bust, and the fear subsided—only to be replaced by the economic downturn that ushered in the millennium, pushing profits down as advertising fell. Through all of this time, the more worrisome trend is that young people do not read newspapers in anything close to the numbers of earlier generations. What could be done to attract young readers who really are flocking to the Web? And so goes the turbulent economic history of the newspaper.[5]

What will the newspaper of tomorrow look like? Not like that of today. Papers have scrambled to get into the Web business, building often impressive, but seldom profitable sites that channel more readers online. Some of these sites are rich and interactive: *The Washington Post* (**www.washingtonpost.com**), Public Broadcasting Service (**www.pbs.org**), National Public Radio (**www.npr.org**). Perhaps the best example is outside the United States at the British Broadcasting Corporation (**www.bbc.co.uk**). Most of the electronic editions, however, soon became known as "shovelware" in the industry, referring to the practice of simply shoveling the print paper into Web pages, perhaps adding more wire service filler and greater reader input than was possible to include in the print version.[6] Few of the commercial electronic ventures have proved profitable, suffering the same general advertising revenue problems that killed the first generation of dotcom companies.

Meanwhile, the television news picture is similarly turbulent as viewers have more choices in cable channels and the Internet, and the age of TV news consumers continues to rise (meaning that the young audiences prized by advertisers are eluding news programming). Compounding television pressures are corporate owners who demand more profitability from their media investments, and who see news as little different from sports or game shows in terms of its product status. In the heyday of television news, upwards of half the nation's households tuned to one of the three network nightly news shows. The companies that owned those networks regarded news as part of the prestige associated with their brand images and, therefore, allowed greater spending and less income from news divisions than they required from sports or entertainment units. By century's end, TV news audiences were not just shrinking and aging—they were also scattering across multiplying broadcast and cable channels. In the midst of this changing picture, all three pioneering networks were devoured by giant corporations. As of this writing, NBC was owned by General Electric, ABC by Disney, and CBS by Viacom.

CORPORATE PROFIT LOGIC AND NEWS CONTENT

Let's take a look at life on "Planet Viacom."[7] After swallowing CBS and its holdings, Viacom's media empire included: thirty-nine wholly owned TV stations reaching over half of American households and over 200 affiliates reaching nearly all the rest; controlling ownership of the UPN network with its 189 affiliates; controlling ownership of five radio networks including Infinity Broadcasting Corporation, which alone runs 165 radio stations, including six out of the top ten highest grossing channels; a healthy cable collection that includes MTV, VH1, Nickelodeon, Showtime, and Comedy Central; several movie companies including Paramount; dozens of commercial Web sites; a publishing empire that includes Simon & Schuster, the Free Press, and Pocket Books; and theme parks, movie theaters, advertising companies, product promotion and licensing companies, and on and on. *Columbia Journalism Review* has a Web site on media ownership. Viacom can be tracked at **www.cjr.org/tools/owners/viacom.asp**. Other issues connected to media ownership can be followed on the Media Channel at **www.mediachannel.org/ownership**.

One observer likened Viacom to a media mall with CBS as its anchor: "Viacom sees the CBS network as the anchor store of a huge mall—one in which Viacom owns all the stores. With its still-popular shows, CBS will draw in many people who can then be directed to Viacom's many smaller outlets—MTV, Nickelodeon, VH1, and so on. The process should work in reverse, too."[8] The news on CBS quickly became lost as a tiny piece of the profit and synergy picture. When CBS was an independent company, profits were not as important for the news division, which was regarded more as an asset that added prestige to the CBS brand image. Legend has it that owner William S. Paley once told his news division to concentrate on the best reporting possible, and he would make profits from sports and entertainment. Today, the news must perform like the entertainment divisions, with profit pressures cutting away at staff and other resources.

The first direct effect of merger pressures on news content typically comes from budget cuts, which means fewer staff and closing expensive international news bureaus. No matter, international news seemed to be a bore for the key demographic audiences, anyway. At least, that was the conventional wisdom until 9/11, which may have given a few still-viable international news organizations such as CNN (owned by giant Time Warner) a temporary reprieve in their ongoing corporate downsizing operations. CBS had already shut down most of its world bureaus long before 9/11.

The next common pattern following a megamerger is generally a rebranding of the news. Unlike in the days of smaller media corporations when the news was an element of prestige in the brand identification of the company, today's media giants define prestige more in terms of the profits they make for their investors. The role of news in contemporary brand logic is tied to attracting the right demographic audiences to generate the greatest profits. The Viacom merger thus accelerated the fall of the once pioneering CBS news operation (the home of Edward R. Murrow and Walter Cronkite) from corporate flagship to corporate profit problem. Among other things, this meant adjusting news content and delivery formats to fit the lifestyle interests of the audiences already tuning in to entertainment programs. When CBS decided to lower the median age of its audience with programs like *Survivor,* the move set in motion a reformatting of other network programming, including news. A subsequent evening newscast was promoted with a spot in which Dan Rather's concerned voice asked us to stay tuned to find out how safe our hamburgers are, as a conveyer belt of factory produced hamburger patties streamed across the screen.[9]

Another challenge facing CBS news after the Viacom merger was to design news content for the UPN network. This put CBS into the buzz at the winter 2002 press showcase for new television programming in Pasadena, California. It was announced that CBS news executives would oversee creating "niche news content" for UPN. Niche news, like niche advertising, is designed to better deliver the right (i.e., the most lucrative) demographic audience mix to advertisers at low production costs aimed at maximizing profits. According to the *New York Times* media/business correspondent who covered the much-hyped event, the logic of programming niche news content goes like this:

> Network executives yearn to lower the median age for the news, which is about 57 or 58 depending on the network, and replace Immodium and Zoloft ads with ones for the iPod and Mountain Dew. If they cannot attract youth to the current brand of news, they think they can tailor news to be more attractive to youth.[10]

It turns out that UPN had no news programming at all. It had a hard to reach (and harder to keep) audience of desirable white and minority males in the 12–18 and 18–34 demographic groups, thanks to programming such as *Buffy the Vampire Slayer* and *W.W.F. Smackdown!* The goal of getting young people to watch news is a noble one. The real question is whether that news will be of much value after adjusting its content to suit the ratings, profit, and programming brand equation of UPN. One suspects that a better solution would simply be to recycle other Viacom products such as Comedy Central's *Daily Show with Jon Stewart,* which is both funny and informative.

When Viacom's VH1 channel began a news program, the stories involved Mariah Carey's new film opening at the Sundance film festival and the drug problems of Foo Fighters drummer Taylor Hawkins. The show even ended with a clothing credit for the anchor: "Wardrobe courtesy of Anthropologie."[11] Some promise of more political relevance was signaled by a documentary on Hate Rock, offering insights about the role of music in the Aryan supremacist movement. The VH1 vice president for news production observed that "In addition to being awful, neo-Nazis are very telegenic."[12]

Case Study: *All the News That Fits (the Audience Demographics)*

What if the news began telling audiences what they already believe about reality instead of challenging them to think about what is really going on in the world? This delicate question reminds us that we should not ignore the content-bending effects of adapting the news to grab commercially desirable audiences. For example, why was the stock market plunge of 2000–2001 such a surprise to so many investors? Part of the problem, no doubt, was the mass psychology of so many people investing in the market that it was hard to think about the downside. However, the news provided little balance to this crowd psychology. Even a casual reading of business news at the end of the 1990s reveals a balance tipped toward experts and reporters offering what turned out to be bad reasons for investing good money in overpriced technology stocks. True, there were periodic cautionary statements from newsmakers such as guru-investor Warren Buffett and Federal Reserve Chairman Alan Greenspan, but these cautious critics were far outweighed by the daily parade of experts and insiders touting "inside" stock picks that kept audiences tuning in.

Why was the news so out of balance? The answer may lie in the unfortunate practice of news organizations to shape their content to secure ratings. John Cassidy dared to suggest that this backward idea of fitting news content to audience perceptions of reality might apply to business news during the technology boom of the 1990s. According to Cassidy, CNBC was a prime example of a cable channel with a business news emphasis that struggled to hold its audience in the face of growing competition. The cable business news formats soon all came to resemble sports programs, with coverage of the day's winners and losers, sexy anchors and interviewers, regular casts

of insiders, features on star performers (both corporations and their CEOs), and cele-
brations of investor victories:

> Every weekday in the late nineteen-nineties, from early morning, a steady
> stream of town cars made their way from lower Manhattan and midtown up
> the West Side Highway and across the George Washington Bridge. Once in
> New Jersey, the cars . . . deposited their passengers in front of a brick build-
> ing that is home to CNBC. With more than twelve hours of programming to fill
> each day, the CNBC producers couldn't be too picky about whom they put on-
> screen, but they did have some standards. Their ideal studio guest was a for-
> mer beauty queen who covered technology stocks, spoke in short declarative
> sentences, and dated Donald Trump. Since there weren't many of these
> women available, the producers had to settle for middle-aged men who
> revered Alan Greenspan and tried their best to speak in English. The majority
> of CNBC's guests were bullish. Bears weren't banned, but they weren't exactly
> welcome, either. They tended to come off as crotchety, and viewers didn't like
> them.[13]

It was not until several years after the technology bubble burst that CNBC set a new
tone by requiring (in 2004) that its staff divest of all stock holdings—a rule made shortly
after star reporter Maria Bartiromo aired an upbeat report featuring an executive of a
company in which Bartiromo held a substantial amount of stock.

In today's business-driven environment, judgments about what audiences may
need to know are tempered by what marketing research says they want to know
(which is tempered further by how executives interpret that research and decide
what can be done profitably). FOX News architect and former political image-
maker, Roger Ailes, once quipped, "When I die, I want to come back with real
power. I want to come back as a member of a focus group."[14] Focus groups are
those carefully selected samples of consumers who are led through discussions
designed to discover their feelings and fantasies about products, political candidates, and increasingly, the news they consume. The growing use of market research technologies raises important questions about news and democracy. The
search for the demographics that win the election or boost the bottom line also
means excluding large numbers of people from the communication process.
Which explains why entertainment is pitched toward young audiences, and elections target seniors and middle-class families.

The example of marketing economic news to keep hopeful investors tuned in is
just another step in the evolution of news (and the reality it represents) as a
consumer-driven commodity. Consider an earlier trend in consumer marketing of
newspapers that began to reshape their content in the 1980s. As large corporations
bought out the nation's struggling papers during the last two decades, marketing
consultants were brought in to fix the bottom line. For example, the giant Knight

Ridder chain (one of the dominant companies in the newspaper industry) launched a "25/43 Project" aimed at winning back that affluent "demographic" (age group) of television babies who had drifted away from newspaper reading. Focus groups were selected to probe personal concerns and to find market angles that would appeal to new readers.

A former editor at the chain's Boca Raton, Florida, *News* described the effort to make over his former paper as similar to "watching Procter & Gamble develop and test market a new toothpaste."[15] Reporters at other papers in the area dubbed the result "The Flamingo News" for its flamboyant Miami design, which included a pink flamingo on the masthead. Political reporting in the redesigned *News* was derided as "news McNuggets," and another former editor charged the paper with "pandering to people with the attention span of a gnat."[16] However, the editor of the *Boca Raton News* who presided over the marketing makeover claimed that the streamlined approach to news, along with more personalized features, was simply giving people what they want. Other Knight Ridder papers soon followed the lead of the *Boca Raton News,* often to the dismay of their reporters. A song lyric mysteriously appeared on the newsroom bulletin board at a sister paper, the *Kansas City Star,* suggesting that it be sung to the tune of "The Beer Barrel Polka":

> Roll out the Boca, we'll have a paper that's quick
> Roll out the Boca, too many words make you sick
> Keep it all nice and easy
> Makin' more money's the trick
> Now we're gonna roll out the Bocas
> Until the circulation numbers click![17]

Undaunted by such criticism, Knight Ridder executives proudly promoted the company's "customer obsession" campaign at an American Newspaper Publishers Association convention: "We wanted to see what happens if you do everything with the customer in mind."[18] Journalism educators such as Gilbert Cranberg at the University of Iowa challenged Knight Ridder to find a way to win customers without sacrificing good journalism standards in the process. Suggesting that Knight Ridder's 25/43 campaign referred to the IQ of the target audience, Cranberg warned: "The techniques and influence of marketers have degraded political campaigns, and they could degrade the print press. [They are] catering to the self-interest of readers. What about interest in the larger community?"[19]

It appears that James Batten, the chairman of Knight Ridder at the time, was listening. He encouraged some of his papers to find ways to implement the "customer obsession" program without destroying the quality of political journalism in the process. One of the papers to take up the challenge was the *Wichita Eagle*, which launched the "Voter Project" aimed at improving campaign issue coverage and openly encouraging citizen participation in elections, while emphasizing the "community connectedness" of the paper and its readers. Postelection research showed that voters in the paper's circulation area knew more about the issues than did voters elsewhere in Kansas, and the local voter turnout was higher as well.[20] The good news in this case (and in similar experiments at other papers) appears to be that news marketing need not conflict with the interests of democracy. The bad news was reported in a larger study of marketing-driven news organizations by Doug Underwood and Keith Stamm: more papers appear to be moving in the direction of the *Boca Raton News* than the *Wichita Eagle*.[21]

The large Gannett chain inaugurated a "News 2000" program to find out what readers want and to give it to them.[22] In the case of the Olympia, Washington, *Olympian*, readers were surveyed and interviewed at shopping malls (consumer research goes where the consumers are) and took part in public forums with the editors to find out what they wanted in the paper. Based on the input, the entire organization and format of the paper were changed. As with the Knight Ridder program, other Gannett papers have followed suit. Once again, reporters have expressed concerns that the news has been reduced to superficial formulas. Company executives point to increased profits and reader satisfaction as signs of a superior product. Gannett executives even urged journalism schools to train journalists to accept the removal of barriers between newsroom, advertising department, business office, and corporate headquarters.[23]

Among the most surprising casualties of the marketing of news was the resignation of Jay Harris, publisher of one of the most successful and respected dailies in the Knight Ridder chain, the *San Jose Mercury News*. After the highly profitable surge of the 1990s (the *Mercury's* profits ranged between 22 and 29 percent over the decade), the bottom line began to slide, in large part because the recession in Silicon Valley cut into lucrative employment advertising by technology companies. The corporate response was to slash the news budget severely to shore up sagging profits.

A memo from the president of Knight Ridder asked Harris to apply the standard formulas to make the cuts: "I would recommend taking a hard look at the recent reader research. If the *Mercury News* market is similar to our other markets, the research will indicate that the readers will want more local news. The *Mercury News* front pages are consistently local and compelling, while the inside of the A section is very heavily weighted toward foreign news. This may be something to reconsider."[24] Harris knew that a large percentage of his readers were software engineers from other countries. Moreover, the computer business that defined the local economy was a global industry requiring international information. He also knew that corporate headquarters was unyielding in its insistence on maintaining unrealistic levels of profit growth. The inevitable result would be to watch one of the nation's best (and still profitable) papers deteriorate, so Harris resigned in protest. Jay Harris's resignation sent a sobering message to his colleagues in the profession, and he was soon invited to address the convention of the American Society of Newspaper editors. In his speech, he raised these crucial questions:

> When the interests of readers and shareholders are at odds, which takes priority? When the interests of the community and shareholders are at odds, which takes priority? When the interest of the nation and an informed citizenry and the demands of the shareholders for ever-increasing profits are at odds, which takes priority?[25]

THE POLITICAL ECONOMY OF NEWS

Economic pressures have been shaping the news for more than a century and a half. In the view of journalism historian Gerald Baldasty, the most fundamental transformation of news in the history of this country began in the mid-1800s when the political party press began to give way to a commercial press.[26] We will further explore these historical roots of modern news in the case study in Chapter 6. However, the form and magnitude of economic changes in recent years have resulted in a remarkable period of change, making today's news very different than it was even a decade or two ago, perhaps even creating a "new news" as Marvin Kalb calls it.

Audience size and common consumption patterns were two defining elements of the mass media. The fragmentation of audiences and the rise of niche media signal the twilight of the mass media era. There is, however, a sense in which the mass media, or at least a new variant, is still with us: the growing standardization of information at its source. If we combine the declining commitment to producing hard news, we have a prescription for economizing in the industry: more information is produced in generic form, wholesaled to many outlets, and later dressed up or down, as the format of a particular channel and the demographics of its audience dictate. This seeming contradiction between multiplying channels and shrinking diversity and depth of news content is important to understand.

As the global media come under the ownership of a handful of giant corporations, such as Time Warner based in the United States, German-based Bertelsmann, or Rupert Murdoch's News Corporation, the tendency is for the same centrally gathered raw news material to be delivered to more and more outlets in the "media mall." There are, of course, important exceptions: *The New York Times* and *The Washington Post* in the United States, the British Broadcasting Corporation in the United Kingdom, *El Pais* in Spain, *Le Monde* in France, or the *Frankfurter Allgemeine Zeitung* in Germany. These independent, high-quality organizations seldom challenge the political or economic consensus in Washington, London, or Berlin, but they provide detailed reports on important world developments.

ECONOMICS VERSUS DEMOCRACY: INSIDE THE NEWS BUSINESS

It is comforting to think that some overriding sense of responsibility to democracy guides the daily gathering and distribution of news. As the case study indicates, however, the signs increasingly point to the influence of profit motives and market forces. As broadcast television networks, cable channels, Internet portals, news services, and print publications are purchased by industrial giants, it has become common to hear statements such as this one from the chairman of General Electric (GE), the company that bought NBC: "Network news isn't the strategic center of what happens here. . . . News is not the core of the asset."[27]

As noted in Chapter 1, there is no guarantee of optimal information in any political system, including one that displays the First Amendment as a sort of brand guarantee of information quality. As a challenge to conventional wisdom, consider the argument of communication scholar Robert McChesney, whose historical analysis indicates that commercial press systems contain little inherent basis for public service or responsibility. McChesney suggests that if we lift the veil of press freedom, we encounter corporate interests that invoke the First Amendment less often to protect their freedom to publicize politically risky or challenging information than to defend their pursuit of profits against obligations to serve the public interest.[28] Today's byword is *freedom of the market,* which means profits over social responsibility, so corporate owners cut news staffs and world bureaus and rely on cosmetic adjustments to compete in the battle for shrinking rating points, as viewers become harder to attract to the generic information fare.

Explaining Ratings

Just what is a rating point, and why do ratings matter? A rating point reflects the size of the audience watching a program. At the time of this writing, one rating point corresponded to just over a million TV households. The number of households per rating point gradually increases as the number of TV households in the country goes up, meaning that 100 ratings points equals all the TV households. Advertising rates are determined by a combination of the size of the audience (ratings) and its demographic composition of ready buyers for the product. Also, since everyone is not watching TV all the time, the price of ads also reflects the percentage or *share* of actual viewers in a particular time slot who are tuned in to a particular program. For example, according to Nielsen Media Research (the ratings people) the 1999 Super Bowl scored a 44.5 rating and a 67 share, meaning that $44.5 \times 994,000$ households (994,000 was the value of a rating point at that time) were watching, and that this audience consisted of 67 percent of all the households watching TV. Since the Super Bowl is also a social occasion in which people gather to watch, it is tricky to estimate the exact number of people (called "eyeballs") watching. Nielsen put the estimated 1999 U.S. Super Bowl audience at 90 million. Because the Super Bowl is far and away the most watched program on TV (the Academy Awards are a distant second with 55 million viewers), it is highly sought after by advertisers who create clever commercials generally aimed at promoting brand identification. The brands promoting themselves through this media event include, not least of all, FOX TV, which paid a huge amount to the NFL for broadcast rights. The Super Bowl was acquired in large part to boost the FOX brand and to advertise other FOX programs. That is synergy.

Just how much do ratings and audience share affect media company revenues? A 30-second spot during Super Bowl XXXII cost $1.6 million, not counting production costs, which can easily push the figure to $2 million. The same $1.6 million would buy: 4.9 30-second spots on NBC's popular sitcom *Frasier,* 6.3 spots on FOX's *The Simpsons,* 17.6 full-page color ads in the *New York Times,* and 88.9 spots on CNN'S most popular regular program, *Larry King Live.*[29]

The Ratings Decline of TV Network News

In the case of TV network news, the ratings battle is a losing one. As Jon Katz, the media critic for *Rolling Stone* put it, "Forty years ago when television was born, television news consisted of middle-aged white men reading 22 minutes of news into a camera. Today, network news consists of middle-aged white men reading 22 minutes of news into a camera."[30] CBS responded to the ratings-profits challenge by adding Connie Chung to its anchor desk on the evening news while severely cutting its news-gathering and reporting operations and then moving Chung out again when the hoped-for ratings boost failed to materialize. The evening news at CBS, like its competitors at ABC and NBC, routinely scores ratings in the six to eight range, reflecting a steady decline from twice those levels since the 1970s. In the short period between the 1995–1996 and 1997–1998 seasons, ABC suffered a 14 percent ratings drop from 9.2 to 7.9. PBS experienced a 20 percent fall from 1.5 to 1.2.[31]

Fragmented Audiences: The End of Mass Media?

With the exception of the Super Bowl and national crises such as 9/11, it makes little sense to talk about a mass media audience any longer, at least one defined by large numbers of people gathering around televisions and watching the same information fed from a few sources. Consider just a few audience trends that have developed in recent years.

- The original three networks (ABC, CBS, and NBC) captured over 90 percent of prime time television viewers as recently as 1978. By 1997, that share was hovering at 50 percent and still falling.[32]
- In 1975, roughly one-half of all households watched a national network TV news program every night. By 1997, that figure was closer to one-quarter. The number who report "regularly" watching national network news plummeted from 60 percent in 1993 to 42 percent in 1996.[33]
- Even cable news markets are fragmenting. For example, the proliferation of cable news channels has slammed cable news pioneer CNN's already thin au-

dience share by one-third between 1992 and 1997, despite the fact that the number of households receiving CNN tripled during the same period.[34]

- People are less likely to make appointments to watch a favorite news program, preferring, instead, to tune in and out of various sources. For example, the percentage saying their exclusive news source is nightly network or local TV news dropped form 30 percent in 1993 to 15 percent in 1998. More than half of those who watch TV news now do so with a remote control in hand.[35]

- Some slack in conventional news trends appears to be taken up by the Internet. Between 1995 and 1998, the percentage of Americans getting news from the Internet at least once a week increased from 4 percent to 20 percent.[36]

- There is a sharp generational divide emerging in both news habits and content preferences. Three-fourths of 18- to 29-year-olds are excited about the growing diversity of information sources, compared to barely half of those 65 or older.[37]

- More worrisome, only one-third of the younger demographic age bracket enjoys keeping up with the news "a lot" compared to two-thirds of seniors. Also, as noted earlier, the general trends of declining interest in both national and international news are sharper among younger age groups.[38]

What do these audience trends say about the future of news? A pair of media lawyers who work to assemble the business deals that will produce the information products of the future say this about the news of 2005:

> Traditional news formats are becoming increasingly irrelevant, and their economics unsustainable. We want our news and information when we want it, not at a preordained 6:30 time slot. Nearly every day, new competitors set up shop on the Web and on cable. The costs of newsgathering are skyrocketing, and consumers are loath to pay for it. "Why should I pay for anything online?" said one professional during a focus group. . . . "There are sources that give you articles on specific topics for free."
>
> The survivors will not just be broadcast networks, cable news networks, newspapers, or Web sites. They will deliver news anywhere, at any time you want it, through your TV, your laptop, even your Palm Pilot, as portable devices allowing on-line access revolutionize the way people get their news and information. When you watch your favorite cable channel, the announcers will urge you not just to keep watching, but to pick up its magazine, tune in to its radio station, and log on to its Web site.[39]

When viewed from the bottom line, the facts about broadcast news are sobering. At the end of the 1990s, CBS was losing about $70 million per year on its news division, even after years of budget and bureau cuts that left its world news-gathering presence seriously diminished. These losses are figured after the fat profits of news magazines like *60 Minutes* are added in. NBC has been more successful as a TV news operation because the NBC news presence on cable (CNBC and MSNBC) and the

Web enables talent, programming, and the same news stories to be cycled through different outlets. Cross-branding and advertising lure viewers to its other outlets. Even though NBC news was relatively successful because of its early entry into the cable channels, that success came at a familiar price. After the buyout by GE, a new management team at the NBC news division began to phase out international news and other coverage that journalists regarded as important in favor of more stories designed for the personal tastes of the audience demographics. This is called "news you can use" in the trade. Asked if it was really a good idea to pitch stories to Tom Brokaw's aging audience (e.g., medical news, living longer, diet and nutrition), the president of NBC replied enthusiastically, "I hope they're doing that. We're trying to provide programming that we think our audiences are going to be interested in."[40]

When Ted Koppel was asked why his unsuccessful effort to introduce a new and more detailed news report on ABC was titled *The Koppel Report: News from Earth,* he replied:

> The device is intended to differentiate between the kind of newscasts that we do on a daily basis that are designed for quick updates . . . and a different kind of newscast designed to say what kind of important events are happening on earth. . . . If I had come out and admitted that we are producing a newscast which features the things you really ought to be focusing attention on, that would sound sort of preachy and boring. . . . So I am unashamedly admitting that we are using a device which says, "All right, let's pretend we are doing it for an alien intelligence in space."[41]

Serious news aimed at an alien intelligence in space? Any appearance of a grand democratic design in such an information system may be sustained largely by the enduring faith that a free press and a free market create the most perfect results. The reader may still believe that more channels and choices must be inherently better, even if they are owned by fewer parent companies. Let's examine this popular belief.

THE MEDIA MONOPOLY: ARGUMENTS FOR AND AGAINST

Opponents of government regulation of the information industry point to the vast and growing numbers of information outlets that people have available to them. If viewed uncritically, the proliferation of inputs may appear to offer more choice and diversity than any individual could want. National print news magazines can aim articles and advertising at a group as small as the residents of a specific zip code. Despite dire predictions about the end of print with the coming of online information, the number of magazines has actually soared by nearly 50 percent in the past decade to roughly 4,500 titles. In 1990, 557 new magazines were launched, compared with 1,067 new titles in 1998. Much of the growth is propelled by the logic of "brand extensions," through which a successful product like *People* launches a series of spinoffs such as *In Style, Teen People,* and *People en Espanol.*[42]

Who could ask for any more information diversity than that? The trouble is that such brand extensions seldom offer new perspectives. Similar formats are redone for the tastes of different demographics: the old *People* get Madonna and George

Clooney, the young *Teen People* get Britney Spears and Snoop Dog. Basic cable in many markets now offers several home shopping channels for different demographics, often at the expense of C-Span or other public affairs channels. The problem, say critics such as Ben Bagdikian, former dean of the Journalism School at the University of California, Berkeley, is that although information outlets are undeniably proliferating, their ownership is increasingly concentrated, and the first effect of concentration is to push small media promoting noncommercial values out of the way. Successive editions of his book *Media Monopoly* have painted the picture starkly. In the first edition, published in 1984, he warned that fifty big corporations controlled over half the media outlets in the nation. In the fourth edition, in 1992, Bagdikian sounded what seemed like a final alarm, noting that "Despite more than 25,000 outlets in the United States, twenty-three corporations control most of the business in daily newspapers, magazines, television, books, and motion pictures."[43] By the next edition, in 1997, the number of controlling corporate giants had shrunk to just ten.[44] Today's global media giants number five: AOL Time Warner, Bertelsmann, News Corp, Viacom, and Disney. Because the speed of change in the media business far outpaces new editions of this book, the reader may want to follow these trends online with Web sites that are regularly updated by the *Columbia Journalism Review* (click on "Who Owns What" at **www .cjr.org**) or the *Online Journalism Review* (**www.ojr.org**). This media monopoly—or, depending on your view, small oligopoly—has been helped by the government, with little consideration for the diversity of cultural programming or the quality of public information. Consider the most recent governmental assist.

THE TELECOMMUNICATIONS ACT OF 1996

The pace of buyouts, mergers, and alliances was stepped up to dizzying speed by the Telecommunications (TelCom) Act of 1996, which *The Wall Street Journal* heralded as "the first major overhaul of telecommunications law since Marconi was alive and the crystal set was the state of the art."[45] The most highly publicized aspects of the law promised increasing competition and lower rates for consumers in phone and cable services. However, the meat of the legislation was a maze of reduced barriers to ownership of numbers of media outlets (e.g., stations, papers, cable channels), ownership of outlets in different media sectors (e.g., radio, TV, newspapers, cable), and the number of outlets that can be owned by the same company within the same city or media market. Along with these reduced regulations came what was termed a necessary relaxation in community service requirements for distant owners who can now operate multiple outlets in the same local markets.

These ownership restrictions and community service standards were once regarded as firewalls for information diversity and competition in the American democracy. The old thinking was (1) local owners might be more responsive to community values, (2) different ownership of different sectors (types of media) was good for program diversity, and (3) limits on a single company's control of a particular sector would prevent strangleholds on advertising revenues that might put smaller local companies out of business. The new thinking is that markets inherently create diversity through competition and that competition within each company's holdings is driven by the search for audiences and profits. As for public service, if communities want some sort of service from their media outlets, they will support broadcasters who provide it.

This easy reasoning ignores the fact that conglomerates enter communities with the intent of closing down local programming and piping the same music or talk formulas from central production facilities to hundreds of niche markets around the country. During the critical days after 9/11, many local people found that they could not get any information about what was happening in their communities because distant radio corporations had no provision for monitoring the local scenes in which they broadcast. Indeed, some had no news production at all and had to patch into CNN in order to provide communities with any news about the crisis. These realities of community service were glossed over by hasty and shallow debates on media regulation and deregulation.

Therefore, without much public discussion, Congress and President Clinton ended the old regime and announced the new. In what has been termed "The Full Employment Act for Telecommunication Lawyers," a consolidation frenzy was unleashed. This came on the heels of a decade in which few thought that merger mania could get any more intense. For example, before the new law, corporate giants bought out the TV networks (GE swallowed NBC, Westinghouse gobbled CBS, and Disney added Cap Cities/ABC to its portfolio of assets). The world's book publishers were also merged, stripped, and consolidated in breathtaking leaps. But the TelCom Act set the media world spinning even faster. The year following the new law was called the "Year of the Deal" by many in the industry, as indicated by just a few of the deals that the new legislation enabled. Murdoch's News Corporation (which earlier had swallowed FOX, HarperCollins Publishers, and *TV Guide*) bought New World Communications, making News Corp for a short time the nation's largest TV station owner. Westinghouse/CBS bought Infinity Broadcasting, giving it a chain of seventy-seven radio stations to go with its string of other stations, creating multiple outlets in the top ten markets in the country. Viacom bought CBS and all its media holdings, making it the largest TV and radio station owner. Time Warner and Turner Broadcasting merged into the world's largest media company, and not long after, America Online bought Time Warner, making it again the largest. Gannett Newspaper Group bought Multimedia Entertainment to expand its newspaper chain to ninety-two, its TV stations to fifteen, its radio stations to thirteen, and its cable operations to five states, and still growing.[46] Typical of the big picture within most sectors, more than 10 percent (162 of 1,509) of the nation's daily newspapers changed ownership in one year.[47]

These stories unfolded largely as business and financial news, with the focus on corporate profits and growth prospects. What was seldom questioned by the press, whose parent corporations lobbied furiously for the new legislation, was whether the proliferation of choices would really provide the "diversity of voices and viewpoints" promised by Bill Clinton as he signed the bill into law.[48]

The level of media concentration became so worrisome that a grassroots citizen movement emerged (see **www.mediareform.org**) when the Federal Communication Commission moved to relax ownership restrictions even further in 2003. Two of the five FCC commissioners voted against the provisions that would have enabled a single corporation to own a newspaper, three TV stations, eight radio stations, and the cable system in a single market. Hearings were held around the country, and owners of remaining independent media outlets protested that latest rules would surely mean the death of local media. A citizen lobbying campaign targeted Congress, and in an impressive display of bipartisanship, the U.S. Senate voted to block the changes. While the Bush administration regrouped around possible executive measures to restore good relations with its corporate sponsors, FCC Chairman Michael Powell went public with his shock. Robert McChesney described Powell's charge that:

> . . . the rule-making process had been upset by "a concerted grassroots effort to attack the commission from the outside in." Seemingly unaware that a public agency like the FCC could, in fact, be addressed by the public, he expressed amazement that as many as 3 million Americans have contacted the FCC and Congress to demand that controls against media monopoly be kept in place. Capitol Hill observers say that media ownership has been the second most discussed issue by constituents in 2003, trailing only the war on Iraq. Following Brecht's famous dictum, Michael Powell wanted to fire the people.[49]

EFFECTS OF THE MEDIA MONOPOLY: FIVE INFORMATION TRENDS

There are different ways to think about the effects of concentrations of media ownership on news content, some of which we have touched on in earlier discussions. Here are the effects most discussed by communication scholars:

1. Dominance by fewer players in local and regional markets distorts advertising rates, forcing small independent outlets to quit, sell out, or change their formats—resulting in less diversity in music, news, and minority affairs programming.
2. The pressure of corporate self-promotion means less critical coverage of the media industry in general and parent companies in particular.
3. News content shifts to infotainment formats due to the entertainment focus of owners and the economic efficiencies of soft news, "reality programming," and human-interest features.
4. News is regarded less as a public service commitment or a prestige builder for the parent company, and it becomes just another product line in the race for profits.
5. Innovation in packaging and branding disguises declining information diversity and content distinctiveness.

The following sections explore each of these potential impacts of shrinking corporate ownership of the national information system.

Information Trend #1: Less Public Service and Alternative Programming

Even large-capacity cable systems suffer content restriction due to consumer marketing pressures. Cable carriers are eager to find room for new programming competing for lucrative niche audiences for golf, cooking, shopping, business news, travel, Christian programming, and entertainment. While these may seem diverse to some, they exclusively promote consumer values—sometimes approaching 24-hour infomercials for products and lifestyles. One result has been a loss of information diversity in political and public affairs programming. For example, many people have lost C-SPAN, the independent national public affairs network (which was set up as a public service from cable operators as a pledge of good faith in exchange for receiving local monopolies). Between 1993 and 1997, for example, C-SPAN was bumped from more than five million cable households to make room for such offerings as Rupert Murdoch's FOX News Channel, which muscled its way onto cable lineups by paying operators $11 for each cable household it reached.[50]

Those who see unlimited content capacity in the digital future may argue that the jury is still out on the future of cable and Internet competition and information diversity. However, the trends are much clearer and less optimistic in other sectors such as newspapers and book publishing. Despite promises of independence when corporate giants buy competing publishers, the actual trend has been toward consolidating the big companies, while eliminating book lists with sales too small to add much to the bottom line. The newspaper business offers the clearest example of the elimination of competition in once hallowed areas such as city newspapers. Ben Bagdikian notes, for example, that in 1920 there were 700 American cities with separately owned, fully competing daily papers. By the beginning of the 1990s, there were only twelve, and a few dozen others were running under joint-operating agreements in which competing papers shared the same printing and distribution system. Equally shocking is the fact that more than 7,000 cities now have no local paper at all.[51] At the same time, the ownership of the majority of papers has consolidated dramatically, as chains moved in to buy papers of all sizes, often with content results of the kind described in the case study in this chapter.

With the breathtaking consolidation of the broadcast industry following the 1996 Telecommunications Act, local radio and television consolidation has also given new cause for alarm. The advertising rates and coverage offered by single owners of multiple outlets in the same market can create hardships for small local operators, particularly those providing local programming for minorities. The Justice Department soon launched a national investigation of the use of advertising deals to defeat the dwindling number of smaller, local broadcasters.

Information Trend #2: Internal Corporate News Censorship and Self-Advertising as News

Many observers fear that news operations under the profit gun from distant corporate owners become reluctant to report stories that offend their powerful bosses. Indeed, many cite the coverage of the Telecommunications Act in this regard. The overwhelmingly positive business news coverage was accompanied by near silence on the politics of lavish corporate lobbying or the potential information effects discussed here.[52]

It is hard to gather data on the extent of overt censorship, since most such decisions are kept within the corporations, but a few cases have surfaced to illustrate the problem. For example, while covering the 1996 Olympics, sports reporter Bob Costas linked international sports and politics by pointing out that China had various problems of human rights at home and troubles with drug use by athletes in the Olympics. His comments brought a rebuke from corporate headquarters and a formal apology to China from NBC executives. Why? The reason surely did not involve the truth of Costas's comments, which were well documented. As one media journal put it, "since when does a network have to apologize for telling the truth?"[53] In the view of one reporter, NBC apologized because the parent company, GE, had large business deals (electrical infrastructure, hospital equipment, data transmission systems) at stake in China.[54] Even closer to home, NBC had satellite channels (NBC Asia and CNBC Asia) that it hoped to clear with politically sensitive Chinese authorities.

In another case, an ABC news magazine piece on known child molesters working at Disney theme parks (so they could be closer to the kids) was killed before it ever got on the air. Imagine the dramatic lead-in, perhaps from ABC news magazine star Diane Sawyer:

> Disney's Magic Kingdom. Billed as the Happiest Place on Earth. But how safe are you—and more importantly, your children—at Disney's empire in Florida? Our four-month investigation found that Disney's hiring practices actually allowed the employment of convicted pedophiles at its parks and resorts. Is Disney placing your children at unnecessary risk? Stay tuned for our troubling report. . . .[55]

We will have to imagine this buildup because it was never delivered. The president of ABC News, David Westin, killed the story after an internal battle with the journalists who worked on it. This occurred despite familiar assurances that ABC News would maintain complete editorial independence following its buyout by Disney. The reason given by Westin was simply that "the script did not meet ABC News editorial standards" and that the focus on the Disney Company did not enter the decision at all.[56] There was no comment from Disney headquarters. However, an earlier interview given by CEO Michael Eisner at the time of the buyout addressed the general question of conflict of interest involved with a powerful global corporation owning news divisions: "I would prefer ABC not to cover Disney. . . . I think it's inappropriate for Disney to be covered by Disney. . . ."[57]

While this may sound like a reasonably neutral conflict-of-interest policy, it apparently does not apply to good news about the Magic Kingdom. For example, there was an ABC *World News Sunday* feature about an actor who landed a part in the film *Good Will Hunting* made by Disney's Miramax Company. Then there was a story about a real-life horse whisperer, just like the one in the movie of the same name from Disney's Touchstone Pictures. There was a nostalgia piece on the 1950s' sitcom *Ozzie and Harriet,* which just happened to be the subject of a prominently mentioned up-coming documentary on A&E (yep, owned partly by Disney). Perhaps the most bla-tant piece of self-promotion passing as news was a made-up story on whether aster-oids were hurtling toward earth, timed conveniently for airing with the release of the Disney summer blockbuster *Armageddon.* The irresistible headline for the news story was "Are They Really Hurtling to a Spot near You?"[58] One can imagine the Video News Release (VNR) that went to local stations with scary teasers about hurtling as-teroids to be run during prime time programs to alert viewers to stay tuned for the lo-cal news. One can imagine the local news mixing those made-up stories with live shots from the local cineplex and exciting scenes from the movie.

Corporate self-promotion is a growing part of the news. VNR packages are sent to local affiliates to promote late local news features during commercial breaks in prime time entertainment programs. Did they perform a daring operation on *ER?* Local NBC affiliates are alerted to see if they can find a local doctor who performed a similar oper-ation, or, even better, a local resident (best of all, a child) who was saved by it.

In the end, of course, the tendency is for everyone down the line to learn the new rules and anticipate the "dos and don'ts" before disasters like ABC's story on pe-dophiles at Disney even reach the idea stages. When such socialization occurs throughout far-flung media empires, incidents of overt censorship will be lessened simply because the process of self-censorship will take over. William Small, a former president of NBC News and later a professor of journalism, identified self-censorship as the single greatest concern with ever more powerful global corporations controlling news organizations: "If you're an investigative reporter or producer do you hesitate to do a piece on GE's dealings with the Pentagon? Do you say: why should I get GE mad at the news division or at me? We'll never know."[59]

Information Trend #3: More Infotainment and Soft News

In the view of communication scholar George Gerbner, television journalism has be-come "an adjunct of marketing and thus must be more entertaining and more adjusted to the fantasy world of drama and fiction."[60] The entertainment bias in news comes in many forms. Consider, for example, the now obligatory use of theme music to give big stories distinctive moods and the feel of dramatic miniseries. CNN news critic Jeff Greenfield says that scoring the news "would have been unthinkable a generation ago. Once upon a time, we were forbidden to 'lay in' music to dramatize the mood. Now it sounds as if the news divisions have all put John Williams on permanent retainer."[61] Movie composer Williams originally scored the theme music for *NBC Nightly News.* Many composers now work for news shows, earning good payments for themes, and even more in royalties if a big story keeps the theme on the air for weeks or months.

Shelly Palmer is a composer who writes for NBC, among other TV clients. She compared the music that CNN chose for the long-running 1991 news series "Strike Against Iraq" with its theme for the 1999 "Strike Against Kosovo": "The Iraq music was classic war music. It was *Hunt for Red October,* it was *Patton* and *Victory at Sea.* It was very much 'Let's go kick Saddam Hussein's Ass.' The Albanian music is ambiva-lent. It can't make up its mind. It says that there's something bad here, but we don't know what it is."[62] The Kosovo campaign, depicted in many journalistic accounts as vague and ill-conceived, was set to the tune of "Enya's Head Trauma," taken from a CD titled *Relax or Die,* which is track No. 10 in the VideoHelper series. The decisive and triumphal CNN account of the earlier U.S. bombing of Iraq was set to the theme "Emergency Service," taken from the industrial CD *Action, Drama, and Suspense.*

News once preempted entertainment shows for important political events. FOX signaled a new trend when Bill Clinton's reaction to his own impeachment occurred in the midst of a football game. The solution was to split the screen in the Tampa Bay-Washington game to squeeze in historic shots of the president and 101 Democratic members of the House gathering in solidarity on the White House lawn. Sports would not be sacrificed for a political event that occurred for only the second time in national history.

How did the entertainment focus of FOX News evolve? Enter Van Gordon Sauter, former guru at CBS who softened Dan Rather's image and brought emotion to serious news during the 1980s. Sauter later surfaced as president of the news division at the FOX network, a system in which only 34 of 140 affiliate stations carried news when he entered the scene. What sort of news did he have in mind for Fox? Sauter was reported to have this motto on his office wall: "In Nielsen We Trust." A reporter covering the start-up of FOX News witnessed Sauter conducting this impromptu marketing interview with the manager of a bar:

SAUTER: "When you get home, tired after a long day, would you prefer to watch Peter Jennings? Or *Studs?*"

MANAGER: "*Studs,* definitely!"

SAUTER: "You see! We'd never do a newscast like *Studs,* obviously, but we've got to respond to the fact that at 6:30 P.M. in Los Angeles, *Studs* beats all the evening newscasts."[63]

Pushing the Infotainment Envelope: News Magazines   The TV news magazine is one of the oldest infotainment formulas, combining soft features such as celebrity confessionals with consumer rip-offs and dramatic hidden-camera investigations. Beginning in the 1960s with the pioneering *60 Minutes* on CBS, the "newsmags" filled twelve hours of prime time television per week by century's end.[64] The corporate bottom line explains this proliferation of TV news magazines. They generate hefty ratings and advertising revenues at half the cost of entertainment programming.[65] For example, Nielsen Media Research reported during a typical ratings "sweeps" period (when advertising rates are pegged to audiences) that three of the ten most watched shows were news magazines.[66]

According to the trade magazine, *Advertising Age,* the average TV news magazine program grosses $2.7 million, which yields a fat profit on average production expenses of only $700,000, which explains the 142 percent increase between 1995 and 1998 in prime time programming dedicated to these formats.[67] In contrast, the most highly rated entertainment fare may actually lose money due to the costs of expensive talent, lavish productions, and threats by independent producers to take the shows (and their audiences) elsewhere if networks do not pay a premium for them. Therefore, the networks pay heavily for a few popular programming "loss leaders" to build brand images that draw audiences for their profitable in-house productions like the news magazines. As one headline put it, "Reality Is Cheaper than Sitcoms."[68]

Playing up the docudrama and infotainment angles, the TV newsmags skip past politics unless there is a scandal or an attractive personality involved. Instead, they dwell on the human travails of everyday society: drugs, crime, child abuse, diet fads, consumer rip-offs, celebrity scandals, and hidden-camera stings on shady operations. The focus on dramatic plots is maintained by an aversion to letting facts and footage that don't fit the story get in the way. As one team who studied a sample of consumer scare stories from three different programs put it:

> There's a cynical saying in newsrooms: "Never let the facts get in the way of a good story." There is always a temptation to simplify in order to capture and hold an audience. Toward this goal, newsmagazines strive to present clear heroes and villains, as well as a clear moral to every tale. Too often what's lost in the process is the kind of even-handed presentation that the subjects of such investigations deserve.[69]

According to this team of observers, the overriding logic behind these programs is "If you scare them, they will watch."[70] To this maxim, we might also add "If you scare them, they will believe." Research by communication scholar George Gerbner shows that levels of physical threat that people feel in their communities (particularly suburban dwellers) has little correlation with actual crime and violence statistics. However, their sense of danger correlates highly with exposure to television in general, and television news in particular.[71] People most believe what they see on television. According to a "news trust" survey conducted by Gallup, the order of most trusted news sources is TV news magazines (51 percent), nightly newscast (43 percent), local newspapers (40 percent), national newspapers (37 percent), and weekly print news magazines (27 percent).[72]

Pushing the Infotainment Envelope Even Farther: Reality TV   Just one step beyond the news magazines is the realm of reality TV, involving police chases, car crashes, terrifying accidents, and death-defying escapes. This genre can be traced to the original "cops" programs such as *America's Most Wanted,* which, in turn, influenced the escalation of crime drama in both news and news magazines. Reality TV has since colonized many social realities, from relationships and marriage to family disasters, pets, and spectacularly shocking events. FOX continues to blaze new trails in this genre, with such hits as *World's Scariest Police Chases, World's Scariest Police Shootouts, World's Funniest Videos, World's Most Shocking Moments, World's Nastiest Neighbors, When Animals Attack,* and that perennial favorite, *When Good Pets Go Bad.* These programs charted new territory that has expanded in recent years to include *Survivor, Fear Factor,* the *Bachelor,* and the *Bachelorette,* among others.

An early series called *World's Wildest Police Videos* drew high ratings but also drew criticisms for the high number of staged police training exercises that were presented as thrilling and successful real-life chases and arrests. The program began with the somber assurance "What you're about to see in the next 60 minutes is real. Real cops. Real crooks. Real cases. Everything from real training to real shootouts. What you see may shock you, frighten you, anger you." The producers of *Wildest Police Videos* noted that the word *training* was mentioned in the breathless introduction and added that the program was, after all, entertainment, not a news broadcast.[73] This defense, however, ignores the blurring of the line between social reality and dramatized images of society.

Reality-based programs take the authority-disorder bias introduced in the last chapter to a new extreme by dramatizing the personal emotional sense among audiences that society is a dangerous and chaotic place. A writer for a popular police program described a list tacked to the bulletin board at the production facility to remind the video editors and writers of the images they were looking for:[74]

Death

Stab

Shoot

Strangulation

Club

Suicide

This sounds like the same list being used implicitly in TV newsrooms around the country, as local news increasingly turns to a "tabloid" style of reporting bloody crimes and the grisly underside of life in the nation's cities.

The Far Side of Infotainment: Local TV News   Many critics argue that the lowest television life form is local news. Unlike reality TV, it claims to be news, but like cheap entertainment fare, it has little agenda other than drawing audiences with scary and disgusting images of life gone wrong. Recall the discussion from Chapter 1 about the complaint to the FCC that local news has become "toxic." Recall, too, that the FCC does not regard the danger posed by local news to community values as sufficient to adjust the balance between freedom of the press and the licensing standards that protect the public interest. Yet without some compelling monitoring system, the local news continues to blaze new, and ever lower, standards.

Among the specialties of local news in Los Angeles, for example, is live coverage of freeway police chases, which are common occurrences in the maze of southern California freeways. The icon of freeway chases was the bizarre low-speed chase in 1994 involving O. J. Simpson, days after the murder of his ex-wife, Nicole. Now standard news fare, chases boost ratings during live coverage because people buzz about them. There is even a pager service to alert subscribers when one is happening. Chases also become heavily promoted lead stories in regular evening newscasts.

One particularly unfortunate example involved a standoff between police and a man protesting his health care coverage. Several stations interrupted programming to run the event live, complete with helicopter shots of two freeways at a standstill at the beginning of rush hour, and close-ups of the dramatic action on the ground. The FOX affiliate even broke into children's programming, just in time to treat the kids to the horror of the man setting himself and his dog on fire. Still smoldering and on camera, he then put a shotgun under his chin and pulled the trigger. FOX later ran the numbers of counselors for children who were traumatized by watching the incident.[75]

The event drew protests from angry parents and raised questions among journalists about what the news has become. Is news becoming a kind of reality TV that simply shows human dramas as they happen? Should there be some measure of significance and some journalistic judgment exercised? A professor of journalism ethics argued that the media spectacle of a gory self-immolation/shotgun suicide is not news, "It's a show. It's entertainment. Unless you're exercising judgment and taking your tape and editing it, you're not being professional. You have to have that control as a journalist. You're not just a stenographer out there."[76] Yet a news director for an L.A. station defended the incident as news by stressing the role of technology in changing the very nature of news:

> I think what's happened is the technology has progressed to the point that it allows the viewer to see more of the process of gathering news. We used to have to develop film, edit it. But because of our ability to go on line, people are seeing news as it develops. And I'm not sure that's bad. It kind of hits at some of the criticism of the media for slanting the news. You can't say it was slanted when it's live.[77]

Perhaps not, but you can ask why it was shown as news at all.

Information Trend #4: Generic News

A few wholesale news packaging companies supply most of the nation's radio outlets that still care to broadcast news. In Washington, D.C., nineteen stations buy headlines from one of two of these services.[78] In another big city, a radio news director describes how the station owner cut the news staff, eliminated local news, and covered national stories by taking the network feed from satellite. The reason? Shifting to low-budget generic news resulted immediately in "a big gain in cash flow, so the owner can sell the station at a huge profit to one of the big chains, whose owners care nothing about public service to this community. One more journalistic voice is being killed off in pursuit of profits."[79]

TV networks have closed bureaus at home and around the world and turned increasingly to wholesale news suppliers for raw product that they can edit, script, and style in-house. As a result, the world supply of breaking news is generated by a shrinking number of suppliers that few Americans have ever heard of: Independent Television News (ITN), World Television News (WTN, in which Disney/ABC is a major shareholder), Vis-News (owned partly by GE/NBC), and video-swapping systems such as Eurovision and Asiavision. Many of these news wholesalers send "smart camera crews" (i.e., news crews without reporters) to the scenes of news events. TV news producer Av Westin laments this trend as "the video equivalent of paparazzi" who show up "and shoot coverage at every crisis spot at home and abroad and sell it to networks and local stations."[80] The business reasoning is simply that an experienced camera team knows what kind of visuals are likely to sell on the world market, and saving the cost of a reporter means a more profitable operation.

As news wholesalers provide more of the video images, the network correspondents who are edited into the picture are less likely to have witnessed the events on which they appear to be reporting. As a prominent journalist for one of the TV networks put it:

> Instead of racing out of the newsroom with a camera crew when an important story breaks, we're more likely now to stay at our desks and work the phones, rewrite the wire copy, hire a local crew and freelance producer to get pictures at the scene, then dig out some file footage, maps, or still photos for the anchor to talk in front of, or maybe buy some coverage from a video news service like Reuters, AP, or World Television News. If we had our own correspondent and camera covering the story, we'd damn sure get something nobody else had, and be proud of it. But everything now is dollars and cents.[81]

A related development that alarms many journalists is the creation of authenticity by shooting a "stand-up" of the reporter-narrator at a location that has no connection to the actual scene of the story. Although stand-ups in the past were almost always done while the reporter was on assignment, one veteran reporter has observed:

> Now, thanks to advances in technology and declines in network news budgets, reporters are increasingly putting together stories with video from all over the map and voicing over the tape. . . . So the decision of what to say in a stand-up, and where to say it, is usually among the last decisions made before a piece is put on the air.[82]

CBS correspondent Martha Teichner complained that being a reporter once meant witnessing events, learning about them firsthand, and then providing an informed judgment. She describes a now more typical scenario:

> I was asked to do Somalia for the weekend news and I've never been to Somalia and I'm thinking, Oh my god, what am I gonna do? I get every bit of research I can find, but even if I'm correct and accurate, I'm superficial. . . . More and more we're becoming packagers rather than reporters. You weigh the number of times you go out and do it for real against the number of times you narrate, and hope that [the ratio] is satisfactory enough so that you don't feel that you're too compromised.[83]

Ironically, the area that illustrates the generic news trends best of all is the Internet, that exploding domain of seeming endless information diversity. We know that all types of conventional media, from print to broadcast, have rushed to open Web sites, but what are they putting on them? *New York Times* executive editor Joseph Lelyveld cautioned a group of journalism graduates:

> While literally billions of speculative dollars are being amassed, invested and turned into overnight fortunes in this effort to develop and control the means of transmission in the coming age of instantaneous information, investments in the actual gathering of information by conventional journalistic means is in

apparent decline, under the banner of cost control, in all but a handful of traditional news organizations. . . . The Internet . . . is a wonderful place to collect raw data. But it is not, so far, a wonderful place to find reliable and original reporting, real news, except where it has been siphoned off the old.[84]

What the Internet offers is an outlet for often high-quality information from advocacy organizations and citizen activists who seldom get their messages into mainstream media. We shall explore the prospects for this citizen-driven journalism in Chapter 8. The point here is about conventional news: whether in print, on TV, or the Internet, the trend is for more channels to deliver news from fewer sources. Stories are reshaped at the point of broadcast or print by reporters and writers who are often far removed from the original events and whose editors may be paying as much attention to the advice of their marketing consultants as to the political importance or actual meaning of the events themselves. The point is that more channels do not mean more choices. As marketing and communication technologies become more sophisticated, the same news becomes packaged to attract select demographic groups of viewers, listeners, or readers who can be sold to advertisers.

Information Trend #5: Branding the News

In what sense is the news a product? It surely differs from cornflakes and underarm deodorants, yet it shares one important thing with most commercial products: It is marketed effectively through product images, which create the illusion of distinctiveness while often blurring the underlying realities of product quality and differences. One brand of cornflakes conveys the image of crunchiness, another exudes healthiness, and still another evokes an image of family togetherness at the breakfast table. They are all cornflakes.

Similar to other products, the news is packaged. Packages convey images. They dress products up or down. They give off signals about the social status of the people who use particular products. Packages, and more importantly, brand images fit products to the lifestyles of consumers—the pace, swoosh, style, and image of life itself. If we want to keep in touch with world events, we are invited to do so by becoming an "eyewitness," taking an adventure into the world of "action news," inviting a serious "news authority" into our home, or sitting down to start the day by reading "All the News That's Fit to Print."

For example, KING-5 TV is the NBC affiliate in Seattle. Once locally owned, but then sold to the Belo Corp, KING developed a brand identity as "The Home Team." The anchors appear in commercials as though they are a family. The stars do separate spots featuring their families, their community involvement, and how they feel about living in a special place like the Northwest. As for the news, it is mostly the same mix of mayhem, genial weather reports, and local team sports as on the other channels, but it is promoted and delivered with a caring, concerned, nurturing style that reinforces the "home team" image that distinguishes its brand identity.

Consider another branding challenge. Rupert Murdoch, the owner of FOX, decided to launch an all-news cable channel in the already crowded environment of CNN, CNN *Headline News,* MSNBC, and others. For starters, FOX hired Roger

Ailes, former political consultant to Republican heavyweights dating back to Richard Nixon, Ronald Reagan, and George Bush. Ailes later turned from producing TV images for politicians to producing TV programs. He brought Rush Limbaugh to America's airwaves, along with a variety of pioneering infotainment and talk shows such as *The Maury Povich Show, Leeza,* and *A Current Affair.* Now Ailes was charged with creating yet another all-news channel. How did he proceed? His first move was to hire a news star, Brit Hume, a former ABC Washington correspondent with twenty-three years of experience and a big recognition factor. Hume brought instant luster to the emerging FOX brand.

But what would distinguish the overall format of the FOX News Channel from its well-established competition? Murdoch, himself a vocal conservative, put the marketing focus on the popular perception that the national press is politically left. Recall this discussion from Chapter 1. He also keyed in on the low levels of public trust in the news. The result was a decision to brand FOX as "the news you can trust" because it is "fair and balanced." The overarching message or theme of the brand was chosen as "We report. You decide."

The next brand-building challenge was to decide how to communicate these ideas effectively so that people would associate them with FOX and not other channels. First, the themes of "trust," "fairness," "objectivity," and "we report, you decide" were used repeatedly in outside advertising to lure viewers. The same themes were reinforced in on-air self-promotions often featuring viewer testimonials scrolled on the screen:

"Until Fox News Channel, I was about to give up on news."

"Fox News Channel has boldly earned the right to declare they are fair and balanced."

"Finally, objective journalism."[85]

Next, Ailes hired a crew of predominantly conservative hosts. How does this signal objectivity? According to Ailes, it gives FOX a slightly right-of-center perspective that counteracts the liberalism of the other TV news operations. FOX specialized in front-loading its viewer polls and interview segments, as when a *News Watch* program debated the question "Do 'radical environmentalists' receive too-friendly treatment in the liberal media?" A FOX entertainment reporter once said of Clinton Attorney General Janet Reno, "If you dressed her in drag, how could you tell?" A promo for one of the commentary shows had the cohost Sean Hannity defining a liberal as "somebody who thinks he has a right to my hard earned money."[86] And a news scroll during the invasion of Iraq described nations not supporting the war as "The Axis of Weasels."

As noted in the last chapter, news with an explicit political point of view can be a good thing. The problem is that FOX claims its content is objective to create a brand that attracts a right-of-center demographic audience who hear their own beliefs and values confirmed in the news and then decide that this must be objectivity. The people behind the news at FOX seem to know that confounding content with image is exactly what they are doing. As media critic Neil Hickey concluded following his interviews with FOX staffers:

> Nobody can object to a "fair and balanced" news service, nor one that simply "reports" and lets you "decide." Those terms have become a marketing device and a fig leaf for Fox staffers who are otherwise perfectly candid about their right of center convictions.[87]

This discussion does not mean that there are no substantive differences from one news outlet to another. Recall the poll from Chapter 1 showing that viewers of different news programs had very different levels of factual understanding of the Iraq War. There is more detail on the Public Broadcasting Service's *News Hour* than on the *CBS Nightly News*. However, both organizations cover the Washington and world scenes from inside the corridors of power and report mainly what powerful insiders tell them. NPR news is more detailed and carries more lengthy features than generally found on TV or network radio, but the professional norms and news decisions of the reporters are much the same.[88]

As competition increases, different outlets may emphasize one story over another. For example, a study of one day on cable news revealed that CNN, MSNBC, and FOX each gave substantially different amounts of coverage to the top stories of the day: Hurricane Bonnie, developments in President Clinton's sex life, a Wall Street/Russian financial crisis, an investigation of Vice President Gore, and a suspect identified in the bombing of the U.S. embassy in Kenya. At the end of the day, however, they all covered the same stories.[89]

HOW DOES CORPORATE INFLUENCE OPERATE?

Executives at Westinghouse or GE or Knight Ridder or Gannett do not issue many direct orders to distant journalists to cut back on serious coverage of politics and government or to run more sex and crime. The demise of serious news is a mere casualty of sensible-sounding business decisions. As a managing editor of *The New York Times* explained it,

> News coverage is being shaped by corporate executives at headquarters far from the local scene. It is seldom done by corporate directive or fiat. It rarely involves killing or slanting stories. Usually it is by the appointment of a pliable editor here, a corporate graphics conference there, that results in a more uniform look and cookie-cutter approach among a chain's newspapers, or it's by the corporate research director's interpretation of reader surveys that seek simple common-denominator solutions to complex coverage problems. Often the corporate view is hostile to governmental coverage. It has been fashionable for some years, during meetings of editors and publishers, to deplore "incremental" news coverage. Supposedly it is boring, a turnoff to readers, and—what's worse—it requires news hole. The problem with all of this is that government news develops incrementally. And if you don't cover it incrementally, you don't really cover it at all. Incremental is what it is all about.[90]

Journalist and communication scholar Doug Underwood has examined changes in business values of news organizations at the newsroom level, and he finds increasing limits on the content of news that stem from the manufacture and sale of news as a commercial product. Real press freedoms are limited each news day simply because, in his words, "MBAs rule the newsroom."[91] Assignments are made increasingly with costs, efficiency, and viewer or reader reactions in mind. Newspapers, in particular, struggle to survive in the video age; they are run with fewer and fewer concerns about informing the public. As Underwood describes it: "Today's market-savvy newspapers are planned and packaged to 'give readers what they want'; newspaper content is geared to the results of readership surveys; and newsroom organization has been reshaped by newspaper managers whose commitment to the marketing ethic is hardly distinguishable from their vision of what journalism is."[92] The paper that set this trend was *USA Today,* which has been dubbed "McPaper" and "the newspaper for people who are too busy to watch TV." (These trends are examined further in the case study in this chapter.)

Corporations increasingly conduct internal campaigns to get editors and journalists to understand and accept the realities of the news as a business.[93] There is a pervasive management concern that journalists are trained in school to think independently of the business side, and that the traditional dividing line between the editorial and the commercial sides needs to be softened. Among the most dramatic attempts to merge journalistic and commercial sensibilities occurred during the 1990s at the *Los Angeles Times.*

After passing most of the twentieth century as a weak paper, the *Times* rose to national prominence and commercial success during the 1970s and 1980s under the guidance of Otis Chandler, a member of the prominent family who owned it. Then in the late 1980s, southern California entered an economic recession that cut into advertising revenues. Chandler eventually retired from management, leaving the paper to a profit-hungry board of directors. The new management integrated marketing and editorial personnel within the same divisions of the paper. Needless to say, the bureaucratic removal of the "firewall" between the editorial side and the business side of a major news organization stirred considerable controversy in the industry, and that controversy even spilled onto the pages of the *Times* itself.[94] Although the *Times* represented the first reorganization of a prestige news operation around advertising values, the general trend was already sweeping the industry, as described earlier in this chapter's case study.

NEWS ON THE INTERNET: PERFECTING THE COMMERCIALIZATION OF INFORMATION?

Perhaps nowhere is the merger of news and advertising more advanced than on the Internet. For example, CNN and Barnes and Noble have created what the marketing director of Barnes and Noble called a "new paradigm that is not editorial and not advertising."[95] CNN sends the bookseller a list of its top stories of the day, and the book company loads up its books on the subject so that people who access the news site can click on buttons for relevant books to buy. While this sounds like pure consumer benefit, there is a danger that news sites and, more generally, Web sites for many information-related services will filter and emphasize information according to the synergy it has with advertisers.

For example, information searches are far more likely to turn up news sources and information that favor companies sponsoring the sites where the information is provided.[96] The CNNfn site matches travel articles with reservation services and travel agencies keyed to those articles. A page on hair loss in the America Online (AOL) health-information service links to ads for baldness treatments. Amazon.com promoted particular books as "staff picks" after receiving money from the books' publishers. All that a person using the Yahoo! search engine needs to do to make plane reservations is click on "Travel Agent," but the link will go to an agency that pays to be the official travel service of Yahoo! A careful reading of Yahoo!'s own independent ratings of travel services (located in the back pages of the site) discloses that, in Yahoo!'s view, there are better services.[97]

An AOL executive casually dismissed the screening of content according to commercial criteria by saying "Our users don't care what the financial relationship is between us and the provider of the content they see." Another Web site executive said that "Anyone going on line should assume that there is an advertising influence on most of the content they see."[98] Because consumers are generally unwilling to pay for information they take from Web sites, almost all of it is developed in conjunction with advertisers. The increasing dilemma for information seekers is how to evaluate the quality and completeness of the information they get.

The future of a free Internet depends on the degree to which noncommercial information sites develop and find means of supporting themselves. In many cases, charitable foundations such as Ford and Rockefeller have sponsored the communication efforts of nongovernmental organizations (NGOs) dedicated to various political causes, from the environment to human rights. In other cases, activists have donated programming and Web design skills to make low-cost independent political information channels available to other activists. The Independent Media Network (**www.indymedia.org**) began as a single Web site to publicize alternative information during the World Trade Organization protests in Seattle in 1999, and it is now a part of a global network of more than one hundred sites. The question of whether citizens of any political stripe will need to establish their own news services is becoming an increasingly interesting one as we look toward the future of electronic communications.

COMMERCIALIZED INFORMATION AND CITIZEN CONFIDENCE

How far will the trend toward commercialized, consumer-driven news go? How will it affect the quality of public life, from citizen cynicism to common knowledge and concern? According to Neil Hickey, an editor for a prominent journalism review who surveyed the industry, the current state of affairs already gives plenty of cause for concern:

> As competition grows ever more ferocious; as the audience continues to drift away from traditional news sources, both print and television; as the public's confidence in news organizations and news people continues to decline; as

mainstream print and TV news outlets purvey more "life-style" stories, trivia, scandal, celebrity gossip, sensational crime, sex in high places, and tabloidism at the expense of serious news in a cynical effort to maximize readership and viewership; as editors collude ever more willingly with marketers, promotion "experts," and advertisers, thus ceding a portion of their sacred editorial trust; as editors shrink from tough coverage of major advertisers lest they jeopardize ad revenue; as news holes grow smaller in column inches to cosmetize the bottom line; as news executives cut muscle and sinew from budgets to satisfy corporate overseers' demands for higher profit margins each year; as top managers fail to reinvest profits in staff training, investigative reports, salaries, plant, and equipment—then the broadly-felt consequence of those factors and many others, collectively, is a diminished and deracinated journalism of a sort which hasn't been seen in this country until now and which, if it persists, will be a fatal erosion of the ancient bond between journalists and the public.[99]

Perhaps innovations such as the voter project noted in this chapter's case study can help balance the commercial forces that work against serious political news. Yet such experiments with civic journalism have proved controversial. Many journalists object to civic journalism, either as just another marketing strategy in disguise or because it involves too much conscious intervention on the part of journalists in deciding what the news is and how to present it to citizens. For the most part, editors and marketers seem to think that the few noble experiments to improve election issue coverage and offer more in-depth political reporting are up against a basic obstacle: People really do not want more serious news, even when they say they do. In the words of journalism professor Everette Dennis, "I have grave doubts people are really interested in this sort of thing [serious news]. It's a noble cause. I hope it works."[100] Perhaps it would work better if news organizations and government officials took the responsibility of including the public in their communication more seriously.

MEGATRENDS: TECHNOLOGY, ECONOMICS, AND SOCIAL CHANGE

Much of this book focuses on three core elements of political communication: (1) journalism and the news business, (2) the communication strategies of political actors, (3) and the information habits of citizens. However, we cannot ignore how a fourth factor, technology, shapes each of the others in important ways. Some of the greatest changes in news content were created by developments in communication technologies. For example, in the nineteenth century, the development of an overburdened horse-drawn national mail system,[101] followed by the telegraph, invited news dispatches to adopt a "just the facts," or "telegraphic," information structure, launching the "who, what, where, when, why" format for the news. In the twentieth century, first photography, then film, and finally, television put the news emphasis on visual information, creating vivid images that communicate without words.

People talk of the twenty-first century as an age of technological convergence in which word, image, and sound will be translatable, storable, editable, and programmable on devices that will blur the distinctions among television, computers, and telephony. The electronics of a house, from TV to the Internet device, down to the art images on the walls, and even the kitchen toaster may be fully integrated, interactive, and run from a single remote control the size of a palmtop computer. By 2005, according to one expert estimate, more than 25 percent (an estimated nineteen million) of all cable households will have digital cable, meaning that the Internet will always be on, accessible from either TV or the home computer network, and that the speed of Web surfing, shopping, chatting, and data retrieval will be dizzying by today's standards.[102] How will these and the many other coming technological developments change the news? Stay tuned for. . . .

Virtual News? Technology, Society, and Personalized Information

We have seen that the news changes in a dizzying spiral of formats driven by new technologies, political communication strategies, consumer tastes, and warlike corporate competition. As a result, today's news seems exotic and sensationalized compared to that of even a decade or two ago. Yet the images of live-from-the-scene coverage of armed conflicts abroad, video transmitted from missiles as they approach their targets, local news dramatizations of violent crime scenes, hidden-camera sting operations run by news magazines, and presidential campaign appearances that resemble commercials all seem somehow in keeping with contemporary standards of communication. Today's consumer can wake up to a personalized selection of news waiting on her or his computer screen, click on a saved Web address in a browser, and get the latest stock report or sports story, complete with integrated video and animated graphics. For those who would rather hear their newspaper than read it, there is software for translating print into voice, which can then be written on a CD-ROM and played in the car on the way to work. This is the age of information when we want it, how we like it, and automatically updated to suit our tastes, as smart search engines learn our preferences.

In an era in which children play with video laser technology, how could the news avoid imagery and special effects that give it an air of authenticity for a technologically tuned-in society? Because we live in the age of virtual reality (the electronic simulation of real-life experience without leaving the living room), why not "virtual news" that bends events to better suit our feelings and fears? A simpler version of this idea introduced the case study earlier in the chapter. Next, we added the growing integration of entertainment content and information. Recall, too, from the last chapter, the pressures on journalists to create stories that take on lives of their own, sustained by dramatizing sensational elements and inventing provocative questions. News programs and big stories already come with theme music to personalize them, and research departments develop content and formats to make the world seem more *ours*. In short, the news is no stranger to dramatized, clearer-than-life representations that may contain illusory relationships to underlying social and political realities. Now, add to this mix the technologies available to both news organizations and political actors for shaping news to fit the existing feelings, moods, and beliefs of target audiences. It is easy to see how images of the outer world of society and politics can be filtered and shaped to fit comfortably with the inner worlds of the audiences who consume them. One of the early visions of virtual news is Ananova, a cyberanchor modeled in part on British celebrity Victoria Beckham (the former Posh of the Spice Girls). Ananova invites us to choose our daily news mix from a menu that includes *quirky, sporty, light,* and *standard news,* along with email updates on the exploits of our favorite celebrities (see **www.ananova.com**).

Are the Media Breaking Up Society?

What accounts for this trend toward virtual news that loops quickly back on the personal reality of the audience? In part, society and personal information habits are changing. Also, it is simpler and more effective, both economically (for news organizations) and politically (for partisan actors), to measure the feelings of target audiences and to design content to fit them than it is to educate those audiences or stimulate their critical thinking. Technologies of polling and marketing drive these reality loops ever closer to the personal fantasies and lifestyle levels of individuals.

Communication scholar Joseph Turow argues that the technology for targeting consumers and then marketing virtually anything to them—from the brand-extended lifestyle product lines of Ralph Lauren or Victoria's Secret to scary images of new health care reforms or the comforting idea of a more compassionate political candidate—all have the effect of breaking up society.[103] There is a "chicken-and-egg" possibility here that society is fragmenting for other reasons, and communication technologies simply follow the segments and further isolate them.[104] Either way, the segmentation of society into neatly organized consumer groups is great for individuals in pursuit of more emotionally satisfying lifestyles, but it may not be so great for democracy. Many scholars argue that such communication-induced social fragmentation proliferates personal, consumption-centered realities that inhibit mutual understanding, undermine the capacity for consensus, and inhibit the commitment to collective values and public projects on which democracy depends.[105]

PERSONALIZED INFORMATION AND THE FUTURE OF DEMOCRACY

If only democracy were something that thrived inside the heads of each individual citizen, instead of in a shared public life, nothing could be more perfect. However, critics like political scientist James Fishkin argue that even the best dialogue mechanisms in the current communication system, such as opinion polls and talk radio, are often counterproductive because they simply feed unchallenged beliefs and prejudices back to those who hold them. Fishkin argues that a better idea would be to apply the technologies of polling, persuasion, and focus-group deliberation to assemble face-to-face citizen juries who would be exposed to information and expert debate, allowed to question the experts, and then have group deliberation before announcing their opinions in public.[106] Despite several experiments indicating that these deliberative polls have worked in different nations, the political and media trends for informing people, polling them, and using their opinions seem to be moving in the opposite direction: toward less face-to-face deliberation and more personalized information delivery.

The cautionary tales of many scholars and critics do not appear to be diverting the application of communication technologies to the service of democracy. The personalized potential of the digital information age has clearly captured the popular imagination. What is changing most about the news, as many media consultants see it, is that our daily information handouts are becoming more personalized and tailored to individual tastes. The first reaction to this trend may be to celebrate greater individual choice of destinations on the information superhighway, and it is tempting to think that the more personalized the information delivery system, the better for democracy. But is this true?

Perhaps individuals will make their information choices in sensible ways. Perhaps people will not turn away from the tough problems in society and the world. Given the choice to construct increasingly private realities, people may choose to remain informed about the problems of those who cannot help themselves (or who cannot afford the communications technologies required to be in the political loop). However, it is also possible that people will avoid issues that (they think) do not affect them, that seem hopeless, or that require more thought and human concern than they care to give. Research on news habits and political participation patterns is not encouraging. Studies of news consumption from the late 1980s through the turn of the Millenium reveal steady declines in attention to national, international, and local politics. These declines are associated with decreasing likelihood of voting or even registering to vote.[107]

Another concern is that with greater choice, people may seek out only the points of view they already agree with and form virtual communities with only those people who share their religious, economic, social, or entertainment preferences. The home shopping community? The home psychic community? The country music community? Can democracy in America survive more fragmentation and personalization of the political experience? Virtual democracy, anyone?

One aspect of this closing circle of information around the individual is that social reality itself becomes an increasingly personal production. For perhaps the first time in human history, large numbers of people actually have substantial choices over who they are and how they want to be identified socially.[108] As noted by many social theorists, a major reason for this is that the identities once attached to institutional memberships in class, church, business, social clubs, or community associations are weakening. As these elements of personal identity weaken, they are increasingly replaced by choices of lifestyles and communities of consumption.

In some ways, these new prospects for personal identities are liberating, and in other ways, they are stressful and confusing. One thing seems clear, however: Personal relationships to, and uses of, public information are changing. The very things that people regard as news are changing. What counts as news today: *Cops? America's Most Wanted? Oprah?* As early as the beginning of the 1990s, a survey conducted by the Times Mirror

Center for the People & the Press (now the Pew Research Center on People & the Press) revealed that fully half of the respondents said that *America's Most Wanted* was a news show, while only 28 percent said that it was entertainment. In the same survey, 49 percent approved of broadcasting dramatic reenactments in regular news programs if they are clearly labeled as dramatizations. Trying to hold the fading line between news and entertainment was a minority of 44 percent, who objected to the dramatization of news and felt that television news has gone too far in the direction of entertainment.[109]

It is clear that just as the nature of social reality is changing, what matters to people in their lives is also changing. Consider, for example, the aspects of the news that were of most interest to 18 to 29-year-olds at the end of the 1990s: crime (43 percent), sports (30 percent), people and events in the local community (28 percent), health (27 percent), and entertainment (24 percent). Only in sixth place do we find a far dimmer (14 percent) interest in local politics, followed by even smaller interests in general political news and international affairs (10 percent interest in each). As noted earlier, interest in political news is higher in older age groups, but all age groups rate at least three other "soft" news categories above any category of political news.[110]

If we combine the diminished authoritativeness of various information sources noted earlier with the personalization of information indicated in these surveys, a resulting information shift may be a tendency for people to more easily confuse their personal opinions with fact, particularly because information is used to build realities that are more personal and close to home than to imagine social realities shared in common with large numbers of distant strangers. In some respects, the rise of the Internet as a core personal information source may feed this cycle, both by giving individuals increasing control of the realities they choose to participate in and by making it even more difficult to evaluate the quality or authoritativeness of information about those realities that comes straight and unfiltered from cyberspace. Many of these concerns are still speculative, but one thing is clear: The fragmentation of media audiences is occurring at a breathtaking rate.

WHITHER THE PUBLIC SPHERE?

The idea of democracy implies a public life, meaning that people think critically about solutions to common problems. The quality of public input into democratic decisions depends on people sharing public communication forums in which to express their concerns, try out new ideas, and see if they stand the test of everyday debate. The collection of these public spaces, from cafés and taverns to town meetings and book clubs, constitutes what the pioneering communication theorist Jurgen Habermas termed the *public sphere*.[111] Many contemporary observers sense that the public sphere is shrinking or at least splintering perilously in modern society, and that, ironically, the expansion of personal communication technologies is responsible for much of the shrinkage. For example, sociologist Todd Gitlin argues that in place of any coherent public sphere, it makes more sense to think about the proliferation of tiny and shifting "sphericules."[112] These sphericules of interest can be extremely engaging, and they often offer a comforting escape from the pains of society at large. However, if people increasingly use communication technologies to construct and live in their own private worlds, where can people meet and share the concerns and the information required for coherent political discussion, much less for consensus to emerge?

To put it simply, the nature of our political communication process has something to do with how we act together politically—how we define our goals and chart our actions as a nation. At one extreme of national politics are the political crusaders who zealously fill the airwaves with moral ultimatums for everyone to follow. Their flaming on talk shows provides a low-budget media spectacle for the fragmented audiences who tune in, but they evidently set bad examples for the greater numbers who tune out. Many Americans today are more inclined to avoid politics, or at least to seek it close to home, than to welcome open-minded debate in everyday situations about common national concerns.[113]

Today's citizen, in the view of communication scholar Michael Schudson, differs from the citizens of past eras in the acute awareness of a protective armor of personal rights.[114] Prickliness about rights and related identity claims may have the ironic result of further driving wedges between personal lives and the public sphere. Some celebrate the liberation of individuals from oppressive public norms and obligations, while others decry the decline of coherent societies and nations.[115]

These changes in personal relationships to society and public life may explain some of the declining confidence in both national leaders and the press discussed in the last two chapters. Add to this the surrounding fragmentation of many social institutions, from schools and political parties to churches and families, and it is easy to see why many observers conclude that the authoritative basis of public information, itself, seems to be in decline: People simply have fewer common institutional bases for sharing and respecting the same information. These personal information trends are not helped by the politicians and news organizations who use communication technologies to tailor information more to popular emotion and consumer tastes than to challenging alternative perspectives. In short, when viewed from any aspect of the information system—whether from the standpoint of the press, political actors, the people, or technology—it is clear that the information environments in which we live are changing in important ways.

NOTES

1. The quote from the Illinois reporter is from Neil Hickey, "Money Lust: How Pressure for Profit is Perverting Journalism," *Columbia Journalism Review* (July/August 1998): 28.
2. Personal communication, John Zaller.
3. David Laventhol, "Profit Pressures," *Columbia Journalism Review* (May/June 2001): 19.
4. Quoted in Michael J. Wolfe and Geoffrey Sands, "Fearless Predictions: The Content World, 2005," *Brill's Content* (July/August 1999): 111.
5. For earlier episodes in this history, see Gerald Baldasty, *The Commercialization of News in the Nineteenth Century* (Madison: University of Wisconsin Press, 1992).
6. Christopher Harper, "Doing It All: Online Staffers Do a Variety of Jobs," *American Journalism Review* 18, no. 10 (December 1996): 24.
7. See the *Planet Viacom Centerfold* in Mark Crispin Miller, "Can Viacom's Reporters Cover Viacom's Interests?" *Columbia Journalism Review* (November/December 1999): 48–50.
8. Paul Farhi, "In Television, Big Is Now Clearly Better," *Washington Post National Weekly Edition,* September 20, 1999, 21.

9. *CBS Evening News,* January 28, 2002.
10. Alessandra Stanley, "How to Persuade the Young to Watch the News? Program It, Executives Say," *New York Times,* January 15, 2000, C6.
11. Ibid.
12. Ibid.
13. John Cassidy, "Striking It Rich: The Rise and Fall of Popular Capitalism," *New Yorker,* January 14, 2002, 67.
14. Quoted in Elizabeth Kolbert, "Test-Marketing a President," *New York Times Magazine,* August 30, 1992, 19.
15. Sally Deneen, "Doing the Boca: An Interim Report from a Reinvented Newspaper," *Columbia Journalism Review* (May/June 1991): 15.
16. Ibid.
17. Ibid.
18. Quoted in Michael Hoyt, "The Wichita Experiment," *Columbia Journalism Review* (July/August 1992): 43.
19. Ibid..
20. Ibid., 45.
21. Doug Underwood and Keith Stamm, "Balancing Business with Journalism: Newsroom Policies at 12 West Coast Newspapers," *Journalism Quarterly* 69 (Summer 1992): 301–317.
22. Doug Underwood, "The Very Model of the Reader-Driven Newsroom?" *Columbia Journalism Review* (November/December 1993): 42.
23. Ibid., 44.
24. Steve Rossi, "In Their Own Words: The Harris Resignation," *Columbia Journalism Review* (May/June, 2001): 20.
25. David Laventhol, "Profit Pressures: A Question of Margins," *Columbia Journalism Review* (May/June 2001): 18.
26. Baldasty, *The Commercialization of News.*
27. Quoted in Ken Auletta, "Look What They've Done to the News," *TV Guide,* November 9, 1991, 5.
28. Robert McChesney, *Rich Media, Poor Democracy: Communication Politics in Dubious Times* (Urbana: University of Illinois Press, 1999).
29. All figures are from Rifka Rosenwein, "The Anatomy of a Super Bowl Ad," *Brill's Content* (February 1999): 72–77.
30. Quoted in Judith Miller, "But Can You Dance to It? MTV Turns to News," *New York Times Magazine,* October 11, 1992, 33.
31. Karen Bedford, "Public Affairs at PBS: The Pressure Is On," *Columbia Journalism Review* (May/June 1999): 13.
32. Nielsen data reported in Bill Carter, "TV Networks Are Scrambling to Deal with Era of New Media," *New York Times,* May 17, 1999, A17.
33. Roper and Pew surveys reported in Richard Davis and Diana Owen, *New Media and American Politics* (New York: Oxford University Press, 1998).
34. Paul Farhi, "No Longer Exactly on Top of the News: Faced with a Host of New Competitors, CNN Is Struggling to Regain Its Luster and Ratings," *Washington Post National Weekly Edition,* September 8, 1997, 18.
35. Pew surveys reported in Richard Morin, "The Move to 'Net News': Folks Still Want to Know What's Going On, but They're Turning from TV to the Computer," *Washington Post National Weekly Edition,* June 15, 1998, 34.
36. Ibid.
37. Ibid.
38. Ibid.
39. Wolfe and Sands, "Fearless Predictions," 110.

40. Quoted in Abegail Pogrebin, "Lack Attack," *Brill's Content* (February 1999): 93.

41. Quoted in Arthur Unger, "Packaging News for Thousands of Years Ahead," *Christian Science Monitor,* December 22, 1988, 19.

42. See Wolfe and Sands, "Fearless Predictions," 112.

43. Ben H. Bagdikian, *The Media Monopoly,* 4th ed. (Boston: Beacon Press, 1992), 4.

44. Ben H. Bagdikian, *The Media Monopoly,* 5th ed. (Boston: Beacon Press, 1997).

45. From Neil Hickey, "So Big: The Telecommunications Act at Year One," *Columbia Journalism Review* (January/February 1997): 23.

46. Ibid., 24.

47. Ibid., 34.

48. Ibid., 23.

49. Robert W. McChesney and John Nichols, "Up in Flames." *Nation,* October 17, 2003. **www.thenation.com/doc.mhtml?i=20031117s=mcchesney&c=1**

50. Paul Farhi, "Tuning Out C-SPAN," *Washington Post National Weekly Edition,* February 24, 1997, 29.

51. Bagdikian, *Media Monopoly,* 4th ed., 177; see also editor and publisher data reported in Alex S. Jones, "At Many Papers, Competition Is at Best an Illusion," *New York Times,* September 22, 1991, E18.

52. See, for example, Hickey, "So Big," and McChesney, *Rich Media, Poor Democracy.*

53. Hickey, "So Big," 25.

54. Ibid.

55. This dramatic recreation is from Elizabeth Lesly Stevens, "Mousekefear," *Brill's Content* (December 1998/January 1999), 95.

56. Ibid., 98.

57. Ibid., 95.

58. Jennifer Glaser, "Coming Distractions: ABC News Goes to the Movies," *Columbia Journalism Review* (September/October 1998): 13–14.

59. Quoted in Hickey, "So Big," 26.

60. Quoted in Hickey, "So Big," 28.

61. Jeff Greenfield, "When Facts Alone Won't Do," *New York Times,* November 2, 1998, A27.

62. Quoted in Adam Lehner, "Fuller Explanation Department," *New Yorker,* May 24, 1999, 29, "Talk of the Town" section.

63. Tad Friend, "Not Necessarily the News," *Vanity Fair* (October 1992): 190.

64. Bill Carter, "Where Have Television's Big Stars Gone?" *New York Times,* June 14, 1999, C16.

65. Steve McClellan, "TV News Mags Get Prime Shelf Space," *Broadcasting,* November 16, 1992, 4.

66. The period reported was May 1998. See "The Ratings Race," *New York Times,* May 21, 1998, B3.

67. Elizabeth Jensen, D. M. Osborne, Abigail Pogrebin, and Ted Rose, "Consumer Alert," *Brill's Content* (October 1998): 131.

68. Story by John J. O'Connor, *New York Times,* April 20, 1992, B1.

69. Jensen, et. al., "Consumer Alert," 131.

70. Ibid., 130.

71. Interview on National Public Radio, *Morning Edition,* December 17, 1993.

72. Reported by Diane Sawyer, "3000 Minutes," *New York Times Magazine,* September 20, 1998, 89.

73. Howard Kurtz, "Real Cops. Real Crooks. Not Exactly: Some Police Chases on Fox-TV Are not Just the Wildest, but the Woolliest—They're Staged," *Washington Post National Weekly Edition,* May 31, 1999, 31.

74. Debra Seagal, "Tales from the Cutting-Room Floor: The Reality of Reality-Based Television," *Harper's* (November 1993): 51.

75. James Sterngold, "After a Suicide, Questions on Lurid TV News," *New York Times,* May 2, 1998, 1.

76. Richard Schwarzlowse, of the Medill School of Journalism, Northwestern University, quoted in Ibid., A9.
77. Cheryl Fair, news director for KABC, Quoted in Ibid.
78. Ibid.
79. Quoted in Ibid., 29.
80. Quoted in Ibid., 34.
81. Quoted in Ibid., 32.
82. Tal Sanit, "Stand and Deliver: The Art of the Pseudo Stand-Up," *Columbia Journalism Review* (July/August 1992): 15.
83. Quoted in Tal Sanit, "The New Unreality: When TV Reporters Don't Report," *Columbia Journalism Review* (May/June 1992): 17.
84. Ibid.
85. These quotes, and the information about Fox News Channel, are from Neil Hickey, "Is Fox News Fair?" *Columbia Journalism Review* (March/April 1998): 30–35.
86. Ibid., 32.
87. Ibid., 35.
88. For an interesting study showing that NPR reports have grown longer, but at the same time more similar to other news sources in terms of "interpretive journalism," see Kevin G. Barnhurst and Carol M. Liebler, "Political News Reconsidered: National Public Radio and the New Long Journalism." Paper presented at the 1998 Meeting of the American Political Science Association, September, 1998.
89. Elizabeth Jensen, "Alternate Realities," *Brill's Content* (December 1998/January 1999): 79.
90. Gene Roberts, "Drowning in Shallow Waters," *Columbia Journalism Review* (May/June 1996), 55.
91. Doug Underwood, *When MBAs Rule the Newsroom* (New York: Columbia University Press, 1993).
92. Ibid., xii.
93. Iver Peterson, "Newspaper Owners Proselytize Business Sense to Their Reporters and Editors," *New York Times,* June 9, 1997, D3.
94. See, for example, David Shaw, "Cooperation Within Times Viewed with Trepidation," *Los Angeles Times,* March 30, 1998, 1.
95. Saul Hansell, "News-Ad Issues Arise in New Media," *New York Times* December 8, 1997, C10.
96. Saul Hansell and Amy Harmon, "Caveat Emptor on the Web: Ad and Editorial Lines Blur," *New York Times,* February 26, 1999, 1.
97. Ibid., A12.
98. Ibid., A12.
99. Hickey, "Money Lust," 29.
100. Quoted in Elizabeth Kolbert, "Paper Adjusts Reporting by Asking Its Readers," *New York Times,* June 21, 1992, 14.
101. See Richard Kielbowicz, *News in the Mail: The Press, Post Office and Public Information, 1700–1860s* (Westport, CT: Greenwood Press, 1989).
102. Wolfe and Sands, "Fearless Predictions," 111.
103. Joseph Turow, *Breaking Up America: Advertisers and the New Media World* (Chicago: University of Chicago Press, 1997).
104. See W. Lance Bennett, "The UnCivic Culture: Communication, Identity, and the Rise of Lifestyle Politics," *PS: Political Science and Politics* 31 (December 1998): 741–61.
105. In addition to Turow, *Breaking Up America;* see also Stuart Ewen, *PR! A Social History of Spin* (New York: Basic Books, 1996); and Oscar Gandy, "Dividing Practices: Segmentation and Targeting in the Emerging Public Sphere," in *Mediated Politics: Communication in the Future of Democracy,* ed. W. Lance Bennett and Robert M. Entman (New York: Cambridge University Press, 2001).
106. James S. Fishkin, *The Voice of the People* (New Haven, CT: Yale University Press, 1995).

107. Stephen Earl Bennett, Staci L. Rhine, and Richard S. Flickinger, "The Things They Cared About: Change and Continuity in Americans' Attention to Different News Stories, 1989–2002." *Press/Politics.* 9, no. 1 (Winter 2004): 75–99.

108. See Anthony Giddens, *Modernity and Self-Identity: Self and Society in the Late Modern Age* (Stanford, CA: Stanford University Press, 1991).

109. Poll data reported in Bill Thomas, "Finding Truth in the Age of Infotainment," *Editorial Research Reports* (Washington, DC: Congressional Quarterly, January 19, 1990), 35–36.

110. More extensive reporting, including time trends in these surveys, can be found on the Pew Web site: **www.people-press.org/agerpt.htm**.

111. Jurgen Habermas, *Structural Transformation of the Public Sphere: An Inquiry into a Category of Bourgeois Society* (Cambridge, MA: MIT Press, 1989).

112. Todd Gitlin, Lecture, University of Washington, May 20, 1999.

113. Nina Eliasoph, *Avoiding Politics: How Americans Produce Apathy in Everyday Life* (New York: Cambridge University Press, 1998).

114. Michael Schudson, *The Good Citizen: A History of American Civic Life* (New York: The Free Press, 1998).

115. For an extended discussion of these ideas, see Bennett, "The UnCivic Culture."

Chapter 4

How Politicians Make the News

. . . when information which properly belongs to the public is withheld by those in power, the people soon become ignorant of their own affairs, distrustful of those who manage them, and, eventually, incapable of determining their own destinies.

Richard Nixon

There is literally no such thing as an idea that cannot be expressed well and articulately to today's voters in 30 seconds.

Dick Morris

At the close of World War II, the victorious Allied powers met to divide Europe into spheres of influence. These meetings, between Churchill and Stalin at Moscow in 1944 and between Roosevelt, Churchill, and Stalin at Yalta in 1945, were proclaimed in public to be reasoned deliberations that would ensure peace, stability, and freedom in the world for all time. Following Yalta, Roosevelt pointed to the Soviet promise of free elections in Poland as an example of the commitment to democracy that prevailed at the meeting. Stalin echoed Roosevelt's claim with the public assurance that "Poland must be free, independent, and powerful."

In contrast to these lofty images of the meetings and their results, another reality prevailed behind the closed doors of Moscow and Yalta. The agreement at Yalta excluded the Polish government-in-exile from a serious role in forming the new government. With this agreement, the three heads of state knew that there would be no real freedom in the elections that would be held two years later. In fact, their decision paved the way for the tradition of Soviet domination in Poland that persisted until the 1980s.

Churchill's own account of the Moscow session revealed that an atmosphere of brute political bargaining guided the division of the Balkan states. A half sheet of paper was used to jot down the amounts of influence the victors would exert in the territories in question: Romania, 90 percent Russian influence; Greece, 90 percent British influence; Yugoslavia and Hungary, a 50–50 split; and Bulgaria, 75 percent Russian influence. Following the bargaining, Churchill gave the paper to Stalin for his approval. According to Churchill's own account, Stalin simply "took his blue pencil and made a large tick upon it." Whereupon Churchill asked: "Might it not be thought rather cynical if it seemed we had disposed of these issues, so fateful to millions of people, in such an offhand manner?" He proposed burning the paper, but Stalin insisted that Churchill keep it.[1]

There are two realities in the above story. One involves the actual political behaviors and concerns of powerful actors. The other involves the cosmetic presentation of a newsworthy version of the event, a version inspired by concerns about how the actual circumstances might appear to the public. Political actors are confronted constantly with concerns about how the actual politics of an event might appear and whether a more seemly image can be created and used to some political advantage.

THE POLITICS OF ILLUSION

Leaders who disillusion their followers live shorter political lives than leaders who learn to represent situations to their best political advantage. It is hardly surprising, therefore, that the news is filled with strategically constructed versions of events. Nor is it surprising that, with the advent of more sophisticated polling, message development, and marketing technologies, the news often translates the political world into personal terms based on the existing emotions and values of audiences. Indeed, the mark of skill in the political trade is the ability to make the public version of a situation convincing, no matter how actual circumstances may be bent or simplified in the process. As former Secretary of State Dean Acheson once said, the task of public officers seeking support for their policies is to make their points "clearer than truth."[2]

Sometimes, the contrived aspects of news stories are exposed as a result of slips, blunders, leaks, miscalculations, or defections of former insiders. For example, when Gerald Ford pardoned Richard Nixon for his Watergate crimes, Ford lost favor with many Americans who began to suspect that his earlier, seemingly altruistic proposal of amnesty for Vietnam draft resisters was an attempt to buy the sympathy of liberals hostile to Nixon.[3] When the U.S.-backed attempt to overthrow the Castro regime in Cuba ended in a military disaster at the Bay of Pigs in 1961, the Kennedy administration could no longer use the planned cover story that the invasion force of Cuban exiles (with its captured American equipment) had acted independently of the U.S. government.[4] President Eisenhower's repeated denials of U.S. spy flights over the Soviet Union became embarrassingly transparent with the Russian capture of a U-2 spy plane on the eve of a major summit conference.[5] Ronald Reagan's economic explanations lost some of their luster when David Stockman, budget director and chief interpreter of Reaganomics, disclosed that economic figures had been adjusted to fit Reagan's supply-side economic models.[6] George Bush's promise to get tough with China following the Tiananmen Square massacre of student demonstrators in 1989 quickly appeared insincere when a news leak revealed that he had sent a secret diplomatic mission to re-assure Beijing that the incident would not jeopardize U.S.–Chinese relations. Bill Clinton's forceful, finger-pointing denial that he had sex with "that woman" Monica Lewinsky soon became an icon in Republican attacks and news recaps after the steamy details of Monica's own confession were released in the report of Special Investigator Kenneth Starr in 1998. George W. Bush's rationale for the invasion of Iraq eventually became questioned, but too late for people to have made informed decisions about going to war. The case study in this chapter examines the selling of the War in Iraq.

These memorable examples of high-level deceptions point to the importance of news management—both for creating the deceptions in the first place and for controlling the damage if and when they become challenged. News and information management are keys to successful politics and governance. The essentials of political communication begin with assessing vulnerabilities, plugging damaging leaks (and creating useful ones), anticipating possible misunderstandings, and tightly controlling all information that reaches the press. Hindsight reveals that these practices often work surprisingly well: many political deceptions and ill-considered definitions of situations go unmasked in the news until it is too late to stop history from taking an unfortunate turn.

For every timely news revelation on the order of a Watergate or a Bay of Pigs, many more may lie undetected until long after their political effects have been recorded. History tells us, for example, that Lyndon Johnson's justification for large scale American involvement in Vietnam was based on a largely fabricated account of unprovoked attacks on U.S. ships in the Gulf of Tonkin.[7] Johnson, like Roosevelt twenty-five years before him, had searched for an incident that would justify entry into a war. Perhaps it was cruel fate that history made a hero of Roosevelt by providing him an immaculate justification in the Japanese attack on Pearl Harbor, whereas Johnson was forced to resort to the tawdry business of fabricating his own incident. History also tells us of the major role played by the CIA in the 1973 overthrow of the government of Chile. We even learned, many years after the fact, that the Kennedy administration authorized the overthrow of the South Vietnamese government in the early days of U.S. involvement in Vietnam. This revelation took a perverse path to historical disclosure. Feeling that he was both misunderstood and victimized by history, Lyndon Johnson resented being blamed for the credibility gap that undermined public support for his policies in Vietnam. Perhaps in an effort to show that even the glorified Kennedy administration was guilty of a credibility gap, Johnson leaked to a reporter copies of diplomatic cables linking President Kennedy to the assassination of President Diem and the overthrow of his regime.[8]

When the giant Enron corporation collapsed in a heap of accounting fraud and dubious investment schemes, the legacy of recent congressional legislation relaxing corporate accounting standards and other stockholder protections was drowned out by members of Congress holding widely televised hearings in which they angrily charged company executives with heartless betrayals of the public. Among the more telling news portrayals of these hearings was the decision of CNN to run a crawl underneath each member of Congress who appeared on screen to condemn executives from Enron and its accounting firm, Arthur Andersen. The crawl reported the amount that each scolding representative had received in political contributions from Enron.

Aside from reinforcing public cynicism about corporate influence on government, however, this reporting did little to explain how the political path to such corporate abuses had been constructed, nor did it prevent members of Congress from defining the problem in terms of one bad corporation as opposed to the legislation that helped make it possible.

As discussed in earlier chapters, much has changed about the news in recent years, but one important pattern holds: most political news still originates from government officials themselves. In many ways, officials seem an obvious and appropriate source of information about politics, which, after all, often involves activities of government. However, letting officials set the news agenda is not just giving them greater voice in what publics think about and how they think about it, it also enables them to deploy the strategic communication technologies that shape the very realities—the issues, situations, and images of citizen involvement—that are portrayed in the news itself. First, we will see how officials dominate political news, then how they construct news realities, and finally, how journalists attempt to combat the impression that they are being manipulated.

THE SOURCES OF POLITICAL NEWS

There are several ways to think about the impact of politicians' continuing efforts to control images in the news. For example, it is useful to know what proportion of the daily news is directly attributable to such official news control efforts. Even a casual look at the daily paper or the nightly TV news suggests that the bulk of important news is devoted to the official actions of the government and elected officials. True, those actions may be portrayed in the cynical tone of political games or against the backdrop of potshots and spin by opponents, but the fact remains that the majority of political stories are simple condensations of what politicians say and do. In short, the news seems to consist mainly of stories in which at least one point of view is an official one. Many stories are framed by two familiar official angles—Republican and Democrat, for example.

How accurate is this impression that the content of the news is dominated by prepared official messages? Leon Sigal addressed this question in his classic study of the news content of two of America's finest newspapers, the *New York Times* and the *Washington Post*. Common sense might suggest that these prestigious organizations would be among the least likely to take their news as it is served up by official newsmakers. The *Times* and *Post* cover a broad range of political stories in depth, and they have large reporting staffs, which should free them from dependence on press releases and wire service copy as the scripts for news stories. Finally, the *Times* and *Post* have reputations as critical papers that are not afraid of exposing government deception.

As it turns out, these papers are also the leading papers of record for what government officials say and do. How did these leading papers fare against the everyday pressures and temptations to report prepared political information? Among Sigal's findings were the following:

- Government officials (either domestic or foreign) were the sources of nearly three-quarters of all hard news, and only one-sixth of the news could be traced to sources outside the government. The breakdown of news sources looked like this:

Sources	Percent[9]
U.S. officials, agencies	46.5
Foreign, international officials, agencies	27.5
U.S. state, local government officials	4.1
Other news organizations	3.2
Nongovernmental Americans	14.4
Nongovernmental foreigners	2.1
Nonascertainable	2.4

- Less than 1 percent of all news stories were based on the reporter's own analysis, whereas over *90 percent* were based on the calculated messages of the actors involved in the situation.[10]
- The vast majority of news stories (from 70 to 90 percent, depending on how they are categorized) were drawn from situations over which newsmakers had either complete or substantial control. Here is the breakdown of the contexts from which the *Times* and *Post* drew their information:

Sources	Percent[11]
Interviews	24.7
Press conferences	24.5
Press releases	17.5
Official proceedings	13.0
Background proceedings	7.9
Other nonspontaneous events	4.5
News commentary and editorials	4.0
Leaks	2.3
Nongovernmental proceedings	1.5
Spontaneous events	1.2
Reporter's own analysis	0.9

Research by various scholars since Sigal's pioneering study suggests that much the same patterns persist to this day.[12] Even in this age of live event coverage, officials are quickly introduced into reporting from the scenes of wars or crises to provide framing for stories.[13] The level of official domination tends to be even higher on foreign policy issues, where opposition groups and views from other nations are often pushed to the margins. On domestic matters such as abortion, health care policy, or taxes, the views of organized interests enter the news with greater frequency. However, the press tends to index the range of diverse viewpoints in a story to the presence of powerful government actors in Washington who also share those views.[14] By any accounting, the conclusion is inescapable: Even the best journalism in the land is extremely dependent on the political messages of a small spectrum of official news sources. The *Times* and *Post,* no doubt, include more detailed background information (not to mention more coverage of obscure events) than most news outlets, but the basic messages in their stories still represent official views.

Around this core of official spin there are, of course, other trends worth noting. Recall, for example, that journalists have introduced their own voices into the news in increasing volume, commenting upon and interpreting what their official sources say.[15] Moreover, the increase of scandals and journalistic feeding frenzies indicates that journalists have found ways to assert their control over news content, even if these stories often annoy audiences more than they inform them. The irony is that on stories of great consequence such as going to war, journalists are reluctant to insert their own voices and challenge official versions of events—even if there is evidence to support the challenge—unless other influential politicians step forward first.

Why Politicians Work So Hard to Create the Illusions in the News

The economic pressures in the news business described in Chapter 3 leave less space for serious political news than in earlier times. The journalistic bias toward stories that are dramatic, clear in message, and simple of plot also makes politicians reliant on communication professionals who design their messages, keep them "on point," and above all, keep them away from more spontaneous exchanges with press, opponents, and publics. As a result, news content may not always be the best mirror on political reality, yet it can have important effects on how decisions are made, how the public feels about them, and which politicians and groups are perceived as powerful and effective. For these reasons, it is important to understand the manufacture of seemingly naturally occurring news stories by politicians and interests who use publicity to gain recognition, to advance policy agendas, and to damage political enemies.

The Political Impact of Officialized News

The most obvious political effect of news management is the advantage it gives powerful people in getting their issues on the political agenda. Political activists and groups that are not established players in policy processes have much more difficulty making news. A study of grassroots organizations by political scientist Edie Goldenberg showed that it is hard for unofficial actors to develop the credibility, resources, and information control necessary to dominate the news long enough to affect the outcome of issues.[16] When grassroots groups do make the news, it is often in the context of negatively perceived events like demonstrations, sit-ins, and other protest activities that may offend the public and draw easy criticism from public officials.

A long-term effect of officially managed news may be to limit the range of problems, solutions, values, and ideas presented to the American people. The political world becomes a predictable terrain of stereotypes, political postures, and superficial images. Familiar solutions are recycled in melodramatic efforts to solve chronic problems. People come to accept the existence of problems like poverty, crime, delinquency, war, and political apathy as facts of life rather than as the tragic results of the concentration of political power, the exploitative nature of economic relations, and the cynical uses of political communication.

The participation of the news media in promoting the official cover stories about these problems—until those stories are attacked or challenged by opponents—further undermines the chances for the kind of public understanding required for effective political action and real political change. Research reported later in the book shows that news audiences can be quite independent in interpreting the news, but people cannot interpret what they don't see. What they don't see or hear in the news is often linked to effective press management, as described in the case study, *Selling the Iraq War.*

Case Study: *Selling the Iraq War*

"Weapons of Mass Deception" was the headline on Jon Stewart's *Daily Show* after the U.S. military had finished months of unproductive searching for weapons of mass destruction in Iraq. The administration's case for the war had been built on fearful WMD scenarios, capped by Saddam Hussein seeking nuclear weapons that might be used against nations in the Middle East and even in attacks on American cities. The case for war was also built on claims that Iraq had connections to al Qaeda and to the events of 9/11. As the Iraq invasion turned into a messy occupation, it became clear that many of the claims used to convince the public and quiet the opposition had little supporting evidence and a good deal of intelligence information that contradicted them. It even seemed likely that key players in the Bush administration promoted these fearful images to sell a war that they had sought long before 9/11 happened. Enough of this was known to the press in time to generate a healthy public debate before the invasion took place. Few news organizations, however, offered any serious challenge to administration news management efforts. Consider just a few aspects of the political situation surrounding Iraq that were blurred by the administration campaign to sell the war:

- A CIA investigation of administration charges that Saddam tried to purchase bomb-grade uranium in Africa showed that the evidence for the claim had been fabricated. The CIA asked that the claim be removed from a Bush speech during the fall 2002 campaign to raise support for the war. The CIA again pushed successfully for removing the charge from the U.S. Ambassador's speech to the U.N. Security Council later in December. Yet, the uranium charge reappeared at White House insistence in the president's 2003 State of the Union address, signaling the coming war.[17] Months after it was discredited, the charge continued to be spread in news interviews and speeches by other administration officials who simply attributed the claim to British intelligence reports that also proved to be groundless. The repetition of the dubious charge by nearly every top official of the administration in the coming weeks was part of the "strategic coordination" of the administration message as described by White House Communications Director Dan Bartlett.[18] (When the CIA investigator assigned to this case was so moved by this public inaccuracy to explain publicly that the nuclear weapons charge had been discredited, someone in the administration retaliated by leaking the identity of the man's wife, who was working undercover for the CIA. This bit of administration hardball led to a special prosecutor investigation of White House breach of national security law).

- Links between al Qaeda and Saddam Hussein, and between Saddam and 9/11 were asserted repeatedly by high administration officials including President Bush and Vice President Cheney, but no evidence was presented. To the contrary, there was ample evidence that al Qaeda leader Osama bin Laden had condemned Saddam's government as a secular threat to Islamic fundamentalism and that Saddam feared an Islamic threat to his rule. After Saddam's capture, documents were found in his possession ordering Iraqi resistance fighters to refuse to cooperate with any Islamic fundamentalists who entered Iraq in order to avoid stirring an Islamic revolution.[19]

- A book based on interviews with former Bush Treasury Secretary Paul O'Neill claimed that discussions about overthrowing Saddam Hussein were held from the earliest cabinet meetings of the Bush administration, long before the attacks of 9/11. O'Neil charged that 9/11 merely provided the pretext for a war that was already on the agendas of Vice President Dick Cheney, Secretary of Defense Donald Rumsfeld, and the president, among others. According to O'Neill, who had been a trusted Bush political ally, the belief was that regime change in Iraq would provide a model for democracy that would transform the rest of the region. According to O'Neill's account, the main question was how to justify going to war, and the president set a tone of "Fine. Go find me a way to do this."[20] Both Bush and Rumsfeld issued strong denials after the book came out, and the White House retaliated by calling for an investigation of whether O'Neill had broken governmental secrecy laws in providing the book's author with official documents to back up his claims. If those documents supported O'Neill's claim, it would seem that secrecy laws were being used to punish telling the truth—but few reporters raised this issue. Another former top administration official, counterterrorism chief Richard Clarke, also wrote a scathing book claiming that President Bush personally pressured him to find a connection between 9/11 and Saddam Hussein. Jon Stewart satirized the White House response by playing, "Who Let the Dogs Out" with videos of top officials appearing on new interview shows to discredit Mr. Clarke.

As key elements of the administration rationale for the war began to fall apart, White House spinners quickly refashioned their story—after the fact, as it were. What began as a scary scenario linking Saddam to weapons of mass destruction and to the terrorist attacks on the United States eventually settled into the far safer rationale that Saddam was a very bad guy, and the Iraqi people were better off without him. Mr. Bush also explained that he was merely following the policy of regime change that had been in place since the Clinton administration, only he implemented it more decisively.

The question, of course, is whether the American people or Congress would have gone to war on just the argument that Saddam was a bad guy whose regime needed to be replaced. Most Americans agreed with those assessments ever since President Bush's father went to war against Iraq in 1991, but stopped short of throwing Saddam out because of concerns about chaos in the aftermath—concerns that seemed well-founded in the wake of the second war.

Charges of deception were raised by various Democratic presidential candidates in the 2004 primaries, but Mr. Bush dismissed them as just politics, a framing that the press allowed to stand, reducing the issue to one of many that might become important in the fall election. More than a year after what appeared to be a manufactured case for war had been presented to the public, Democratic Senator Ted Kennedy attempted to redefine the terms of debate by making a speech with this bold claim: "The administration capitalized on the fear created by 9/11 and put a spin on the intelligence and a spin on the truth to justify a war that could well be one of the worst blunders in more than two centuries of American foreign policy." He charged that the war was marketed like a "political product" to help elect Republicans, and that "If Congress and the American People knew the whole truth, America would never have gone to war."[21] Needless to say, Kennedy was quickly dismissed as a liberal throwback, and few in the press would invoke his words to reframe the war story. The censorship campaign described in the case study in Chapter 1 was immediately geared up by House Majority Leader Tom DeLay, who said that "His hateful attack against the commander-in-chief would be disgusting if it were not so sad," adding that Kennedy had "insulted the president's patriotism." Apparently it is not possible for patriots to make mistakes or engage in undue deception if they truly believe their cause is just.

For more than a year and a half, the White House held advantage in the game of news framing, even as its frames kept changing to accommodate information that did not fit the old ones. As noted in Chapter 2, however, journalists are ultimately the ones who write the frames for news stories. Evidence challenging the administration claims about an imminent threat from Iraq was available to journalists from the early days of the administration campaign to drum up support for the war.[22] For example, an interesting set of responses by experts to Mr. Bush's claims about Iraq in his 2003 State of the Union address has been collected by the Institute for Public Accuracy, and can be found at **www.accuracy.org/2003**. Most of these counterpositions were available to the press at the time of the address.

Senator Kennedy's assertion that the administration had marketed the war as a partisan political product should have come as no surprise to journalists or other political insiders. In a good piece of investigative reporting (lamentably not followed up by the *Post* or other news organizations), two journalists for the *Washington Post* describe a systematic media campaign that began in August 2002 with the formation of the White House Iraq Group (WHIG) aimed at rolling out communication strategy for the coming war. WHIG's "strategic communications" task force planned publicity and news events for a campaign that would start in September after most Americans (and Congress) had returned from their summer vacations. As White House Chief of Staff Andrew Card put it in an interview that the *New York Times* ran in September 2002, "From a marketing point of view, you don't introduce new products in August."[23]

The selling of the war went according to plan. The nation's talk shows on the weekend after Labor Day 2002 were filled with administration officials staying on message and reading from a script that turned out to be more scary fiction than fact.[24] On NBC's *Meet the Press,* Vice President Cheney raised the specter that Saddam's nuclear, chemical, and biological weapons presented an immediate danger to the United States. Condoleeza Rice acknowledged on CNN's *Late Edition* that solid evidence was scarce, but that waiting only increased the risk. Her punch line: "We don't want the smoking gun to be a mushroom cloud." Donald Rumsfeld warned the audience on CBS's *Face the Nation,* "Imagine a September 11 with weapons of mass destruction. It's not 3,000, it's tens of thousands of innocent men, women, and children."[25] Why did this campaign pass through the press so easily, being reported just as it was scripted? Stay tuned for the case study in Chapter 5.

NEWS IMAGES AS STRATEGIC POLITICAL COMMUNICATION

Walter Lippmann observed over sixty years ago in his classic work on public opinion, "the only feeling that anyone can have about an event he does not experience is the feeling aroused by his mental image of that event."[26] There is little check on the kinds of images created for political situations when the information received by the masses of people on the outside is controlled by a few people on the inside. As Secretary of State Acheson reminded us, the effective public official does not attempt to educate or convey "objective" images; the official's goal is to represent issues and events in ways that gain support, shape action, and influence outcomes.[27]

If the images contained in official political positions were mere entertainment fare floating about in the electronic ether, there might be less cause for concern. As long as the images in the news are treated as real, however, people may be inclined to respond to them. Even, and perhaps especially, those images with the most dubious links to reality can generate actions in the real world, actions that have real effects: the election of corrupt leaders, the acceptance of oppressive laws or ideas, the labeling of social groups, support for wars such as Iraq, or tolerance of chronic social and economic problems. Thus, news images of the political world can be tragically self-fulfilling. Dominant political images can create a world in their own image—even when such a world did not exist to begin with.

The fact that political actors make a practice of creating images for political situations does not mean that the news is filled with wild, diverse, and highly imaginative political stories. Most political images are based on familiar symbols, formulaic plots, standard slogans, and simple rhetoric.[28] The world of political images is built from predictable symbolic transformations: the new into the old, the startling into the familiar, the self-interested into the public-spirited. Even threats and crises come wrapped in stereotypes of enemy aggression, American firmness, peace through strength, productive and serious discussions, and so on. Political language, in the view of Murray Edelman, thrives on banal, predictable, formulaic images that undermine critical thinking in public communication.[29] Both the familiar pronouncements and partisan squabbles of authorities become substitutes for detailed analyses of situations.

There is, therefore, a profound irony in news making. The newsworthiness of a political image often lies not in some independent check on its accuracy or importance but in its past success as a news formula. In this world of media reality, newsworthiness becomes a substitute for validity, and credibility becomes reduced to a formula of who applies what images to which events under what circumstances. Ordinary logic tells us that the more standardized an image, the less valid and meaningful is its application to unique, real-world situations. On the other hand, what David Altheide and Robert Snow have termed *media logic* tells us that reality *is* the image constructed for it as long as that image remains dominant and uncontested across different mainstream communication channels.[30] A corollary of this logic is that if other authorities in positions to affect the outcome of a situation challenge an existing official position, the news will tend to dramatize the conflict (generally in personalized terms), leaving the audience to decide what the issues and their merits really are.

These and other aspects of media logic flow from the basic news information biases outlined in the last chapter. Those biases help explain the evolution of the information and press-management strategies used by newsmakers to get their views across in the news.[31] Failure to control the news is often equated with political failure. As the campaign manager for a presidential candidate put it, "the media is the campaign."[32] Or, as a key presidential advisor explained, there is no political reality apart from news reality. That assessment came from one of Ronald Reagan's top aides (and later secretary of state in the Bush administration), James Baker, who was asked by an NBC correspondent why the president seemed so unwilling to compromise on a tough budget proposal he submitted to Congress. Baker said that compromise was undesirable because, in the media, "everything is cast in terms of winning or losing."[33] Thus, the president could not back down, no matter how unrealistic his position. To be seen as unrealistic was preferable to being perceived as a loser because being perceived as a loser would make him a loser.

124 Chapter 4 / How Politicians Make the News

NEWS BIAS AND PRESS-GOVERNMENT RELATIONS

The news often fails to put sustained focus on important questions because its space is filled with the stories that best fit the information biases and the media logic uniting journalists and politicians. When ready-made news that fits these biases comes along, the news space is filled with it. When supplies of such news run thin, news organizations may go out and stir it up.

This dynamic explains why the relations between press and public officials are so uneasy, yet why neither press nor politicians can get their jobs done without often high degrees of cooperation. Journalists routinely turn to public officials for definitions of developing situations, and as illustrated by the Iraq War campaign, newsmakers often provide tailor-made news fare.

The military have proved particularly impressive news managers in recent years. In the view of many current top brass who were young officers in Vietnam, that war was not so much a military defeat as a media-led national loss of will. After the relatively open access enjoyed by the press in Vietnam, today's journalists have gradually become conditioned to spoon-fed news handouts during wars and interventions. As then Chairman of the Joint Chiefs of Staff Colin Powell put it before the Panama invasion in 1989, "Once you've got all the forces moving and everything's being taken care of by the commanders, turn your attention to television because you can win the battle or lose the war if you don't handle the story right."[34] Handle it they did, both in Panama and even more impressively in the Gulf War against Iraq in 1991. In the words of Michael Deaver, who elevated press management to an art form in the Reagan White House, "If you were going to hire a public relations firm to do the media relations for an international event, it couldn't be done any better than this."[35] In the words of Hodding Carter, a press relations officer from the Carter administration, "If I were the government, I'd be paying the press for the kind of coverage it is getting right now."[36] The lessons from the first war against Iraq were extended in the second by embedding journalists with military units, providing audiences with historic and captivating scenes from live combat with little context or interpretation. As one correspondent put it following the first Iraq war, "We have sort of become adjuncts of the government. The line between me and a government contractor is pretty thin."[37] Another complained that each journalist who accepts the terms of government news management becomes "an unpaid employee of the Department of Defense, on whose behalf he or she prepares the news of the war for the outer world."[38] Despite the presence of more than a thousand U.S. news people throughout the Persian Gulf region in 1991, one observer concluded that "To get at the real story in the Gulf, reporters did not have to travel to the front. They did not even have to travel to Saudi Arabia. Most of the information they needed was available in Washington."[39] The war in Afghanistan in 2001–2002 was even more carefully managed in terms of information control. This information management, combined with the press censorship pressures described in the case study in Chapter 1 made it difficult to learn anything that was not crafted by administration information offices. The Iraq War of 2003 carried news management to the point that the press settled comfortably into its managed status and elevated officials such as Defense Secretary Donald Rumsfeld to the status of celebrities.

THE GOALS OF STRATEGIC POLITICAL COMMUNICATION

It is clear that controlling political images in the news is a primary goal of politics, and, as such, it is important to understand what this entails. Most public relations experts agree that successful image making involves:

- Being clear about your client's political goals—damaging an opponent, improving the client's leadership image, or representing an environmental regulation as stronger than it will appear to opponents.
- Understanding the client's vulnerabilities so that opponents cannot turn the strategic communication back on its sponsors. For example, taking a moralistic stand against an opponent's sexual indiscretions may be ill advised if there are similar behaviors in the client's own past.
- Identifying the audience(s) most important for accomplishing those goals. Perhaps the main audience is a small demographic group that voted against the client in the last election, or the audience may be the key members of Congress who need to be convinced that there is public support for voting against health care reform.
- Using polling and market research to develop a message and a delivery strategy that reaches those audiences in ways that promote the goals of the campaign.

The core of the strategic communication process involves developing and communicating a message that promotes the political goals of a campaign by appealing to a targeted audience and holding the symbolic high ground if it comes under attack. The message construction aspect of the process can be further broken down into four important parts:

1. Composing a simple theme or message for the audience to use in thinking about the matter at hand. Call this *message shaping.*
2. Saturating communications channels with this message so that it will become more conspicuous than competing messages. Call this *message salience.*
3. Constructing a context of credibility for the message by finding a dramatic setting and recognized sources to deliver it, followed by endorsements from prominent supporters. Call this *message credibility.*
4. Delivering the message with the right scripting (particularly sound bites) and postdelivery *spin* to lead journalists to pick the right category for accentuating the message. For example, when a president signs a law and says "this is an important victory for taxpayers in America," an obvious frame for the story is "President scores political victory." Effective news management helps journalists accentuate the message by putting it inside that frame, which becomes the central meaning communicated by the story. Call this *message framing.*

Although these four components of political image making work together in actual political communication, it is useful to consider them separately in order to see what each one contributes to the definition of a political situation.

Message Shaping

The content of a political message is usually simple; it is both emotionally and intellectually accessible. Political messages generally begin with a key phrase, idea, or theme that creates a convenient way for people to think about a political object, be it an issue, an event, or even a person. For example, Franklin Roosevelt appealed to the hopes of the masses by using the simple term *New Deal* to refer to his complex patchwork of untried economic programs. Borrowing these characteristics of simplicity and idealism, John Kennedy added the power of familiarity when he presented his programs to the people under the title of *New Frontier.* Ronald Reagan used *New Federalism* to label his efforts to dismantle Roosevelt's New Deal, Kennedy's New Frontier, and Johnson's Great Society. When Bill Clinton stole the Republican thunder in his support for welfare reform, he spoke of *New Beginnings.* George W. Bush invoked the concept of an *Axis of Evil* to put the American public on notice that the War on Terrorism, along with the nation's defense build-up, would continue after Afghanistan. This example illustrates that simplicity, alone, does not good communication make.

Effective political themes and slogans invite people to bring their own meanings to a situation. Thus, an image is an impression anchored partly in symbolic suggestion and partly in the feelings and assumptions that people have in response to that suggestion. Research by communication scholars Doris Graber, Marion Just, Russell Neuman, Ann Crigler, Michael Delli Carpini, and Bruce Williams, among others, shows that people actively construct personal meanings from the evocative symbols and images of media coverage.[40] When people begin to supply the facts and feelings necessary to complete an image, the symbolic message component of political communication seems increasingly real and convincing. This explains why some of the most simplistic and insubstantial ideas produce some of the most heartfelt understandings. For example, when Richard Nixon's campaign strategists assessed his presidential prospects in 1968, they concluded that the biggest problem was the widespread perception that he was a loser. In response, the campaign introduced the symbolic suggestion that there was a "new Nixon," borrowing a classic advertising ploy to revive sagging products. The "new Nixon" became a much-discussed term that created for many people a concrete reference for new political actions that otherwise might have seemed ambiguous or deceitful.[41]

Message Salience

Lots of catchy messages elude popular imagination because they fail to capture widespread attention. The need for a message to capture attention explains why the second goal of image making is to saturate communication channels with the message and to "stay on message" in those communications. The goal of message salience explains why advertisers spend billions of dollars to chant their simple jingles and slogans over and over again in the media. This explains why month after month of the Clinton-Lewinsky scandal involved opponents feeding talk show pundits and journalists a steady message of SEX, SEX, SEX, while justifying this dubious political information by amplifying the Republican congressional message of CLINTON LIED, CLINTON LIED, CLINTON LIED.

Because the environment is full of competing messages, communication consultants are careful to remind (and script) their political clients that whenever the message *du jour* does go out, it must be "on point," which means not complicating the idea, not drifting to other topics, and punching the current political theme until the strategic campaign of the moment has run its course.

Even when they follow their professionally crafted scripts, and *stay on message,* powerful figures may end up the victims of the same news media that helped promote them in the first place. Journalists may simply stop covering an actor who, in their estimation, is no longer delivering the message in dramatic or effective ways. For example, after covering the hundredth campaign appearance with the same speech, journalists may downplay the candidate's message in favor of raising questions about the audience reaction, the delivery, or the wisdom of the campaign communication strategy itself. Alternatively, reporters can reduce the strength of an actor's political signal by boosting the coverage given to opponents' messages. Such are the perils of life in the symbol business; today's truth may become tomorrow's travesty. As discussed later in the chapter, establishing good relations with the press helps to assure that messages will be reported rather than commented upon by journalists in their stories.

Although media decisions about what to play up or down often seem arbitrary or capricious, there are patterns. David Paletz and Robert Entman discovered three conditions surrounding the presidency that seem to affect whether the media will pass along a president's messages without commentary or whether they will dilute message salience with critical commentary or opposing views.[42] The first condition involves the media status of the president. If it is early in his term and he is effective in projecting a strong media image, the news is more likely to give strong emphasis to his chosen messages. Second, the more solemn the occasion or the more important the issue, the more undivided attention his messages will receive. Finally, the greater the perceived elite and public support the president has, the more salient his messages will be. As Paletz and Entman put this last point, "the greater the opposition is believed to be, the more emboldened network correspondents are in their analysis."[43] The Bush administration Iraq War campaign benefited from strong press coverage because the president had presided over a grave national crisis early in his term, and opponents were initially reluctant to face charges of being unpatriotic by challenging his war message.

In view of these patterns, it is easy to understand why politicians are so concerned with their images. In a sense, they are right in thinking that image is everything. Images feed on each other. To the extent that politicians can create appealing leadership images, salience is more likely to be conferred on their specific political pronouncements. To the extent that issues can be made to seem important by calling them "crises," opposing voices are more likely to be drowned out. To the extent that public favor can be won, future messages will receive less criticism, thereby escalating the spiral of popularity, thereby increasing future message salience, and so on.

Message Credibility

Even a public bombarded with salient political messages cannot always be relied on to accept them—even if they hear them often. Salient political messages are more likely to be supported when they are accompanied by some measure of their validity. Most political communication employs some logic, evidence, or authoritative endorsement. In addition, politicians often use staged dramatic settings such as the Oval Office or the deck of an aircraft carrier to lend weight to their announcements. Shocking events may be used to push messages, as when killing sprees are followed by renewed appeals for tougher gun control laws, or terrorist attacks renewed efforts to topple Saddam Hussein.

Message Framing

Simply creating, repeating, and supporting a message are not enough to assure a successful communication strategy. The news is not just an information bulletin board; it is, more importantly, a storytelling process. Stories become pegged to central ideas or categories of meaning, such as sex scandal, government waste, natural disaster, election horse race, terrorism, or weapons of mass destruction, just to name a few. For example, during the Clinton-Lewinsky sex scandal, Republican opponents in Congress were successful in getting across the message that Clinton lied under oath. However, the question for many members of the public and for many members of Congress was whether or not his lying rose to the level of an impeachable offense. Clinton offered a more persuasive framing of the story as a personal matter between him and his family which justified lying to save public embarrassment.

SYMBOLIC POLITICS AND THE TECHNIQUES OF IMAGE MAKING

The goals of image making are fairly straightforward: design a theme or message to spark the imagination, make sure that message dominates communication about the matter at hand, surround the message with a context of credibility, and tell or act out a story that offers the best framing for the message. Simple though they may appear, these goals are not easy to attain.

Effective image making requires a sophisticated understanding and use of communication technologies such as polling, message development in focus groups, market research to see how the message plays, and news management to get the message into the news with the right framing. There is, of course, a good deal of time, energy, resources, and personnel devoted to image making in politics. It has been estimated that anywhere from 30 to 50 percent of the large and well-paid White House staff is involved with media relations in some form.[44] The major preoccupation of the average member of the House of Representatives is running for the next election.[45] The Defense Department spends billions of dollars annually from its huge budget on public relations.[46] The U.S. Army even runs a special school to train its corps of public relations officers.[47] In view of these efforts, one observer has concluded that "the vast, interlocking federal information machine has one primary purpose: the selling of the government."[48]

In the view of communication scholar Jarol Manheim, the technologies of image making today are so advanced that the term *strategic communication* better expresses this sophistication than does the more traditional term *public relations*.[49] What do the political communication experts do? To put it simply, they use symbols in ways calculated to best satisfy the goals of image making.

The Political Uses of Symbols

Symbols are the basic units of most human communication. Words are symbols that stand for objects and ideas. Flags, emblems, and uniforms are symbols of nationalism, group, or authority. Specific people can even symbolize general human attributes like heroism, patriotism, beauty, or greed. Because of the existence of symbols, it is possible to communicate about something without having the object of communication immediately present. Thus, the word *tree* is a symbol that permits communication about trees whether or not a tree is present. The term *nuclear war* permits communication about something that does not exist anywhere except in the human imagination. Because a major preoccupation of politicians and interest groups is how to represent actual situations in the most favorable terms, it is obvious why symbols are so important. Through the skillful use of symbols, actual political circumstances can be redefined.

In order to understand how symbols are used and what makes them effective or ineffective, it is useful to know something about their psychological effects. Every symbol affects us in at least two ways, one *cognitive* and the other *affective*. The cognitive effect refers to the thought and logic engaged by a symbolic message. Affect involves the emotions and feelings triggered by the message. The cognitive associations with a message can be narrow or broad. For example, the term *freedom* has multiple associations for nearly everyone. In contrast, the term *congressional delegation* has a narrow, specific meaning. On the affective side, a symbol may elicit little emotional response or may evoke great outpourings of feeling. For example, the term *freedom* can be used in highly emotional ways, whereas *congressional delegation* provokes relatively little emotion from most people under most circumstances. (However, the term *Congress* can provoke considerable emotional reaction these days.) Symbols that convey narrow meaning with little emotion are called *referential symbols*. Symbols that evoke broad categories of meaning accompanied by strong emotions are called *condensational symbols*.[50] We have even invented symbols to help us talk about symbols!

The kind of image created for a political situation depends on what the key actors want the public to do in the situation. A faction interested in broadening the scope and intensity of public involvement may picture a situation in condensational symbols, whereas a faction seeking to narrow the scope and intensity of public concern can be expected to use referential terms. For example, groups who opposed U.S. involvement in Vietnam represented the bombing of North Vietnam in condensational terms, emphasizing savage destruction, government lying, and dangerous expansion of the war. The government, on the other hand, sought to minimize public concern with the details of the war. Public relations officers in the White House and the Pentagon invented an entire vocabulary of referential symbols to blunt the meanings and feelings attached to military actions. Thus, bombing raids on North Vietnam were referred to as *protective reaction strikes,* a term so narrow and bloodless that only its creators understood precisely what it implied.

In today's high-technology warfare, it is common to hear that enemy positions in Iraq were *removed* with *surgical* precision. Such terms make the news soothing to home audiences, but they may be of little consolation to the people in the battlefield killed near a target that was being surgically removed. *Collateral damage* and *friendly fire* are political code terms to minimize public outrage at the mistaken targeting of innocent people.

Whether a particular symbol has referential or condensational effects depends partly on the symbol and partly on how it is used. In the right context, even the most innocuous referential term can be transformed into a powerful condensational symbol. For example, in the early days of the Vietnam War, the Pentagon used the term *missing in action (MIA)* to refer to the troops missing and unaccounted for in combat. For years, this symbol was a descriptive term with a specific meaning and little emotional charge. Over the years, however, the number of MIAs grew, and many Americans became increasingly disturbed by the failure of anyone to account for these loved ones. Also during this time, the country became polarized into prowar and antiwar factions, making for a highly charged emotional atmosphere. Caught in the middle of this situation, Richard Nixon searched for some effective way of justifying his continued war policies despite broad opposition to them. Suddenly Nixon had his issue. He explained to the public that the breakdowns in his peace negotiations had been due largely to the refusal of the North Vietnamese to promise an accounting of prisoners of war and MIAs. He told the public that he could not end the war and turn his back on those brave soldiers. Seemingly from out of nowhere came demonstrations and endorsement of his position. Bumper stickers proclaimed the plight of the MIAs. In the space of a few months, the change of usage transformed MIA from an obscure referential term to a powerful condensational symbol. The lesson is important: Symbols are not static; their effects (both cognitive and affective) depend on how they are used in specific contexts.

Defining the Political Situation

The flexibility of symbols is a great resource for politicians bent on transforming the real world of politics into a world of realistic political images. So great are the possible gaps between symbol and reality that actors sometimes propose truly absurd or transparent definitions of situations. The frequent absence of feedback or commentary in the news can make the ridiculous appear to be acceptable, if not sublime. For example, a local police department's increase in radar patrol activity triggered angry citizen protests against that spine-chilling condensational symbol, the "speed trap." The department launched a public relations effort to cool off the citizens, reassuring them that the radar activities were no more than "accident prevention patrols" and that worried motorists could call a special number to find out where these patrols were located each day (presumably so that the motorists would be sure to avoid having accidents in those areas).[51]

In another case, the owners of a nuclear power plant that leaked radioactive gas were determined not to let the incident become a major news story like the one that haunted the nuclear power industry following an earlier leak at Three Mile Island in

Pennsylvania. The leak at the Louisa, Virginia, plant was followed by an eleven-hour communication blackout during which time press briefings were scripted for simultaneous delivery at the plant site and at the Nuclear Regulatory Commission headquarters in Washington, D.C. The announcement stated that the plant "burped" a small amount of radioactive gas into the atmosphere. To clarify, the company spokesperson said, "It wasn't a leak, it was more like a burp."[52] The choice of a ridiculous metaphor worked, as the story died quickly.

There are two morals to the above stories. First, if politicians can code complex, ambiguous, or unpopular realities into simple, clear, and pleasing symbols, they probably will do it. Second, grasping what is going on behind the scenes becomes more difficult when the press fails to take issue with the resulting credibility gap. The interplay of politicians' efforts to define political situations and the likelihood of the press to take issue with those definitions largely determines the effectiveness of efforts to manage the news. Political actors try to improve their chances in the news-management game by controlling the terms on which they interact with the press.

NEWS MANAGEMENT: FROM STAGING TO DAMAGE CONTROL

The press displays an odd pattern. In some cases, news organizations seem to be easily seduced by the public relations tactics designed to create the grand illusions (historic deceptions) of political news. In other cases, the press turns petulantly critical, putting the news focus on personal scandals, politicians' failures, and partisan attacks. This odd alternation between being spun and providing knowing commentary may mean that news organizations have only a dim sense of their obligations to the public.[53] In crafting stories, members of the press are more likely to pay attention to each other, to the politicians and political insiders they associate with every day, and to the audience research messages that filter through their editors.

As a result of this reference system, journalists are most tuned into the significance of news within insider political circles. Therefore, it is the maneuvering, spinning, and leaking from within these circles that keep the main stories going from day to day. Even though this odd system may undermine public confidence in both press and politicians, it has become central to the conduct of politics as outlined in earlier chapters. What keeps this illusory news system spinning? The following pages explore various news-making situations, from canned new releases and staged events, to those less controlled situations that can sorely test the spin doctor's art.

Prepackaged News Stories

As it becomes more difficult to get and keep the attention of journalists, newsmakers, and their consultants have developed ever more sophisticated techniques for monitoring public opinion and managing the news flow from the offices of government, business, and interest organizations. According to one estimate, the number of communications professionals in America (150,000) now exceeds the number of journalists

(130,000), and the gap is growing.[54] Consider just two applications of improved technologies for communicating about politics: prefabricated news and strategic polling.

Video News Releases   One result of the growth of the professional communications industry is that television newsrooms today are deluged with so-called VNRs (video news releases) that tempt understaffed and budget-strapped organizations to run public relations materials packaged in news formats. From pharmaceutical companies hawking new wonder drugs to members of Congress trying to remain visible in their home districts, the production of canned news material has become a staple of daily life.

VNRs have been termed the "Hamburger Helper" for news organizations. They generally arrive at newsrooms via satellite feeds similar to the raw feeds that bring the news gathered by actual reporters and wholesale news suppliers. The difference is that VNRs deliver strategic messages wrapped in news packages produced in public relations, advertising, political consulting, or corporate communications offices. The VNR generally arrives in two parts: a completed news segment that can either be run as is or used by producers in the newsroom to understand the story, and a so-called B-roll, which contains the raw footage and a script that can be used to build a story at the station.

A study of TV newsroom decision makers by Nielsen Media Research (the ratings people) revealed that all 110 of those surveyed had put VNRs on the air in the last year. Nielsen also tracks the audiences for various VNRs thanks to hidden electronic codes embedded in the footage. Nielsen reported that a Lockheed Martin Corporation story on the first flight of its F-22 fighter jet was watched by 41 million people. The "news story" fashioned for the release of a Nieman Marcus Christmas catalogue was delivered to an audience of 91 million. Perhaps the most successful VNR to date was the one touting Pfizer's wonder drug Viagra, a VNR that was fed to some 800 stations. According to the estimate of the proud public relations executive who produced it, it was viewed all or in part by 210 million folks.[55] Advertising as effective as such free and authenticating news coverage cannot be bought at any price.

Strategic Polls: The Public as Target   Polling exemplifies another information area in which advancing communications technology is often not used with regard for the highest interests of democracy. Despite advances in opinion polling and the proliferation of survey organizations of all stripes, polls are not typically reported in ways that might help people better understand and participate in political situations. Research by political scientists Alan Monroe, Lawrence Jacobs, and Robert Shapiro indicates that neither politicians nor journalists generally use polls to create more enlightened policy dialogues that might engage the general public. In fact, there is evidence that politicians use polls less often than in earlier years to guide their policy thinking. Today, they most often cite polls as helpful for finding the right language to sell already-made decisions to the public.[56]

Even when news organizations conduct independent polls, they often use them to play up extremes and conflicts, along with incessant ratings of politicians. In the words of Jacobs and Shapiro, polling reports resemble "the journalistic equivalent of a drive-by shooting." Only the numbers that support the dramatic focus of a news story tend to be reported. There is also a tendency in news organizations to exaggerate changes in opinion where there are often none at all. Also, in an estimated 40 percent of all references to polls in news stories, no numbers are reported at all.[57] Political actors have learned to play on these journalistic uses of polling to leak their own polls and to commission seemingly independent surveys to suit their political aims.

Controlling Events: From Staging to Damage Control

Many newsmakers have the resources required to produce professional media events: writers, media directors, costume consultants, access to dramatic settings, and an attentive press corps ready to cover official announcements and events. Careful preparation of events enables control over key elements of the news story: the scene (where), the status of the actor (who), the motives, or ends, the political action is to serve (why), the means through which the action will accomplish its ends (how), and the significance of the political action itself (what). However, some situations are too spontaneous, and some actors are too poor in skills or resources to control the news event. Thus, political manipulation of the news runs along a continuum from fully controlled news events at one end, to uncontrolled events (the political handler's worst nightmare) at the other extreme.

Pseudo-events: Fully Controlled News Situations

Fully controlled media presentations are often called pseudo-events.[58] Pseudo-events disguise actual political circumstances with realistic representations designed to create politically useful images. A pseudo-event uses careful stage setting, scripting, and acting to create convincing images that often have little to do with the underlying reality of the situation. By incorporating fragments of an actual situation into a dramatized presentation, a pseudo-event tempts the viewer to fill in the blanks and build a complete understanding out of fragmentary facts. According to Daniel Boorstin's definition, a pseudo-event has four characteristics:

1. It is not spontaneous but comes about because someone has planned, planted, or incited it.
2. It is planted primarily for the immediate purpose of being reported.
3. Its relation to the underlying reality of the situation is ambiguous.
4. It is intended to be self-fulfilling.[59]

George W. Bush's aircraft carrier landing discussed in the case study in Chapter 2 was a classic pseudo-event: (1) It was anything but spontaneous: it required practice, costuming, and even holding the carrier off the coast; (2) the event was staged purely for newsmaking purposes; (3) the relationship between the swaggering president and his dubious military record was rendered ambiguous by the self-contained performance, and (4) the images of a confident leader and a victory in war were self-fulfilling in the sense that evidence to the contrary was excluded from the performance, and only the claims and images within the staged scene could be judged by the audience—that is, as long as the news coverage mirrored the scripted event.

How effective are pseudo-events in shaping the news? A well-conceived event has such strong story lines that it becomes hard for reporters to find alternative news angles. Even when truly significant spontaneous occurrences find their way by accident into a carefully staged performance, the overall theme of the performance is often strong enough to downplay the spontaneous elements in the plots of resulting news stories. In 1970, for example, Richard Nixon shared his Thanksgiving dinner with a group of wounded Vietnam veterans. The event served the dual purpose of counteracting his image as a cold person and promoting support for his new interest in the human side of the war (i.e., the fate of missing, captured, and wounded troops). When many of the invited soldiers decided to spend the day with their families, the empty places in the White House dining room were filled with staff members from the local naval hospital. On cue, the press was ushered in for a brief picture session. After the dinner, an enterprising reporter decided to interview the soldiers who sat at Nixon's table. During these interviews, the reporter discovered the bombshell news that Nixon had mentioned, that a daring attempt had been made to rescue American prisoners from a North Vietnamese POW camp. This disclosure was big news on several accounts. First, the raid involved an offensive mission into North Vietnam, risking a possible escalation of the war during a period of intense peace efforts. Second, the secretary of defense and other officers of the administration had lied repeatedly under oath during congressional testimony, claiming that no such raids had taken place. Finally, the raid had been a failure, indicating possible breakdowns in U.S. intelligence and special forces capabilities. Despite the importance of these factors, the reporter and his editors at the *Washington Post* decided to lead the story with the "President spends Thanksgiving with the troops" angle and to use this as the headline. Nixon's disclosure was buried in later paragraphs of the article.[60]

During a time of chaos in the aftermath of the Iraq War, George W. Bush flew from his Texas ranch to join the troops for Thanksgiving, producing a big news story around the angle that Mr. Bush had effectively fooled the press as to his whereabouts. The image projected by this and visits to Iraq by other administration officials was that Iraq was far safer than news images of chaos made it appear.

Partially Controlled News Situations

Some political situations are not as easy to control as Thanksgiving dinner with the troops or a landing on an aircraft carrier. Many public settings have an element of spontaneity in them. For example, press conferences can be controlled insofar as choice of time, place, and opening remarks, but they always contain some risk of unexpected or hostile questions from the press. In other cases, an official may be surprised by an issue and asked to comment, even though he or she is unprepared to do so. Perhaps such hard-to-control features explain why modern presidents hold far fewer press conferences than their pretelevision-era predecessors.

When the comforting script of a pseudo-event is unavailable, political actors must resort to other means of protecting desired images. A common means of handling partially controlled situations is to anticipate and prevent possible moments of spontaneity in advance. For example, press conferences are often structured tightly to promote desired messages and prevent spontaneous distractions. In a press conference, opening remarks are intended to set the tone and make the headlines, reporters can be called on or ignored, time limits can be imposed, and stage settings can be manipulated. Some officials grant interviews only if certain ground rules are agreed to by reporters. Those ground rules often stipulate that some sensitive remarks may be branded as off the record and thereby censored from reporters' stories. In general, the handlers for most politicians plan public appearances to avoid spontaneous settings, particularly those with reporters present.

Sometimes the most effective means of operating in a hard-to-control situation is to stay out of public settings and release information through an anonymous news leak. Leaks are useful for delivering messages in many unstable situations. In some cases, an official may favor a policy but not know how the public will react. An anonymous leak describing the policy gives the official a chance to change course if the opposition is too strong. In other cases, the information leaked is privileged or secret, thereby presenting problems for any kind of formal public release. In other cases, a political message is not important enough to be guaranteed coverage if released through normal press channels or presented as a pseudo-event. If the right reporter is given a scoop based on the information, however, the chances are pretty good that the story will receive special attention. Strong emphasis given to a story by one news outlet may prompt others to cover it the next day. This use of leaks was acknowledged humorously when Ronald Reagan opened a press conference by saying that he did not have an opening remark because his planned statement was so important that he had decided to leak it instead.

Leaks also offer control over one of the most important variables in partially controlled situations: timing. The timing of a leak or a press release is crucial. For example, it is common wisdom that bad news is best released on weekends when reporters are off duty, news programs are scarce, and the public is distracted from worldly concerns. In other cases, the issue of timing means getting the jump on opponents who may attempt to plant their own images about a situation. Consider the case of a Reagan administration budget leak. The year was 1983. The proposed budget was a political disaster. There were huge deficits where Reagan had promised a balanced budget. There were painful cuts in already weakened social programs. To top it all off, the country was in serious economic trouble. The news management goal was to soften the blow of more bad news. Normally, the budget is delivered to the press on a Friday with a strict embargo not to publish any stories about it until after the president delivers his budget message to Congress and the nation on Monday. The early release allows reporters to digest the huge mass of information in order to write stories around the president's message. The embargo ensures that the president's message will be the salient news theme at the start of the week. The Reagan media staff evidently decided that the budget was such a potential news disaster that the budget director leaked the budget on Friday by "forgetting" his copy in a congressional hearing room following a high-level congressional briefing. In a few hours, the budget had found its way into the hands of newspeople without the usual embargo. The story that would have dominated Monday's headlines was, instead, scattered across the less-visible weekend news channels. By Monday, the budget was old news. When asked about the apparent leak, White House Communication Director David Gergen denied it and explained that the embargo stamp had been omitted "accidentally" from the budget books taken to the briefing.[61]

Another advantage of leaks is that the source is often protected by journalists who strike a deal of secrecy to obtain the story. This means that leakers often have an important degree of control over how the story will be told. Because journalists must generally craft the story to make it appear self-contained and removed from its source, leaked stories can often be highly damaging to targeted opponents simply because the whole story and the politics behind it are not told.

Uncontrolled News Situations

Few things strike more fear in the heart of a politician than a news story that has gotten out of control. Sometimes control of a story is lost because the underlying reality of a situation is simply too big to hide, as was the case with Lyndon Johnson's increasingly empty assurances that the United States was winning the war in Vietnam. In some cases, former insiders blow the cover on a story, as happened when John Dean delivered his damaging Watergate testimony against Richard Nixon or when former war strategist Daniel Ellsberg leaked secret government documents about Vietnam. In many instances, a story gets out of control when a politician fails to handle the pressures of a partially controlled situation. A classic case in point was Gerald Ford's blunder during a presidential debate when he claimed there was no Soviet domination in eastern Europe.

Whatever the reason for loss of control, the *damage control* imperative is to once again contain reality behind a screen of politically advantageous and controlled images. Although there is no magic formula for turning out-of-control situations into fully controlled public relations bonanzas, there are important news management techniques that politicians ignore only at their peril. Presidents not only experience more media pressure than most politicians, but they also have more resources to manage the press. Thus it is not surprising that the most sophisticated methods for news control have emerged from presidential press operations. As research by John Anthony Maltese shows, the White House press operation grew phenomenally both in size and sophistication during the half-century from Truman to Clinton.[62] The case study and the presidential profiles in the next section illustrate the key ingredients of presidential news management.

NEWS MANAGEMENT STYLES AND THE MODERN PRESIDENCY

When Harry Truman ordered atomic bombs to be dropped on Japan in 1945, he personally broke the news to a White House press corps that numbered twenty-five reporters. Bill Clinton arrived in Washington to find that more than 1,700 reporters cover the White House, and a total of 2,800 people including television producers, technicians, and other crew members were allowed to pass through the press entrance of the president's residence.[63] It is hard to imagine any politician interacting with such a crowd in the absence of considerable staging, planning, and scripting, and so the White House press operations have grown along with, and sometimes ahead of, the press corps.

Richard Nixon created the White House Office of Communications with the aim of controlling the flow of information out of the entire executive branch and staging events that would reduce the press to passive transmitters of political messages. This idea of "going over the heads of the press" to communicate directly with the people has been termed *going public* by political scientist Samuel Kernell.[64] These goals were disrupted in Nixon's case when the Watergate affair and a series of congressional investigations aroused a press pack that followed a trail of scandal that led eventually to the Oval Office.

Elected on a promise to restore trust in government, Jimmy Carter neglected news management with a possibly foolish determination to run a White House that was open to the press. With plot assists from a struggling economy, opponents in Congress, and an embarrassing 444 days of news about Americans being held hostage in Iran, the media helped the voters send Carter out of Washington with unpopularity levels approaching those suffered by Richard Nixon in the polls. It was not until the Reagan presidency that the White House Office of Communications was fully developed into the well-oiled public relations machine that helped turn Reagan into the Great Communicator.

Ronald Reagan

The textbook on how to manage the news was written during the Reagan administration. It is open for others to follow. Few politicians may attempt or even want to manage the press as completely as the Reagan communication staff did, but relations between press and politicians will never be the same again. What does the textbook say about media management for politicians? The first step is to adopt the proper frame of mind. As former White House Communication Director David Gergen put it: "To govern successfully, the government has to set the agenda; it cannot let the press set the agenda for it."[65] How did Mr. Gergen achieve this goal? According to an analysis by Mark Hertsgaard, here is the step-by-step method:[66]

1. Weekly long-term strategy meetings of policy officers and press handlers to plan the future news agenda and assess the results of ongoing media control efforts.

2. Daily meetings of the White House communication group to decide, as one member put it, "What do we want the press to cover today, and how?"[67] According to Michael Deaver, one of the masterminds of the press operation in the Reagan years: "We would take a theme, which we usually worked on for six weeks—say, the economy. The President would say the same thing, but we had a different visual for every one of [the regularly scheduled media events]."[68]

3. As the previous step indicates, *repetition* is the key. Feed the press the same message with a new (and therefore newsworthy) visual setting to satisfy the media need for changing video footage and new photo opportunities. As Deaver recalled, "It used to drive the President crazy because the repetition was so important. He'd get on that airplane and look at that speech and say, 'Mike, I'm not going to give this same speech on education again, am I?' I said, 'Yeah, trust me, it's going to work.' And it did."[69]

4. Put out the line of the day to all the other potential newsmakers in the executive branch to "make sure we're all saying the same thing" to the press.[70] During the

Reagan years, the line of the day was sent out over a computer network to all administration offices. All that any official had to do was call it up on his or her screen before meeting with reporters.

5. Coordinate the day's news via conference calls to top administration officials to make sure they understand the line of the day and to orchestrate which officials will say something, when they will say it, and who will keep their mouths shut, as in "Look, the President's got a statement tomorrow, so shut up today, goddammit, just shut up, don't preempt the President, [we'll] cut your nuts off if you leak anything out on this one. . . ."[71]

6. Work the press and call reporters and their bosses to see if they understood the story correctly. This has become known as "spin control." During the Reagan years, the White House made it a regular practice to call the national TV network executives just prior to their nightly newscasts to check on what they were running and to offer additional clarification on the stories.

7. Weekly seminars held for the spokespeople of the various federal bureaucracies to educate them on how to present the administration to the press.

8. A heavy volume of opinion polling and market research to see what was on the public mind and how the president could tap into it through the news. The White House even conducted its own market research on the public images of such news people as news anchor Peter Jennings, columnist George Will, reporter Sam Donaldson, and a host of others in order to decide to whom to give scoops, to whom to give interviews, and whom to treat more or less deferentially. In assessing marketing chief Richard Wirthlin's award-winning performance, one observer concluded that the mapmaker of the public mind "probed just about every aspect of public affairs on a scale unmatched in U.S. history."[72]

There you have it. Follow the eight easy steps, set the media stage, introduce a president who is comfortable with the TV lights and cameras, and you have the Great Communicator, someone whose message is on point, salient, credible, and effectively framed. The Reagan press management plan was so effective that chief image maker, Richard Wirthlin, was crowned Advertising Man of the Year in 1989. He did not receive his industry's top award for his creative work for General Foods or Mattel Toys, but for his accomplishments as director of consumer research for Ronald Reagan.[73] Another measure of the success of the Reagan press program is that even when the press attempted to be critical, the efforts seldom produced results that stuck to the so-called Teflon coating that seemed to protect the president from the press.

The classic case of news management operating with even a critical press involves CBS News correspondent Lesley Stahl, who put together a long report showing the gaps between Ronald Reagan's carefully styled news images and his actual policies in office. Stahl was nervous about the piece because of its critical tone and the practice of the White House Communications Office to call reporters and their employers about negative coverage. The phone rang after the report was aired, and it was "a senior White House official." Stahl prepared herself for the worst. In her own words, here is what happened:

> And the voice said, "Great piece."
> I said, "What?"

And he said, "Great piece!"

I said, "Did you listen to what I said?"

He said, "Lesley when you're showing four-and-a-half minutes of great pictures of Ronald Reagan, no one listens to what you say. Don't you know that the pictures are overriding your message because they conflict with your message? The public sees those pictures and they block your message. They didn't even hear what you said. So, in our minds, it was a four-and-a-half-minute free ad for the Ronald Reagan campaign for reelection."

I sat there numb. I began to feel dumb 'cause I'd covered him four years and I hadn't figured it out. Somebody had to explain it to me. Well none of us had figured it out. I called the executive producer of the *Evening News* . . . and he went dead on the phone. And he said, "Oh, my God."[74]

There it was. The textbook news management system worked even with uncooperative reporters. TV is the medium through which most people get their news. When politicians and their handlers are careful to stage their public appearances for the right production values (i.e., to convey the right visual images), reporters are denied the video evidence they need to back up a hard-hitting script. As one of the Reagan news wizards put it bluntly, "What are you going to believe, the facts or your eyes?"[75]

George Herbert Walker Bush

It is clear that George Bush's (1989–1992) White House did not set out to manage the media as completely as the communications group did during the Reagan era. Even Lesley Stahl could be heard almost complaining about the "night and day" difference, saying about the Bush administration that "This White House doesn't care if the president gets on the evening news or not."[76] Another reporter responded by saying, "That's not an impeachable offense—yet—but it does raise some interesting questions. Not least for the White House press corps, which seems to be looking back on the slick, well-packaged Reagan presidency with a touch of—can it be?—Nostalgia."[77]

Media criticism of Bush's unwillingness to manipulate the press became too much to tolerate, and the White House soon brought back the media team that got him elected. For example, former public relations executive Sig Rogich, who had produced several Bush campaign commercials in 1988, came to the White House as Special Assistant to the President for Activities and Initiatives (i.e., chief image maker).[78] Rogich was rewarded for helping to restore the Bush image by being named ambassador to Iceland. In 1992, Bush once again forgot the lessons of news and image management, and Mr. Rogich was recalled from Iceland to produce Bush campaign commercials. However, Rogich and the other image doctors arrived too late; the Bush media-management team was far too disorganized during the 1992 campaign to save the president's image or his reelection.

Bill Clinton

Although Clinton displayed little enthusiasm for it, news management became an early preoccupation of the Clinton political operation. Indeed, it had to be, considering the attacks on his draft record and his sex life during the 1992 campaign. Yet Clinton flirted dangerously with ignoring the press, sometimes trying to circumvent the news altogether. During his first election campaign, when the press became too concerned with Clinton's personal problems, the candidate went directly to the people through appearances on *60 Minutes,* MTV, various talk shows, and specially produced electronic town hall programs that created the illusion of intimacy with audiences. When his media image improved, the Clinton news team staged events like the direct-to-the-voter bus tours that sparked considerable positive coverage from the press. However, after the election, Clinton apparently continued to seethe about the personal press attacks he had suffered during the campaign. Convinced that as president Clinton could go over the heads of the news media, the Clinton team closed off the hallway between the press room and the White House press office and kept the presidential press pack at a distance. The results were devastating. Clinton became the object of massive journalistic criticism. As the *Washington Post* editorial page editor Meg Greenfield put it, she had never seen an administration "pronounced dead" so early.[79]

At last, Clinton brought none other than David Gergen on board to manage his press operations. When Gergen was allowed to implement press management techniques, Clinton's news control visibly improved. However, Clinton's continuing personal frictions with the press corps did not make Gergen's job easy, and he was never given the freedom to run the Clinton press operation that he had been granted under Reagan. This reluctance to give full reign to the "Sultan of Spin" (as Gergen was dubbed by journalists) remains puzzling in light of a report that the communication style that Clinton most admired was that of Ronald Reagan.[80]

Despite the rocky relations with the press that continued through the impeachment ordeal of his second term, Clinton managed to communicate fairly effectively by continuing to "go public." His staff staged numerous controlled events—including ceremonies on the White House lawn, world travels, weekly radio talks, and frequent announcements of policy goals and accomplishments—that gave him opportunities to share his easy media style with audiences who continued to support him with remarkable levels of approval. One of those gatherings on the White House lawn later came back to haunt Clinton: The scene of the president giving a warm hug to Monica Lewinsky later became endlessly replayed as one of the news icons condensing the scandal for television audiences. Yet Clinton's familiar on-screen character of the humble "comeback kid" continued to overcome those damaging images in the eyes of a majority of citizens, even as his resilience astounded political opponents and the press alike.

George W. Bush

For all of its conflicts with the press, and perhaps due to the run of crises and scandals it had to confront, the Clinton administration communication strategy maintained a fairly traditional emphasis on spinning the daily news through direct encounters between communication officers and the national press corps. The George W. Bush administration shifted its press strategy to an event-based news making program that often left the press on the sidelines to transmit well-controlled dramatic images to their audiences. The Bush communication staff of forty-four was roughly the size of Clinton's (forty-two), but they were deployed differently. Where Clinton had twenty-four of these working in the national press office, the Bush press contact staff was half that size. A majority of the communications staff were employed as "event planners, speech writers, and media affairs specialists whose job it is to reach out to journalists beyond the beltway."[81]

Mr. Bush spent much of his early term in office continuing to make quasi-campaign appearances around the country, using events as contexts for messages about policy proposals such as education and tax cuts. The strategic focus was less on briefing and informing the press corps than on offering them controlled events containing political messages that the president had little interest in expanding beyond their sound bite salience. Presidential communication scholar Martha Kumar explains the Bush shift toward communication and event strategies and away from press office activities: "The difference is that communications operations are about persuasion, while the press office is about information. The Bush people want to develop a message and stay on it. They use the press office to deliver that message and not answer a lot of questions about it."[82] The result was that the administration suffered few leaks, gave few interviews, and seldom got caught (as the Clinton administration often did) trying to explain differences among statements from different officials. Bush's first press secretary Ari Fleischer summed it up by saying, "When the administration has something to announce, it will announce it."[83]

One week of the Bush presidency involved six days of cross-country stops, including opening the 2002 Winter Olympics in Salt Lake. The Olympics made big national news, but many of the lesser stops received little or no coverage from the national press corps. The White House communication strategy was aimed elsewhere: to secure regional coverage that it regarded as more valuable in terms of its goal of getting messages to voters that it needed to cement for the upcoming election more than two years off. For example, a stop in Florida at Eglin Air Force Base produced a controlled but noisily friendly crowd of military personnel for his message asking Congress to support his defense spending increase. This pseudo-event received an impressive eighty-six television reports in Florida's seven broadcast markets according to Video Monitoring Service.[84]

After 9/11 happened, the Bush team controlled the news with a vengeance. With a combination of intimidation (see the case study in Chapter 1) and well-managed events of the sort described in the case study in Chapter 2, the administration exercised a remarkable degree of control over events that seemed constantly on the verge of spiraling out of control. Perhaps the Bush team recalled how press coverage turned against the president's father only months after he rode a then record wave of popularity following the Gulf War. As with all press control operations, the potential for a press feeding frenzy to turn against Mr. Bush awaited the next scandal, economic downturn, crisis in Iraq, or well-orchestrated campaign by the Democrats.

Because politicians and reporters come into such intimate and often uneasy contact, the news game frequently extends beyond the methods of news control previously described. Personal social relations and occasional displays of intimidation also affect what gets reported. The next section explores some of these less formal aspects of press relations.

PRESS RELATIONS: FEEDING THE BEAST

Beyond the choice of symbols, the staging of news events, and the development of a news management strategy, the daily working relations between reporters and news-makers can play a major part in the willingness of reporters to transmit all the news that politicians deem fit to print. Most newsmakers strive to maintain cooperative relations with the press by scheduling press conferences and issuing releases at times convenient for making deadlines; offering scoops and exclusive interviews to friendly reporters; and even wining and dining a press corps eager to bask in the limelight of the famous and powerful. It may be that former ABC and current FOX news correspondent Brit Hume was more critical of Bill Clinton than George H. W. Bush because he was more comfortable with Bush's brand of politics. (Recall from an earlier discussion that Hume later became the top journalist anchoring the right-of-center marketing strategy for FOX news.) However, it should not be overlooked that Hume's personal stock also plunged sharply from one administration to the next. He went from being a favored news carrier, and sometime tennis partner for Bush, to being barred (along with the rest of the press corps) from the corridor that linked the press room to the White House press office in the early (i.e., pre-Gergen) Clinton administration. One should not underestimate the degree to which the personal treatment of journalists can shape the tone of news coverage, particularly inside the closed social world of the nation's capital.

Care and Feeding

Perhaps it is no accident that members of the Clinton press staff referred to the press corps down the hall and past the locked door as "the beast." Yet locking the door between the White House press room and the communication offices only made the beast angry. Simple courtesies, by contrast, can pay big dividends in terms of controlling the timing, content, and amount of coverage. For example, shortly after Ronald Reagan became president, he attended a major North-South economic summit conference in Mexico. Reagan's foreign policy prowess was under its first major test, and there were many potentially damaging criticisms of U.S. policies among the Latin American delegates. (At the time, the region suffered under several U.S.-backed wars, dire poverty, and numerous failed economic development initiatives.) Although a huge press entourage accompanied Reagan, few of those reporters ventured beyond the comfortable American compound to find out how other countries viewed such problems in the region. Few negative stories came from a well-fed and carefully handled U.S. press corps. As one observer put it:

> Reagan brought an enormous White House press corps. If the spokesmen for the poorer countries thought that meant access to the American media, which rarely discuss the issues of development, they were in for a surprise. "We'll try to feed you as often as possible," Secretary of State Alexander Haig promised at an early briefing in the makeshift White House press room, situated in the basement of the hotel where most of the American reporters stayed. The Reagan administration did feed the media, and many American journalists' accounts of what happened [at the conference] came straight from that official source. Some

members of the White House press spent an entire week without meeting a single foreign delegate.[85]

In contrast, as noted previously, the Clinton administration closed itself off from the Washington journalism corps—quite literally, by shutting the door between the press room and the White House communication offices. Other affronts to the comfort level of journalists further compounded press relations, including the firing of key staff in the White House travel office with whom reporters had developed helpful personal relationships in earlier administrations. The so-called Travelgate scandal surrounding the Clinton reorganization of the travel office was one of the first negative news stories on the administration, and it continued to pop up in the news years later.

Cooperation with the media extends beyond the care and feeding of reporters to the scheduling of major news events so they don't conflict with entertainment programming that generates ratings and revenues for the TV networks. Times have changed since the golden days of broadcasting, when a political broadcast gave prestige to a network and saved the production costs of live programs. According to an analysis by Joe Foote,

> During 1934, the year Congress was writing the Federal Communications Act, the two networks managed to find free time for 350 speeches by Congressmen and Senators, an average of nearly one program a day. . . . These political broadcasts substituted in many ways for news programs that were just then coming into their own and demonstrated the networks' commitment to public service.[86]

Now the problem of media access is a much more delicate economic matter resolved for the most part by running political messages during the regularly allocated news slots on the broadcast networks. Politicians' attempts to communicate with the American people at other times can cost a network upward of $200,000 for every thirty-second commercial spot it loses when a political broadcast preempts an entertainment program. Failure to cooperate with corporate economic realities can cool political relations with the media, as David Gergen explained about his experiences in the Reagan White House:

> I would never call and say we're going to do a speech on Tuesday night at 8 o'clock without first asking what's on the air that night. Our television guy would look it up and determine how much of a problem it was going to be with the network. It was idiotic, if they've got *Dynasty* on, to try to schedule something. That has to be a matter of discretion [otherwise] you heard from them. They would tell you very informally that this is a problem for us. "And this is part of the scorecard we have with you guys." I was aware at all times what our relative standing was with the network—whether we were in good standing, bad standing. You could take too much. You could go out and try to gouge them, play them as the enemy, etc. I felt there was a different way to play. If you do it very professionally, you'll get more out of them.[87]

Later, when Gergen became special communication counsel to President Clinton, he would find press relations a bit more challenging. Perhaps because of the icy relations between the Clinton staff and the Washington press corps, or perhaps because the media felt too easily manipulated during the Reagan years, two of the three major networks refused to carry Clinton's first press conference live.[88] However, even in the rocky era of Clinton press relations, the president remained the subject most likely to motivate the three big networks to preempt prime time (7 P.M. to 11 P.M.) programming. In the first year-and-a-half of the Clinton presidency, one or more networks preempted their prime time schedules for eleven events. Seven of those occasions featured Bill Clinton in controlled (e.g., Oval Office speeches, State of the Union addresses) or semicontrolled (e.g., press conferences) events. Two involved the death and funeral of a former president, Richard Nixon. One involved a major earthquake in Los Angeles. The final occasion, and, incidentally, the one that received the largest prime time preemption, was a low-speed freeway police chase involving former football-star-turned-actor, O. J. Simpson. That episode was witnessed by a captive audience of ninety-five million people who had tuned in their chosen Friday night programs.[89]

Intimidation

Even in the most clubby of relations between political sources and the journalists who cover them, some exercise of intimidation may come into play. Indeed, the interplay of intimidation and cooperation strategies can be quite sophisticated, as indicated by another example from the media-management lore of the Reagan years. When the war in El Salvador became dramatic enough in the early 1980s to warrant regular news coverage, the venerable *New York Times* sent a bright young reporter named Ray Bonner to cover it. Unfortunately, Bonner was inexperienced in the fine points of press-government cooperation and had the audacity to develop contacts among rebel leaders fighting the U.S.-backed government. Some of Bonner's early stories suggested that the rebels had considerable popular support, while the regime proclaimed "democratic" by U.S. officials had engaged repeatedly in terrorism, torture, intimidation, and massacre of its own people. Such intrusive realities contradicting the daily line of the White House became too much for the administration to bear. Not only was Bonner snubbed repeatedly at the U.S. embassy in San Salvador (a serious problem for a journalist dependent on official reactions to all stories), but *Times* Executive Editor Abe Rosenthal paid a visit to San Salvador, where he held a meeting with U.S. ambassador Deane Hinton. According to a "well-placed" reporter on the *Times,* Ambassador Hinton "became hysterical" about Bonner's critical reporting and flagrant disregard for the daily news images preferred by the administration. Although Rosenthal denied being influenced by the embassy, he recalled Bonner from El Salvador.[90]

Bonner's replacement was a reporter with no experience in the region. No sooner had the *Times* made the change than the embassy changed its press strategy to one of cooperation and opened its arms, doors, and reception rooms once again to the news-hungry press corps. A new press officer was appointed, and daily briefings on the war were resumed. The briefings were warm, witty, and filled with newsworthy quotes. The result of a new era of cooperation? *Times* coverage swung clearly toward the official definition of the situation with the story of the day making the headlines of the day. Coverage of grassroots issues and popular sentiments in El Salvador all but disappeared in the new era of cooperative relations. The successful attack on an organization as prestigious as the *New York Times* sent shock waves through the rest of the media. According to a reporter for another paper, Bonner's transfer "left us all aware that the embassy is quite capable of playing hard ball," and as a result, "people treat it carefully. If they can kick out *The Times* correspondent, you've got to be careful."[91]

The irony—and the moral—of this story is that more than a decade later, and long after the wars had ended, much of Bonner's early critical reporting was backed up with independent evidence. After the war ended, teams of United Nations investigators discovered mass graves in El Mozote, the site of one of the early Salvadoran army massacres of civilians reported by Bonner. Other sources reported that U.S. officials involved in directing the war knew about such incidents at the same time they were publicly denying them and discrediting the journalists who reported them. A front page *New York Times* article in 1993 finally confirmed what the *Times* had removed Ray Bonner for reporting a dozen years earlier:

> The Reagan Administration knew more than it publicly disclosed about some of the worst human rights abuses in El Salvador's civil war and withheld that information from Congress, declassified cables and interviews with former government officials indicate.
>
> Charges that Reagan officials, and to a lesser extent the Carter and Bush Administrations, may have covered up evidence of abuses to win Congressional approval of about $6 billion in aid were revived with the release this week of a United Nations-sponsored report.[92]

After the government and the press finally set the record straight in 1993, a colleague of Bonner's offered the consolation that it took the Roman Catholic Church hundreds of years to reverse its condemnation of Galileo for (among other things) claiming that the sun and stars did not revolve around the earth. He sent a message to Bonner in the form of a headline: "Bonner and Galileo Still Right after All These Years."[93] It is nice to know that the record was finally set straight. However, correcting misinformation from 1981 twelve years after the fact surely captured little interest on the part of most Americans. Indeed, that is the great lesson of news management: Information is political, and the construction of images that fit political agendas is the object of the news game. Thus, the Bush administration intimidation campaign against critics of its Iraq policies may have been good politics, but the results were bad for public comprehension of a fateful war.

GOVERNMENT AND THE POLITICS OF NEWSMAKING

As explained in the first chapter, the news remains, for all its failings, crucial to governing. At the same time, the relationships among the key players in the American information system—the people, politicians, and the press—have entered a vicious political cycle:

- As the space for serious news shrinks due to economic calculations, political actors must rely on communication consultants and professional media staff to develop strategies to capture that precious space for their messages.

- How do they capture news space? By using technologies of market research and persuasion to stage, script, and spin news for its most dramatic media effect.
- Given the changes in the news business, the newsmaking potential of political messages and staged events goes up as the complexity and information richness of their messages goes down.
- Stories are increasingly told to, by, and for political insiders, leaving citizens out of the democratic picture. The result is a spiral of public disillusionment with both politics and the news.

In short, we have entered an age in which the demand for news drama fuels the strategic communication process, and the media operations of politicians, government offices, and interest organizations generally supply more than enough news to meet the demand.[94] Much as they may resent their own side of the news game for its shallowness and artificiality, politicians who think their positions are secure enough to rest their news-management operations often wake up to their own demise in the news. The case of George Bush losing his popularity so soon after winning the Gulf War is just one case in point.

To make matters worse, the advent of the twenty-four-hour news cycle means that the news never sleeps. There must be developments even when there are none to report. As journalists become ever more active in keeping stories going, they need reactions and dramatic material from political actors. Failure to "feed the beast" with new installments of a story can result in being on the losing end of a story fed by opponents, instead. In those rare cases in which the supply fails to anticipate demand, journalists are pressured to crank up a story of their own to fill the news space. For example, the presidential election of 2000 was more than a year-and-a-half away, and the primaries had not even been held, when Republican candidate George W. Bush was declared the front-runner by the national press, and incumbent Democratic Vice President Al Gore was declared to have a problem-plagued campaign. In the 2004 presidential election, the amazing rise of former Vermont Governor Howard Dean was soon tempered by stories that he was unelectable because he was too liberal or too angry. Perhaps he was simply too preoccupied communicating directly with the growing ranks of his supporters through the uses of Internet technologies to spend resources trying to manage the Washington press corps.

Those who market ideas for a living learn quickly that dramatized events, spin, rumor, and reaction are helpful to journalists trying to operate within the low-budget, high-hype constraints of the twenty-four-hour news cycle. A classic example was the masterfully produced Gulf War against Iraq in 1991. Vast national and international audiences witnessed live shots of bombing behind enemy lines, followed by battle briefings from the military commanders themselves. Like so many other events on the planet, war can now be brought to us live, in our own homes, complete with rock-and-roll sound tracks, dazzling computer graphics, and instant analyses from experts who resemble the color commentators on sports events. Not surprisingly, the audience ratings for the Gulf War were extremely high and, despite legions of journalists on the scene in the Persian Gulf, almost all the material needed to supply the nonstop news spectacle was supplied by government press managers in Washington. The Iraq War of 2003 managed to top its predecessor by embedding reporters in military units, creating a sense of breathless identification with the soldiers in combat, and leaving the high-level impressions of how the war was going almost entirely to the Defense Department and the White House.

Reporters are well aware that most of what they cover is heavily managed, but they generally try to create the impression that they are on the outside of events looking in. Sometimes these efforts create almost comical results in which the news intrudes upon and shapes the very realities that it appears to represent. A memorable example of this occurred when the United States joined a humanitarian United Nations mission to bring food to Somalia in 1992. The first troops to hit the beaches met with a surrealistic scene. Navy Seals in full camouflage attire and battle gear were startled by journalists, television cameras ablaze, who had already secured the beaches to record the landing for the nightly news back home.[95] Even when journalists attempt to resist the spin, as on the election campaign trail where the same speech is delivered day in and day out, the results often leave journalists awkwardly inserting themselves in stories to the point that they overshadow the politicians they are covering.

This news system does not make many of its players look good. Polls typically show press and politicians competing for last place in the race for public approval. Meanwhile, politicians quietly bemoan the low levels of public understanding of most issues and the selfish attitudes of citizens that hamper solutions for many public problems. This syndrome was summed up by West Virginia Senator Jay Rockefeller who told a group of reporters:

> Voters . . . are angry with politicians like me. And they're angry with you in the media. Well, let me tell you something. The voters are no bargains, either.[96]

In this age of mediated politics, power is, to an important extent, a communication process that must be monitored and maintained by political actors. As a result of the technologies of strategic communications (polling, market research, news and image management), the news is not just a record of events, it is an event in and of itself—an integral part of the political process linking politicians and people in the struggle for government power.

NOTES

1. From William Pfaff, "Yalta Only Symbol," *Seattle Post-Intelligencer,* January 26, 1982, A11.
2. Dean Acheson, *Present at the Creation: My Years in the State Department* (New York: Norton, 1969), 375.
3. See W. Lance Bennett, Patricia Dempsey Harris, Janet K. Laskey, Alan H. Levitch, and Sarah E. Monrad, "Deep and Surface Images in the Construction of Political Issues: The Case of Amnesty," *Quarterly Journal of Speech* 62 (April 1976): 109–126.
4. See Bruce Miroff, *Pragmatic Illusions: The Presidential Politics of John F. Kennedy* (New York: Longman, 1976).
5. See David Wise, *The Politics of Lying* (New York: Vintage, 1973).
6. See William Greider, "The Education of David Stockman," *Atlantic* (December 1981): 27–54.
7. See Richard Barnet, *Roots of War* (Baltimore: Penguin, 1972).

8. For a more detailed discussion of this incident, see Wise, *Politics of Lying,* Chapter 5.

9. Leon V. Sigal, *Reporters and Officials: The Organization and Politics of News Reporting* (Lexington, MA: Heath, 1973), 124. (Percentages total slightly over 100 due to rounding.)

10. Ibid., 122.

11. Ibid., 122.

12. See, for example, Daniel C. Hallin, Robert Karl Manoff, and Judy K. Weddle, "Sourcing Patterns of National Security Reporters" (paper presented at the annual meeting of the American Political Science Association, San Francisco, August 30–September 2, 1990) and Jane Delano Brown, Carl R. Bybee, Stanley T. Wearden, and Dulcie Murdock, "Invisible Power: Newspaper Sources and the Limits of Diversity," *Journalism Quarterly* 64 (1987): 45–54.

13. Steven Livingston and W. Lance Bennett, "Gatekeeping, Indexing, and Live Event News: Is Technology Altering the Construction of News?" *Political Communication* 20, no. 4 (October-December 2003): 363–80.

14. W. Lance Bennett, "Toward a Theory of Press-State Relations in the United States," *Journal of Communication* 40, no. 2 (1990): 103–27.

15. Thomas E. Patterson, "Doing Well and Doing Good: How Soft News and Critical Journalism Are Shrinking the News Audience and Weakening Democracy—and What News Outlets Can Do About It," Harvard University: Joan Shorenstein Center on Press, Politics, and Public Policy, 2000.

16. Edie Goldenberg, *Making the Papers* (Lexington, MA: Heath-Lexington Books, 1975).

17. "Bush Knew Iraq Info Was Dubious," CBS News, July 10, 2003. **www.cbs.com.**

18. Walter Pincus, "Little Words, Big Implications: 'Strategic Coordination' May Have Led to an Allegation about Iraq Being Repeated," *Washington Post National Weekly Edition,* April 11–17, 2003, 11.

19. James Risen, "Hussein Warned Iraqis to Beware Outside Fighters, Document Says," *New York Times,* January 14, 2004, A1.

20. Richard W. Stevenson, "Bush Disputes Ex-Official's Claim That War With Iraq Was Early Administration Goal," *New York Times,* January 13, 2004, A22.

21. Sherly Gay Stolberg, "Kennedy Says War in Iraq Was Choice, Not Necessity," *New York Times,* January 15, 2004, A13.

22. See, for example, Robert M. Entman, *Projections of Power: Framing News, Public Opinion, and U.S. Foreign Policy.* (Chicago: University of Chicago Press, 2004).

23. Barton Gellman and Walter Pincus, "Errors and Exaggerations: Prewar Depictions of Iraq's Nuclear Threat Outweighed the Evidence," *Washington Post National Weekly Edition,* August 18–24, 2003, 6.

24. "With Few Variations, Top Administration Advisors Present Their Case," *New York Times,* September 9, 2002. **www.nyt.com.**

25. Todd S. Purdham, "Bush Officials Say Time Has Come for Action in Iraq," *New York Times,* September 9, 2002. **www.nyt.com.**

26. Walter Lippmann, *Public Opinion* (New York: Free Press, 1922), 9.

27. Acheson, *Present at the Creation.*

28. See Murray Edelman, *Political Language: Words That Succeed, Policies That Fail* (New York: Academic Press, 1977).

29. Edelman, *Political Language.*

30. See David L. Altheide and Robert P. Snow, *Media Logic* (Beverly Hills, CA: Sage, 1979).

31. See, for example, Mark Hertsgaard, *On Bended Knee: The Press and the Reagan Presidency* (New York: Shocken, 1989). Also, Jarol B. Manheim, *All of the People, All the Time: Strategic Communication and American Politics* (Armonk, NY: M. E. Sharpe, 1991).

32. Quoted by F. Christopher Arterton, "Campaign Organizations Face the Mass Media in the 1976 Presidential Nomination Process" (paper presented at the annual meeting of the American Political Science Association, Washington, DC, September 1977), 4.

33. NBC News, "White Paper on the Reagan Presidency," December 30, 1981.
34. Quoted in Bob Woodward, *The Commanders* (New York: Simon & Schuster, 1991), 155.
35. Quoted in *New York Times,* February 15, 1991, A9.
36. Quoted in an interview on C-SPAN, February 23, 1991.
37. Quoted in *Extra!* May 1992, 3.
38. Quoted in Michael Massing, "Debriefings: What We Saw, What We Learned," *Columbia Journalism Review* (May/June 1991), p. 23.
39. Ibid., 24.
40. See Doris Graber, *Processing the News: How People Tame the Information Tide,* 2nd ed. (New York: Longman, 1988); Russell Neuman, Marion Just, and Ann Crigler, *Common Knowledge* (Chicago: University of Chicago Press, 1993); and Michael Delli Carpini and Bruce Williams, "Television in Political Discourse" (paper presented at the annual meeting of the American Political Science Association, September 1991, Washington, DC.
41. For a detailed discussion of how this worked, see Joe McGinniss, *The Selling of the President* (New York: Pocket Books, 1969).
42. David L. Paletz and Robert M. Entman, *Media Power Politics* (New York: Free Press, 1981), 69–70.
43. Ibid., 70.
44. Wise, *The Politics of Lying.*
45. David R. Mayhew, *Congress: The Electoral Connection* (New Haven, CT: Yale University Press, 1974).
46. See J. William Fulbright, *The Pentagon Propaganda Machine* (New York: Vintage, 1970); also Barnet, *Roots of War.*
47. Wise, *The Politics of Lying.*
48. Ibid., 273.
49. Manheim, *All of the People, All of the Time.*
50. For the classic discussion of symbols in politics, see Murray Edelman, *The Symbolic Uses of Politics* (Urbana: University of Illinois Press, 1964).
51. This incident involved the Bellevue, Washington, police department and was reported on KIRO News Radio, Seattle, February 16, 1982.
52. United Press International (UPI) wire story, reported in the *Seattle Post-Intelligencer,* September 26, 1979, A2.
53. See Susan Herbst, *Reading Public Opinion: How Political Actors View the Democratic Process* (Chicago: University of Chicago Press, 1998); and Robert M. Entman, *Democracy Without Citizens* (New York: Oxford University Press, 1989).
54. See Mark Dowie, "Torches of Liberty." Introduction to John C. Stauber and Sheldon Rampton, *Toxic Sludge Is Good for You* (Monroe, ME: Common Courage Press, 1995).
55. Jeff Pooley, "Tricks of the Trade: Hamburger Helper for Newscasters," *Brill's Content* (December 1998/January 1999), 46.
56. See Richard Morin, "Public Policy Surveys: Lite and Less Filling," *Washington Post National Weekly Edition,* November 10, 1997, 35.
57. See Richard Morin, "Which Comes First, The Politician or the Poll?" *Washington Post National Weekly Edition,* February 10, 1997, 35.
58. Daniel Boorstin, *The Image: A Guide to Pseudo-Events in America* (New York: Atheneum, 1961).
59. Boorstin, *The Image,* 11–12.
60. Wise, *The Politics of Lying,* 3–16.
61. AP wire story, *Seattle Times,* February 8, 1982, A3.
62. John Anthony Maltese, *Spin Control: The White House Office of Communications and the Management of Presidential News* (Chapel Hill: University of North Carolina Press, 1992).
63. Source: Office of the Press Secretary for the President, 1992.

64. Samuel Kernell, *Going Public,* 3rd ed. (Washington, DC: CQ Press, 1997).
65. Quoted in Mark Hertzgaard, *On Bended Knee: The Press and the Reagan Presidency* (New York: Farrar, Straus & Giroux, 1988), 33.
66. The following overview of Hertsgaard's analysis, Ibid., is organized along the lines suggested by Steven Livingston of George Washington University.
67. Hertzgaard, *On Bended Knee,* 35.
68. Ibid., 48.
69. Ibid., 49.
70. Ibid., 36.
71. Ibid., 36.
72. Source: Hedrick Smith, *The Power Game: How Washington Works* (New York: Ballantine, 1988).
73. From Jack Honomichl, "Richard Wirthlin, Advertising Man of the Year," *Advertising Age* (January 23, 1989).
74. From Smith, *The Power Game,* 409.
75. Ibid., 407.
76. Quoted in David Ignatius, "The Press and the President," *Seattle Times* (from the *Washington Post*), May 28, 1989, A16.
77. Ibid.
78. See Honomichl, "Richard Wirthlin."
79. Quoted in David Shaw, "Dire Judgment on Clinton Started Just Days into Term," *Los Angeles Times,* September 16, 1993, A1.
80. Ann Devroy and Ruth Marcus, "Guess Who Clinton's Picked to Be His Presidential Role Model," *Washington Post Weekly Edition,* November 23–29, 1992, 14.
81. Ryan Lizza, "The White House Doesn't Need the Press," *New York Times Magazine,* December 9, 2001, 108.
82. Quoted in Ibid.
83. Ibid.
84. Elisabeth Bumiller, "Presidential Travel: It's All About Local News," *New York Times,* February 11, 2002, A21.
85. Sanford J. Ungar, "North and South at the Summit," *Atlantic* (January 1982): 7.
86. Joe Foote, "The Network Economic Imperative and Political Access," *Political Communication Review* 10 (1985): 2.
87. Quoted in Ibid., 9.
88. Noted in "Seven Days," special *Newsweek* look at a week in the life of Bill Clinton (engineered, of course, by David Gergen). *Newsweek,* July 12, 1993, 17–25. Press conference incident noted on page 24.
89. From data displayed in Elizabeth Kolbert, "We Interrupt This Program . . . ," *New York Times,* June 26, 1994, E18.
90. Reported by Michael Massing, "About-Face on El Salvador," *Columbia Journalism Review,* November/December 1983, 42–49. Quotes from p. 45.
91. Ibid., 46.
92. Clifford Krauss, "How U.S. Actions Helped Hide Human Rights Abuses," *New York Times,* March 21, 1993, 1.
93. Ibid., 34.
94. Jarol B. Manheim, *All of the People, All the Time: Strategic Communication and American Politics* (Armonk, NY: M.E. Sharpe, 1991).
95. Although the Pentagon had authorized this publicity spectacle in advance, the unruly press pack tailing the Seals created such chaos that camera crews were finally ordered to shut down the lights and cease the coverage.
96. Richard Morin, "Budget Czars for a Day," *Washington Post National Weekly Edition,* November 23–29, 1992, 36.

Chapter 5

How Journalists
Report the News

Journalists today find fault with most everything that politicians say and do. The press no longer even has much respect for public officials' private lives—even their bedroom behavior is fair game for news stories.

Thomas Patterson

. . . People may expect too much of journalism. Not only do they expect it to be entertaining, they expect it to be true.

Lewis Lapham

It is obvious why politicians attempt to control the news. The journalistic response to news control is more complicated. When citizens, parties, and interests are fully engaged in an issue, the news is likely to report diverse political views, and we see a healthy democracy through the news window. More often, however, popular participation is limited, and political insiders attempt to control the public agenda by managing the news. In these cases, the press offices of government and political interests continue to dominate what is reported as *hard news*. At the same time, the space for hard news is shrinking due to the economic equations noted in Chapter 3. The drift toward sensationalism magnifies the tendency of journalists to turn against politicians at the hint of a slip, a rumor, or a cheap accusation from an opponent. Even politicians who have managed the news effectively may suddenly find the press biting the hand that feeds them (recall "feeding the beast" from the last chapter).

This strange American news pattern alternates between publicizing political spin and trying to trap politicians in slips and scandals. Far from enhancing public respect, the press game conveys an air of smug insiderism. Even when the press pack attacks, the displays of adversarialism are largely ritualistic, providing little insight beyond puncturing the image of the target *du jour.* Thus, "gotcha" journalism often comes across to audiences as posturing—as a game that journalists play to make themselves appear independent and adversarial.

In the early stages of the 2000 presidential primary campaign, for example, the press tried to trap George W. Bush into confessing his alleged history of drug use. No matter what Bush said, the journalistic response was generally "gotcha." He was damned if he admitted it and damned if he denied it. Just exactly what was the point of it all? One of the few newsmakers to try to put a point on the story was Jesse Jackson, who argued that the issue of cocaine use in itself was not as important as the possible inconsistency of a rich white man getting away with using cocaine, and then, as governor of Texas, favoring harsh prison penalties for poor minorities who used crack. For the most part, however, the mainstream press seemed to think that playing "gotcha" was point enough in the news game. As for Jackson, he soon found himself enmeshed in a scandal story of his own involving a child out of wedlock.

The press also played "gotcha" with Al Gore during the 2000 election. Leading news organizations such as the *Washington Post* and the *New York Times* ran incorrect and out-of-context versions of Gore's remarks on his involvement with facilitating access to the Internet and helping establish a program to clean up toxic waste sites. He soon became branded in the national press as "serial exaggerator" (a term supplied by the Bush communication team). Late night comedians made him a national laughingstock. Between February and June of 2000, a sample of 2,400 national news articles showed that 76 percent of the stories contained charges that Gore lied, exaggerated, or was somehow involved in scandal. The students and teachers at the New Hampshire high school where the most damaging press misquote originated tried in vain for months to fix the inaccuracy and came away discouraged. A media literacy class at the school compared their tape of the Gore visit with national coverage and issued a press release titled "Top Ten Reasons Why Many Concord High Students Feel Betrayed by Some of the Media Coverage of Al Gore's visit to their school."[1]

In the 2004 presidential race, the press anointed former Vermont Governor Howard Dean as the early front-runner, and then just as quickly changed the narrative in response to Democratic party insiders who pronounced him unelectable. Dean suddenly became a candidate who was too angry and hotheaded for voters, and who could not challenge President Bush on Iraq (even though Dean's rise to the top in the first place was based largely on his opposition to the war). Dean suffered a surprising defeat in the Iowa caucuses, and the press had new front-runners to take to the next primary, creating new plot material for the familiar horse race story that journalists tell in every election.

This chapter explores why so much journalism falls into the two broad categories of (1) reporting the official lines of the day and (2) then playing personal "gotcha" games, often with the same officials and news makers. This dynamic is at the core of the authority-disorder syndrome discussed in Chapter 2, and it contributes in various ways to the other news biases as well. Both of these reporting tendencies present serious problems for citizens and their relation to government. On the one hand, the tendency to open the gates to officials and their carefully managed messages is hard to reconcile with the common assumption that the media are (or at least have the potential to be) objective, independent, professional, and even adversarial in their relations with news sources. The problem of a free press relying so heavily on what officials (and more importantly, their handlers and their opponents' handlers) feed it is so perplexing that the reasons have been explored by a number of researchers in the fields of communication (e.g., Jay Blumler, Michael Gurevitch),[2] sociology (e.g., Herbert Gans, Gaye Tuchman),[3] and political science (e.g., Bernard Cohen, Timothy Cook).[4]

The second tendency of the press to then bite the hand that feeds it is in many ways equally puzzling because the resulting adversarialism is more often personal than substantive. As Thomas Patterson has pointed out in the larger analysis from which the epigram that opens this chapter was drawn, the resulting news content is an odd mix: a narrow range of political ideas, interspersed with cranky criticisms of politicians and the games they play. Patterson describes the rising levels of journalistic negativity as follows:

> . . . negative coverage of politics has risen dramatically in recent decades. Negative coverage of presidential candidates, for example, now exceeds their positive coverage. . . . By 1990, negative coverage of Congress and its members was over 80%. Each president since 1976—Carter, Reagan, Bush, and Clinton—has received more negative coverage than his predecessor. Federal agencies have fared no better; in the 1990–1995 period, for example, not a single cabinet-level agency received more positive than negative coverage. As portrayed by the press, America's public leadership is universally inept and self-serving.[5]

Although different researchers propose different specific reasons for why the news comes out in this odd way, all seem to agree that the general answer is a combination of four factors: (1) the economics of the news business, (2) the dependence of journalists on sources who control the information that journalists need, (3) the routine news gathering practices of reporters and their news organizations, and (4) the professional norms and codes of conduct that grow up around those organizational routines. Since we have discussed the political economy of the news and the information management strategies of news sources extensively in earlier chapters, we turn in this and the next chapter to a close look inside journalism itself.

WORK ROUTINES AND PROFESSIONAL NORMS

Organizational routines are the basic rules and practices that journalism schools and news organizations train reporters and editors to follow in deciding what to cover, how to cover it, and how to present the results of their work. Journalistic routines give the news its reassuring familiarity and create a steady supply of news product in a competitive marketplace. *Professional norms* are those moral standards, codes of ethics, and guidelines about inserting one's voice and viewpoint into a story that enable journalists to make personal decisions. In addition, these codes of the profession enable news organizations to justify what they produce. Both of these factors are shaped strongly by the business pressures explained in Chapter 3. The recent wave of economic change sweeping the news industry not only introduced changes into reporting practices, but created serious strains in important journalistic norms such as objectivity, as discussed in Chapter 6.

It is increasingly clear that the everyday work routines inside news organizations bias the news without necessarily intending to do so. Our first order of business (and the focus of this chapter) is to show how the everyday practices of journalists and their news organizations contribute to the authority-disorder bias, as well as to personalized, dramatized, and fragmented news. In addition to explaining how reporting practices bias the news, it is important to understand why these habits persist and why neither the press nor the public seems to grasp their true political significance. For example, many members of the press continue to defend their reporting habits as being largely consistent with the professional journalism norms of *independence* and *objectivity*. These standards may go by different names such as accurate, fair, unbiased, or nonpartisan, but the point is that a surprising number of American journalists continue to espouse some notion of objectivity. The peculiar nature of objectivity is so important to understand that the next chapter is devoted primarily to its origins and its defining consequences for American news. In the discussions of professional norms and work routines in this chapter and the next, the critical focus is on how they contribute to the news biases outlined in Chapter 2 and to the capacity of politicians to make the news as described in Chapter 4.

First, a word of clarification is in order about the intent of this critical discussion. In many instances, the practices and professional standards of American journalism have been commendable. In a few celebrated cases, for example, reporters and editors have even gone to jail in order to protect the confidentiality of sources or to defend the principle of free speech. Moreover, routine news coverage of some political issues and situations is rich and full of diverse viewpoints. For example, both reporting and entertainment media treatments of abortion politics have been as full of information, as rich in competing viewpoints, and as diverse in the social voices represented as we can expect a democratic communication system to be.

In other respects, however, the professional norms of independence and objectivity have backfired. In fact, American journalism may have become trapped within an unworkable set of professional standards, with the result that the more objective or fair reporters try to be, the more official (and other) biases they introduce into the news.[6] A five-nation study of political journalists by Thomas Patterson and a group of international colleagues produced a startling finding: Although the American press is arguably the most free or politically independent in the world, U.S. journalists display the least diversity in their decisions about whom to interview for different hypothetical stories and in what visuals they chose for those stories. Patterson concluded that the strong norms of political neutrality or independence among American journalists actually homogenize the political content of their reporting. By contrast, reporters in countries such as Italy, Britain, Sweden, and Germany (the other nations studied) are more likely to regard political perspectives as desirable in covering events. As a result, journalists in other nations tend to cover the same events differently—that is, by interviewing a broader range of political sources and using different visual illustrations.[7]

WHEN ROUTINES PRODUCE HIGH-QUALITY REPORTING

It is important to remember that the news does not report every story the same way, nor do the news biases apply equally to every issue covered in the news. One of the fascinating discoveries in studying the role of the press in politics is that journalists using similar news gathering methods can end up reporting stories that range from highly biased to very useful to citizens. This is because reporting is an interaction among the various factors that shape the information system: the sources of news, the economics of the business, and the public reactions to stories.

When is more information rich, diverse, and broadly based news coverage likely to emerge in the U.S. system? News content is most diverse, detailed, and open to competing views when public officials are willing to debate issues openly for extended periods. In such cases, the news organizations cover issues in depth and follow the political process through the halls and hearing rooms of government with citizen input in tow. (Recall the discussion of *indexing* from Chapter 1). We find this relatively open and detailed coverage in a handful of historic cases such as Vietnam or Watergate investigations, and more often in coverage of the moral issues that rage through American politics. Abortion, civil rights, gun control, flag burning, and other enduring moral controversies are most likely to capture the popular imagination, pit politicians and parties against each other, expand the range of political viewpoints, and take the public on extended tours of government at work. In these cases, the news may show citizens how issues move from elections to legislatures, to executive offices, to courts, to regulatory agencies, and at times spill over into the streets in sustained political conflicts.

By contrast, officials tend to handle complex issues of economics, energy, war, foreign policy, and other areas of elite power politics more guardedly. As a result, issues that are arguably the most important to America's future are apt to be reported in the fragmented and officialized language that keeps people guessing about what is going on and why. Many important events receive detailed media attention only after poorly understood policies have already become facts of life.

As noted earlier, studies of the role of the press during the Vietnam War explain that the critical press coverage in the later years of the war was less the singular product of liberal or crusading journalists than a result of news organizations reporting views critical of government policies *after* those policies were attacked by important figures in Washington.[8] In the more typical cases of the Gulf War and the Iraq War, most members of Congress were cautious in expressing their doubts about going to war, and the majority of Washington elites quickly joined the rallying public after the fighting broke out. As a result, the media paid little attention to opposition views or even to unpleasant reminders of the realities of the war itself, such as the untold deaths of Iraqi soldiers and civilians, or even the totals of American casualties. Even though there were numerous national demonstrations against going to war, the major TV news organizations decided not to cover them. During the Gulf War in 1991, for example, the networks ran a mere 29 minutes on antiwar protests compared to 2,855 minutes covering the war.[9] To put this in perspective, they gave about the same amount of airtime to antiwar protesters as to interviews with tourists and businesspeople on how the war affected their travel plans.[10] The case study in this chapter provides an analysis of why the press overwhelmingly reported images favorable to administration war policies on Iraq II during the time in which public opinion on that war mattered most: from the period before the war began in 2002 to the crucial 2004 presidential primaries.

Case Study: *Top Ten Reasons the Press Took a Pass on the Iraq War*

If the first Iraq war (generally called the Gulf War) was named Desert Storm, the second might be called Perfect Storm. The run-up to the 2003 war witnessed an extraordinary convergence of factors that produced near perfect journalistic participation in government propaganda operations. At least ten factors converged in Perfect Storm fashion to push the press pack to write stories that seldom contested administration framing even though gaps in the credibility of that framing were available to knowledgeable reporters at the time (see the case study in Chapter 4).[11] Here are the ten factors that created this perfect propaganda storm:

1. *9/11* happened. The national public was softened by those horrific events to accept almost anything that might produce closure, leading to restrictions of civil liberties on the domestic front and the rise of empire discourse from those in the administration (Wolfowitz, Perle, Cheney, Rumsfeld) who had long harbored fantasies of a militarist reassertion of American power. Where was the press after 9/11? Apparently too wrapped in its cultural-patriotic storytelling to find credible sources to challenge that vision. Thus, the administration was able to push a weak case for war based on fantastic assertions of an al Qaeda–Iraq link, and the even stealthier innuendos that Saddam Hussein was somehow involved in the 9/11 attacks—a connection that 71 percent of the public attributed to the administration as late as the summer of 2003.[12]

The capacity of the administration to successfully push deceptions and misrepresentations through a docile press to an emotionally volatile public may stand as the most ruthless press control operation in history—an operation that achieved such sophistication that at least three distinct press-management factors must be counted separately.

2. Master scripting and directing by Karl Rove. The Rove White House communication operation made Reagan press management under Deaver and Gergen seem modest by comparison. No news management opportunity was missed, from the Top Gun carrier landing, to edgy insertions of Iraq into the War on Terror. Even the president's deer-in-the-headlights media presence was countered as described in the case study in Chapter 2 with the relentless spin that he in fact has a natural "swagger."

3. Beyond spin: outright intimidation. Intimidation of journalists and news organizations began within hours of the 9/11 catastrophe, as described in the case study in Chapter 1. This intimidation campaign continued through the aftermath of the War in Iraq. When whistle-blowers came forward—such as the investigator of the Iraq-uranium connection, or former Treasury Secretary Paul O'Neill—they were swiftly shouted down in public and intimidated with personal reprisals.

4. The press was embedded with the military. Scratch a good journalist and one is likely to find a vicarious adventurer who seeks to be at the scene of the action telling a Big Story. Apparently one could not be closer to the Iraq War story than inside a tank hurtling across the desert toward Baghdad. Nearly every respected journalist (including those too old to go into action, themselves) initially hailed the military embedding as a ringside ticket to great journalism, a perspective that would bring the uncensored reality of war to the American people. Only later did some journalists admit what they might have seen beforehand: that the Big Story was dictated from Washington, and the scenes from inside the tanks were little more than B-roll filler that authenticated a story told by the government. If the embedding operation was as telling about the dramaturgy of the press as about the press-control proclivities of the administration, the next factor moves us even farther into the realm of press responsibility.

5. Telling the story that promises maximum drama *and* most likely plot advancement. When journalists make story choices, they favor narrative elements that are most likely to advance a coherent, dramatic story into the future. In some cases, those choices produce stories that ignore potentially damning evidence to the contrary. Those cases typically involve looking away from sources less likely to deliver future installments and favoring (usually official) sources more prepared to deliver regular updates. Consider the reporting decisions to downplay the volume of doubt linking al Qaeda—and, more generally, 9/11—to Iraq. Consider, too, the volume of doubt about Saddam's weapons of mass destruction. Although doubts were reported, they were pegged largely to foreign sources and domestic protesters that were dismissed insultingly by Rumsfeld and company. Finally, consider the widespread journalistic decisions to avoid complicating the Iraq-terrorism narrative with stronger evidence of links between al Qaeda, 9/11, and Saudi Arabia—stories that continued to go begging for major coverage even after a postwar revelation by Saudi officials that al Qaeda operatives conducted training operations as late as July 2003 on Saudi farms, and even after the administration refused to release an intelligence report allegedly linking al Qaeda to prominent members of the Saudi political elite. Seymour Hersh published an early investigative report in the *New Yorker* presenting evidence against the Iraq connection, while pointing something of a smoking gun at Saudi Arabia.[13] These rare acts of investigative journalism were virtually ignored by the larger press community because standard Washington sources offered nothing to advance those stories, serving up, instead, daily installments on Saddam and terrorism. What would it have taken for the press to turn those potential blockbuster alternatives into serious frame challenges to the administration? Did I mention the Democrats?

6. Where were the Democrats? Apparently the defeated Democrats had been advised to offend no one and to take no political risks. Although this advice might be questioned as making them seem even more offensive by looking weak and indecisive, they apparently paid enough for their professional communication counsel to follow it. Thus, the party left criticism to a few isolated representatives and to a pack of presidential candidates who criticized each other more often than they criticized the president. News organizations are so dependent on prominent official sources to advance challenges to a leading news frame that the strategic silence of the Democrats all but killed media deliberation about the war.

Why were the concerns of presidential primary candidates such as Howard Dean or Dennis Kucinich not enough to reframe the story? Because the U.S. press is taken with reporting only who and what the Washington consensus anoints with *gravitas*. Most contestants in the Democratic primary pack may as well have said nothing. Without major figures weighing in, strong antiwar sentiment among the public went largely unreported. Consider a small case in point. In January 2003, I was called by a *Newsweek* reporter who asked the stunning question (as I paraphrase it): "We in the press have become aware of a substantial antiwar movement. Why do you think we are not reporting it?" Why, indeed, did the press fail to report organized large-scale opposition? I explained that the failure to report on the antiwar movement was due to the dependence of the press on official opposition, or on partisan engagement of institutional processes to bring grassroots voices into the news cast. A couple of weeks later, candidate John Kerry raised a trial balloon question about the advisability of war over continued inspections and military quarantine. Kerry was a prominent senator, and he was regarded by the press at the time as the leading candidate for president. Sure enough, the *New York Times* promptly noted the rise of a substantial antiwar movement in the very same paragraph. Kerry, however, promptly went into the hospital, other Democrats stared blankly at Bush's post-9/11 popularity ratings, and so went the opening for the antiwar movement to have a prominent voice in the public sphere. Subsequently, on February 15, 2003, when some ten million people across the globe raised their voices in what may well be the largest coordinated public demonstrations in world history, the American press allowed the president to dismiss it as the ramblings of a "focus group" to which he would not respond.

7. The absence of credible progressive think tanks. News stories are often advanced through reactions from experts at think tanks who promote the political policy objectives of those who fund these high-level opinion-making operations. The conservative right has enjoyed considerable media success through a combination of (1) aggressive news management (see point 2 above), (2) dense networking of radio and TV talk pundits and conservative rapid response e-mail lists to create a public "echo chamber" to support policy initiatives and attack opponents (see point 3), and (3) timely delivery of think tank reports and experts to journalists when new initiatives are launched, or when old ones suffer MADS (media attention deficit syndrome) and need new life. Perhaps it is because of funding disparities between left and right—or simply because of the dim capacities of the left to understand how the press works—that there was virtually no coordinated expertise to counter Bush administration war frames. (The Brookings Institution has been so closely identified with promoting the doctrine of Democratic moderation that it seldom advances progressive media positions.)

8. Press construction of a spectator public. It is some consolation that publics form their opinions only in part through the cueing of voices in the news. In their lives outside of media representations, people surely look elsewhere for clues about what to think. Perhaps the most impressive thing about public opinion as measured by polls up to the eve of the invasion was that clear majorities favored war only if the administration could build an international coalition (one suspects that a "coalition of the willing" that included Palau and Tonga over France and Germany was not what they had in mind).

As the news narrative built toward inevitable war, opposition levels in the polls were reported only as footnotes for the record. It seems that polls and protests were not enough for the press to turn the public into players in the media spectacle. Once again, journalists forgot that publics can take active roles in the news story of democracy. Thus, when the tide of public opinion rose predictably into a patriotic rally with the outbreak of the war, it would have been easy to conclude that the public supported the rationale for the war all along. Unfortunately, questions about just what the public was supporting would have been hard to air in the midst of a national patriotic rally that was led as much by a cheerleading press as by the administration.

9. Press ethnocentrism. More than any other Western democratic press system, the U.S. press is remarkably closed to world opinion. Perhaps this reflects the press's implicit mirroring of the confusing popular cultural impulses of isolationism and patriotic intervention. The inward turn of American journalism may also reflect the unwillingness of most politicians (a.k.a. leading news sources) to risk their patriotic credentials either by questioning the values and motives behind government decisions to use force, or by crediting outsiders when they do so. In any event, international reactions of outrage to the administration's "you're either with us or against us" stand on Iraq were duly noted for the news record and then easily spun away by administration news sources and journalists alike. While news features reported on boycotts of French wine and the renaming of french fries as freedom fries, many commentators adopted a condescending tone for discussing the din of international criticism. No national news organization was more aggressive in its patriotic support for the Iraq War—or its vitriolic condemnation of administration critics, foreign and domestic—than FOX.

10. The FOX Effect. This is the last, and I think, the least important factor explaining why the press faithfully reported so many administration claims that could have been challenged. Because of the levels of patriotic cant from FOX reporters, anchors, and talk show hosts, alike, many observers felt that FOX exercised a chilling effect on a competition that was worried about ratings losses among audiences allegedly swept with patriotic fervor. It is true that new standards of jingo-journalism may have been set by the FOX anchor who described antiwar protesters in Switzerland as "hundreds of knuckleheads," or by the decision to run a crawl at the bottom of the screen branding nations that refused to join the "coalition of the willing" as the "axis of weasels."[14] FOX's hyperbolic reporting notwithstanding, we should not forget the stiff competition among television news organizations during the first Gulf War to display their patriotic bona fides—long before FOX news was a gleam in the eyes of Roger Ailes and Rupert Murdoch.[15] If FOX's competition effectively took a pass on critical journalism, I would argue that the effects of factors 1 through 9 were considerably more important than looking over their journalistic shoulders at the FOX effect.

In retrospect, I suspect that, just like their Gulf War forebears, the Democrats remained largely silent during the Iraq War in hopes of an economic downswing or a scandal that would offer safer grounds for attacking a seemingly popular president. If the economy staggered under the Bush tax plan, or if a trail of smoking deception about the Iraq War somehow reached the Oval Office, the press would quickly turn on the man they endowed with Texas Swagger and send him into early retirement like they did his father a decade before. Such a reversal of political fortune would not likely be due to much dogged reporting, it would happen because the press had found a better story.

The emerging conclusion about mass-mediated democracy is that news debates tend to be more open and informative when the government itself is already functioning ideally—that is, when government officials are openly debating and investigating public policies in front of the news cameras. On the other hand, when elites are not debating policy options in public, journalism routines result in narrowing or closing the news gates on stories that might be quite important to the public interest. The weakness in the American information system appears to be those crucial and all-too-common cases where government officials do not confront difficult issues or choices. Should information be shaped so thoroughly by what elites and elected officials are doing in public? Perhaps the press should pay more attention to the stories that politicians (and the public) are avoiding.

The differences in reporting about different kinds of stories are not accidental. They reflect the way the news system in a country is organized. There is a relationship between what journalists believe about their jobs and how they go about them. While recognizing that conceptions of the role of the press in society affect the daily routines of news gathering, it is easier to discuss these two related aspects of the news separately. The focus of this chapter is to show how the professional code of the U.S. press actually perpetuates the kinds of biases and public discontents that becoming professionalized is supposed to prevent. The remainder of the present chapter explores how news organizations work: where they find sources, how they assign stories, and what shapes the development of those stories.

HOW REPORTING PRACTICES CONTRIBUTE TO NEWS BIAS

Much like any job, reporting the news consists largely of a set of routine, standardized activities. Despite some obvious differences involving the nature of assignments and personal writing styles, American reporters (as noted earlier) tend to cover news events in remarkably similar ways. A fascinating example of how these work routines affect news content was discovered by Timothy Cook in a study of international crisis coverage in the United States and France. In the months after the Iraqi invasion of Kuwait, crucial international diplomatic efforts attempted to prevent the looming war. When news of these efforts broke, television networks in both countries assigned their reporters to get reactions from key sources. American newscasts flipped through the "golden triangle" of Washington news beats: the White House, State Department, and Pentagon. Even though there was no official U.S. reaction to be had, the reporters were pressured to say something, and they effectively invented the kinds of vague pronouncements that one might expect from officials in sensitive political posts at the early stage of a world crisis. By contrast, French reporters (who do not operate with a U.S.-style beat system) interviewed various political party leaders and generated a comparatively broad range of political views about the meanings and implications of the diplomatic talks.[16]

The existence of standardized reporting behaviors and story formulas is not surprising when one considers the strong patterns that operate in the news environment. For example, the events staged by political actors tend to reflect the predictable political communication goals outlined in Chapter 4. Moreover, most mass media news organizations tend to impose fairly similar constraints on reporters in terms of acceptable story angles, deadlines, and news gathering resources. Also, reporters are subject to the standardizing influence of working in close quarters with one another, covering the same sorts of events under the same kinds of pressures.

In short, reporters confront three separate sources of incentives to standardize their reporting habits:

- Routine cooperation with (and pressures from) news sources
- The work routines of (and pressures within) news organizations
- Daily information sharing and working relations with fellow reporters

Each of these forces contributes to the development of standardized reporting formulas that favor the incorporation of official political messages in the news, interspersed with the feeding frenzies that may undermine the officials themselves. These reporting patterns also lead reporters to write personalized, dramatized, and fragmented news stories. We will now explore each source of everyday pressure on journalists.

REPORTERS AND OFFICIALS: COOPERATION AND CONTROL

Most political events are so predictably scripted that reporters can condense them easily into formulaic plot outlines: who (which official) did what (official action), where (in what official setting), for what (officially stated) purpose, and with what (officially proclaimed) result. For example:

> President ———— met at the White House today with President ———— from ———— to discuss mutual concerns about ————. Both leaders called the talks productive and said that important matters were resolved.

It does not take a careful reading to see that such a formula is virtually devoid of substance. The pseudo-events that provide the scripts for such news stories are generally designed to create useful political images, not to transmit substantive information about real political issues. Because such events are routine political occurrences, reporters quickly develop formulas for converting them into news whenever they occur. Compounding the temptation to report official versions of political events is the fact that reporters live in a world where divide and conquer is ever present. Careers are advanced by receiving scoops and leaks and are damaged by being left out in the cold, excluded from official contact. Like it or not, reporters must depend on the sources they cover. When those sources are powerful officials surrounded by an entourage of eager reporters clamoring for news, it is always possible that those who report what officials want them to will be rewarded, whereas those who fail to convert key political messages into news will be punished.

In view of the patterned nature of political events combined with the press tactics of politicians, it is not surprising that the news seems to emerge from formulas that virtually write themselves.[17] Of course, knowing the formulas does not mean that reporters will always use them. However, in a workday world filled with short deadlines, demanding editors, and persuasive news sources, the formulas become the course of least resistance. Even when a formula is abandoned, there is seldom enough other information available in a typical political setting to construct another story.

In the illusory world of political news, formulas describe official actions, and the seal of official approval becomes a substitute for truth and authenticity, which in turn makes the formulas seem legitimate.[18] Robert Scholes developed these ideas a bit further when he said:

> Perhaps the credulous believe that a reporter reports facts and that newspapers print all of them that are fit to print. But actually, newspapers print all of the "facts" that fit, period—that fit the journalistic conventions of what "a story" is (those tired formulas) and that fit the editorial policy of the paper. . . .[19]

Anyone for changing that famous slogan to "All the News That Fits, We Print"? The formulas used to select and arrange facts in the news are produced largely through the mutual cooperation of reporters and newsmakers. These partners may not share exactly the same goals or objectives, but together they create information that satisfies each other's needs. It is all in a day's work.

THE INSIDER SYNDROME

In addition to developing work habits that favor official views, reporters are also human beings. Behind the occupational roles are people who sometimes identify with the newsmakers they cover. Because reporters have regular contact with officials under stressful conditions, it becomes easy for them to see these officials as sympathetic characters. Of course, when officials go out of their way to antagonize the press, as the Nixon administration did during the early 1970s and as the Clinton administration did for most of its first term, it is more difficult for reporters to identify with the officials. When officials court the favor and understanding of reporters, they are often paid back with sympathetic coverage that sticks close to the officials' political line.[20] Such coverage is easily justified as an objective account of the officials' public actions.

Yet another aspect of the subtle working relations between reporters and officials is that journalists who cooperate with powerful officials often receive recognition and flattery and are taken into the confidence of those officials. In the intensely political environments in which most of our news occurs, nothing is valued as much as power. If one cannot possess power (and there always seems to be a shortage), then the next best thing is to be on the inside with the powerful—to be seen with them, to be consulted by them, to socialize with them, and perhaps even to have them as friends. As Tom Bethell put it:

> To be on close terms with elite news sources is to be an "insider," which is what almost everyone in Washington wants to be. It is interesting to note how often this word appears on the dust jackets of memoirs by Washington journalists. But Nixon—his great weakness!—didn't like journalists and wouldn't let them be insiders. . . . Kissinger, on the other hand, was astute enough to cultivate the press, and he survived—not merely that, was lionized as "the wizard of shuttle diplomacy." (Is it not possible that the most awesome "lesson of Watergate" . . . will be a social lesson?)[21]

The perils of being a Washington insider were summarized by Tony Snow, a Detroit news columnist and former speechwriter for George H. W. Bush: "We spend a lot of time hanging out with the high and mighty. It's intoxicating. In Washington, access to people in power is important, if nothing else for social reasons, for name dropping."[22] As the distinguished reporter Murray Kempton put it: "It is a fundamental fact about journalism, and might even be a rule if it had the attention it deserves, that it is next to impossible to judge any public figure with the proper detachment once you begin calling him by his first name."[23]

Ellen Hume, a journalist and scholar of the press, says that she has come to feel that journalists can be "more powerful than any elected official" and that something "urgently" needs to be done to "dynamite" the insiders out of their privileged positions.[24] Steve Goldstein, Washington correspondent for the *Philadelphia Inquirer,* suggested term limits for Washington journalists. If news organizations would agree to rotate their stars out of Washington, the power of the "unelected media elite" might be diminished. Even more important, says Goldstein, media term limits:

. . . might counteract the potential for disconnection, whereby the correspondent suffers a loss of understanding of issues that Americans really care about. Federal policy-making and the impact on the folks at home is supplanted by the view from Washington. There is a difference between Here and There. In Sodom-on-the-Potomac the political culture is secular, while most of America is religious. Here the character issue is often framed as: Did he/she sleep with her/him/it? Out there, the issue is often one of fairness, justice, integrity. All the sleaze we print doesn't fit.[25]

All of this said, setting a term limit for the Washington media elite is challenging. Two or four years may not be enough time for a newcomer to understand the political mazeway and develop the contacts that enrich his or her reporting. However, in six or eight years, the Washington lifestyle of expensive dinners, exotic foreign travel, and power parties may have already taken hold of the reporter's sensibilities. Goldstein suggests that the press should develop stronger professional norms against insiderism that journalists could call upon to make a personal decision about when to leave:

. . . one thing is clear. It's time for the journalist to move on, or be moved, when he or she thinks that presenting America as seen through Washington's hellish prism is more important than helping readers understand decisions made on Capitol Hill that will change or affect their lives.[26]

In a lighter vein, Goldstein suggests the following "self-test" for Washington reporters. Offering apologies to David Letterman, he lists the "top 10 telltale signs that a journalist has been in Washington too long":

10. You cannot recall the area code of your hometown.
9. Your best sources are at other news organizations.
8. You go to Duke Ziebert's a second time [a restaurant notorious as a meeting spot and watering hole for the power elite].
7. You think a regional story refers to Upper Northwest [a district in Washington, D.C.].
6. The conductor of the Marine Band salutes you.
5. You reject an interview with the mayor of your hometown because it conflicts with Gridiron rehearsal [a Washington journalist's club that puts on an annual show in which press and politicians satirize each other].
4. *The Capitol Gang* [a TV pundit gathering] offers honorary membership.
3. Larry King calls you by your first name.
2. You cover the story by watching CNN.
1. You become eligible for Redskins' season tickets.[27]

However, before thinking that journalists and the officials they cover are too cozy, or that they are any cozier than in earlier eras, it is important to remember that "cozy" is hardly the way most of them would describe their relationship. Many politicians today describe their relations with the press as regrettably antagonistic and, therefore, necessarily guarded. Reporters often complain that they never get close to officials and must fight through the "spin patrol" of handlers, consultants, and flaks. It is surely the case that today's political scene is, in many ways, far less cozy and (in the special sense of "gotcha" journalism) more adversarial than that of thirty years ago, before Watergate or Vietnam. Just because many prominent journalists and officials of yesterday were more likely to be friends, drink and party together, and go off the record after 5 P.M., this does not mean that press relations today have lost their cooperative aspects or their insider aspirations.

REPORTERS AS MEMBERS OF NEWS ORGANIZATIONS: PRESSURES TO STANDARDIZE

If reporters' relations with officials breathe new life into old news formulas, their own news organizations reinforce the use of those formulas. Novice journalists experience constant pressures (subtle and otherwise) from editors about how to cover stories.[28] These pressures are effective because editors hold sway over what becomes news and which reporters advance in the organization. Over time, reporters tend to adjust their styles to fit harmoniously with the expectations of their organizations.

In many cases, these organizational expectations are defended by journalists as simply preserving the "house style" of the news organization—the tone, editorial voice, and format that makes one news outlet distinguishable from another. (Recall this discussion from Chapter 3.) This level of formula reporting is as unobjectionable as it is inevitable in any kind of organization that has standard operating procedures. However, there are deeper levels at which organizational preferences for story formulas do matter. To an important extent, there are industry-wide norms about story values that define what is news and that, in turn, open the news to the kinds of biases outlined in Chapter 2. For example, one young reporter serving an apprenticeship with a major big-city newspaper talked about the somewhat mysterious process of having some stories accepted and others rejected without really knowing the basis for many of the decisions. Equally mysterious were the conversations with assignment editors in which the editor seemed to know what the story was before it had been covered. Over time, the socialization process works its effects, and young reporters learn to quickly sense what the story is and how to write it. Beyond the style of this or that news organization, the whole media system begins to emulate particular formats, themes, and news values.

For the most part, political censorship is rarer than the shading of news formats to fit marketing and audience research. Bending news genres to fit commercial values and socializing reporters to recognize how potential stories fit the familiar formulas are the roots of the news biases discussed in Chapter 2. In all of their variations, however, organizational pressures result in news that typically fits a formula.

Why Formulas Work

Standardized news is safe. Managers in news organizations must constantly compare their product with that of their competition and defend risky departures from the reporting norm. As Epstein observed in his classic study of television network news, even TV news assignment editors look to the conservative wire services for leads on stories and angles for reporting them.[29] The wires cover the highest portion of planned official events and stick closest to official political scripts. Following the daily lead of the wires becomes the most efficient way to fill the news hole.

Other organizational arrangements also strongly influence standardized reporting. Among the most powerful standardizing forces are daily news production routines. Newspapers and news programs require a minimum supply of news every day whether or not anything significant happens in the world. Perhaps you have seen a television news program on a slow news day. In place of international crises, press conferences, congressional hearings, and proclamations by the mayor, the news may consist of a trip to the zoo to visit a new "baby," a canned report on acupuncture in China, a follow-up story on the survivor of an air crash, or a spoof on the opening of baseball spring training in Florida. Slow news days occur during weekends or vacation periods when governments are closed down. News organizations run fluff on slow days because their daily routines report official happenings from the news centers of government.

The News Hole

In order for a news organization to function, it must fill a minimum "news hole" every day. Producing a large amount of cheap, predictable news normally means assigning reporters to events and beats that are sure to produce enough acceptable stories to fill the news hole by the day's deadline. During normal business periods, the public relations machinery of government and business fills these organizational needs by producing events that are cheap, easy to report, numerous, and predictable.

With the advent of twenty-four-hour news channels and Web sites linked to papers and broadcast organizations, the news hole has become a gorge. Pressures increase to update stories many times a day, in contrast to once or twice a day in the old era of morning and evening news. The journalistic credo of "advancing" a story has become an obsession for many organizations. Reporters learn to ask leading or challenging questions, often based on little more than trying to elicit a reaction from a newsmaker in an effort to generate new material to report. "President Bush denied rumors today . . ." becomes a familiar lead in a news age with an ever larger news hole to fill.

Beats

Filling the daily news hole on time means that news organizations must figure out how to make the spontaneous predictable. The obvious solution to this problem is to anticipate when and where the required amount of news will happen every day. Because this task is made difficult by the size of the world and the smallness of reporting staffs, the solution is to implicitly adjust the definition of news so that things that are known to happen on a regular basis become news. Reporters can be assigned to cover those things and be assured (by definition) of gathering news every day. As a result, the backbone of the news organization is the network of beats, ranging from the police station and the city council at the local level, to Congress, the Supreme Court, and the presidency at the national level. Beats produce each day's familiar run of murders, accidents, public hearings, press conferences, and presidents entering helicopters and leaving planes.

Special Assignments

To break the daily routine, some reporters are given special assignments to cover big stories such as elections or spontaneous events like assassinations and floods. However, the expense of special-coverage assignments dictates that even the truly spontaneous must be translated into familiar formulas. If an event is important enough to justify special coverage, then it must be represented in dramatic terms. Even assassinations, invasions, and floods quickly become scripted. For example, when it became clear that the United States was planning an invasion of Haiti in the summer of 1994, television news organizations readied large libraries of canned material on the island nation and extensively scripted their coverage well in advance.

Because special coverage is costly and must be kept going, even no news often becomes news. Frank Cesno, Washington Bureau chief for CNN, told of his week of special coverage when John F. Kennedy Jr.'s airplane was missing in July 1999. He personally anchored much of the coverage and spent a good bit of it announcing that there was not much news from the search-and-rescue teams. However, making the decision to go live and assigning the story the top priority for the network required being on the air and keeping the news flowing.[30]

Bureaus

In addition to beats and special-coverage assignments, many large news organizations have developed a third news-gathering unit, the geographically assigned crew. For example, television networks have news crews (a correspondent and video and sound technicians) stationed in large cities like Chicago, New York, Houston, Los Angeles, and Miami. The assumption is that enough news will be generated from these areas to warrant assigning personnel to them. The use of geographical assignments reflects another way in which organizational routines have shaped the definition of news into a convenient formula. Because national news cannot all come from Washington, reporters must be assigned to other locations. But what other locations? Any location chosen suddenly becomes a defining center for national news. As Epstein discovered in his study of television network news, almost all non-Washington news originates from the handful of cities where the networks station their crews.[31]

To an important extent, the reliance on bureaus has decreased in the past decade. As the profit imperative has been felt at both print and broadcast organizations, expensive bureaus are often the first things to be cut. Among American television news operations, only CNN has retained a substantial network of world information-gathering outposts—in large part because CNN also runs an international channel that demands serious world coverage. All the others have dropped bureaus and reporting staff. The result is that ABC, CBS, and NBC have increasingly settled for buying their raw product secondhand from a variety of world TV wholesale news suppliers. In the newspaper business, pressures to cut luxuries such as remote bureaus have been equally intense. Many big-city papers have been purchased by large conglomerates, which feed all the papers in the chain the same material from centralized bureaus. The few remaining independent big-city papers increasingly rely on secondhand suppliers such as the *New York Times* and the *Washington Post,* which continue to maintain extensive bureaus and sell their stories to smaller organizations. The overall trend is an increasing consolidation of the information channels on which media organizations rely for their daily supply of news.

Public Relations and News

As noted in earlier chapters, the public relations industry has grown in size and technological sophistication in recent decades. The goal of many public relations and communications campaigns is to place news stories that advance the images and political goals of clients. As news organizations reduce staff, shrink bureaus, and become more conscious of budgets, the supply of public relation (PR) events and news releases becomes more attractive as news material. Indeed, PR wires run into most newsrooms, and public relations workers (who often have experience as journalists) work up contacts with journalists and supply them with story ideas and sources. As a result, packaged pieces on personalities, movies, entertainers, and more generally, staged events in communication campaigns become featured in the news.

REPORTERS AS A PACK: PRESSURES TO AGREE

As a result of the increasingly routine nature of news gathering, reporters tend to move in packs. They are assigned together to the same events and the same beats. More than most workers, they share close social experiences on the job. Together they eat, sleep, travel, drink, and wait, and wait, and wait. They also share that indescribable adrenaline rush of "crashing" a story—hurtling through those precious minutes between the release of key information and the deadline for filing the story. As a result of such intimate social contact, reporters tend to develop a sense of solidarity. They learn to cope with shared pressures from news organizations and news sources. They come to accept news formulas as inevitable, even though they may cynically complain about them in between mad scrambles to meet deadlines. They respect one another as independent professionals but engage in the social courtesies of comparing notes and corroborating story angles.

In his insightful description of press coverage during the 1972 election, Timothy Crouse called the reporter's social world "pack journalism."[32] He concluded that reporters come into such close contact while under such sympathetic conditions while covering such controlled events that they do not have to collaborate formally in order to end up reporting things the same way. Once a reporter has been assigned to a routine event for which news formulas are well known, there is a strong temptation to produce a formula story. Added to this are a tight deadline and an editor who will question significant departures from the formula used by other reporters; as a result, the temptation to standardize becomes even stronger. Finally, put the reporter in a group of sympathetic human beings faced with the same temptations, and the use of formulas becomes easily rationalized and accepted with the social support of the group.

So strong are the pressures of the pack that they have been felt even by a trained sociologist who posed as a reporter in order to study news gathering from an insider's perspective. While working as a reporter for a small daily paper, Mark Fishman was assigned to the city council beat. He quickly fit into the routine of writing formula stories that mirrored the council's careful efforts to create an image of democracy in action—complete with elaborate hearings, citizen input, serious deliberations, and formal votes. In a rare case when an issue before the council got out of control and turned into a hot political argument, the reporters at the press table reacted strangely. Ignoring a bit of news that did not fit the mold took some social prompting from various members of the pack. As Fishman described it:

> The four members of the press [including Fishman] were showing increasing signs of impatience with the controversy. At first the reporters stopped taking notes; then they began showing their disapproval to each other; finally, they were making jokes about the foolishness of the debate. No evidence could be found in their comments that they considered the controversy anything other than a stupid debate over a trivial matter unworthy of the time and energy the council put into it.[33]

Fishman noted the strength of group pressure operating against independent news judgment: "Even though at the time of the incident I was sitting at the press table [as a reporter] making derisive comments about the foolishness of the council along with other journalists, it occurred to me later how this controversy could be seen as an important event in city hall."[34]

Just as Fishman succumbed to the pressures of the pack while still recognizing them at a conscious level, most reporters are aware of group pressure but seem unable to escape it. In a study of the Washington journalism corps, the nation's reporting elite, Stephen Hess found that reporters regarded pack journalism as their most serious problem.[35] As Hess noted, however, pack journalism will persist as long as news organizations establish their routines around the predictable actions of officials.

Although the pack generally feeds on the handouts offered by spin doctors and political handlers, it can also turn on the unprepared or vulnerable politician. Cases of the pack devouring its political prey are legendary: Lyndon Johnson fell to a feeding frenzy over the Vietnam War; Richard Nixon lost control of the press during the Watergate crisis; Jimmy Carter was himself held hostage in the Oval Office by the press for 444 days during the Iranian hostage crisis of 1979–1980; Gary Hart withdrew his presidential candidacy in 1984 when the press pack took up his challenge to prove that he was having an extramarital affair; the first George Bush plummeted from his standing as most popular president in the history of modern polling as the press pack followed the Democrats in attacking him for an economic recession; and Bill Clinton saw the customary presidential honeymoon period curtailed prematurely by a feeding frenzy. The growing chaos and criticism surrounding the Iraq crisis provided openings for the press pack to turn on George W. Bush, but those openings were balanced against the somber fact that the country was at war.

Whether the members of the press pack accept their daily news handouts with equanimity or bite the hand that feeds them, the problem remains much the same: The resulting news becomes standardized and distorted. Two cases discussed earlier (the Vietnam War and Watergate) have been defended—even glorified—by media scholars as golden moments in which the free press exposed government lying and corruption. Even these two exceptions, however, point to the rule of pack journalism. Evidence of problems in both situations existed long before the stories became big news; the pack resisted giving big play to critical stories for a long period after reportable issues were available; and the pack feeding frenzy was set in motion by (in the case of the Vietnam War) increasingly public splits among high-level elites or (in the case of Watergate) congressional investigations of the various improprieties of the Nixon White House.

FEEDING FRENZY: WHEN THE PACK ATTACKS

Although the political content of the mainstream press may be remarkably uniform, it does not always follow the scripts of politicians. What is often mistaken for a critical, independent press is a phenomenon popularly known as the "feeding frenzy."[36] When politicians become caught up in personal crises, scandals, or power struggles, the news media may descend like a pack of hungry dogs to devour the political prey. Add the hint of a sex scandal or produce the proverbial smoking gun of political corruption, and the frenzy can bring down the high and mighty.

Few politicians have felt the sting of the feeding frenzy as repeatedly as Bill Clinton. The news was spiced during the 1992 election by charges of Clinton's extramarital affairs, pot smoking, draft dodging, and other personal issues. Clinton's character became a major preoccupation of the press during the campaign.[37] The resulting challenge for the Clinton communication team was to reassure voters about the character defects raised in the news and reinforced by opponents during the primaries and the general election. The fact that Clinton survived the nearly nonstop negative news and then won the election struck Ian Weinschel, a Republican media consultant, as something close to a miracle. He likened Clinton to the crash test dummy of American politics: "I've never seen anybody come back from being attacked in that fashion. It's like going through a car crash with no seat belts and then going through the window and hitting a wall and walking away. It's absolutely astounding."[38]

After the election, Clinton and his staff remained bitter about their treatment by the press during the campaign. When they came to Washington, it seemed as if they felt that they could govern much as they had won the election, by going over the heads of the press through electronic town halls, controlled news events, and heavy polling and image construction. The daily world of Washington politics proved different than the campaign trail, where paid advertising and controlled events stand a better chance of countering press attacks. The now famous decision to close the corridor between the press room and the White House communication office amounted to a declaration of war on journalism's elite corps. The icy relations left the press pack surly and ready to pounce at the hint of a scandal or personal failing. Clinton's run of personal incidents continued after the inauguration, and the press pounced on such items as Clinton's expensive haircut aboard an idling Air Force One on a Los Angeles International Airport taxiway and a scandal in the management of the White House travel office that was quickly dubbed "Travelgate" in the media.

So short was the presidential honeymoon and so notable were the feeding frenzies of the press pack that a number of publications questioned those abrasive press relations. For example, the *Los Angeles Times* ran a three-part series under the title "Covering Clinton: Did Media Rush to Judgment or Merely Reflect Reality?" In the first article, entitled "Not Even Getting a 1st Chance," reporter David Shaw observed:

> The media battered Lyndon B. Johnson over Vietnam and savaged Richard Nixon over Watergate, but perhaps never in our nation's history—certainly not in its recent history—has a President so early in his term been subjected to a greater barrage of negative media coverage than Bill Clinton endured in his first 239 days in office.[39]

The second article in the series opened with the observation that "Twelve days after President Clinton took office—with *only* 1,448 days left in his term—Sam Donaldson of ABC News was on a weekend talk show saying 'This week we can all talk about, 'Is the presidency over?' ''[40]

The third article suggested that a large part of the problem was that the Washington reporters were taking their isolation from an upstart White House staff personally, and they were reminding the administration that the power game in American politics involves the press. In that article, *Newsweek's* White House correspondent Eleanor Clift found it suspicious that even the prestige press linked Clinton to the fiasco in Waco, Texas, when an assault by a federal force on a religious cult resulted in the fiery deaths of eighty-six cult members. Despite headlines blaming Clinton, Clift noted a national poll in which 93 percent blamed cult leader David Koresh for the disaster. Clift said that she remembered thinking at the time, "The other 7 percent are in the White House press room."[41]

Another reflective piece was titled "The White House Beast" after the derisive nickname given the press corps by George Stephanopoulous, who was Clinton's early (and disastrous) communication director, and now serves as a pundit for ABC News. As *Washington Post* correspondent Ruth Marcus put it in that article, "The White House press corps is like this large, dysfunctional family. It's weird. It's not normal. Half the time I'm at the White House, my attitude is: No one would believe this."[42]

There are at least three reasons for the series of feeding frenzies that plagued the Clinton presidency from the start. As these factors often contribute to other feeding frenzies, they are stated here in more general terms:

- Cooperative relations between the president's communication staff and the press had broken down. (See the discussions of press-politician cooperation earlier in this chapter and in Chapter 4.)
- The communication staff seemed to think it unnecessary (or beneath the dignity of the office) to follow the basic rules of news management in response to the initial outbreaks of negative coverage, as outlined in Chapter 4. They provided few packaged stories to interrupt the negative news, and they had no apparent game plan to spin the incidents that kept the feeding frenzies going.
- The charged and actual offenses involving the president resulted in numerous uncontrolled news situations.

Whether Bill Clinton operated out of some sort of political death wish or simply had more skeletons in his closet than the average politician, only future psychoanalysts and historians will be able to say. As the third factor suggests, the press frenzy clearly fed on personal episodes that invited questions about Clinton's character and leadership. However, the magnitude of the Clinton frenzies and their occurrence so early in his presidency points to the important roles played by the first two factors as well. Clinton supporters also accused political opponents of feeding the frenzies with well-orchestrated accusations. With the exception of the sex scandals and a questionable real estate deal, however, many of the incidents clearly resulted when Clinton's media handlers left their boss out of position in poorly controlled situations (such as the haircut and the Waco fiasco) that could have been controlled more effectively.

With the exception of the stories that David Gergen was allowed to manage during his brief stay in the Clinton White House (recall the earlier discussions of Gergen's news management style), press relations for much of the Clinton first term remained rocky. For example, influential *New York Times* correspondent (now an influential columnist) Maureen Dowd listed the numerous instances of poor press handling on the part of the press office staff during a European trip commemorating the fifty-year anniversary of D-Day. She recounted a reflective moment at a British pub after a missed deadline: "Sipping champagne ordered by the *Paris Match* reporter, I fantasized about replacing the corner dartboard with the head of one of Clinton's prepubescent press-minders."[43]

After the stunning Democratic party defeat in the 1994 congressional elections, the White House began to address its communication problem.[44] Slowly and grudgingly, the communications office became more responsive to the journalists down the hall. The decision to hire Mike McCurry as press secretary proved to be the single best press relations move of the administration. At least when the Lewinsky scandal broke later on, the president was put at a distance from reporters, and the daily briefings from the White House were as effective as could be hoped for in the midst of a frenzy that was well beyond the capacity of routine press management to control.

Even well into his last term, however, Clinton managed to find small ways to antagonize the press corps. On the eve of the Lewinsky scandal, for example, the White House reduced the number of 1997 press Christmas parties from four to two, and in the process, cut the guest list in half. The news organizations, themselves, had to decide who would be excluded from one of the "A ticket" Washington social events of the year. The parties increasingly drew media executives from New York, along with nearly 2,000 journalists, spouses, and hangers-on, who, as Howard Kurtz described the scene,

> . . . got to nibble on shrimp and lamb chops, visit the open bar, and pose for official photos with the president and first lady, who had to stand through four grueling two-hour sessions of greeting those who often give them less than flattering reviews. Even jaded journalists enjoy having these prestigious souvenirs mailed to them. . . . [45]

Even as the Clinton team strived to restore routine press relations in many areas of the news process, it seemed to forget that the goodwill of journalists is something that must be cultivated, particularly during the holidays.

THE PARADOX OF ORGANIZATIONAL ROUTINES

The problem with routine news gathering is that most of the news on most of the channels starts looking pretty much the same. The paradox is that because there are many papers, radio programs, and television broadcasts from which audiences can receive the daily news, it is hard for competing organizations to establish a competitive edge in the news market. In short, routine reporting of news may be efficient, but it limits the share of the market that any media source can capture. For example, if all the news on television is pretty much the same, each network should capture an equal share of the audience, all other things being equal. Thus, efficiency may impose an unintended ceiling on audience share, which limits the growth of profits in the news organization—and news is, after all, a business. The ways around this dilemma involve marketing strategies, budget cutting, and the various other business moves described in Chapter 3—none of which improve the quality of news.

Breaking out of the news routine toward more independent, less sensational news has not been attractive to news organizations because it is not clear what the alternative would look like even if it were profitable to worry about. For example, television executives may point to the *News Hour* on the Public Broadcasting Service (PBS) as an example of how more in-depth reporting only drives audiences away. Some critics argue, however, that the PBS news, while more detailed, and more likely to broadcast hard news over soft, is otherwise very similar in content to that available on the commercial networks. Why should audiences seek a bigger dose of the same product?

Because news is largely the result of convenient conventions between politicians and journalists, it is not clear where to look for guidance in reforming the product. Any new format would surely draw criticism from politicians and other news organizations, and it might startle the public, risking the possible loss of audience share. As a result, the media do not like to think too much about tampering with the standard news gathering routines. Instead, the competition in most news markets tends to be waged in terms of marketing strategies, brand images, and other matters of style over substance.

Should the Market Rule the News?

After receiving a survey of audience reading habits, the management of one major daily paper reportedly issued a memo to reporters calling for more "fine examples" of rapes, robberies, and auto accidents on page 1.[46] Whether the marketing strategy involves more human-interest stories or more stereotyped coverage of political heroes in action, the result is the same as far as political information goes: The news trends are toward replacing coverage of government and civic affairs with sex, personality, lifestyle, entertainment, sports, weather, and mayhem.

The contribution of the news doctors to standardized news raises a number of important questions, including the following:

- Should news be based on market considerations, or should it be based on some independent criteria of importance and newsworthiness?

- Because some people (i.e., enough to turn a profit) watch or read news about fires, murders, accidents, and political scandals, does this necessarily mean that (a) they want more of it (b) they think these things are important (c) they think these things belong in the news (d) they do not want alternatives to formula news (e) they would not be engaged by news that actually *explains* more about politics and society?

Such questions are dodged by news doctors and media executives, who reply simplistically that they are only interested in making the news more relevant to people. It is doubtful that current marketing surveys really measure popular demand at all.[47] For example, most media surveys are designed with the assumption that formula news is a given. Audiences are not asked if they would prefer alternatives to news formulas; they are simply asked which news formulas they like best. Thus, the standard excuse that the news reflects what the people want might be stated more properly as "the news reflects what people prefer among those choices that we find profitable and convenient to offer them." This is not the same thing as saying that the news is responsive to popular demand.

WHEN JOURNALISM WORKS

Within the limits of business pressures and journalistic routines, there are clearly some news organizations that seem to make greater commitments to news content that displays more diversity, detail, and coherence. Journalists turn out to be among the most self-critical of professionals. Perhaps because they receive such volumes of criticism from all sides (public opinion, politicians, other journalists, and media scholars), they sometimes experiment with news formats in an effort to try to improve the quality of their product. Although these changes are often modest in their impact, they are worth noting.

Fighting the Mayhem? A Hopeful Trend in Local TV News

In Austin, Texas, the news looked pretty much the same on all the channels: more mayhem than at least some local journalists felt accurately reflected life in the increasingly cosmopolitan Texas capital. Then, ratings leader KVUE-TV broke from the pack. News executives decided that they would screen the mayhem stories for their social or political significance before making an automatic story assignment based on the "if it bleeds, it leads" principle. For example, before a crime story would be shown on KVUE, it had to meet at least one of five significance criteria:

1. Does action need to be taken?
2. Is there an immediate threat to safety?
3. Is there a threat to children?
4. Does the crime have significant community impact?
5. Does the story lend itself to a crime prevention effort?[48]

Soon after these standards were developed, they were put to a test by a Saturday night brawl in a local town that resulted in a triple shooting and murder. KVUE investigated the incident and judged that none of its significance criteria was engaged. The station held its ground and did not report the story, while its competitors gave it the prominent play generally assigned to such a good example of local mayhem. As the news director at Austin's K-EYE put it simply, "When somebody's killed, that's news."[49] Perhaps it was easier for KVUE to try a new kind of journalism in Austin because it was already the ratings leader. However, the ratings for the new format made for happy news executives. The ratings for the first full month of the experiment were the best ever for the station's 10 P.M. newscast.

A more general look at national trends shows that KVUE is not alone in its efforts to improve the quality of local TV news. For example, KARE in Minneapolis features a lengthy report on an important issue of the day, and its ratings have risen. KAKE in Wichita has twice the national average in issue coverage and is also doing well in the ratings. WCTV in Tallahassee goes where others have closed operations (such as reporting on state government) and leads its market. These examples are from a larger study of sixty-one stations in twenty cities conducted by Columbia University's Project for Excellence in Journalism.[50]

The most interesting finding from the study is that serious news tends to be compatible with good ratings primarily when a station makes a commitment to breaking completely with the mayhem format. In other words, stations that incorporate a mix of serious issues and mayhem are not as likely to be rising in the ratings as stations that either make serious news their dominant format or that continue to go with "more mayhem most of the time." This interesting finding was summarized and interpreted this way:

> The stations least likely to be rising in the ratings were those in the middle, which were often hybrids—part tabloid and part serious. This suggests that audiences are not schizophrenic—they are segmenting. There is a group that embraces news full of revelation, scandal, and celebrity. There is another group that prefers a more sober, information-based approach.[51]

With the exception of five out of the eight stations in the high-quality group that were experiencing rating gains, the rest of the picture was decidedly mixed. Indeed, the overall profile of the 8,500 stories from the 600 broadcasts monitored on the 61 stations in the study was not an optimistic portrait of a revolution sweeping local TV:

> Despite the good news, the study found that most local newscasts are far from excellent. The general picture of local TV news is superficial and reactive— journalism on the run. Almost half (46%) of all stories were about commonplace events. Less than 10% originated from ideas in the newsroom. Of stories involving controversy, many (43%) gave only one side.[52]

Although this study found a somewhat more reassuring crime volume (28 percent) than other research (using different samples) has found, the substantive problems with local news still seemed large. The Project for Excellence team cited major failings on the local scene with "sourcing, getting both sides of the story, thinking ahead."[53]

Reforms on the National Scene

Although there is hardly a tidal wave of reform sweeping the media, a few developments are worth noting. For example, some news organizations have developed "agenda" features that provide more in-depth analysis of national problems. These agendas are generally relegated to the status of minor features and set apart from the normal news, however, rather than driving the daily news agenda. In many cases, these independent agendas reflect pressures for sensationalism, as illustrated by the many special segments on dramatic examples of government waste during the 1990s. A more positive development is the "adwatch" coverage that many news organizations have introduced to help people decode and think critically about the political advertising during election campaigns.

Even when news organizations vow to improve the quality of coverage, however, other pressures in the information system often intrude. For example, CBS announced a policy in the 1992 presidential campaign to reverse the trend toward shrinking "sound bites" (those direct statements by candidates and politicians that are sandwiched in television news packages). According to a study by Daniel Hallin, the length of the average sound bite hit an all-time low of under ten seconds during the 1988 campaign.[54] The CBS goal of running at least 30 seconds of direct statement from the candidate in each story was soon abandoned, however, as it became clear that the media managers who run campaigns had learned to script their candidates' performances with those 10-second political marketing jingles in mind.[55] As a result, the length of the sound bite shrank even further in 1992 to 8.4 seconds. Although it seems impossible to shrink candidate statements much farther, they weighed in at a puny 7.2 seconds in the 1996 election according to a study conducted midway through the campaign by the Center for Media and Public Affairs.[56] The 2000 election held firm at 7.3 seconds, with candidates getting only 11 percent of campaign news time.[57] Election night TV coverage has reduced the role of reporters familiar with campaigns and candidates in favor of greater face time for star anchors and pundits who now talk in clipped, rapid fire exchanges.[58]

The shrinking sound bite and rapid pace of TV talking heads are signs that it is hard to change news formats in the direction of more information-rich fare. The sound bite trend reminds us that not all of the inhibitions to change arise from inside news organizations. Candidates hire communication consultants who are also quite comfortable shrinking ideas to fit media formats. Critics argue that the now standard 30-second ad spots used in election and issue campaigns permit candidates to skip over the details of their proposals and aim at often volatile public emotions.[59] Yet many media consultants like former Clinton advisor Dick Morris see no such problem. According to Morris, "There is literally no such thing as an idea that cannot be expressed well and articulately to today's voters in 30 seconds."[60]

DEMOCRACY WITH OR WITHOUT CITIZENS?

Recall from Chapter 1 that political communication scholar Robert Entman has argued that our mass-mediated democracy is in danger of becoming a *democracy without citizens*. This is in part because most news coverage is driven by forces that involve people more as passive consumers than active citizens.[61] For both politicians and journalists, the public has become more of a market to be tested, persuaded, and sold than an equal partner in communication and government. The reality of much opinion and participation is anchored in electronic images that move people psychologically in private worlds that may be detached from society and face-to-face politics.[62]

The irony in this is that the technology exists to communicate more information, farther, faster, from more sources, and to more people than ever before. At the same time, the political and business pressures operating behind the news may create just the opposite results. Perhaps the electronic age would not be so worrisome if politicians and the press used the potential of today's electronic technology to communicate critical ideas to people. The question is how to move politicians and journalism away from the paths of least political and economic resistance in their communication strategies.

In short, it is not hard to imagine how the news could be more citizen-oriented than it is. For example, the press could keep more citizen voices in reporting on important issues—even when public officials attempt to manage, downplay, or ignore those voices. News organizations could require their reporters and editors to run more direct statements from newsmakers and less commentary from journalists. News organizations also could minimize the writing of vapid "meta-narratives" such as the campaign horse race, or the authority-disorder plot that can be applied to almost any generic political situation.

Above all, citizens and their activities should be covered in the news even when officials are not engaged with the issues or viewpoints in question. News organizations could include citizens in their reports and create paths from the broadcast or the news page to Web sites where audiences can learn more about what they can do to make a difference. A good example of such a citizen-oriented news site is the BBC's *iCann* citizen information project (**www.bbc.co.uk/dna/ican/**). What do you think? What kind of news would best fill the needs of a *democracy with citizens?*

NOTES

1. "Al Gore and the 'Embellishment' Issue: Press Coverage of the Gore Presidential Campaign." Kennedy School of Government Case Program. C15-02-1679.0.
2. See, for example, Jay G. Blumler and Michael Gurevitch, "Politicians and the Press: An Essay in Role Relationships," in *Handbook of Political Communication,* eds. Dan Nimmo and Keith Sanders, (Newbury Park, CA: Sage, 1981), 467–93.
3. Herbert J. Gans, *Deciding What's News* (New York: Pantheon, 1979); Gaye Tuchman, *Making News* (New York: Free Press, 1978).
4. Bernard C. Cohen, *The Press and Foreign Policy* (Princeton, NJ: Princeton University Press, 1963); Timothy Cook, *Governing with the News* (Chicago: University of Chicago Press, 1998).
5. Thomas E. Patterson, "Doing Well and Doing Good: How Soft News and Critical Journalism Are Shrinking the News Audience and Weakening Democracy—And What News Outlets Can Do About It," Joan Shorenstein Center on the Press, Politics, and Public Policy, Harvard University, December 2000, 10.
6. See the argument in Robert W. McChesney, *The Problem of the Media: U.S. Communication Politics in the Twenty-First Century.* (New York: Monthly Review Press, 2004).

7. Thomas E. Patterson, "Irony of a Free Press: Professional Journalism and News Diversity" (paper prepared for the annual meeting of the American Political Science Association, September 3–6, 1992, Chicago). See also, Patterson's *Out of Order* (New York: Knopf, 1993).

8. See, for example, Dan Hallin, *The Uncensored War* (Berkeley: University of California Press, 1989); and W. Lance Bennett, "Toward a Theory of Press-State Relations in the United States," *Journal of Communication* 40 (Spring 1990): 103–27.

9. *Extra!,* (May 1991), 19.

10. Ibid., 5.

11. Also see Robert M. Entman, *Projections of Power.* (Chicago: University of Chicago Press, 2004).

12. Paul Krugman, "Bush and Blair, So Far, Face Different Fates," *International Herald Tribune,* July 30, 2003, 7.

13. See Entman, *Projections of Power.*

14. Ken Auletta, "Vox Fox," *New Yorker,* May 26, 2003, 64.

15. See Daniel C. Hallin and Todd Gitlin, "The Gulf War as Popular Culture and Television Drama," in *Taken By Storm: The Media, Public Opinion, and U.S. Foreign Policy in the Gulf War,* ed. W. Lance Bennett and David L. Paletz, Chicago: University of Chicago Press, 1994), 149–66.

16. Timothy Cook, "Domesticating a Crisis: Washington Newsbeats and Network News after the Iraq Invasion of Kuwait," in *Taken by Storm: The Media, Public Opinion, and U.S. Foreign Policy in the Gulf War,* ed. W. Lance Bennett and David L. Paletz, (Chicago: University of Chicago Press, 1994), 105–30.

17. See, for example, the numerous accounts of reporters, including Lou Cannon, *Reporting: An Inside View* (Sacramento: California Journal Press, 1977); Robert Darnton, "Writing News and Telling Stories," *Daedalus* 104 (Spring 1975): 175–94; and Lewis Lapham, "Gilding the News," *Harper's* (July 1981): 31–39.

18. For an excellent discussion of this syndrome, see Tuchman, *Making News.*

19. Robert Scholes, "Double Perspective on Hysteria," *Saturday Review* (August 24, 1968): 37.

20. For a detailed analysis of how this pattern occurs, see Leon Sigal, *Reporters and Officials* (Lexington, MA: Heath, 1973).

21. Tom Bethell, "The Myth of an Adversary Press," *Harper's* (January 1977): 36.

22. Ibid., 31.

23. Quoted in David Owen, "The Best Kept Secret in American Journalism Is Murray Kempton," *Esquire* (March 1982): 50.

24. Steve Goldstein, "How About Term Limits for the Unelected Elite," *Columbia Journalism Review* (May/June 1994): 35.

25. Ibid., 35.

26. Ibid., 35.

27. Ibid., 36.

28. See, for example, Warren Breed's classic study, "Social Control in the Newsroom," *Social Forces* 33 (May 1955): 326–35.

29. Edward Jay Epstein, *News from Nowhere* (New York: Vintage, 1973).

30. Frank Cesno, Joan Shorenstein Center brown bag lunch, Kennedy School of Government, Harvard University, September 21, 1999.

31. Epstein, *News from Nowhere.*

32. See Timothy Crouse, *The Boys on the Bus* (New York: Ballantine, 1973).

33. Mark Fishman, *Manufacturing the News* (Austin: University of Texas Press, 1980), 80–81.

34. Ibid., 81.

35. Stephen Hess, *The Washington Reporters* (Washington, DC: Brookings Institution, 1981), 130.

36. See Larry Sabato, *Feeding Frenzy* (New York: Free Press, 1991).

37. See W. Lance Bennett, "The Cueless Public: Bill Clinton Meets the New American Voter in Campaign '92," in *The Clinton Presidency,* ed. Stanley Renshon, (Boulder, CO: Westview Press, 1995).

38. Quoted in Maureen Dowd, "How a Battered Clinton Has Stayed Alive," *New York Times,* March 16, 1992, 1.
39. David Shaw, "Not Even Getting a 1st Chance," *Los Angeles Times,* September 15, 1993, A1.
40. David Shaw, "Dire Judgments on Clinton Started Just Days into Term," *Los Angeles Times,* September 16, 1993, A1.
41. David Shaw, "Did Reporters Let Their Feelings Affect Their Coverage?" *Los Angeles Times,* September 17, 1993, A1.
42. Jacob Weisberg, "The White House Beast," *Vanity Fair* (September 1993): 169.
43. Maureen Dowd, "Beached," *New York Times Magazine* (June 19, 1994): 18.
44. For an excellent historical capsule of Clinton administration press relations, see John Anthony Maltese, "The Communication Strategies of the Clinton White House" paper presented at the March 1999 annual meeting of the Western Political Science Association, Seattle, Washington.
45. Howard Kurtz, "The White House Trims Its Guest Tree: The Austerity Move Miffs Journalists Who May Be Deleted from the Clinton's Holiday Party List," *Washington Post National Weekly Edition,* November 3, 1997, 31.
46. Fergus M. Bordewich, "Supermarketing the Newspaper," Columbia Journalism Review (September/October 1977), 27.
47. See, for example, Philip Meyer's criticism of market research and defense of more reliable social science investigations in his article, "In Defense of the Marketing Approach," *Columbia Journalism Review* (January/February 1978): 61.
48. Reported in Joe Halley, "Should the Coverage Fit the Crime? A Texas TV Station Tries to Resist the Allure of Mayhem," *Columbia Journalism Review* (May/June 1996): 27–32.
49. Ibid., 28.
50. Based on studies by the Project for Excellence in Journalism at Columbia University, as reported in Tom Rosenstiel, Carl Gottlieb, and Lee Ann Brady, "Local TV News: What Works, What Flops, and Why," *Columbia Journalism Review* (January/February 1999, special section), **www.archives.cjr.org/year/99/1/pej/main.asp.**
51. Ibid.
52. Ibid.
53. Ibid.
54. Daniel C. Hallin, "Sound Bite News: Television Coverage of Elections, 1968–1988," Woodrow Wilson Center Paper, 1991.
55. See John Tierney, "Sound Bites Become Smaller Mouthfuls," *New York Times,* January 23, 1992, 1; and Richard L. Berke, "Mixed Results for CBS Rule on Sound Bite," *New York Times,* July 11, 1992, 7.
56. Mitchell Stephens, "On Shrinking Soundbites," *Columbia Journalism Review* (September/October 1996): 22.
57. Center for Media & Public Affairs. September 28, 2000. **www.cmpa.com/pressrel/electpr5.htm.**
58. Thomas E. Patterson, "Diminishing Returns: A Comparison of 1968 and 2000 Election night Broadcasts." Shorenstein Center on Press, Politics & Public Policy. December 2003. Available at **www.shorensteincenter.org.**
59. See, for example, Kathleen Hall Jamieson, *Dirty Politics* (New York: Oxford University Press, 1992).
60. The statement is from Morris's memoir *The New Prince,* quoted in a review by Andrew Sullivan, "As the Focus Group Goes, So Goes the Nation," *New York Times Book Review,* June 13, 1999, 8.
61. Robert M. Entman, *Democracy Without Citizens: Media and the Decay of American Politics* (New York: Oxford University Press, 1989).
62. Dan Nimmo and James E. Coombs, *Mediated Political Realities,* 2nd ed. (New York: Longman, 1989).

Chapter 6

Inside the Profession: Objectivity and Political Authority

> *"Objectivity" demanded more discipline of reporters and editors because it expected every item to be attributed to some authority. No traffic accident could be reported without quoting a police sergeant. No wartime incident was recounted without confirmation from government officials.*
>
> *"Objectivity" placed overwhelming emphasis on established, official voices and tended to leave unreported large areas of genuine relevance that authorities chose not to talk about. . . . It widened the chasm that is a constant threat to democracy—the difference between the realities of private power and the illusions of public imagery.*
>
> Ben Bagdikian

Can the news be objective? Should it be? If you ask most people what's wrong with the press, the common answer is that journalists fail in their obligation to be fair or objective. (Recall the discussion in Chapter 1.) The bias question is confounded by the fact that most people view the world through their own political biases and think that perspectives deviating from their views are unbalanced. Because there are so many different views operating in the public on almost any issue, the quest for news coverage that strikes a majority as fair, balanced, or objective appears to be an impossible dream. However, the paradox of converting something as value-driven as politics into generic news does not stop people from demanding this of journalists. As explained in Chapter 1, it is commonly assumed that the problem of news bias involves journalists abandoning their professional norms and practices to insert their personal prejudices into their reporting. In this chapter, we will consider the disturbing possibility that the most serious biases in the news occur not when journalists abandon their professional standards, but when they cling most responsibly to them.

JOURNALISTS AND THEIR PROFESSION

Some things have changed and other things have stayed much the same in the ways journalists view their jobs. For example, the speed of communication has increased greatly in the past quarter century, and journalists correspondingly sense the importance of getting the news out quickly. In the early 1970s, 56 percent of journalists surveyed regarded getting information to the public quickly as extremely important. By the 1990s, 69 percent felt that news speed was a top priority. Perhaps due to the pressures to produce news quickly, the perceived need to provide analysis of complex problems in the news dropped from 61 percent to 48 percent. The avoidance of complex stories may, in turn, account for a somewhat diminished sense of the importance of investigating government claims—long the hallmark of journalism's contribution to democracy. The perceived importance of investigative reporting dropped from 76 percent to 67 percent from the 1970s to the beginning of the 1990s.[1] Perhaps the soul searching of the profession in recent years accounts for a bit of a rebound to over 70 percent in a 2002 survey.[2]

Yet for all the change, one feature of the profession that has remained nearly constant since the rise of a professional press in the 1920s to the present day is the overriding commitment to objectivity—the idea that there is some essential reality that can be reported and that it should be reported through the words and facts offered by authoritative sources.[3] The irony is that this notion of objectivity is not easy to defend: officials are known to have biases, facts are easily disputed, and the news can never include all the viewpoints that may be important to understanding events. As charges of press bias have become more intense in recent years, many journalists backed away from the term *objectivity* and used words such as *balance* and *fairness*. Whatever its name, there is a broad, exceptionally American, cultural ideal to cast politics in broad public-interest terms and essential procedures that are free of, well, "politics." Journalists are both the carriers of this ideal and its major casualties.

Some observers have claimed that journalists are not so much committed to objectivity as they are to a scientific approach to reporting the world as a defense mechanism that protects them against criticism in a nearly impossible job. Sociologist Gaye Tuchman called objectivity a "strategic ritual" that offers a defense against career-threatening moments in which a risky report might receive the brunt of official or other public condemnation.[4] The curious result of seeking a common reality is perhaps the most standardized reporting system in the free world—a system that blurs the lines between objectivity and political authority, and between fact and political spin.

THE PARADOX OF OBJECTIVE REPORTING

"If only the press would be more objective. . . . " Every embattled politician since George Washington has accused the press of adversarial coverage, and most members of the public seem convinced that the news, at worst, has a liberal, rather than an establishment, slant.[5] Nowhere in this popular view is there much room for the idea that the news follows the lead of powerful elites and well-organized interest groups, while underreporting the interests of large numbers of silent Americans.

This chapter confronts the paradox of objective journalism by showing that the news is biased not in spite of, but precisely because of, the professional journalism standards intended to prevent bias. The central idea is that the professional practices embodying journalism norms of independence and objectivity also create conditions that systematically favor the reporting of official perspectives. At the same time, the postures of independence and objectivity created by the use of these professional practices give the impression that the resulting news is the best available representation of reality. In short, professional journalism standards introduce a distorted political perspective into the news yet legitimize that perspective as broad and realistic.

DEFINING OBJECTIVITY: FAIRNESS, BALANCE, AND TRUTH

Journalists sometimes substitute terms such as *accuracy, fairness, balance,* or *truth* in place of *objectivity* to describe the prime goal that guides their reporting. Objectivity is a tough standard to achieve, particularly with so many critics and citizens charging that journalists today do not even come close to achieving it. Accuracy, balance, and fairness are softer. They seem to be more reasonable reporting goals in light of all the obstacles to objectivity:

- The values inherent in political events
- The deceptions of newsmakers
- The difficulty of achieving a wholly neutral point of view
- The impossibility of covering all the sides and gathering all the facts
- The rush to meet unreasonably short deadlines

Because of these difficulties, the press is sure to come under fire no matter how hard it tries to present the facts. To many embattled journalists, accuracy, balance, or fairness sound like more defensible goals. One sign of the times is that the Society of Professional Journalists' code of ethics dropped the word *objectivity* in 1996 after many years of featuring it as the core principle. However, journalist and historian David Mindich notes that *objectivity* was replaced in the code with terms such as *truth, accuracy,* and *comprehensiveness.* In his view, the decision to replace *objectivity* with these synonyms signals that many journalists are tired of defending an embattled word, yet remain committed to its meaning and guiding spirit.[6] There is strong evidence that no matter which name it goes by, the vast majority of journalists subscribe to an ideal of objectivity. For example, in a 1999 national survey conducted by the Pew Center, three-quarters of journalists polled agreed that their ideal standard is to report the "true, accurate, and widely agreed upon account of an event."[7]

Changing the names of reporting ideals might be more laudable if there were also changes in the actual practices that create the news information biases discussed in Chapter 2. The new terms, however, refer to much the same journalistic practices that once passed under the lofty claim of objectivity. Moreover, fairness, accuracy, or balance may be even more misleading than objectivity as a description of news content. At least objectivity stands in sharp contrast to the reality of personalized, dramatized, fragmented, and authority-oriented (whether normalized or chaotic) news. *Fairness* or *accuracy* are fuzzier terms that invite rationalizing these information bias as the best we can hope for given the limits within which well-meaning journalists operate.

Consider, for example, the case for the term *fairness*. One may say, isn't presenting the facts offered by both sides and giving them equal time about as close to accuracy as we can get? Isn't *fair* a better description of this approach than *objective?* Consider the number of dubious assumptions on which the term *fairness* rests. First, there is the problem of limiting complex, multisided issues to two sides. Then there is the question of which two sides to admit through the news gate. The two sides that appear in most stories are anything but a broad sample of possible viewpoints. For example, fairness in reporting presidential addresses means that the opposition party will be given an opportunity to reply. Fair enough, right? But this definition is based on the poorly examined, commonsense notion that the two political parties are the two most legitimate other sides in American politics. This assumption is reinforced every time journalists build a story upon it, yet the gradual weakening of ties to parties by both voters and candidates in recent years raises serious doubts about this premise.

A second hallmark of fairness is equal time (as in allowing both sides to present their positions). Given equal time, the information edge goes to the most predictable, stereotypical, official pronouncements in almost every case. New ideas take more time and effort to communicate intelligibly than old, familiar ideas. The press could devote extra time to make new ideas accessible to people, but that would seem unfair to the dominant actors and their supporters. It is safer to stick with an easy idea of fairness that involves granting equal time to the statements of the two most vocal—and often most stereotypical—sides.

All this raises the possibility that seemingly simple ideas such as balance and equal time are not as simple as they may appear. To raise just one more troublesome issue, should balance be achieved in every news story or over a period of time? That is easy, you say. Indeed, most people look for balance in every story, meaning that they cry foul if a report emphasizes one point of view over another. However, as noted above, what if one point of view is seldom heard, and it is more complicated than the already established positions? Why not give new perspectives more time, without interruption from a perspective that is heard every day? Recall the example from Chapter 1 in which CNN's reports of civilian casualties in the war in Afghanistan had to be balanced with constant reminders of American deaths in the terror attacks of 9/11.

When people encounter new ideas alongside familiar ones, the psychological tendency is to discount the new and to embrace the old. When we look at fairness this way, the attempt to achieve balance within every story between new ideas and familiar political formulas hardly seems fair at all. If the goal of the news is to present information so that new perspectives can be grasped along with the old, then a new conception of information balance over time might replace the currently popular assumption that balance within each story is the ideal.

THE ORIGINS OF PROFESSIONAL JOURNALISM STANDARDS

Because the ideas of accuracy, balance, truth, and fairness have their roots in what was originally called objective reporting, the following discussion will use the term *objectivity* to preserve historical continuity. If the reader prefers the alternate terms, feel free to substitute them, but bear in mind that the words may change, but the underlying practices remain much the same.

A review of journalism texts by David Mindich finds a common set of perspectives and practices that reporters are taught and that bring objectivity into their daily work. These defining ingredients of objectivity include: *detachment, nonpartisanship, reliance on "facts," balance, and the use of the inverted pyramid* writing style (which puts the most important facts in the lead paragraph).[8] The following discussion shows how the ideal of objectivity is embedded in these defining journalistic methods, and thus remains a key to understanding the general workings of news organizations. The standards and practices that embody objective journalism include the following:[9]

1. The professional journalist assumes *the role of a politically neutral adversary,* critically examining both sides of an issue and thereby assuring impartial coverage. Journalists see adversarialism as an important counterpoint to becoming too close to their sources, assuring detachment and balance in their reporting. As discussed in the last chapter, the adversarial role has been corrupted by "gotcha" journalism in recent years, but many journalists and scholars continue to think of this as adversarialism.

2. The journalist resists the temptation to discuss the seamy sensationalistic side of the news by *observing prevailing social standards of decency and good taste.* Standards of taste establish boundaries as a story makes its way toward becoming "objectified." Like adversarialism, this norm has also become strained with the increase of sex scandals and tabloid coverage in the mainstream press. Many critics wonder if news organizations are losing their commitment to sticking to important issues and avoiding rumor and gossip.

3. The truthfulness and factuality of the news is guaranteed by *the use of documentary reporting practices* that permit reporters to transmit to the public "just the facts" that can be observed or supported with credible sources.

4. News objectivity is also established by *the use of a standardized format for reporting the news: the story.* Stories serve as implicit checks on news content by requiring reporters to gather all the facts (who, what, when, where, how, etc.) needed to construct a consistent and plausible account of an incident. Because stories are also the most common means of everyday communication about events, they enable the public to judge the consistency and plausibility of news accounts. Within the story format, journalists use other conventions, such as writing in an inverted pyramid style, meaning, as noted earlier, that the most important elements of the story appear in the lead paragraph.

5. Because they share the above methods, news organizations often favor the idea that reporters should be generalists, not specialists. The use of standardized reporting formats enables any reporter to cover any kind of story, further separating reporters from personal bias vis-à-vis the subject matter of the news. The

practice of training reporters as generalists, as opposed to specialists, also helps to minimize undesirable interpretive tendencies in news reporting.[10] In recent years, specialization has appeared in areas such as the environment, health, science, and technology, but many key areas such as business and politics still favor generalists.

6. The above practices are regulated and enforced by the important practice of *editorial review,* which is a check against violations of the practices and norms of the profession.

These reporting standards are so familiar and sensible that they seem to have been put there to serve obvious and laudable purposes. Indeed, it is difficult to imagine any other function for adversarial roles or documentary reporting or standards of good taste than improving the quality and objectivity of the news. Yet the accompanying case study suggests that the evolution of norms such as objectivity, fairness, and balance had more to do with the somewhat haphazard course of the developing news business than with the rational or determined pursuit of truth. In short, practices were dictated more by historical, technological, or business circumstances than by rational human design. The resulting reporting practices later became rationalized as good and even noble things.

The historical story of these modern reporting standards involves a radical shift over the course of the nineteenth century from a press supported largely by political parties to one supported by business models based on the sale of advertising. Journalism historian Gerald Baldasty describes this transformation in these terms: "In the early nineteenth century, editors defined news as a political instrument intended to promote party interests. By century's end, editors defined news within a business context to ensure or increase revenues. News had become commercialized."[11] From this commercialization and its continuing evolution to this day, come what we now understand to be sensible and proper ways to report on the world we live in.

Case Study: *The Curious Origins of Objective Journalism*

It is tempting to think that modern journalism practices derive logically from the norm of objective journalism. However, there is considerable evidence that the practices preceded the norm. The first modern journalism practices can be traced to mid-nineteenth-century economic and social conditions surrounding the rise of mass-market news.[12] According to David Mindich's historical analysis, various components of objective journalism emerged at very different points in time and often under odd circumstances. For example, the "inverted pyramid" style may have originated with a nonjournalist, Secretary of War Edwin Stanton, who wrote a series of important communiqués about the Civil War.[13]

Mindich claims that the foundations for all the practices that go into objective reporting were established, one at a time, by the end of the 1800s.[14] However, the idea that what many reporters were already doing might be called "objective journalism" did not appear until after the turn of the century. In many ways, this retrospective ideal of objectivity can be viewed as both an ennobling claim on the part of a journalism trade looking to become a profession, and as a rhetorical appeal to an increasingly educated middle-class news audience who responded favorably to those claims about professionalism.

In the early days of the American republic, the news was anything but objective. Most newspapers were either funded by, or otherwise sympathetic to, particular political parties, interests, or ideologies. Reporting involved the political interpretation of events. People bought a newspaper knowing what its political perspective was and knowing that political events would be filtered through that perspective. In many respects, this is a sensible way to approach the news about politics. If one knows the biases of a reporter, it is possible to control for them in interpreting the account of events. Moreover, if reporting is explicitly politically oriented, different reporters can look at the same event from different points of view. The idea was that people would encounter different points of view and bring them into face-to-face debates about what the best course of action might be—an idea that came directly from some of the nation's founders such as Jefferson.

The commitment to political analysis in news reporting began to fade as the nature of politics itself changed after the age of Jackson from the late 1830s on. As Baldasty notes, politicians became less dependent on party papers to communicate with voters as, among other things, strict norms against candidates campaigning directly in public began to change.[15] With these changes, party financial support for papers began to dry up. The early papers were modest operations with small local readerships. These small and increasingly impoverished newspapers could not compete for large audiences as the nation and its communication system grew.

As the country grew, the economics of the news business changed. For example, the population began to move to the cities, creating mass audiences for the news. Also, the expansion of the American territory during the nineteenth century created a need for the rapid and large-scale distribution of national news. Breakthroughs in printing and communication technologies made possible the production of cheap mass media news that could be gathered in the morning on the East Coast and distributed by evening on the West Coast.

These and other patterns in the development of the nation produced dramatic changes in the news. By 1848, a group of newspapers made the first great step toward standardized news by forming the Associated Press (AP).[16] Pooling reporters and selling the same story to hundreds, and eventually thousands, of subscribing newspapers meant that the news had become a profitable mass-market commodity. Of course, the broad marketability of the news meant that it had to be stripped of its overt political messages so that it would be appealing to news organizations of all political persuasions. An early prototype of objective reporting was born. Moreover, the need to send short messages through an overloaded mail system was followed by the transmission of national news over telegraph wires that also dictated a simplified, standardized reporting format. The *who, what, where, when,* and *why* of an event could be transmitted economically and reconstructed and embellished easily on the other end.

As the market for mass media news grew, the demand for reporters grew along with it. Whereas writing a persuasive political essay required skill in argumentation and political analysis, it was far easier to compose stories, which are the basic media for communicating about everyday events. The *use of stories* also guaranteed that the news would be intelligible to the growing mass news audience.

In this manner, the overlapping effects of communication technology, economic development, and social change gave rise to large-scale news-gathering and news-marketing organizations. Along with these organizations came a standardized set of reporting practices. As mentioned previously, news services like the AP ushered in the *documentary report.* The use of wire transmission, along with untrained reporters, promoted the shift to *the story form.* The discovery that drama sold newspapers promoted the first *adversarial reporting.* Early reporters were rather like agents provocateurs, stirring up controversy and conflict in order to generate dramatic material for their stories.

As news bureaucracies grew in response to the papers' economic success, editorial review practices became expedient means of processing the huge flow of news. *Standards of good taste* guaranteed that a news product would be inoffensive to the mass market. Much of today's news format in the mainstream establishment press evolved at the turn of the century with the growth of a large educated middle class of affluent consumers who wanted serious reporting and bought the household products that were advertised along with the news. There was initially stiff competition between this highbrow press and the tabloids or "scandal sheets" (also known as the yellow press) at the turn of the twentieth century. These highly sensationalized versions of news were marketed to a less-educated working-class population seeking escape as much as information from the media.

By the 1920s, urban life and local politics became dominated by an affluent middle class of business and professional people with formal educations. Representing the news as objective, nonpartisan, and tasteful was an effective marketing ploy geared to the lifestyle of this group. Consider, for example, the early slogans of the *New York Times,* "All the News That's Fit to Print" and "It Will not Soil the Breakfast Cloth."[17] This professional image dressed existing practices in a new style. This image also became a convenient means to discredit the muckrakers on the journalistic left and the sensationalistic scandal sheets on the political right.[18]

Finally, there was a growing expectation among intellectuals following World War I that democracy was in trouble and could be saved by a professional press dedicated to the mission of providing objective information to the public.[19] This noble purpose helped define a movement for a professional press and a code of objective journalism. Led by persuasive spokesmen like Walter Lippmann,[20] journalists began to regard objective reporting as both a description of their existing work practices and as a high moral imperative.

In these ways, journalism, like most professions, developed a set of business practices first, and then endowed those practices with an impressive professional rationale. Successive generations of reporters began to regard their work as a skilled occupation that should demand higher status and better wages. The move toward a professional status both enhanced the social image of reporting and paved the way for higher wages by restricting the entry of newcomers off the street into the journalism ranks. Professionalism meant that formal training and screening could be required for skills that had been acquired formerly on the job.[21] As a result, journalism programs emerged at universities and began to formalize and refine the received practices as professional standards.

Perhaps the best capsule summary of this curious transition of journalism from a business into a profession is Lou Cannon's observation that what began "as a technique became a value."[22]

PROFESSIONAL PRACTICES AND NEWS BIAS

Each of the defining elements of objective journalism makes a direct contribution to news bias. Each component of news objectivity creates conditions favorable to the reporting of news filtered by Washington officialdom. This should not be surprising in light of the previous capsule history of the news profession. The basic practices that later became known as professional journalism were developed to sell mainstream social and political values to a mass audience. As diverse political perspectives gradually disappeared from the news or became discredited as not objective, it became easier to convince people that the officiated political perspective that remained was somehow objective. The logic of such a claim is simple: As one reality comes to dominate all others, that dominant reality begins to seem objective. The absence of credible competition supports the illusion of objectivity. The following discussion shows how each element of objective journalism actively promotes narrow political messages in the news.

THE ADVERSARIAL ROLE OF THE PRESS

If the media were truly adversarial in their dealings with politicians, they would face a serious dilemma: The news could end up discrediting the institutions and values on which it depends for credibility. To a remarkable degree, then, maintaining the illusion of news objectivity depends on the heavy reliance on official views to certify reports as credible and valid. As sociologist Gaye Tuchman put it:

Challenging the legitimacy of offices holding centralized information disman-
tles the news net. If all of officialdom is corrupt, all its facts and occurrences
must be viewed as alleged facts and alleged occurrences. Accordingly, to fill the
news columns and air time of the news product, news organizations would have
to find an alternative and economical method of locating occurrences and con-
stituent facts acceptable as news. For example, if the institutions of everyday life
are delegitimated, the facts tendered by the Bureau of Marriage Licenses would
be suspect. One could no longer call the bureau to learn whether Robert Jones
and Fay Smith had married. In sum, amassing mutually self-validating facts si-
multaneously accomplishes the doing of newswork and reconstitutes the everyday world of offices and factories, of politics and bureaucrats, of bus schedules
and class rosters as historically given.[23]

It is equally true, of course, that the news would also lose its image of objectivity
if reporters openly catered to the propaganda interests of public officials and government institutions. If neither extreme adversarialism nor or its polar opposite support
the illusion of news objectivity, then there is an obvious implication: most adversarial
behavior on the part of the press should reveal itself as ritualistic, and in keeping
within the cooperative interests of reporters and officials. A ritualistic posture of antagonism between press and government creates the appearance of mutual independence while keeping most news content to political perspectives certified by authorities. Such ritualistic posturing dramatizes the myths of a free press and an open
government that have long defined American democracy. It is the nature of rituals to
evoke such myths and beliefs without challenging them.[24]

Adversarialism as Ritual

If the adversarial relationship is a ritual that both mystifies and legitimizes the reporting of narrow political messages, then the following characteristics should be observed: (1) The incidence of criticism and confrontation should occur regularly, as a
matter of everyday reporting orientation, as opposed to just when there is a serious political issue at stake; (2) challenges and charges will aim to provoke personal mistakes
or political confrontations between politicians rather than deeper investigations of issues, (3) charges against officials will be restricted to them personally and generally
separated from their institutions and offices, and finally, (4) these characteristics
should pertain equally to routine news coverage (e.g., reporters' beats) and nonroutine
coverage (e.g., crises and scandals).

As illustration of these points, consider C. Jack Orr's study of earlier presidential
press conferences.[25] Analyzing data from a sample of Kennedy, Johnson, and Nixon
press conferences, Orr found that the proportion of hostile or critical questions was
virtually constant across presidents, conferences, issue categories, and political contexts.[26] Not only did the incidence of confrontational questions fall into a routine pattern, but nearly all hostile questions were personal in nature. Many of those personal
questions signaled clear deference to office and institution. Moreover, questions that
could have been phrased as strong issue concerns often contained open invitations to

the president to redefine the issue or dismiss the entire question. Based on these patterns, Orr concluded that the adversarial postures of press and president create a dramatic image of journalistic aggressiveness while communicating a subtle message of institutional deference.

In an age in which personal image and public approval are key elements of political power, politicians increasingly avoid even ritualistic skirmishes with the press pack. As a result, fewer press conferences have been held in recent decades, indicating that presidents prefer to deliver their messages to the public in more controlled settings. With news organizations increasingly keying on the most personal and dramatic aspects of politicians' lives, stepping in front of the pack can prove challenging to a president. For example, George H. W. Bush stepped to the podium with a world leader to announce the results of important talks (part of the politician's ritual) only to be asked about whether he had had a love affair a few years earlier. When Bill Clinton introduced Supreme Court nominee Ruth Bader Ginsberg to the press, she told a moving story about her difficulties as a woman in a male-dominated world. After her statement, the opening question from the press pack challenged the president's political motives for her appointment and so angered Clinton that he lectured the journalists on their common decency.

Broad ritualistic elements have also been observed in the reporting of less routine events such as scandals and crises—to the extent that a number of observers have argued that crises and scandals are becoming routine news events, complete with standard reporting formulas.[27] For example, Altheide and Snow showed how a scandal involving an aide to Jimmy Carter was cast quickly into a standard reporting formula that emphasized political damage to the president while offering little measure of the importance of the issue itself.[28] Similar patterns ran through the Whitewater scandal involving Bill and Hillary Clinton, as they were subjected to guilt by association with a number of shady dealings. Despite saturation coverage implying the possibility of serious wrongdoing, few members of the public ever understood what the scandal was about.

Tag Team Journalism

The format of virtually every news interview and talk program is designed to promote adversarial displays, from the stage settings that place press and politicians in confrontational poses, to the tag team question-and-answer formats, to tone of voice and terms of address. Programs such as *Hardball* with Chris Matthews (MSNBC) are examples of frenzied adversarialism. The journalists on these TV shows not only display little respect for politicians, but they seem to delight in being rude to each other as well.

For their part, politicians contribute to the enduring antagonism by routinely attacking the press as liberal, biased, or hostile. Such attacks frequently appear in elite publications and occupy the agendas of business, government, and journalism symposia.[29] Occasionally, such charges are dramatized through formal political attacks, such as the ones during the McCarthy era and the Nixon administration. One analyst found the Nixon-Agnew attacks on the press so ritualized that he interpreted them in terms of ethological concepts of animal aggression and territorial defense.[30]

None of this means that politicians or the press take their often antagonistic relations lightly. Indeed, the mark of a good ritual is that those involved are deeply moved by it. For example, Bill Clinton raged in a *Rolling Stone* interview with William Greider that he was the most poorly treated and misrepresented of presidents.[31] Clinton was hardly alone. The list of presidents claiming this distinction is a long one dating from George Washington and Thomas Jefferson to Lyndon Johnson and Richard Nixon. Few have taken their press treatment as personally as Nixon, who kept a personal enemies list, which included a good number of journalists who were singled out for wiretaps, IRS audits, and other special punishments.[32] Although the press ritual can be quite animated and engrossing, both for those who play it and for the audiences who watch it, this should not distract us from understanding what this ritual accomplishes: narrowing the focus of human attention to convincingly exclude large categories of experience from public discourse.

The Uneasy Partnership Between Reporters and Officials

For all of the structure and routine that define the news, there are still times when the press provides a fairly wide range of critical information to the American people. As explained in Chapter 1, some information diversity enters the news through journalistic routines such as *indexing* content to the degree of conflict among actors whom journalists regard as having potential impact on the course of a story. All the same, narrating the state of society and politics is a delicate business, and journalists have considerable choice over how to build up and how to end these stories. This means that press-government rituals still have an edge to them. Indeed, both sides have enough to gain and lose to make the displays of aggression genuine.[33]

The ritual works as long as neither side undermines its credibility by raising questions about the system that legitimizes their roles. Even Watergate, long regarded as the model of modern investigative reporting, stopped short of challenging the authority of government or pushing too far into institutional failings, such as flaws in the secrecy and espionage systems that may have contributed to presidential abuses of power. For the most part, the press pack settled for the limits established by congressional investigations. The press ultimately pronounced the normalizing conclusion that "the system worked."

Watergate: The System Worked!

The Watergate scandal is a classic example of a watchdog press in action. Watergate involved nearly two years of intensive press scrutiny of President Richard Nixon and his aides. The core issues at stake were whether the White House illegally spied on the Democratic Party during the 1972 election campaign and whether the president knew about it and subsequently tried to cover it up (another illegal activity). Although the situation contained major questions about the potential for official misuse of the huge national security system that has evolved since World War II, the press deflected these issues in favor of asking whether Nixon had personally remained pure and uncorrupt in his use of the state security apparatus. Curiously absent from the barrage of coverage was the simple question of whether anyone should be expected to remain pure when given the chance to wield such great power with so little public accountability. In short, little attention was paid to the institutional flaws that might tempt a president to use CIA personnel to spy on his domestic opposition and then obstruct subsequent FBI investigations of those illegal activities. When, over a dozen years later, even more shocking institutional angles were opened up, the press was uninterested in pursuing them. Evidence from mysteriously sealed FBI files pointed to the possibility that the CIA may have abused its own institutional cover of legal secrecy by running a double-agent operation, spying on both the Republicans and the Democrats![34] This important lead raised the additional possibility that the mysterious leaks from the anonymous informant Deep Throat (who fed investigative reporters Woodward and Bernstein key information) were the result of this CIA operation. This, in turn, signals the important possibility of institutional power struggles between the CIA and the president—power struggles that would never be revealed to the American people in the absence of media scrutiny.

Despite these rich possibilities for a story that might go well beyond the personal failings of one flawed president, the press avoided them all in favor of reporting the steady stream of leaks from Deep Throat along with the activities of various congressional investigations at work on the case. This brand of investigative reporting ignored questions about institutional problems or abnormalities in favor of dramatizing the personal culpability of the most publicly visible actors involved.[35] Whereas all institutional paths led to questions of change and reform (questions the press chose largely to avoid), the personal drama held out the promise of returning the political system to normal as soon as the individuals were accused, charged, and removed from office. True to the chosen normalizing plot, when Nixon resigned from office under threat of impeachment, NBC correspondent Roger Mudd led the nation in the cheer "The System Worked!"

The melodramatic resolution—a tearful Nixon saying goodbye to the White House staff and an upbeat ending of good news for the system—seemed to make sense at the time. In retrospect, however, it seems that the news exonerated a system containing the institutional weaknesses that permitted the abuses of power to occur in the first place. Even at the level of personal melodrama, "The System Works" seems an ironic ending. After all, the system pardoned the worst offender, gave light sentences to most of the others, and turned many criminals into millionaires and media celebrities in the process.

In the more than quarter century since Watergate, a kind of balance between deference to authority and adversarialism still exists, but it has been thrown off by a loss of perspective on how to strike that balance. With the increase in "gotcha" journalism, authorities are routinely challenged on personal grounds involving their morality, their gamesmanship, or their credibility. Whether this is more a cause or a consequence of lowered public trust in government is a good question. What is clear is that news audiences see journalists as less objective than at any point since polling has tracked this issue. Popular objections to journalists advancing stories with sensationalism and negativity also challenge another tenet of the modern-day journalism profession: the commitment to standards of decency and good taste.

STANDARDS OF DECENCY AND GOOD TASTE

Standards of decency and taste seem designed to keep the focus of news on important issues and away from the seamy, sensationalistic aspects of political life. These standards have clearly changed in recent years. The sex-drenched coverage of the Clinton-Lewinsky affair suggests a tabloid trend in the press. During that scandal, audiences learned of oral sex in the Oval Office, presidential semen stains on a blue dress, and graphic sexual accounts published in the report of special prosecutor Kenneth Starr. Such a media spectacle would be hard to imagine even ten years earlier.

While an earlier era of media morality would have avoided such things, current moral standards seem to involve publicizing them with expressions of shock and disapproval. Even as they drag up seamy details, journalists are also quick to pronounce moralistic judgments. It would have been useful during the Lewinsky affair to do a count of the number of raised eyebrows on the Sunday morning news shows or the numbers of shocked and disdainful expressions uttered by Sam, Cokie, and George. Whereas an earlier generation of journalistic morality police may not have published such material in the first place, a later generation driven to sensationalism will publish first and then decry its sorry content.

Although the media seem to have become obsessed with the private lives of politicians and other public figures, there are other areas that are avoided with great consistency. For example, graphic images of gruesome death, profane language, erotic art, or depictions of the human anatomy seldom appear in the news. (And when they do, they often cause a stir, as illustrated by the live coverage of the freeway chase-suicide described earlier in the book.) When such material is publicized, it is generally preceded by disclaimers such as, "The following video contains images that may be disturbing to some viewers. Viewer discretion is advised."

Even as it evolves, there remains a curious strain of middle American morality and taste that the mainstream press long ago adopted as part of its professional code. Even coverage of scandals generally carries the moral message of family values and the enduring obligation of politicians to uphold them. As for the collection of things regarded as too tasteless, offensive, or obscene to include in the news, excluding them legitimizes the middle-class values that may often be at odds with the actual events that reporters witness. To put it bluntly, reporters and editors may censor their coverage to bring news images in line with social values and sensitivities. The practical application of standards of good taste creates two paradoxes for news content. First, standards of taste have a bias in favor of precisely those status quo values that the bulk of political propaganda promotes.[36] Moreover, the avoidance of offensive ideas removes from public awareness many undesirable but true aspects of the real world. As a result, the definitions of and the solutions for the problems represented in the news, however artificial, may appeal to the ideals of the middle-class, church-going public.

The Morality Police

Censoring news according to standards of taste runs counter to a key feature of politics. Politics is the primary social activity through which widely divergent values and morals come together in struggles for dominance and legitimacy. The selective attention to preferred morals not only passively promotes the work of propagandists, as mentioned previously, but it actively distorts the values and issues at stake in many situations. In this latter role, standards of taste may lead to overt censorship of some aspects of news events, thereby making journalists active agents in shaping the definitions of political situations. Should journalists join forces with society's morality police? Consider the following cases and decide for yourself.

A classic example of how standards of taste can affect the definition of political events is illustrated by the news coverage of a statement made by Agriculture Secretary Earl Butz during the 1976 presidential campaign. While flying between campaign appearances, Butz made a blatantly racist remark to a group of reporters. This remark was not only significant on its own merits due to its appalling racist content, but it was also pertinent to the campaign because it was offered in response to a question about Republican election strategies. Although the statement contains offensive language of the sort not often found in scholarly writing (not to mention news stories), its political magnitude can be conveyed only by quoting it directly. When asked about the efforts of the Republican party to mobilize the black vote, Butz remarked that it was pointless to worry about the black vote because blacks were unconcerned about politics. He then summarized his view of the concerns of blacks as follows: "I'll tell you what coloreds want. It's three things: first, a tight pussy; second, loose shoes; and third, a warm place to shit."[37]

It is arguably in the public interest to publicize a racist remark uttered by a U.S. cabinet officer while campaigning for the president who appointed him. However, the professional press regarded Butz's offense to good taste as a higher consideration than his offense to political sensibilities. The pervasive commitment to the decency code was reflected in a simple fact: Not one major news outlet ran the Butz remark at the time it was made. Only when the statement was quoted later at the end of a rambling article on the campaign in the (then) underground magazine *Rolling Stone* did the respectable press have to acknowledge that the incident had in fact happened. Even when major press and broadcast outlets ran the story, only one major daily paper (the Madison, Wisconsin, *Capitol Times*) used the verbatim language. In defense of their use of inoffensive euphemisms in place of the real language, editors and news producers pronounced the litany of the decency code. An editor at the *New York Times* put it this way: ". . . we recognized that if we used this series of filthy obscenities then we'll probably use the next." The editor of the *Des Moines Register* said he found the remark so offensive and so atrocious that "I couldn't bring myself to give it to people with their breakfast." The editor of the *Washington Post* produced a tortured chain of logic leading to the conclusion that only if the president himself had uttered the remarks would he have printed them, but lesser officials did not merit such a violation of the journalism code.[38]

The impact of the statement was lost when euphemisms were substituted for the actual language. As a result, the Ford campaign was spared the painful embarrassment of this rare lapse from its agenda of carefully staged and scripted performances. When the national press finally acknowledged the incident, Ford had little choice but to fire Butz.

However, one suspects that Butz's desire to exit the situation gracefully and Ford's wish to minimize his political losses could not have been satisfied any better than through the delicate treatment accorded to the episode by the journalistic community.

Sex, Death, and Censorship

The decency code is so entrenched that it even applies to coverage of important health and biological issues. For example, it took over two years for the mainstream media to explain that one way in which the dreaded disease AIDS (acquired immune deficiency syndrome) is spread is through anal intercourse. The threat posed by a large-scale, life-threatening AIDS epidemic would seem to call for rapid delivery of as much explicit information as possible to the public. Yet in the early, panicky years of the disease, the decency code governed information content about AIDS. Early stories suggested that the disease was transmitted "not through casual contact," and through the "exchange of bodily fluids." As one editor put it, "We would make the reader guess what was going on rather than use the term 'anal intercourse' . . . We wouldn't spell it out." A television reporter recalls receiving pressure from her producer to refrain from using explicit language in response to a few phone calls from morally offended viewers. It took years for consensus to emerge in the media that informing the public about health risks was more important than censoring offensive language from the news.[39]

What is the obligation of the press to communicate information that people may not want to hear, read, or see? Imagine, for a moment, that you were an editor for a news organization covering the Gulf War in 1991. The United States just routed the Iraqi army from Kuwait City, and the fleeing army has been attacked by American airpower, creating a scene that was widely described as "the highway of death." The carnage was so distressing that some of the American pilots involved asked the commanders to stop it. Behind the scenes, a high-level debate was raging about whether to go on with the war, knowing that it would produce a massacre of the enemy's disorganized army, or whether to stop it and leave the enemy with a substantial portion of its fighting force intact for the future. A photojournalist visited the highway of death and took a terrifying picture of the remains of an Iraqi soldier burned alive with a hideous expression on his face, his arms raised in the macabre position in which he died while trying to climb out of his flaming vehicle. It was an image right out of a horror movie.

Would you run the picture? Why not run a picture in the news that is no worse than an image that millions of people might pay money to see in a horror movie? More to the point, why not run a photo that appeared in leading English and French newspapers on the grounds that it brought home the fact that at least 100,000 Iraqis died in the war, and people should be forced to consider the human consequences of decisions to go to war? However, the newspaper and magazine editors of America never even had the chance to struggle with these issues because the leading photo wire service that had the option to buy and distribute the picture censored it at the source. The picture never even went out over the wires.

The AP editor explained that he did not buy and distribute the photo because he already knew what the reaction of newspaper editors would be: "Newspapers will tell us, 'We can't present pictures like that for people to look at over breakfast.' "[40] The picture editor at *Time* magazine later said this about the picture: "It's dramatic. It's horrific. It says it all about war." However, he admitted that even if he had seen it in time, *Time* probably would not have printed it because, "Whenever we run a picture like that, we're heavily criticized. We get a lot of reader mail."[41]

Should such images be part of the news? Are they worse than images commonly shown in movies? How should the news limit its representations of reality? The case of the photo of the Iraqi soldier and many similar episodes from the Gulf War raise the troublesome question of whether people in a country at war should see comforting images of war as they prefer to think about it, or whether they should be stimulated, even shocked, into thinking about the consequences of the political decision to go to war.

Notice that the decisions of both the wire service editor and the picture editor at *Time* magazine hint at the economic costs of running the photo. The wire editor in effect said that nobody would buy it anyway, so there was no point in wasting the money to acquire and distribute it. The *Time* editor noted that subscribers would object to it. Their reasoning suggests that, as with the grand principle of objectivity, the moralism of the press also has economic roots. As explained in the case study, a key part of the market strategy of the turn-of-the-nineteenth-century press was to appeal to the moral sensibilities of the most affluent, rapidly growing, and untapped mass news market: the middle class. Since that time, the news has continued to present a restricted picture of American society in two ways: First, by representing the world through middle-class values, the news became an implicit model for social propriety; second, by introducing selective moral perspectives into news coverage, the press tacitly became the legitimator of the same values it helped to promote.

The strength of middle-class moralism in the news business is formidable. For example, even a tabloid paper like the *New York Daily News* did not print the word *syphilis* until 1931, long after it had become a major social problem. Similarly, the prototype of the highbrow family newspaper, the *New York Times,* refused to review Kinsey's landmark study of sexual behavior until years later when it had been certified by the academic community as a serious scholarly work. One also suspects that human sexual behavior was a significant and widely practiced phenomenon long before the *Times* endorsed it as a subject worthy of discussion.[42]

As the frenzied coverage of the Clinton-Lewinsky sexual activities indicate, the standards for reporting on the private lives of public figures are clearly changing. Yet many other areas of moral standard-bearing are still protected by mainstream journalism. As with other reporting codes and practices discussed in this chapter, filtering the real world through the value lenses of middle America lends the news a familiar, safe quality. This morality filter contributes to the illusion of objectivity not because the resulting news content mirrors the diversity of the social world, but because it reflects the values of the news audience.

DOCUMENTARY REPORTING PRACTICES

Objective reporting assumes that journalists do not embellish their stories, advocate particular interpretations of ambiguous events, or otherwise make up the news. These principles define the practice of documentary reporting. Reporters trained in the documentary method report only the information that they have witnessed and only the facts that credible sources have confirmed. Although the goals of documentary reporting are hard to fault, in practice the method creates a trap for journalists confronted with staged political performances. Only in rare cases when performances are flawed or when behind-the-scenes staging is revealed, can reporters document in good professional fashion what they know otherwise to be the case: The news event in question was staged for propaganda purposes. The problem, as Daniel Boorstin has pointed out, is that manufactured news events, or pseudo-events, contain their own self-supporting and self-fulfilling documentation. Thus the documentary method highlights the very aspects of events that were designed to be reported, blurring the underlying reality of the situation.[43] The paradox of the documentary method is clear: The more perfectly an event is staged, the more documentable and hence reportable it becomes.

In response to this dilemma, news organizations have begun to expose some of these planned media events.[44] However, the proportion of stories exposing media events is minuscule in relation to those based on media events. This imbalance between reported and actual occurrences of staged events has a distorting effect similar to adversarialism. However, by exposing even a fraction of the political manipulation in the news, journalists may reassure the public that they are monitoring such manipulation and alerting the public when it occurs.

A more common practice reflecting the "new cynicism" that seems to characterize the press in recent times is to frame political situations as games between manipulative actors. This tendency has been described by various scholars, including Kathleen Jamieson and Thomas Patterson, as noted in Chapter 1. The focus on political motives and maneuvers may or may not capture the essence of contemporary politics, but it conveys an essence of politics that seems both to ring true for many disillusioned citizens, who, perhaps correctly, see the press as part of the game. As a result, the documentary method has bent in ways that reflect the odd changes that have resulted in "gotcha" adversarialism and steamy moralism. Reporting the political game, rather than the institutional safeguards or social values at stake in it, may continue to look like objective reporting to journalists, but it may undermine the sense of news authority on the part of audiences.

THE USE OF STORIES AS STANDARDIZED NEWS FORMATS

Although adopting the story as the basic news unit also had economic roots, stories quickly became justified under the norm of objective journalism. Stories can be defended as standardized and mechanical means of communicating information. This representation gives journalists a claim to a universal methodology of objective reporting. The problem with this definition is that it is a very selective rendition of what storytelling is all about. Telling a story requires choices about what information to include, what words to assign to the included information, and how to tie together all the chosen symbols into a coherent whole. These choices in turn depend on assessing the audience, deciding what point to make to that audience, and choosing what plot techniques (flashbacks, sequencing, character development, climax, etc.) will best make that point. In short, stories are not mirrors of events.[45]

A well-constructed story may be plausible, but plausibility and truth in the world of storytelling have little necessary connection.[46] An obvious implication of these features of storytelling is that they give reporters room to emphasize dramatic and narrative aspects of events.[47] Epstein suggests that the use of artistic (i.e., literary and dramatic) forms in news construction is encouraged by editors, one of whom even issued a memo containing formal instructions about how to incorporate dramatic structure into stories.[48] Gans notes the frequency with which reporters "restage" aspects of stories to heighten their dramatic qualities.[49]

The dramatic license in storytelling creates a tension: The wholesale invention of news plots would place enormous strains on the norm of objective reporting. This tension between the value of dramatic news and the commitment to documentary reporting helps explain the receptivity of news organizations to events that are staged dramatically by news sources. Staged events are designed to be documented, and their dramatic features are built in. So important is the dramatic element in political performances that they are often judged for newsworthiness on this criterion. Gans observed that

> an exciting story boosts morale; and when there is a long drought of exciting stories, they [reporters] become restless. . . . Some magazine writers, left "crabby" by a drought of dramatic domestic news, joked about their readiness to be more critical of the President and other public officials for their failure to supply news that would "make adrenalin flow."[50]

The Limited Stock of News Plots

The use of stories further constrains news content by promoting the use of standardized plots in news reporting. Any communication network based on stories will become biased toward particular themes. For example, criminal trials are dominated by such familiar plots as mistaken identity, victim of circumstances, and others relevant to the legal judgment of cases.[51] The national obsession with the O. J. Simpson murder case in 1994 and 1995 can be explained in part by the rich set of plots and subplots that ran through the developing story: murder, circumstantial evidence, allegations of framing, the fallen hero, the abusive relationship, sex, and celebrity. Add to these dramatic ingredients the element of race, and an already big human-interest story became even richer with political plot possibilities. One newspaper headline even proclaimed: "Modern Shakespearean Tragedy Rivets Nation."[52]

When a unique event engages familiar dramatic themes, the stage is set for an interesting story. This principle of communication holds true whether in a conversation between friends or in a journalistic account about lofty national issues. Storytelling between friends frequently centers on recurring themes that define the relationship and express the identities that the individuals have created in it. In politics, consensus and legitimacy can be promoted through the frequent use of dominant values, beliefs, and myths of the political culture.[53] Gans has noted the news is dominated by a remarkably small number of recurring themes. These plot devices include ethnocentrism (America first, America-the-generous, America-the-embattled, etc.), altruistic democracy, responsible capitalism, and individualism, among others.[54]

Political performances scripted around routine themes legitimize the status quo at the price of severely limiting the range of political discourse.[55] The formula-story syndrome enables reporters to use plots to screen and organize facts so that few details are left dangling, and the resulting story can be viewed as an exhaustive representation of reality. This naive approach to objectivity gives news writing a mystical quality described by Robert Darnton:

> Big stories develop in special patterns and have an archaic flavor, as if they were metamorphoses or *Ur*-stories that have been lost in the depths of time. . . . News writing is heavily influenced by stereotypes and by preconceptions of what "the story" should be. Without preestablished categories of what constitutes "news," it is impossible to sort out experience.[56]

Just as stories lock in the narrow political messages of routine news events, they can introduce distortions into investigative reporting. Stories, by definition, encapsulate events, making them seem self-contained and independent of external forces. Yet the tips provided by inside sources to investigative reporters are often (one suspects, usually) motivated by the source's own political considerations. These motives are seldom included in the stories fashioned by reporters. Recall, for example, the earlier discussion that the Watergate story based on the investigative reporting of Woodward and Bernstein may have been only part of a much larger political scandal (see Chapter 2). The source of the inside information necessary to keep the story unfolding seemed to provide only information that would turn the story toward the Oval Office. Epstein noted that there might have been other political actors, perhaps inside the CIA, who could have been caught up in the Watergate scandal had the reporters not encapsulated the issues in a story centered on the president and his men.[57]

We will probably never know who provided the information that trapped Nixon within the damaging Watergate story. It is ironic that the reporting practices involved prevent our finding out who did it or why. The obvious need to protect the confidentiality of sources is not the only, or even, the most important reason why the political contexts of news stories are seldom disclosed. The elevation of the story form to a professional practice places an even more subtle prohibition on revealing the politics behind political news. It would be devastating to the simple view of news reality to show that behind every story lies another story that comes much closer to revealing the true politics of the situation. As Epstein explained, the story-behind-the-story approach to news reporting would blow the cover off the normative claim that objective reality can be encapsulated somehow in stories.

REPORTERS AS GENERALISTS

Stories play another role in journalism as a universal reporting methodology employed by all reporters whether of politics, sports, or business. Reporters are trained as generalists who are able to write stories on any subject. Although a small percentage end up reporting in a specialized area such as science or fashion, the majority change beats periodically and pride themselves on their ability to cover any news story.[58]

The emphasis in the profession on training reporters as generalists has obvious origins and payoffs. As Gans noted,

> . . . the news is still gathered mostly by generalists. One reason is economic, for general reporters earn less and are more productive. Beat reporters can rarely produce more than one story per television program or magazine issue, while general reporters can be asked, when necessary, to complete two or more assignments within the same period.[59]

Despite these obvious economic advantages, generalism is justified almost exclusively in normative terms. A key element of the journalism code is informing the average citizen. The use of generalists who tell simple stories is justified as the best means of presenting comprehensible information to the average person.

Keeping It Simple

If a reporter has any special expertise on a topic, he or she may run the risk of complicating a story or violating the story form altogether by lapsing into technical analysis. Editors and news producers seem to widely believe that the general public cannot follow news produced by specialized reporters. For example, Epstein reported this response by an NBC News executive to a Justice Department suggestion that the TV networks use correspondents with special knowledge of ghetto problems to cover urban riots: "Any good journalist should be able to cover a riot in an unfamiliar setting. . . . A veneer of knowledgeability in a situation like this could be less than useless."[60] In another case, Gans reported a comment by an executive producer to his economics reporter following a good story on a complicated subject. "You scare me with your information; I think we'll put you on another beat."[61] Gans also noted that many specialists shared a general anxiety that they were becoming too knowledgeable for the tastes of their audiences or their superiors.

Although generalism is justified normatively as a necessary concession to a mass audience, the audience may pay a high political price in exchange for the alleged gains in news comprehension. Generalist reporters are often at the mercy of the news source. In technical areas, they are seldom qualified to ask critical questions.[62] As a result, reporters may have to ask news sources for guidelines about appropriate questions. Even when generalists are assigned to fairly straightforward political stories, they may have to fashion their stories almost entirely from official pronouncements and the story angles pursued by other reporters.[63] Because generalists are more dependent on their sources than are specialists, the odds are even greater that they will report fabricated events. Moreover, generalists may be less likely than specialists to spot flaws in performances that would make it possible to expose the contrived nature of an event. For example, Gans noted of generalists:

> Not knowing their sources well enough to discount self-serving information, they may report an opinion or a hopeful guess—for example, the size of an organization's membership—as a statistical fact. In this way, enterprising politicians sometimes get inflated estimates of their support into the news. . . . Occasion-

ally, general reporters may cover only one side of a story without ever knowing that there are other sides.[64]

This generalization about generalism applies even to areas in which we might expect more perspective and sophistication. For example, business reporting reflects news values that seriously neglect the political or social impacts (or the inner politics) of corporations in modern life. Instead, business news tends to be a mix of shallow reports of mergers and profit analyses, alongside personality profiles of corporate celebrities such as Donald Trump or Bill Gates. As noted by Diana Henriques of the *New York Times,* one of the relatively few investigative business reporters in the mainstream news business, even business editors at prestige news organizations, often have little sense of big business as a social or political force. Indeed, because these editors often parachute into the business desks as generalists with little understanding of economics or the inner workings of corporations, their news assignments and decisions about what to run reinforce the tendency to report a shallow mix of profit and loss and profiles of companies and executives. Lacking much depth or perspective, such business news implicitly promotes the myths of business virtue and the superior rationality of free markets.[65]

When the giant Enron Corporation went bankrupt in 2001 and the unbelievable story of its shady pyramid schemes and corrupt accounting practices came to light, there was little in the business press to prepare the public for the spectacle. Even the *Wall Street Journal* investigation of Enron the year before stopped short of blowing the whistle on the company because the journalist assigned to the story could not understand how the company actually worked. Similarly, the political story of Enron's involvement in shaping Bush administration energy policy was not even hinted at until after the collapse of the company in a cloud of deception and corruption.

THE PRACTICE OF EDITORIAL REVIEW

It is hard to imagine that the practice of editors' reviewing, checking, and approving reporters' preliminary accounts of events could be criticized. The review policies of most news organizations are represented as ensuring that the professional practices discussed earlier will be used in reporting the news. In a sense, editorial review does serve this function, thereby also ensuring the news distortion produced by these journalistic practices. Editorial review exerts its own influence on the political content of the news as well. Editors are not just the overseers of news production; they are accountable to management for the competitive position of their news product in the marketplace. As a result, editors and owners (or managers) typically develop guidelines that their reporters must follow in order to be successful and professionally respectable in their eyes. Studies of the internal workings of news organizations make it clear that these often subtle editorial pressures are major influences on reporters and on the political content of news.[66]

These editorial pressures would not be so worrisome if they were idiosyncratic, giving each news organization its own perspective and encouraging reporters to be different. However, the safest editorial course is often to cover the same stories in the same ways as other organizations but to package them differently, using concerned anchors, catchy theme music, or bold headlines to attract the audience. It is no secret that most editors take their leads from the wire services and the prestige papers such as the *New York Times,* the *Washington Post,* and, increasingly, the *Wall Street Journal.* The reliance on the wire services and the prestige papers as implicit standardizing mechanisms applies to both print and broadcast media.[67] In addition, editors tend to standardize their product further by comparing it to the competition. It is easier for them to justify similarities in the coverage of stories than to account for differences between organizations. To put it simply, the transparency of the objectivity or fairness claim becomes most evident when the coverage of one organization differs from the others and, as a result, journalists must defend it against queries by publishers, politicians, and the public. The best defense of objectivity is contained in the implicit standardization of editorial review practices.

The obvious political consequence of standardized editorial policies was captured nicely by Edwin Diamond, who noted that editorial practices reinforce the worst tendency in the news business to stereotype stories. News stereotypes conform to the major plot outlines of fabricated news performances and give the news its obvious status quo bias. As Diamond notes, none of this bias can be attributed directly to political motives on the part of reporters. To the contrary, the professional standards of journalists cleanse the news of such motives; yet, somehow, the resulting product does seem to display a particular slant:

> The press isn't "racist," though as the skins of the participants become darker, the lengths of the stories shrink. The press isn't "pro-Israeli," though it is very sensitive to Jewish-American feelings. The press isn't afraid of the "vested interests," though it makes sure Mobil's or Senator Scott's denials appear right along with the charges. The paranoids are wrong: there is no news conspiracy. Instead there are a lot of editors and executives making decisions about what is "the news" while constrained by lack of time, space, money, talent, and understanding, from doing the difficult and/or hidden stories.[68]

In short, the editorial review standards pointed to as the fail-safe mechanism for preventing news distortion are, paradoxically, the very things that guarantee it.

OBJECTIVITY RECONSIDERED

A number of observers (including many journalists when they are not being pressured by critical academics) have argued persuasively that whatever the news is, it is not a spontaneous and objective mirror of the world. Nevertheless, it would be a mistake to leap from this to the conclusion that neither the ideal of objectivity nor professional reporting practices matters. Professional standards still work in several ways that are worth noting. For example, high-minded norms such as objectivity, even if they are not clear themselves, hide the connection between the news and its economic, organizational, and political contexts. Above all, the objectivity norm gives the press the look of an independent social institution. Moreover, even though actual reporting practices distort the political content of the news, they can be rationalized and defended conveniently under the objectivity code, thereby obscuring their political effects. In this fashion, journalistic norms and reporting practices operate together to create the aforementioned information biases in the news—biases that are well hidden behind the facade of independent journalism.

As explained earlier, claims about "objective" reporting rest on very shaky foundations. For every source included, another is excluded. With each tightening of the plot line, meaningful connections to other issues and events become weakened. Every familiar theme or metaphor used in writing about an event obscures a potentially unique feature of the event. Even though it is impossible for the news to be objective, it is important that it seem objective or, in the terms of the trade, "believable." Perhaps most important of all, the practices and perspectives that go into it, the appearance of objectivity or believability depends heavily on striking the right balance between adversarialism and deference toward official sources. It is this balance that seems most in danger of tipping in ways that damage the credibility of news.

How the "New News" May Undermine the Credibility of Journalism Itself

The interesting question is, Why has the news focus shifted in recent times from generally authority-affirming accounts that paint a picture of a normal, orderly world, to more often authority-challenging accounts that describe a world plagued with disorder, intrigue, and mayhem? As explained in Chapter 2, even though representations of authority and social order appear to have tipped toward the negative in recent years, the reason may have little to do with whether officials are really more venal, government is more corrupt, or levels of social disorder are objectively higher. Instead, the increasingly negative images of public authorities and social disorder can be traced at least partly to commercial news pressures for more sensationalism, emotion, and drama and to generate new story developments to feed the twenty-four-hour news cycle.

Recall the argument by sociologist Gaye Tuchman from earlier in this chapter: The illusion of news objectivity depends on journalists treating the world of officialdom as authoritative. If this is true, then "gotcha" journalism may have the effect of undermining the very essence of news objectivity. No matter how much journalists dedicate themselves to the ideal (by whatever name it goes), the legitimacy of the news may suffer under the burden of "gotcha" adversarialism. This is not to imply that achieving credibility by blindly reporting the pronouncements of officials is a good idea either. It is simply to say that the ideal of objectivity may be flawed, no matter how journalists try to pursue it in a given era. What matters is not debunking objectivity but understanding that the endless debate about it may keep people from seeing that the underlying biases in the news are created by the very efforts of journalists to achieve it.

It is also important to understand that just as the basic practices that define objectivity evolved over the course of the nineteenth century, and just as the idea of objectivity became a solid foundation of American journalism in the twentieth century, the pace of change in the news business will surely continue to affect both the ideal and the practice of objective journalism in the twenty-first century. Changes such as the twenty-four-hour news cycle or the introduction of marketing people into the editorial offices of news organizations are characteristic of kinds of changes that have spurred the historical evolution of reporting practices and news values discussed throughout this chapter. In short, what accounts for any particular change in the news may be a combination of economic, technological, and social conditions. The results of such change may appear far from rational or coherent. Yet journalism, as much as any profession, continues to try to make sense of its practices and even glorify them with such sobriquets as objective reporting.

When journalists and their audiences grow as far apart in their perceptions of whether a defining concept like objectivity is really being practiced properly, we know that serious tensions exist among the different elements of the news system. Those who produce news and those who consume it appear to have different understandings of what they are doing. In the process, they may have lost an important measure of respect and understanding for each other. Is objectivity possible, or even desirable? That is a question for the reader now to decide. One thing, however, is sure: We live in a time where there is little consensus on just what good reporting might be.

NOTES

1. Trends of surveys of American journalists taken in 1971, 1982–1983, and 1992, reported in David H. Weaver and G. Cleveland Wilhoit, *The American Journalist in the 1990s* (Mahwah, NJ: Lawrence Erlbaum, 1996).
2. Indiana University, Knight survey reported by the Poynter Institute. **www.poynter.org/dg.lts/ id.28823/content.content_view.htm**.
3. John W. C. Johnstone, Edward J. Slawski, and William W. Bowman, *The News People: A Sociological Portrait of American Journalists and Their Work* (Urbana: University of Illinois Press, 1976). Also, Charles J. Brown, Trevor R. Brown, and William L. Rivers, *The Media and People* (New York: Holt, Rinehart and Winston, 1978); and Stephen Hess, *The Washington Reporters* (Washington, DC: Brookings Institution, 1981).
4. Gaye Tuchman, "Objectivity as Strategic Ritual: An Examination of Newsmen's Notions of Objectivity," *American Journal of Sociology* 77 (1972): 660–79.
5. See, for example, Edith Efron, *The News Twisters* (Los Angeles: Nash, 1971); and Doris Graber, *Mass Media and American Politics* (Washington, DC: Congressional Quarterly Press, 1980), chapter 10.
6. David T. Z. Mindich, *Just the Facts: How "Objectivity" Came to Define American Journalism* (New York: New York University Press, 1998), 5–6.
7. Pew Center survey, March 1999, **www.people-press.org/press99sec1.htm**.
8. Mindich, *Just the Facts,* 8.
9. For a review of these professional norms, see John Tebbell, *The Media in America* (New York: Mentor, 1974); Johnstone, Slawski, and Bowman, *The News People;* Gaye Tuchman, *Making News: A Study in the Construction of Reality* (New York: Free Press, 1978); and Michael Schudson, *Discovering the News: A Social History of American Newspapers* (New York: Basic Books, 1978).
10. In recent years, the much-touted specialist has entered the reporting ranks. However, the use of specialists continues to be restricted to a few subject areas like science and economics. Also, specialists are employed by a relatively small number of big news organizations. Because the bulk of political reporting continues to be done by generalists who rotate assignments periodi-

cally and who refrain from introducing technical or theoretical perspectives in their reports, the practice of generalism merits inclusion here.

11. Gerald J. Baldasty, *The Commercialization of News in the Nineteenth Century* (Madison, WI: University of Wisconsin Press, 1992).

12. For supporting evidence for this claim, see, among others, Meyer Berger, *The Story of the New York Times* (New York: Simon & Schuster, 1951); Frank L. Mott, *The News in America* (Cambridge, MA: Harvard University Press, 1952); Edwin Emery and Henry Ladd Smith, *The Press in America* (New York: Prentice-Hall, 1954); Tebbell, *The Media in America;* and Schudson, *Discovering the News.*

13. See Mindich, *Just the Facts.*

14. Ibid.

15. See Baldasty, *The Commercialization of News in the Nineteenth Century,* chapter 2.

16. For discussions of the origins and impact of the wire services, see Bernard Roscho, *Newsmaking* (Chicago: University of Chicago Press, 1975); Mott, *The News in America;* and Emery and Smith, *The Press in America.*

17. Schudson, *Discovering the News,* chapter 3.

18. Upton Sinclair, *The Brass Check* (Pasadena, CA: Author, 1920). Also, Berger, *The Story of the New York Times;* and Tebbell, *The Media in America.*

19. For a history of this period and its ideas, see, among others, Harold J. Laski, "The Present Position of Representative Democracy," *American Political Science Review* 26 (August 1932); 629–41; John Diggins, *Mussolini and Fascism: The View from America* (Princeton, NJ: Princeton University Press, 1972); and Schudson, *Discovering the News.*

20. See the following books by Walter Lippmann: *Drift and Mastery* (New York: Kennerly, 1914); *Liberty and the News* (New York: Harcourt Brace, 1920); *Public Opinion* (New York: Free Press, 1922); and *The Phantom Public* (New York: Harcourt Brace, 1925).

21. Tebbell, *The Media in America,* chapter 12.

22. Lou Cannon, *Reporting: An Inside View* (Sacramento, CA: California Journal Press, 1977), 35.

23. Tuchman, *Making News,* 87.

24. See, for example, Murray Edelman, *The Symbolic Uses of Politics* (Urbana: University of Illinois Press, 1964); Peter L. Berger and Thomas Luckmann, *The Social Construction of Reality* (New York: Anchor, 1966); and W. Lance Bennett, *Public Opinion in American Politics* (New York: Harcourt Brace Jovanovich, 1980), chapters 13 and 14.

25. C. Jack Orr, "Reporters Confront the President: Sustaining a Counterpoised Situation," *Quarterly Journal of Speech* 66 (February 1980): 17–32.

26. Ibid., 22.

27. See, for example, Harvey Molotch and Marilyn Lester, "Accidents, Scandals, and Routines: Resources for Insurgent Methodology," *Insurgent Sociologist* 3 (1973): 1–12; Molotch and Lester, "News as Purposive Behavior: On the Strategic Use of Routine Events, Accidents, and Scandals," *American Sociological Review* 39 (February 1974): 101–12; Murray Edelman, *Political Language* (New York: Academic Press, 1977), chapter 3; Todd Gitlin, *The Whole World Is Watching* (Berkeley: University of California Press, 1980), chapters 2 and 7; Graber, *Mass Media and American Politics,* chapter 8.

28. David L. Altheide and Robert P. Snow, *Media Logic* (Beverly Hills, CA: Sage, 1979), chapters 3 and 4.

29. See, for example, Howard Simmons and Joseph A. Califano, Jr. eds., *The Media and Business* (New York: Vintage, 1979).

30. Henry Beck, "Attentional Struggles and Silencing Strategies in a Human Political Conflict: The Case of the Vietnam Moratoria," *The Structure of Social Attention: Ethological Studies,* eds. M. R. A. Chance and R. R. Larson (New York: Wiley, 1976).

31. Jan S. Wenner and William Greider interview with Bill Clinton in *Rolling Stone* (December 9, 1993): 40–45.
32. For a fascinating look at Richard Nixon's ins and outs with the press, see Marvin Kalb, *The Nixon Memo* (Chicago: University of Chicago Press, 1995).
33. It is not hard to understand why politicians often become personally embittered over their treatment by the press. Although it often seems that politicians adopt a sour-grapes attitude about the adversarial norm itself, the politician's typical complaints that news coverage is arbitrary, gratuitous, and unpredictable may be reasonable and valid perceptions of journalists' ritualistic behaviors.
34. See, for example, Phil Stanford, "Watergate Revisited: Did the Press—and the Courts—Really Get to the Bottom of History's Most Famous Burglary?" *Columbia Journalism Review* (March/April 1986): 46–49.
35. For a more detailed analysis of the spoon-fed aspects of Watergate investigative reporting, see Gladys Engel Lang and Kurt Lang, *The Battle for Public Opinion: The President, the Press, and the Polls during Watergate* (New York: Columbia University Press, 1983). The Langs also provide extensive documentation on the overwhelming emphasis, both in the White House and among the press, on Nixon's personal image and popularity during the Watergate saga.
36. See Jacques Ellul, *Propaganda* (New York: Vintage, 1973).
37. Quoted in *Rolling Stone* (October 7, 1976): 57.
38. For these and other editors' responses, see Priscilla S. Meyer, "Hello, Rolling Stone? What Did Butz Say?" *Wall Street Journal,* October 7, 1976, 18.
39. "AIDS and the Family Paper," *Columbia Journalism Review* (March/April 1986): 11.
40. Quoted in David Walker, "The War Photo That Nobody Wanted to See," *Photo District News* (August 1991): 16.
41. Ibid.
42. Tebbell, *The Media in America,* 141.
43. Daniel Boorstin, *The Image* (New York: Atheneum, 1961).
44. See Edwin Diamond, *Good News, Bad News* (Cambridge, MA: MIT Press, 1978).
45. See W. Lance Bennett, "Storytelling in Criminal Trials: A Model of Social Judgment," *Quarterly Journal of Speech* 64 (February 1978, pp. 1–22); and W. Lance Bennett and Martha S. Feldman, *Reconstructing Reality in the Courtroom* (New Brunswick, NJ: Rutgers University Press, 1981).
46. Bennett and Feldman, *Reconstructing Reality in the Courtroom,* chapter 4.
47. James David Barber, "Characters in the Campaign: The Literary Problem," in *Race for the Presidency: The Media and the Nominating Process,* ed., John Barber (Englewood Cliffs, NJ: Prentice-Hall, 1978).
48. Edward Jay Epstein, *News from Nowhere* (New York: Vintage, 1973), 4–5.
49. Herbert Gans, *Deciding What's News* (New York: Vintage, 1979), 173.
50. Ibid., 171.
51. Bennett, "Storytelling in Criminal Trials," and Bennett and Feldman, *Reconstructing Reality in the Courtroom.*
52. *Atlanta Journal and Constitution* (June 18, 1994), 1.
53. See Murray Edelman, *Political Language* (New York: Academic Press, 1977); and W. Lance Bennett, *Public Opinion in American Politics* (New York: Harcourt Brace Jovanovich, 1980).
54. Gans, *Deciding What's News,* chapter 2.
55. See Tuchman, *Making News;* and Mark Fishman, *Manufacturing the News* (Austin: University of Texas Press, 1980).
56. Robert Darnton, "Writing News and Telling Stories," *Daedalus* 104 (Spring 1975): 189.
57. Edward Jay Epstein, "The Grand Cover-Up," *Wall Street Journal,* April 19, 1976, 10.
58. Johnstone, Slawski, and Bowman, *News People.*
59. Gans, *Deciding What's News,* 143.

60. Epstein, *News from Nowhere,* 137.
61. Gans, *Deciding What's News,* 143.
62. Ibid.
63. Ibid.; also Crouse, *Boys on the Bus.*
64. Gans, *Deciding What's News,* 142.
65. A summary of remarks by Diana Henriques at a seminar on "Corporate Power: You Can Run, but You Can't Hide," Shorenstein Center, Kennedy School of Government, Harvard University, October 12, 1999.
66. See, for example, Breed, "Social Control in the Newsroom," *Social Forces* 33 (May 1955): 326–35; Walter Geiber, "Across the Desk: A Study of 16 Telegraph Editors," *Journalism Quarterly* 33 (Fall 1956): 423–32; Epstein, *News from Nowhere;* Crouse, *Boys on the Bus;* and Gans, *Deciding What's News.*
67. For discussion of the impact of wire services on newspaper coverage, see Crouse, *Boys on the Bus;* and Sigal, *Reporters and Officials.* The impact of the "wires" on television news is discussed extensively in Epstein, *News from Nowhere;* and Gans, *Deciding What's News.*
68. Diamond, *Good News, Bad News,* 228.

Chapter 7

The News Audience: Information Processing and Public Opinion

To give citizens a choice in ideas and information is to give them a choice in politics. If a nation has narrowly controlled information, it will soon have narrowly controlled politics.

Ben H. Bagdikian

The post-baby boom generation—roughly speaking, men and women who were born after 1964 and thus came of age in the 1980s and 1990s—are substantially less knowledgeable about public affairs, despite the proliferation of sources of information. Even in the midst of national election campaigns in the 1980s and 1990s, for example, these young people were about a third less likely than their elders to know, for instance, which party controlled the House of Representatives.

Robert D. Putnam

Increasing numbers of people are tuning out the news because they find it negative, distressing, or discouraging (recall the discussions in Chapters 1 and 3). Unfortunately, this escape from the news is too often an escape from politics and civic life as well. Communication scholar Roderick Hart argues that the way we communicate may even make people feel "saintly" about abandoning politics.[1] Like the politicians, pundits, and critics they hear in the news, many citizens adopt the identity of outsiders battling a hydra-headed monster of government—a system run amok. For many, cynicism becomes an angry stance against a political communication process that offers little beyond targeted messages aimed at shaping opinion, shifting votes, or raising and lowering the chorus of public discontent. This does not mean that people necessarily buy all or even most of what the politicians are selling. It does mean, however, that when they enter the political arena, the language and choices they find are products of the communication processes outlined in this book.

The most distressing escape from the news and politics has been among young people. According to Robert Putnam, quoted at the opening of this chapter, each generation of young Americans entering society in the last several decades has been less informed, less inclined to follow politics in the news, and less likely to participate in political life than the last. This pattern of generational rejection of politics is unlike anything witnessed in modern times. Here is how Putnam describes it:

> Today's generation gap in political knowledge does not reflect some permanent tendency for the young to be less well informed than their elders but is instead a recent development. From the earliest opinion polls in the 1940s to the mid-1970s, younger people were at least as well informed as their elders were, but that is no longer the case. This news and information gap, affecting not just politics, but even things like airline crashes, terrorism, and financial news, first opened up with the boomers in the 1970s and widened considerably with the advent of the X generation. Daily newspaper readership among young people under 35 dropped from two-thirds in 1965 to one-third in 1990, at the same time that TV news viewership in this same age group fell from 52 percent to 41 percent. Today's under-thirties pay less attention to the news and know less about current events than their elders do today or than people their age did two or three decades ago.[2]

This chapter explores two citizen information trends that have a common source. First, the failure of both news and politics to engage and motivate people—particularly younger citizens—has contributed to alarming information and participation gaps in the American democracy. Second, those who continue to try to find meaning in news content are often frustrated with the negativity, sensationalism, and disconnection from their own political concerns and action options. In both cases, the news frustrates the formation of informed publics on which the quality of democracy depends. On most issues, publics are poorly informed, and those who do follow events are disproportionately older, white, conservative males.[3]

It may be too simple to blame politics and the media for the public disconnection. It is clear that most people would rather spend their time in public as consumers than citizens. The culture of hostility toward politics and government, while fanned by politicians and media cynicism, surely runs deep in contemporary American culture. Audience attention seldom strays far beyond very personal concerns. For example much as television news producers try to create content to lure the commercially attractive female age 18 to 34 demographic, that group is still the most likely (45 percent) to watch news with the remote in hand, and switch channels when not interested in the next story.[4] The following section explores the link between news and these qualities of citizen life.

NEWS, CITIZEN INFORMATION, AND PUBLIC OPINION

People cannot make contact with distant others or form a coherent body of public opinion without embracing some issues and ideas in common. Consider just three of the many ways in which news content matters:

1. *The formation of publics.* In an age in which people may have more in common as talk show or television audiences than as workers, neighbors, or members of political parties or other social institutions, they pick up their political cues and public identities most easily through media experiences. As a result, individuals seldom join together as publics without reliance on media cues and images.

2. *Political awareness and importance of issues.* News coverage varies in the volume of attention devoted to a few dramatic issues and the scant attention to many others. This emphasis affects the importance that people assign to issues and whether they know enough to even form meaningful opinions.

3. *Shaping political thinking and behavior.* Not all political messages in the news affect individual thinking, but some do. Marketing research is aimed at finding messages that appeal to popular thinking, and communication consultants are paid to develop strategies to get those messages into the news. Even if only a small percentage of voters or "issue publics" change their feelings about a candidate or an issue, that change can affect the outcome of an election or an issue campaign.

The questions of how much and in what ways people rely on media cues still divide many scholars, but few today are willing to admit—as many did just a few decades ago—that the media have only minimal effects on individuals.[5]

THE CITIZEN'S DILEMMA: WHO AND WHAT TO BELIEVE

In considering whether to become involved in public life, people confront a dilemma: If they ignore or discount what they hear from the officials and opinion leaders who make the news, they become isolated and unable to contribute to that most precious citizen resource in a democracy—public opinion. By contrast, people who overcome their cynicism and become part of public life often feel pressured to adjust their views to the available media agenda of issues and credible positions.

Whether they choose isolation, consensus, or escape, people complain that their opinions are often dashed by government inaction, political promises that turn out to be false or misleading, and policies that sounded better in the news than when put into action. These experiences account for the rising tide of political discontent measured in polls and in elections over the past quarter century.[6] What traps people in this dilemma is that the national political communication process is more often one way than two way, providing little room for grassroots exploration of alternative agendas and programs for public action. Even many citizen revolts—such as the movement to impose term limits on elected politicians—turn out to be organized by interests with ties to traditional politics and big money.

Not surprisingly, this dilemma affects people differently. Some adopt a familiar ideology or party line and embrace it meaningfully, whether or not it seems to be solving real-world problems. Some abandon politics altogether and step behind a shield of isolation and cynicism. Others decide that participating in public life, for all its dilemmas, is better than leading an isolated existence. One hope for greater public input in defining the agendas of government and society is the use of the Internet to develop and communicate public opinion.

INTERNET VERSUS MASS MEDIA: WHY MAINSTREAM NEWS STILL MATTERS

With the advent of the Web and the Internet, many citizens may end up turning to alternative information channels that deliver politically packaged information that is better integrated with personal interests and various citizen action options. The promise of the Internet for politics lies in low-cost, interactive, and politically focused communication that facilitates rather than discourages citizen engagement. Although more people, particularly young people, are turning to interactive media, the "reality" of politics continues to be shaped by mass media news and the information management strategies of political actors.

Consider the interplay of different media levels in the rise of Howard Dean in the presidential primaries of 2004. Dean's sudden surge from a long shot to the frontrunner can be attributed in large part to his campaign's deployment of interactive technologies that informed and mobilized large numbers of supporters very rapidly (see the case study in Chapter 8). However, the campaign team neglected the management of mass media images. Soon after building Dean up as the leading candidate, the national press hatched a story that Dean was hot tempered and too "angry" to attract enough voters to defeat the cool George Bush. The Dean team played into that worrisome story following his defeat in the Iowa caucuses when campaign manager Joe Trippi reportedly urged Dean to give a fiery speech to rally his disappointed young campaign workers. The hot speech violated all the rules of performing on the cool medium of television. The news cameras captured frenetic bursts of finger pointing and arm waving that built to a strange yell that soon became a media icon. The "Dean scream" traveled through the news, talk shows, comedy programs, and the Web, capturing the candidate in an image that will forever join the ranks of bad media moments.

PROCESSING THE NEWS

In the view of political scientists Russell Neuman, Marion Just, and Ann Crigler, "The traditional view of the way citizens gain information from the media is dominated by imagery of a vegetative audience, passively absorbing media influence."[7] Because they cite me as holding this view, let me set the record straight: There is considerable evidence that individuals actively select, filter, and personalize the meanings that they draw from the news. Yet whether such engagement makes people feel better about society, relate to others, or act effectively as citizens remain open questions. Moreover, the failure of news to motivate those who are not already interested in the political process, means that the escape from public life (particularly among younger citizens) continues to grow. Communication scholars Thomas Patterson and Philip Seib argue that the most important function of the media may not be to directly inform citizens, but to first attract their attention and interest. Once people have developed an interest in politics, they are more likely to seek out information that is often available in the media environment.[8]

Without the guidance provided by political interest and curiosity, the information environment can seem overwhelming. One of the pioneers in understanding how people "tame the information tide" is political scientist Doris Graber. Her research on how people process the news reveals that many personal factors shape what people pay attention to and what they think it means: personal interests in the issue or problem; the influence of friends who provide news updates and interpretations; and eventually, the personal frames or models of society that people develop to recognize familiar aspects of news stories. Her latest work is aimed at how to reconnect young citizens with information that engages and motivates them to act politically. She concludes from a research on how the brain processes information that more visual, interactive television and Web-based formats contain the potential to reconnect young citizens.[9]

Most research shows that people develop personal interpretive strategies that help them actively *construct* meanings from the news. In some cases, these constructions can be quite surprising and removed from the apparently intentional meanings in the news (or entertainment) content itself. For example, communication scholar John Fiske found that homeless people residing in a shelter often produced "oppositional readings" of popular television shows, cheering for the bad guys and rejecting the good guys—mirroring the way that "proper society" had rejected them in real life.[10]

Sociologist William Gamson shows that people explore news issues in often remarkable depth through everyday conversation, applying various interpretations that were not contained in the news stories they consumed. For example, some people overcome the sense of isolation from events by applying "collective action" frames that address issues of justice, common identities, and the possibilities for social action. Gamson acknowledges that breaking out of the sense of isolation often associated with news frames is easier for people with direct personal experience with an issue. People without direct experience are far more influenced by the framing in news stories.[11]

Following in this tradition, the studies by Neuman, Just, and Crigler have sharpened our understanding of how people interact with news information. For example, people are less likely to regard even heavily covered issues as important if they feel powerless to do much about them. People are more likely to wade through dense and complex stories if they contain information about "what you can do about the problem."[12] It also turns out that the medium matters. Contrary to common stereotypes, people actually learn more from television coverage of most issues than from newspaper coverage. It seems hard for most people to decode and organize the greater detail of newspaper coverage unless they already have a personal interest in the issue and, following Graber's earlier finding, unless they have some personal frame of reference to help sort through the dense newspaper format. News magazines are much more accessible than newspapers and nearly as informative as television, perhaps because they offer more of an overview and a thematic perspective in a weekly format than in daily newspaper installments. This research may provide a simple explanation for why the vast majority of people prefer television as their primary news source: They actually learn more from it.[13]

WHY PEOPLE PREFER TV: AUDIO AND VISUAL INFORMATION

As noted earlier, people generally learn more from television than from other news media. Not surprisingly, TV is the runaway favorite news source across all the standard demographic divides. Among the general public, TV beats newspapers as the *most important* (not necessarily the only) news source by better than a 2 to 1 margin (56 percent rely primarily on TV, compared to 24 percent for newspapers, 14 percent for radio, and only about 1 percent for magazines). The margin of TV to newspapers goes up to 3 to 1 for women (and better than 4 to 1 for women over age 30), and the 2 to 1 TV preference for whites jumps to 6 to 1 for nonwhites.[14] If we relax the standards a bit, 75 percent say they regularly watch some television news program, with local news leading the way in most age and sex demographic categories.[15]

Americans love TV. Some surveys claim that people, on average, get more satisfaction from television than from a wide range of other pursuits, including sports, eating, hobbies, and even sex![16] Most people watch TV with the explicit expectation of having a pleasurable or emotionally stimulating experience. Perhaps the most interesting commentary on the centrality of television is from a study of people (680 households, 1,614 individuals) whose TV sets were either stolen (19 percent) or broken (81 percent). In 24 percent of these households, people experienced something like a mourning reaction, and 68 percent reported psychological troubles ranging from anxiety symptoms (39 percent) to moderate discomfort (29 percent).[17]

Doris Graber notes these and other studies as indicators that TV stimulates the human brain in more comprehensive ways than other print and electronic media do—with the exception of interactive streamed media on the Web. Graber cites research on human brain functions and information processing to conclude that information is not compartmentalized, but continually integrated across different kinds of sensory input. TV, unlike most other news media, gives us words, sounds, and sights to work with. This enriches the sense of understanding and knowing more about televised situations.[18] The important question, of course, how those who produce television news approach their responsibility to carefully select the pictures and sounds that go along with the words.

NEWS FRAMES AND POLITICAL LEARNING

For all that individuals may bring to bear in interpreting the news, there is considerable evidence that news content can greatly affect (if not determine) the thinking of the average person. Recall two important effects that none of the above studies appears to refute. The work of Iyengar and Kinder (see Chapter 2) showed that just making the news made issues seem more important than issues that are not covered, confirming the hypothesis that the news often tells people what to think about.[19] A follow-up series of experiments by Iyengar found that the personalized or "episodic" *framing* of stories directed audiences to think in short-term, emotional, and personalized ways about issues such as economics and social policy. What is missing in most news coverage, according to Iyengar, are more "thematic" approaches to framing social problems that might encourage people to think about the social, political, and economic forces that affect them.[20]

It seems safe to conclude that the news biases described in Chapter 2 invite people to think in personalized terms about distant social and political issues. Within this personalized world, individuals surely introduce their own thinking. However, it is not clear what kind meaningful collective identifications (the first step toward political power) can arise among isolated individuals employing this sort of personalized interpretation. In short, people may not be able to think their way toward effective action just by adopting an independent frame of mind. To the contrary, independent thinking may breed isolation and thus be counterproductive. In the next chapter, we will explore the kind of independent and analytical thinking that can help decode the news in more useful ways.

As noted previously, the most compelling evidence suggests that people interpret the news in more analytical and socially connected ways when they have had direct experience with the issues in question. Recall, too, that people are less likely to find issues in the news important when they feel powerless, and more likely to engage with challenging stories that explain what average people can do to make a difference. From this we may conclude that the sense of being left out of politics may partly explain why so few people are informed about politics and government.

Most Americans score poorly on basic citizen knowledge tests such as the one developed by Michael Delli Carpini and Scott Keeter.[21] Critics of these tests, such as Doris Graber, argue that they more resemble trivia tests than they measure the kind of practical understandings that might help people navigate through real political situations.[22] Yet the names of elected officials or the number of votes required in the House or Senate to overturn a presidential veto are not the only things that are vague in the minds of most people. Few people pay close attention to much of what they see in the news. A survey by the Pew Research Center tracked public attention to more than 670 news stories over a ten-year span and found that only 5 percent of the stories attracted close attention from those polled.[23] The case study in this chapter raises the question of whether Americans have something of an attention deficit disorder when it comes to politics.

Case Study: *National Attention Deficit Disorder?*

In a recent analysis of the economics of the news, James Hamilton suggests that the conventional "who, what, where, when, and why" of journalism is actually determined by another, more important, set of "five W's:" "Who cares about information? What are they willing to pay, or others willing to pay to reach them? Where can media outlets and advertisers reach them? When is this profitable? Why is this profitable?"[24]

What he concludes from this is that economic markets do not create conditions favorable to the open exchange of democratic ideas. Markets aim to deliver consumers to sponsors by nearly any means that work. What gets the attention of consumers may not be what matters to citizens. What media organizations do with audience attention once they have it may have little to do with informing and encouraging political involvement. It is hard to decide what comes first: the marketing of soft features and shocking stories that kill audience interest in more serious information, or a more general withdrawal form civic life that leaves news producers searching for anything to grab audience attention. Either way, the result is a national spiral of inattentiveness to many of the most monumental issues facing the nation.

Consider just a few of the media attention patterns that Hamilton reports in his survey of the habits of news audiences. Less than 10 percent of men and women aged 18 to 34 regularly view a nightly network news program, compared to 23 percent of men and 32 percent of women over age 50. TV news magazines (*20/20, Dateline, 60 Minutes*) outdraw network news audiences in three of six crucial demographic categories (men and women age 18 to 34, and women age 35 to 49). FOX Cable News beats National Public Radio audiences in five of the six key demographic categories; only women aged 35 to 49 listen to NPR more (16.9 percent) than watch FOX (15.9 percent). Cops programs beat NPR in every demographic category except men over age 50. And more than four times as many people watch talk programs such as Oprah and Dr. Phil than follow the PBS *News Hour with Jim Lehrer.* Not surprisingly, few Americans claim to follow politics closely.[25] Only one of the six key demographic categories tracked by news marketers (males over age 50) registered a majority claiming to follow politics most of the time.[26]

Attention was so thin during the 2000 election that the World Wrestling Federation's *Smackdown!* drew four times the audience as the first debate among the Democratic candidates (and *Smackdown!* barely made the top hundred in the week's television rating charts).[27] A general survey in the 2000 election asked voters to identify presidential candidates by three background characteristics (e.g., a former governor of Texas). Only 12.7 percent of the public correctly identified all three, and fully 30.3 percent were unable to identify even one (including the former governor of Texas who went on to become president).[28] Similar levels of disinterest ran through the entire campaign. A majority of people did not become very interested in the election until after it was over, and Americans woke up to discover that there was no clear winner.[29]

The lack of interest in elections is reflected in the media sources that people pay attention to.[30] For example, young voters ages 18 to 29 are seven times more likely (21 percent to 3 percent) to learn about elections from comedy TV shows than voters over age 50. Older voters are twice as likely to pay attention to elections through network news or newspaper coverage. Trends from 2000 to 2004 show that attention to cable and comedy is on the rise, and attention to network and print sources is in decline.

There is some potential for improvement as both voters and candidates begin to find each other on the Internet. The percentage of citizens using the Internet to follow elections increased from 24 to 33 percent between 2000 and 2004, with the greatest gains among young voters. Regular Internet users were among the most informed about candidates and their issues.

A counterargument to the attention deficit syndrome is that measuring whether people attend to the details of news events is like a trivia test that fails to tap how people actually understand politics. Some political scientists claim that people learn what they need to know from talk shows and entertainment programs—at least they learn enough about key issues to form opinions and participate meaningfully in public life.[31]

What is the quality of the information and reasoning on which such distracted participation rests? Recall the discussion from Chapter 1 on the misperceptions about the Iraq War among different media audiences. Even those who watched news programs varied greatly in their understandings of the basis for going to war. Viewers of FOX news were more then twice as likely as viewers of the *News Hour* on PBS to have the basic facts wrong about such key issues as the connections between Iraq and terrorism. This raises the question of whether such unfounded or ungrounded opinions fully qualify people to participate in public life. The even more difficult question is whether politicians prey on public inattentiveness to create poorly informed support for policies they promote.

The political attention crisis is greatest among young citizens. For example, during the hot Democratic primaries of 2004, interest among those under age 30 was cold: 64 percent reported that they were not interested, and few had heard about even the most heavily reported campaign developments. Only 15 percent knew the answer to one of two basic factual questions about the backgrounds of prominent candidates, compared to 37 percent of people aged 30 to 49, and half of those over age 50.[32]

What remains true despite—or perhaps because of—this national attention deficit is that people continue to regard the news as ideologically biased in the ways described in Chapters 1 and 2. Americans at either end of the ideological spectrum are the most likely to see campaign coverage as biased. Conservative Republicans think the news favors the Democrats by a margin of 47 percent to 8 percent, and liberal Democrats think that campaign news favors the Republicans by a margin of 36 percent to 11 percent. The overwhelming majority (67 percent) still seek political information from sources that do not have a particular point of view, and just a quarter (25 percent) say they prefer news that matches their political point of view.[33]

One conclusion about these trends is that most Americans lack the basic personal interest and orientation needed to help them think and act effectively. Perhaps this general lack of internal political bearings fuels the fruitless quest for unbiased information about politics, resulting in continuing confusion among those in the middle and charges of bias from ideologues at both extremes. While people seek illusive general truths about politics, news marketers grow more desperate to attract the attention of viable consumer demographics. The result is news increasingly aimed at targeted audiences. Such news leaves many and sometimes most citizens out of the information equation. Perhaps that is the great irony of the American information system: whether it comes from politicians at the source or from content packaging at the point of transmission, information is increasingly aimed at small demographic groups, leaving increasingly large majorities out of the democratic conversation. The attention deficit syndrome is reinforced equally by the public, politicians, and news organizations as they struggle to make sense of politics in the marketplace of ideas.

NEWS AND PERSONAL EXPERIENCE: WHAT GETS THROUGH

As noted earlier, when people have direct experience with issues, whole new avenues of information and ways of thinking often open up. For example, someone who enjoys camping in the wilderness may subscribe to specialized publications promoting environmental awareness and begin thinking about how to join with others in various kinds of creative political action. Alternatively, someone who enjoys hunting in the wilderness may subscribe to other specialized publications to learn how to combat the environmentalists who wish to restrict the use of firearms in nature.

For the majority of people, however, most issues and events are encountered more through media exposure than through personal experience. In addition, people are busy with their personal lives and with the political issues in which they have a direct interest. Thus, it takes a great deal of information presented repeatedly in the media to get the attention of the average person.

To reduce this information processing to its simplest terms, we can say that after repeated exposure to an issue or problem, simple recognition sets in. If someone has a personal interest in the matter, he or she may next categorize, or frame, the object of attention to help keep it in focus and to begin thinking more clearly about it. After people have begun to form categories, they can place finer details and bits of information in the categories and begin to shade their thoughts and opinions. At this point, we can begin to say some things about how people process information from the news. Following the development of attention, interest, and some basic categorization schemes, people may pick up and evaluate news information in the following ways:

- Reacting to *cues* or labels (left, right; Republican, Democrat; hawk, dove; environmentalist, gun lover, terrorist, etc.).

- Assimilating factoids or bits of information that are often offered in support of the broad political cues and labels.
- Attending to emotions in news reports that motivate greater attention and learning.
- Fitting all this mediated information processing into the central organizing principles (values, interests, lifestyle choices) that make up the individual's personal life experiences.

In short, people tend to form their thinking about the big items repeated frequently in the news (major issues, candidates in elections, chronic social problems) using these general (intellectual) labor saving devices: cueing, factoid gathering, weighing positive and negative claims about those factoids, and finally, judging the information gathered against personal experiences. These commonly used information strategies provide a bridge in the debate about whether people think for themselves or whether the news does their thinking for them. The answer is that people creatively incorporate the cue and information structures of media representations (news, political advertising, editorials, punditry, etc.) into their personal thinking. Each individual develops a strategy for selecting (and tuning out) information about politics but relies as well on the common information pathways in order to make contact with the more general ideas and themes that we call public opinion. Thus, we are able to move from the individual to the public with this approach, reminding ourselves that it may be less important what individuals think in private than whether some part of that thinking can be linked meaningfully to public opinion. Consider how each of these information processing patterns operates.

Pattern 1: Taking Broad Interpretive Cues from the News

Most of us simplify busy lives by screening political information through familiar and trusted reference groups. We take cues from leaders, political parties, interest groups, and other familiar news sources who interpret (frame) news events and offer opinions that may guide thinking about a confusing world. In addition, stereotypes, slogans, and old-fashioned name calling can provide the basis for simplifying our thinking about otherwise complicated realities.

Research by political scientist John Zaller demonstrates that the more closely people follow an issue in the news, the more their opinions follow the cues offered by leaders of the political parties, recognized ideological groups, and other prominent political viewpoints.[34] This means, in effect, that the more informed people are about issues in the news, the more their opinions conform to those expressed by elites, government officials, interest groups, and parties.

Perhaps even more startling, these generalizations apply most strongly to more educated people, who tend to pay more attention to the news—the so-called informed public. Although this is an ironic way to think about being informed, it is less surprising when we recall that the information that goes into the news is largely provided by government officials and other prominent elites.

This does not mean that hearing one statement containing a familiar symbol or information source typically molds understanding of an issue. On the contrary, most people live with a serious state of information overload. They tend not to pay much attention until an issue or event reaches saturation coverage and continues to make the news regularly for an extended period of time with prominent spokespersons taking increasingly clear and simple positions. Once this signal-to-noise ratio (recall the discussion from Chapter 4) becomes very high, people begin to accept the kinds of broad cues discussed earlier to help organize their thinking. Thus, the ability of the Bush administration to dominate the news leading up to the Iraq War and repeatedly link Iraq to weapons of mass destruction and terrorism led majorities of Americans to conclude that Iraq represented an immediate threat.

Pattern 2: Gathering Factoids

Even when people are knee-jerk liberals, conservatives, Republicans, Democrats, or Rush Limbaugh ditto heads, they tend to search for some supporting reasons to accept the cues they get from their favorite political references. This is where factoids come in, those bits and pieces of information that fill in emerging understandings of a situation. This is also where news management becomes crucial, with forces on both sides trying to keep a story going and to add elements that reinforce their preferred interpretations while countering those of the other side. For example, in political campaigns where the field of candidates narrows and media scrutiny becomes ever more intense, there is a daily battle in which each side tries to build up its own message while tearing down the images of the other side.

In the political trenches, the lines between news and advertising, information and propaganda, have become increasingly hard to draw. Media consultants often try to insert news and documentary-type images into TV ads while setting up news events with advertising values in mind. The synergy between news and advertising can be important in getting public attention and influencing opinions. When themes from advertising hit the news, they gain an important element of "facticity" (objectivity or legitimacy) that can break down resistance.

During the great health care reform battle of 1994, for example, groups in the health care, insurance, and pharmaceutical industries spent millions of dollars on advertising to create doubts about possible negative effects of the president's call for universal health care. A barrage of commercials sent emotional messages about rising costs, government bureaucracy, diminished quality of care, and long waits for treatment to the politically important middle-class audience (most of whom already had health insurance).

Among the most memorable ad campaigns were the "Harry and Louise" spots produced by the health insurance industry, whose member companies stood to lose a great deal from any plan that regulated their profits or required them to extend coverage to people with expensive health problems such as cancer or AIDS. The millions of dollars they spent on the slick Madison Avenue spots were minor compared to the billions that the big insurance companies had at stake in the reforms. Harry and Louise were depicted as a sympathetic middle-aged, middle-class couple of the sort that appears in TV series and other commercials. They worried about what they would lose under the proposed reforms, and each ad in the series introduced a new element of doubt about the leading plans, particularly the one championed by Hillary and Bill Clinton.

Meanwhile, behind the scenes the health care industry was spending widely on lobbying and campaign contributions to key members of Congress to pry their support away from the president's plan. Not surprisingly, the authoritative opposition voices from Congress that were heard in the news echoed the same elements of doubt raised in the advertising.[35] A public opinion one-two punch (as in patterns 1 and 2) had been set in motion.

On the other side, the Clinton forces ran their own ads to counter the daily attacks (including their own series of Harry and Louise commercials in which the couple is bedridden following a medical calamity, Harry loses his job and the health coverage it provides, and Louise turns against him). Through it all, both the Clintons and many members of the administration delivered speeches, appeared at rallies, and gave interviews with reporters to reinforce important bits of supporting information underlying their plan.

These opposing campaigns produced something of a draw in terms of public reactions. After more than a year of concerted news and advertising information blitzes, a strong majority of 74 percent favored the idea of universal coverage, a cornerstone of the Clinton plan.[36] At the same time, only 33 percent backed the Clinton plan, while 76 percent said they were unwilling to accept less choice in doctors or hospitals, and 74 percent believed that universal reform would lead to rationing.[37] Perhaps most telling of all was the discovery made by the White House polling team led by Stanley Greenberg that after all the sides had weighed in, the public actually understood less about the Clinton plan than they did at the time it was unveiled.

The moral of this story is that once the big information cues such as president and Congress, Republicans and Democrats, big government and small government, have structured the information picture (pattern 1), the fine details added daily in the news and advertising can make a big difference (pattern 2). As Robert Teeter, one of the gurus of the information and opinion management business, put it: "People don't decide based on some great revelation. They form their views based on thousands of little bits of information that shake out from television ads and news stories."[38]

Pattern 3: Tuning in to Feelings and Emotions (Weighing the Positives and the Negatives)

The first two patterns of information processing are seldom enough to account for public reactions to news. In most cases, people would not even attend to stories if there were not some emotional hook or charge in them. It is not surprising in this light that the communication strategies employed by warring political factions can turn downright nasty. This often happens in election campaigns and big national policy battles. The emotions in the long-running national fight over abortion policy come to mind here.

Not only do advocates for a cause challenge factual claims and attack the character of opponents, but they frequently plant doubts that have little basis in fact. Indeed, when the battle rages for the emotions of the public, the question of what is true or relevant is often the least of considerations. The key concerns of strategic communication become, what gets people's attention, and then what creates or resolves doubts in their thinking? Although media managers often have more freedom with advertising, they can obtain the greatest effects when the same messages cross over and become part of news stories.

This is not to suggest that emotions are bad or even less relevant than facts in their thinking about politics. To the contrary, research by George Marcus, Russell Neuman, and Michael MacKuen shows that, in many cases, some degree of emotional arousal must occur in order for people to pay attention to other kinds of information in a situation. In some cases, the emotional (or affective) information that people receive may be far more important for their thinking and acting than facts (or cognitions).[39] These important understandings also help explain why TV is more important than other media for most people.

However, the use of emotion in political communication is often not aimed at enhancing critical thought or judgment, and the reporting tendencies of the press do not always favor the citizen as much as they favor communication strategists bent on winning their immediate political battles. For example, given the tendencies of the press to indulge in feeding frenzies as described in Chapter 5, allegations and charges from one political camp can often turn into news nightmares for another. The failure to counter even the most scurrilous charge planted in the news can begin to gnaw at people and take root in their opinions, even if they try to ignore the dirt and concentrate on substantial information. All this explains one of the great puzzles of political communication: Negativity often works even though a large majority of the public claims that they hate negative communication and that they try to screen it out of their thinking.

An important word of caution is in order here: Negative communication does not always work. A classic case is the difference between the George Bush election campaigns of 1988 and 1992. Both were extremely negative campaigns, with conservative estimates of the negative message content running at 50 percent or more of Bush's ads and news statements and increasing to as much as 75 to 80 percent in the closing days.[40] Yet Bush won one of those campaigns quite handily and lost the other one quite convincingly. To simplify the reasons greatly, negative campaigning is successful in part if the opponent (or the victim, as it were) understands the importance of information pattern 2 and counters every bit of negative information with bits of information that deflect it, raise doubts about the other side, or refocus public attention on something else. Where Bush's 1988 opponent Michael Dukakis seemed to lack a strategic response to the negative attacks of 1988 (thus allowing them to sink in), Bill Clinton in 1992 developed a wink and a shrug that suggested that perhaps Mr. Bush's use of negative tactics meant that he was a bit desperate.

In short, when people encounter negative information that goes uncountered, they tend to incorporate the negativity into their thinking even if, consciously, they try to avoid it. In the view of opinion experts Barbara Farah and Ethel Klein, people make the best sense they can of the information they have available to them, even when that information is negative, of questionable reliability, or generally distasteful.[41]

Pattern 4: Individuals Judge New Information Against their Personal Experiences

A popular school of thought about citizen information-processing suggests that people are lazy information processors or cognitive misers.[42] Citizens rely mainly on gut feelings, personal experience, and their immediate life circumstances to screen information and reach judgments about politics. In this view, much information from the outer world is discounted simply because it does not dent this shell of personal experience. Thus people take shortcuts in processing information and arrive at judgments about politics that have been described by political scientist Samuel Popkin as "low information rationality."[43] Such experienced-based reasoning about politics explains why people cannot remember many facts about particular stories in the news, yet draw cues, supporting factoids, and feelings from news coverage as the basis for judgments that often turn out to be fairly stable and meaningful.

Charting the terms of public engagement reminds us that beneath the rough indicators and simple judgments recorded in opinion polls are meanings that people construct in the process of arriving at their opinions on issues. These important areas of personal meaning remind us that for individuals in society, the news may be about things that go well beyond just making judgments that feed into elections or policy debates on various issues. The news also contains information that matters for people as they make various personal choices, live their lives, and adjust their emotions through the often turbulent flow of daily events in a complex world.

USES AND GRATIFICATIONS: OTHER REASONS PEOPLE FOLLOW THE NEWS

Thus far we have viewed news information in its most obvious democratic context: People follow the news to gather information that may help them in thinking about politics, forming opinions, and taking more effective political action. However, as noted earlier and illustrated in the case study, there are clearly other reasons people follow the news:

- *Curiosity and surveillance:* scanning for information that may be useful in everyday life (news of airline fare wars, weather forecasts, inflation reports, home mortgage rates).
- *Entertainment and escape:* following interesting dramas that develop around crime stories (O. J. Simpson) and political scandals. For example, were members of the Bush administration too cozy with Enron officials like CEO Kenneth Lay to whom the President referred as "Kenny Boy"? In other words, people can simply enjoy the spectacle of politics.
- *Social and psychological adjustment:* keeping contact with society and our own places in it (How is my world and where do I stand in it?).

As explained in Chapters 1 and 3, news organizations understand that people have much broader uses for the news and adjust their coverage accordingly. As popular tastes and interests shift, the news generally follows, creating tensions with the democratic ideal of citizen-friendly news information. Critics argue that such pandering to base public tastes only fuels the spiral of declining news values. Others counter that people will select and convert information to their own uses regardless of the standards that news or entertainment organizations attempt to maintain. For example, studies of popular American television programs in other countries show that viewers often find meanings that American audiences are far less likely to support, including confirmation of some rather nasty beliefs about greed, violence, corruption, and other images of life in the United States.[44]

A great deal of research has been conducted on the so-called uses and gratifications of news and entertainment programming. Most recently, the focus has been placed on highly personalized decodings of media content.[45] However, for purposes of illustrating the idea that news attracts attention for a variety of reasons, it is helpful to think about some broad alternative uses of the news that many people share in common. Traditional research on the various uses and gratifications associated with the news can be summarized under the three broad categories just listed.[46] It is important to see these activities as part of an extended notion of media politics, in the sense that people drawn by whatever reason to follow news stories may engage in ways that lead to meaningful new understandings of the political world or their places in it. Because all these uses and gratifications can have important personal and political consequences, they are worth exploring in more detail.

Curiosity and Surveillance

People are blessed with curiosity, which can be a source of sheer pleasure or amusement as well as a means of spotting new information that might be useful in coping with everyday reality. Research has shown that human curiosity is piqued by things (e.g., situations, ideas, scenery, films, art, and news) that contain a mixture of familiar and novel stimuli and features.[47] On the one hand, repeated exposure to completely familiar stimuli results in the formation of subconscious mental "scripts" that make it possible to respond to situations without really thinking about them.[48] Curiosity and attention are minimized in such scripted situations. On the other hand, stimuli that are completely foreign may be so dissonant and hard to assimilate that people tend to ignore, avoid, or misinterpret them.[49]

Even though the political messages in the news are fairly predictable, the events, plots, and characters are constantly changing. Human curiosity is engaged by new events and novel twists on old themes. Moreover, some of the events in the news may have an impact on the people who follow them. Thus, many people find it useful to scan the news just to keep potentially important events under surveillance. News is the perfect blend of the familiar and the novel. There is an intrinsic satisfaction in seeing how a familiar theme will develop in a new plot or whether an old plot will develop a new twist. For example, how will freedom of choice—a theme familiar to every American—be adapted to fit such contexts as abortion, drug use, pornography, or the regulation of cigarette smoking in public places? As long as new events keep happening in the world, people will be drawn to the news as a means of applying, testing, and adjusting their understandings about reality.

However, the news may satisfy our curiosity too easily when familiar political scripts confirm popular beliefs and stereotypes that people have scripted into their own thinking. For example, if the news persists in portraying the problems of the Third World in terms of the virtues of development versus the stigma of underdevelopment, the news audience may fail to perceive many of the problems caused by rapid economic development in Third World societies—problems such as the destruction of culture, the growing dependence of poor countries on the economies of rich countries, and the corruption that often accompanies economic growth in repressive regimes. All these problems contribute to the political and economic instability of those Third World countries that have entered the seemingly endless process of development. Despite its limitations, the development metaphor is written into each chapter of the development saga by government officials and the reporters who cover them. It becomes easy for people to tune out such familiar stories in the news when little new information is presented in ways that shake familiar plots.

Indeed, the refocusing of attention on growing inequalities between northern and southern nations lies at the heart of the rising global protest movement, which has staged demonstrations in cities around the world where trade and development agencies hold their meetings. Other activists have turned the brand images against the corporations that created them by cleverly waging *logo campaigns* against corporations such as McDonald's, Nike, and Coca Cola to bring news attention to global problems involving environmental change, labor abuses, and human rights.

The news is often the most satisfying when it contains periodic information that is directly relevant to people. The reactions to such reporting differ in two interesting ways, from reactions to more abstract stories. First, people are more likely to think in action-oriented terms about personally relevant stories. The more distant world of political news often leaves people with little option but to exercise their beliefs in a purely private fashion. Second, people express much less confusion and displeasure about news stories that satisfy curiosity with information than can be applied to their immediate concerns. Consider, for example, some typical reactions, in a survey conducted by the author, to a report on the financial troubles faced by four major airlines. The report outlined the various consequences for travelers, employees, and the economy if the airlines went bankrupt. Such information would seem to be relevant to a broad range of people. In fact, everyone in the sample of 375 respondents who chose to discuss the report found some personal use for the information. The range of uses was quite broad. For example, some people were alerted to possible difficulties in future travel arrangements, as indicated by this reaction: "I was disturbed by the fact that the failure of several airlines could result in increased inconvenience in travel." People who had already made travel plans were moved by the report to take direct action, as this response explains: "I found the story disturbing, as I have plane reservations in the spring with one of the airlines that may go bankrupt, so I plan to check with my travel agent about possibly changing airlines." Others found even more intimate applications for the information in the story, as revealed in these reactions: "I found the story disturbing, as I have a friend that's been employed for several years by another of the airlines mentioned," and it is "reassuring that I am employed by an airline that is doing very well. The loss is our gain." It is significant that the airline story did not lead anyone to question its relevance or newsworthiness.

Political surveillance also goes on in many long-running political news stories. Consider the Clinton impeachment scandal in this context. Curiosity and surveillance help explain shifts in opinion on such issues as whether Clinton lied about his affair with Lewinsky, and, if he did, how that should affect his impeachment. This indicates that even when people have formed opinions on something, they may continue to monitor the news to see if new information either confirms or challenges their judgments.

Entertainment and Escape

The news may represent itself as fact, but as illustrated in Chapters 2 and 3, it is communicated to the public with all the trappings of fiction: short, intense scenes; literary rather than analytical treatments; the nearly uniform use of the story format; and the emphasis on drama, emotional conflict, and larger-than-life characters. The news may portray real events, but this portrayal often discourages analytical or instrumental uses for the information it presents. This result is not an inevitable property of narratives, which can, if presented in the right ways, actually provoke thoughtful reflection and action. Indeed, some news narratives appear to have this critical potential, as when people are engaged in sustained and important national deliberations.

Most stories in the news do not go on long enough, however, nor do they contain angles that people identify deeply enough with, to stimulate much thought or critical action. It is, in these cases, easy to become engaged by the sheer drama of news events. The news makes everyday happenings seem larger than life. Most news reports invite us to escape for a minute or two into a world filled with pathos, tragedy, moral lessons, crisis, mystery, danger, and occasional whimsy. The escape into this dramatic world is made all the easier when the happenings involve people like us or people about whom we have strong positive or negative feelings.

Each day's news menu offers a large supply of complete minidramas for our entertainment pleasure. We can step into one fascinating fantasy for a minute or two—experiencing a brief sense of other lives and other worlds—and then move on to the next one. One moment we are a member of a guerilla band on maneuvers in a far-off war, the next we move in with the survivors of an earthquake, and then suddenly we are transported into the nightmare of a bank robbery and murder captured on the closed-circuit video system. At last, the string of high-tension episodes is broken by a commercial that gives us a chance to regain our bearings, grab a snack, and get ready for the next installment of our evening's journey into real-life adventure.

Vicarious involvement in the news is often even more compelling than more conventional forms of escape via drama and literature. News dramas, after all, are represented as real, serious, important, and worthy of everyone's attention. Fiction, by contrast, does not involve real spies, real robbers, or real earthquakes. Fiction can at times command our attention, but it seldom combines intensity, universality of appeal, and realism the way the news does. A best-selling novel may sell a million copies during its lengthy run on the best-seller list, whereas most everyone in the nation may be riveted by the news on a single day such as 9/11.

The seriousness or realism of the news is, paradoxically, a key to understanding its power as an escape medium. The general acceptance of the news as factual, important, and objective makes it easy for people to give themselves over to serious involvement with it. Having done this, the individual is swept away by images and ideas that are often both stranger and more dramatic than fiction. For example, few novels contain plot twists like the ones in the news story about a band of thieves posing as police officers who were forced by circumstances to try to arrest a group of policemen disguised as a gang of thieves. The real police were—you guessed it—on the trail of the thieves who were posing as police. If a novelist were to submit such a plot to a publisher, it would probably be rejected as incredible or unrealistic. When it becomes news, however, no plot is too incredible to be engrossing. All plots are credible precisely because they are news. Thus the issue of credibility or realism, a major obstacle to people becoming involved in fiction, is transcended easily by stories in the news, no matter how bizarre they may be. The fact that news stories are thought to represent real situations adds to their entertainment value in at least one other respect. When dramatic incidents involve real people—people who feel, suffer, think, and die—this creates a direct bond of human sensibility with the audience. Whereas fiction writers struggle to create such bonds through words and imaginary actions, the news generates them routinely by simply recording dramatic excerpts from real lives. Thus few novels or movies about the horrors of war can rival the routine nightly installments on the Vietnam War that Americans witnessed between 1965 and 1970. Fictional accounts of political power and intrigue may achieve a measure of credibility, but few can match the daily revelations about power and corruption in the White House that filled the news at the time of the Watergate scandal. The unfolding horrors of 9/11 will forever be etched in the minds of those who witnessed them.

In fact, the news is so dramatic that it increasingly supplies the plot material for novels, films, and new entertainment forms like the docudrama. Novels have been written about murders, robberies, hijackings, and kidnappings, subjects that first captured the popular imagination in the news. Journalistic treatments of terrorism, political corruption, military operations, and spy escapades have spawned movies by the score. Even the activity of journalism has inspired entertainment fare, as in the case of Woodward and Bernstein's book and film versions of *All the President's Men*—a highly dramatized account of how the two daring reporters conducted their famous Watergate investigation. Nowadays, the people who often arrive at the scene of a news event after the reporters are book agents and movie deal-makers. Such a trend only enhances the news as an escape medium and further undermines its potential to inform us realistically about contemporary life. One observer of this trend of life-based reality dramas dominating entertainment media called his book *Life: The Movie*.[50]

As Walter Lippmann pointed out many years ago, the world of politics, as viewed by the public, will always be somewhat dramatized and fictionalized.[51] Politicians who control the flow of information will attempt whenever possible to shape news to their advantage. However, when the media actively seek dramatized reality to feed to a receptive audience, the only check on the representation of political reality is removed. *When politicians, press, and public all judge political performances more in terms of dramatic criteria than moral standards, the conscience of the polity is lost.*

In the world of political drama, the performance may count more than the success or failure of action because, in many cases, the performance *is* the action as far as the public is concerned. Consider some other cases of actions that were either made or broken by the quality of the surrounding dramatic performances. When John Kennedy admitted to botching the Bay of Pigs invasion, a majority of Americans forgave him on the strength of his compassionate and convincing apology. Yet when Jimmy Carter took responsibility for the aborted attempt to rescue the American hostages from Iran, his popularity plunged. Carter, unlike Kennedy, had failed to script a dramatic performance that fit his role properly into the surrounding adventure saga. In short, Carter gave a bad performance. When Richard Nixon was a candidate for vice president in 1952, he faced the nation on television to address charges of political corruption. He won millions of voters' hearts with his careful script, his calculated stage setting, the fine supporting role of his faithful wife, and his emotionally delivered reference to his innocent little dog, Checkers. By contrast, when Nixon again faced corruption charges over two decades later, his performance was flawed, petulant, personal, and poorly rehearsed. He failed to produce the all-encompassing script and well-rehearsed supporting cast that might have represented some salvation from the otherwise tawdry reality of the Watergate affair.

In many ways, Bill Clinton's every appearance during the Lewinsky scandal was subject to the public's critical judgment about both his character and his ability to stay in character. The steady stream of jokes from late-night comedians (that were often recycled the next day at the office, in computer chat rooms, and in e-mail) can be thought of as part of the national play of politics. Like most play, political play is both entertaining and serious.

Even though Bill Clinton was the one on trial, both in the court of public opinion and in the Senate, the news and talk about the scandal also focused playful attention on its colorful cast of characters. Monica Lewinsky was not alone in becoming a household name; she was joined, most notably, by Kenneth Starr and Linda Tripp—a trio of characters whose motivations the public viewed dimly. In August 1998, Gallup observed that "both Monica Lewinsky and Ken Starr have extremely low personal ratings, which continue to decline. When she first emerged into public view in January 30 percent of Americans had a favorable view of Lewinsky and 50 percent an unfavorable one. Today only 13 percent feel favorably toward the former intern, and 72 percent unfavorably." Gallup also noted that "Throughout the year roughly one-quarter of Americans have had a favorable view of Ken Starr, but his unfavorable rating has grown from 24 percent in January to 54 percent today."[52]

In this company, Clinton fared rather well. As Gallup reported in March 1998, "Clinton's favorability rating . . . is well over twice as high as those of the other major participants in the developments of the last eight weeks, including [Kathleen] Willey, Lewinsky, [Paula] Jones and Special Prosecutor Kenneth Starr."[53] Clinton may have been buoyed not only by a general sense that everyone close to the scandal became tarnished by it, but also by the public's belief that the motives of these other characters were far from pure. Indeed, it is hard to discount the social importance of the discussions that went on about such matters as why Starr, the self-styled Puritan, released a report filled with pornographic material, or what kind of friend was Linda Tripp pretending to be as she bugged her intimate conversations with Monica?

If the dramatization of political reality is a key to understanding the fortunes of public life, it is no less important for understanding the private political worlds of individual citizens. Vicarious political experience may be different from direct participation, but it is nonetheless a valid form of experience. As a result, escape and entertainment are far from being meaningless pursuits. Whatever their other effects may be, political dramas can help people open up their fantasies and subconscious feelings, assisting them in easing psychological tensions and social strains. The escape and entertainment functions of the news thus pave the way for important social and psychological adjustments.

Social and Psychological Adjustment

When people escape into the world of drama found in the news, they do not necessarily leave all their concerns behind them. Although our inclinations for direct action may be inhibited by the one-way communication channels of the mass media, we respond psychologically to the people and issues in news reports. It is, in fact, remarkably easy to identify with actors in the news, respond to them emotionally, and imagine that we are somehow part of their experiences. In a fascinating discussion of the rise of nations, political scientist Benedict Anderson argues that, to an important degree, the society of strangers beyond our daily, face-to-face worlds is a product of imagination fueled by the media.[54]

Human beings spend a good deal of both their waking and sleeping time creating imaginary scenarios in which they explore wishes, hopes, fears, and desires. Through fantasies, we can rehearse unfamiliar social roles and anticipate encounters with other people. Fantasies also enable us to contain powerful feelings like anger, sexual desire, or fear when it is inappropriate to express them openly in a particular situation. In other situations, fantasies help in making choices about how best to express those feelings in public.

A healthy fantasy life is essential for adjusting to the conditions and people we encounter in real life. The news, with its powerful images, emotional themes, and colorful characters, is a rich source of fantasy material. One can step into a news plot and imagine what it would be like to be rich, poor, powerful, weak, female, male, sexy, brave, or intelligent. By taking the real world into the privacy of our minds via the news, we can explore feelings and relate to people in ways that might not be comfortable or possible in real life.

The emphasis on drama, emotional themes, powerful images, and strong personalities makes the news a convenient medium for working out psychological tensions and social conflicts. People do not even have to leave their living rooms in order to encounter real people about whom they have strong feelings and issues that seem to affect their well-being. In their encounters with this imaginary society, people can form impressions of their community, their nation, and their places in them. By making connections between personal concerns and events and personalities in the news, people can express feelings and think about their problems in uninhibited and often satisfying ways. This vicarious resolution of social and psychological strains is all the more effective because the realities of news stories are usually too distant for people to experience directly—thus the feelings and understandings people develop in response to the news are seldom subjected to reality testing.

Fantasies require very little anchor in reality in order to thrive. In fact, because fantasies involve by definition the suspension of ordinary reality, they can spring from the barest of suggestions and the least substantial of images. As far as our fantasy life goes, what does it matter what our favorite newscaster is really like in private life? As long as he or she displays the right style, manner, or looks, we feel comfortable inviting him or her into our home and listening as we would to a trusted friend imparting all the news that has transpired since our last meeting.

Because fantasies feed on such minimal information, and because the news transmits such condensed, ambiguous images, it should not be surprising to learn that people generate very different fantasies from the same story. Who knows what it is really like to be the guerilla fighter dashing through the jungle, locked in a life-or-death struggle for the freedom of her country? Some might imagine that she is a romantic figure, with the virtues of bravery, charisma, morals, and intelligence—the sort of person they would secretly like to be. Others might imagine her as a bloodthirsty heathen—an immoral foe who threatens their values and lifestyles. Same news story, different fantasies.

Part of the fantasy element in the news is caused by the heavy emphasis in politics on fantasy themes of power, community, order, and security.[55] Such concerns are central to the social and emotional well-being of the average person. A political speech without an emphasis on power, community, order, or security would be an atypical and in all likelihood ineffectual statement. These fantasy themes of politics are transmitted from political performances to the mass audiences by the news. In fact, mass media journalism tends to focus on fantasy themes, which represent the most dramatic and universally appealing components of political performances. Fantasy themes are about the only medium through which a lengthy political performance can be condensed into a meaningful news-length capsule.

Consider, as an example, television news coverage of a presidential inauguration. High rituals of state such as inaugurations, campaigns, funerals, and State of the Union addresses are good vantage points for viewing fantasy themes in action. These rituals are designed to appeal to the popular imagination with images of strength, community, security, and new beginnings. Inaugurations are always occasions for bringing people together, reminding them that they are one nation with common bonds, and calling for renewed commitment to the goals of prosperity, harmony, peace, and security. Because most people are concerned at some level with prosperity, harmony, peace, and security, it is comforting to have related fantasies evoked time and again by each new leader chosen to preserve and protect these elements of the American fantasy, more commonly referred to as the American dream. Inaugural speeches are open invitations for new presidents to pull out all the symbolic stops in an effort to kindle the deepest fantasies that define the political community.

Ronald Reagan was faced with a challenge when he mounted the platform to address the nation in 1980. The country was plunging into recession, national pride was at an ebb, and people saw a future with little promise. Drawing on the themes that got him elected, Reagan exhorted the country to step back into the past as a means of finding the values and spirit with which to face the future. He chose the perfect setting for such a speech. Standing at the West Front of the Capitol, Reagan pointed to the great gallery of national monuments in Washington, D.C. As he mentioned great heroes and episodes from the nation's past, he could evoke their physical presence by indicating those shrines. Mentioning George Washington is one thing, but presenting the dramatic image of the Washington Monument and its stunning reflecting pool is an even more effective way to engage the imagination of the audience.

In order to realize the full potential of the images in his speech, Reagan needed a little help from the media. He could, of course, talk about the great monuments and symbols of state that surrounded him, but how much more effective it would be if the media incorporated pictures of those things as though they were part of the script for the performance. Reagan and his media advisers must have anticipated what the journalists would do. All the White House needed to do was announce the time and place of the performance and issue an advance copy of the script, and the media could be relied on to do the rest. As the following excerpt from Ernest Bormann's analysis of inaugural coverage by CBS television indicates, journalist and political actor joined forces smoothly to maximize the fantasy potential in the event:

> Toward the close of the speech Reagan noted that this was the first time the ceremony was held on the West Front of the capitol, then he said, "Standing here, one faces a magnificent vista (The director called up a long shot of the magnificent vista), opening up on this city's special beauty and history. At the end of this open mall (The director had the camera pan up the open mall) are those shrines to the giants on whose shoulders we stand. Directly in front of me, the monument to a monumental man: (Cut to a shot of Washington monument) George Washington, father of our country. . . ." After an encomium to Washington, Reagan said, "Off to one side (Cut to a shot of the Jefferson Memorial), the stately memorial to Thomas Jefferson." After some words of praise for Jefferson, Reagan continued, "and then beyond the reflecting pool, the dignified columns of the Lincoln Memorial (Camera moves to Lincoln Memorial)." When Reagan next directed his audience's attention to the "sloping hills of Arlington National Cemetery with its row upon row of simple white markers bearing crosses or Stars of David . . ." the director had the camera focus on the Cemetery.[56]

With this kind of interplay between political images and news emphasis, it is little wonder that news provides a rich source of fantasy. Two characteristics of such fantasy play are the formation of strong expressions of feeling and opinion (stronger than would ordinarily be acceptable in real-life situations) and the development of vicarious relationships with the actors in news stories. Communication theorists have used the term *parasocial relationship* to refer to the often intimate emotional bonds that people can establish with the distant actors on the other end of one-way mass media relationships.[57]

It is also worth considering that the Clinton scandal engaged people at deeply personal levels involving not just drama and entertainment but also emotions and social identities. For example, the social and emotional dimensions of the scandal may be found in the striking divide in reactions of lower and higher income groups. Pew Center surveys show a generally negative relationship between the income level of respondents and their approval of Clinton as president: Low-income groups were more likely to approve of Clinton's performance in office and less likely to think he should be impeached. For example, Clinton's August 1998 approval ratings ranged from 59 percent among the highest income groups to 69 percent among the lowest.

Is this just economic self-interest at work? Perhaps low-income groups believed they had economically benefited from Clinton's policies and supported Clinton while discounting the Lewinsky spectacle. Another related explanation might be that these differences among income groups merely echo the effects of political partisanship. Economic gains and some interaction with party loyalty may well be at work here, but there is still strong evidence that different social and economic groups felt very differently about how they separated their support for the job Clinton was doing as president from their feelings about Clinton as a person. Pew asked respondents to choose among the following statements: "I like Bill Clinton personally and I like his policies"; "I don't like Bill Clinton personally but I like his policies"; and "I don't like Bill Clinton personally and I don't like his policies." Here again, sharp differences were clear among income groups. Whereas only 19 percent of the highest-income group and 24 percent of the next-highest group agreed that they liked Bill Clinton personally and liked his policies, 43 and 47 percent of the two lowest-income groups agreed. In contrast, 76 percent of all respondents earning more than $50,000 said they disliked Clinton personally compared with 53 percent of those earning between $20,000 and $30,000 and 44 percent of those earning less than $20,000.

These findings suggest that approval of Clinton was strongly associated with different income groups' assessments of Clinton as a person. Thus, for many lower-income Americans, Bill Clinton appears to have represented something of a sympathetic character despite the sexual scandal. He is, after all, a child of a lower-class background, and he used that fact quite publicly to build his image as "The Man From Hope." Clinton's symbolic profile as a poor child who rose to the White House perhaps matters more to poorer Americans than does his sexual behavior, or perhaps his sexual behavior seems less inconsistent with that group's expectations of how presidents should act. Poorer Americans, therefore, apparently reacted to the Lewinsky scandal in part based on their symbolic understanding of Clinton-as-a-person, signaling not just policy differences among income groups but their different emotional constructions of the narrative itself.[58]

Such reactions to people and issues in political reporting can be important for emotional adjustment and maintaining a sense of emotional belonging in a vast and often conflicted society. Whereas people often feel pressure not to express their true feelings in real-life settings, they can rail against injustice and political folly through private interactions with the media. A range of clear-cut, simplified, and easily accessible social ties and antagonisms is displayed on a daily basis in the news. The social and emotional adjustment functions served by media politics may be more satisfying than the corresponding outlets for emotional expression and social bonding in everyday life.

THE FUTURE: CITIZENS, INFORMATION, AND POLITICS

The ways in which people engage with news suggests a complex picture of political communication. On the one hand, when issues saturate the news and entertainment media, as have topics as disparate as abortion politics and the Clinton scandals, people may engage at deep levels. However, it is not always clear that this engagement translates into obvious effects on public policies.

The temptation always exists for political actors to propose magical solutions and fantastic political scenarios through the use of myths, stereotypes, scapegoats, and other symbolic devices. When the media tell such stories because they fit the news values that organizations are looking for, there are few restraints on the fabrication of political reality. Under such circumstances, political actors can manage issues, conflicts, and crises by simply throwing symbols at them—symbols that may be irrelevant to the matters at hand yet provoke powerful emotional responses from the public.

Hope for escaping this information confinement of political illusion and social isolation is provided by the research introduced earlier showing that people can be skeptical and reach their own interpretations. However, in the current news system, people all too often reach the conclusion that they have been deceived by politicians and government. Still, as William Gamson notes, there is evidence that when people tap into personal experiences with political issues, they can begin to identify with others who have common experiences and think in terms of political actions that might make a difference.[59] Moreover, as noted earlier, news that points to citizen action alternatives also stimulates greater citizen interest and makes information easier to store and use. Together, these two ideas send a message to journalists to cover more of the experiences that ordinary citizens have with the issues that make the news and to surround those experiences with information about the political options available to concerned citizens.

If young people are to return to politics, the new interactive media will have to offer richer visual and participatory information formats. It would also help, of course, if political leaders spoke to young citizens. Most electoral and issue campaigns offer few messages to young citizens, either because they are thought to be hard to reach, or because they are regarded as so tuned out that their participation will not have much impact, or both. While mainstream politics and news largely ignores the youth audience, many young people are finding alternative channels of information and action. The global social justice movement of recent years indicates greater interest among young activists than at any time perhaps since the 1960s. Yet without some connection to more traditional political participation such as voting, or to broader information channels such as mass media news, it is unclear how this movement will grow in public support or how it will affect government policies.

Will news organizations change their patterns of coverage voluntarily? Perhaps not. Because we are talking about an information system, it makes more sense to think about related changes that might occur in all three areas of press, government communication practices, and citizen information use. The next chapter addresses changes that would bring each set of actors in the system closer to constructing the kind of information order that would serve the needs of contemporary democracy.

NOTES

1. Roderick Hart, *Seducing America: How Television Charms the Modern Voter* (New York: Oxford University Press, 1994), 22.
2. Robert D. Putnam, *Bowling Alone: The Collapse and Revival of American Community* (New York: Simon and Schuster, 2000), 36.
3. See James T. Hamilton, *All the News That's Fit to Sell: How the Market Transforms Information into News* (Princeton, NJ: Princeton University Press, 2004), Chapter 3.
4. Ibid, 103.
5. See, for example, Dan Nimmo and David L. Swanson, "The Field of Political Communication: Beyond the Voter Persuasion Paradigm," in *New Directions in Political Communication: A Resource Book,* ed. Swanson and Nimmo, (Newbury Park, CA: Sage, 1990), 7–47.
6. See the more detailed discussions in W. Lance Bennett, *The Governing Crisis: Media, Money, and Marketing in American Elections* (New York: St. Martin's Press, 1992).
7. W. Russell Neuman, Marion R. Just, and Ann N. Crigler, *Common Knowledge: News and the Construction of Political Meaning* (Chicago: University of Chicago Press, 1992), 8.
8. Thomas Patterson and Philip Seib, "Informing the Public." Report to the Press Commission, Institutions of Democracy project of the Annenberg Foundation Trust. Commission meeting at Rancho Mirage, California, February 5–8, 2004.
9. Doris A. Graber, *Processing Politics: Learning from Television in the Internet Age* (Chicago: University of Chicago Press, 2001); see also, *Processing the News: How People Tame the Information Tide,* 2nd ed. (New York: Longman, 1988).
10. John Fiske, *Television Culture* (London: Methuen, 1987).
11. William Gamson, *Talking Politics* (New York: Cambridge University Press, 1992), 179.
12. Neuman, Just, and Crigler, *Common Knowledge,* chapter 7, especially p. 111.
13. Ibid., Chapter 5. See also, Graber, *Processing the News.*
14. National opinion sample taken in 1996 for the *News in the Next Century Project* (Washington, DC: Radio and Television News Directors Foundation). Reported by Doris Graber in *Processing Politics: Learning from Television in the Internet Age,* 3.
15. Hamilton, *All the News That's Fit to Sell,* 90.
16. See, for example, Robert Kubey and Mihaly Csikszentmihalyi, *Television and the Quality of Life: How Viewing Shapes the Everyday Experience* (Hillsdale, NJ: Lawrence Erlbaum, 1990).
17. Charles Winick, "The Function of Television: Life without the Big Box," in *Television as Social Issue,* ed. Stuart Oskamp, (Newbury Park, CA: Sage, 1988), 217–37.
18. Graber, *Processing Politics.*
19. Shanto Iyengar and Donald R. Kinder, *News That Matters* (Chicago: University of Chicago Press, 1987).
20. Shanto Iyengar, *Is Anyone Responsible? How Television Frames Political Issues* (Chicago: University of Chicago Press, 1991).
21. See, for example, Michael X. Delli Carpini and Scott Keeter, *What Americans Know About Politics and Why It Matters* (New Haven, CT: Yale University Press, 1996).
22. Graber, *Virtual Political Reality.*
23. Pew Research Center Database, "Public Attentiveness to Major News Stories, 1986–1998."
24. Hamilton, *All the News That's Fit to Sell,* 262.
25. Ibid., 90.
26. Ibid., 85

27. Thomas E. Patterson, *The Vanishing Voter: Public Involvement in an Age of Uncertainty* (New York: Vintage Books, 2003), 16.

28. Hamilton, *All the News that Fits,* 85.

29. Ibid., 18.

30. "Political Information Sources and the Campaign." Pew Internet and American Life Project. **www.pewinternet.org/reports/reports.asp?Report=110&Section=ReportLevel1&Field=Level1I&ID=475.** Report of January 11, 2004.

31. Matthew Baum. "Sex, Lies, and War: How Soft News Brings Foreign Policy to the Inattentive Public." *American Political Science Review* 96; no. 2 (2002): 91–109.

32. Ibid.

33. Ibid.

34. John Zaller, *The Nature and Origins of Mass Opinion* (New York: Cambridge University Press, 1992).

35. For the magnitude of this information campaign, see the report "Well-Heeled," published by the Center for Public Integrity, Washington, D.C., 1994.

36. *Newsweek* poll reported in Steven Waldman, Bob Cohn, and Eleanor Clift, "How Clinton Blew It," *Newsweek* (June 27, 1994): 28.

37. Polls reported in Melinda Beck, "Rationing Health Care," *Newsweek* (June 27, 1994): 30.

38. Quoted in Maureen Dowd, "Bush's Top Strategists: Smooth Poll-Taker and Hard Driving Manager," *New York Times,* May 30, 1988, 11.

39. George E. Marcus, W. Russell Neuman, and Michael MacKuen, *Affective Intelligence and Political Judgement* (Chicago: University of Chicago Press, 2000). See also, W. Russell Neuman, Michael B. MacKuen, George E. Marcus, and Joanne Miller, "Affective Choice and Rational Choice" (paper presented at the annual meeting of the American Political Science Association, Washington, D.C., September 1997).

40. See the more detailed discussions in Bennett, *The Governing Crisis,* especially Chapters 1 and 4.

41. Barbara G. Farah and Ethel Klein, "Public Opinion Trends," in *The Election of 1988: Reports and Interpretations,* ed. Gerald M. Pomper, (Chatham, NJ: Chatham House, 1989), 103.

42. Arthur Lupia and Matthew McCubbins, *The Democratic Dilemma: Can Citizens Learn What They Need to Know?* (New York: Cambridge University Press, 1998).

43. See Samuel Popkin, *The Reasoning Voter: Communication and Persuasion in Presidential Campaigns,* 2nd ed. (Chicago: University of Chicago Press, 1994).

44. See, for example, Tamar Liebes, "Cultural Differences in the Retelling of Television Fiction," *Critical Studies in Mass Communication* 5 (1986): 277–92.

45. For an overview of trends in the field, see Elihu Katz, "Communications Research Since Lazarsfeld," *Public Opinion Quarterly* 51 (1987): 25–45.

46. For an introduction to the "uses and gratification" concept, see Jay G. Blumler and Denis Mc-Quail, *Television in Politics: Its Uses and Influences* (Chicago: University of Chicago Press, 1969). Also, Lee B. Becker, "Two Tests of Media Gratification: Watergate and the 1974 Elections," *Journalism Quarterly* 53 (1976): 26–31.

47. See, for example, Dan Berlyne, *Conflict, Arousal, and Curiosity* (New York: McGraw-Hill, 1960).

48. For an explanation of how such scripts are formed and how they work, see Roger Schank and Robert Abelson, *Scripts, Plans, Goals and Understanding* (Hillsdale, NJ: Lawrence Erlbaum, 1977).

49. For a discussion of how new stimuli become incorporated into a mental picture, see W. Lance Bennett, "Perception and Cognition: An Information-Processing Framework for Politics," in *The Handbook of Political Behavior,* vol. 1, ed. Samuel Long, (New York: Plenum, 1981).

50. Neal Gabler, *Life: The Movie: How Entertainment Conquered Reality* (New York:Knopf, 1998).

51. Walter Lippmann, *Public Opinion* (New York: Free Press, 1922).

52. See Lydia Saad. "Clinton's Options in Grand Jury Testimony Appear Limited, but Not Lethal," *Gallup* (August 15, 1998) **www.gallup.com/poll/releases/pr980815.asp**.
53. Frank Newport, "Public Views Willey Charges as Little Different from Those of Other Women," *Gallup* (March 20, 1998) **www.gallup.com/poll/releases/pr980320.asp**.
54. Benedict Anderson, *Imagined Communities* (London: Verso, 1983).
55. "Fantasy theme" is a concept coined by Ernest G. Bormann in his article "The Eagleton Affair: A Fantasy Theme Analysis," *Quarterly Journal of Speech* 59 (1973), pp. 143–59.
56. Ernest G. Bormann, "A Fantasy Theme Analysis of the Television Coverage of the Hostage Release and the Reagan Inaugural," *Quarterly Journal of Speech* 68 (1982): 137–38.
57. See, for example, Donald Horton and R. Richard Wohl, "Mass Communication and Para-Social Interaction," *Psychiatry* 19 (1956): 219–29; see also Mark R. Levy, "Watching TV News as Para-Social Interaction," *Journal of Broadcasting* 23 (Winter 1979): 69–80.
58. These conclusions and the data in this section are from Lawrence, Bennett, and Hunt, "Making Sense of Monica."
59. William Gamson, *Talking Politics* (New York: Cambridge University Press, 1992).

Chapter 8

All the News That Fits Democracy: Solutions for Citizens, Politicians, and Journalists

News from the Past
Where the press is free, and every man able to read, all is safe.
Thomas Jefferson

News of the Future
The new market-oriented communications and information system that is currently gaining ground within liberal democracies is being sold to the general public on the promise that it will enlarge people's choices and increase their control over their lives, that it will be both liberating and empowering. . . . [Yet] the new market oriented system . . . addresses people predominantly through their identities as consumers. . . . In the process, the system marginalizes or displaces other identities, in particular the identity of citizen.
Graham Murdock and Peter Golding

Understanding the information system in the United States is made difficult by the layers of belief and mythology that have built up to defend the very things that may be weakening the core of that system—the news. As discussed throughout the book, common sense is not always the best guide to discovering how things work. We learned, for example, that the popular belief in liberal press bias is not only off the mark, but it may actually keep people from recognizing more serious biases. The biases outlined in Chapter 2 run far deeper than ideology; they actively discourage many citizens of different political persuasions from engaging creatively with the political world around them. We also examined the myth that sensational news is what the public wants. This is, at best, a half truth, but its widespread acceptance gets in the way of seeing that cheap sensationalism is precisely the kind of news that satisfies corporate profit demands, even when large numbers of people tune it out. The irony is that the factors that have produced this disconnection between news and democracy are often pointed to as foundations of American freedom itself:

- Private (corporate) ownership of the media
- Popular resistance to government support for public broadcasting—compounded by the erosion of public responsibility regulations on commercial broadcasters
- The continuing belief by citizens and journalists that news should be objective or politically neutral makes it difficult to think about reinventing a journalism that better suits our democracy

These defining conditions of the American press are accepted with nearly religious faith by many Americans. Yet many of the same Americans also find fault with the journalistic product. Is there some relationship between these defining features of our news system and the unsatisfying results it produces? This chapter explores these curious tenets of the American free press in order to introduce more productive ways of thinking about improving our political information system. Consider how each of these core elements of the American press system may actually limit the range and depth of the news.

THE NEWS ABOUT THE PRIVATE MEDIA SYSTEM

Americans too easily regard private ownership of public information as a good thing. Economic competition is easily imagined to produce informational diversity and quality. Yet markets often present opportunities for concentration of ownership and control, resulting in oligopoly or monopoly. This is why democratic governments everywhere regulate key markets—in order to protect the people from the many unhappy coercions of unchecked economic power. Most Americans today take for granted that they will not have to work in sweatshop conditions for starvation wages or that the new toaster they buy will not likely burn down the house. Government regulations concerning labor and product safety have become invisible guarantees of decent lives that few would argue with. Yet there is surprisingly little public concern about protecting the quality of ideas that ultimately define the quality of democracy.

As discussed in Chapter 3, the largely private ownership of the news business in the United States does not advance causes such as the diversity or citizen-friendliness of information. When John Stewart Mill long ago discussed the importance of a *marketplace of ideas* for democracy, he thought about how to design election and press systems that would bring ideas into public debate and link them to governing.[1] Most democracies still think seriously about how to best represent and stimulate the thinking of the many diverse publics that make up complex societies. Unfortunately, the American faith in the rule of markets means that there is not much serious policy-level thinking about just what kind of press system citizens should have.

Even when scholars and journalists engage with this important question, there is little interest from government or most citizens in imposing public responsibility guidelines (beyond moral codes) on private media corporations. Public information standards in this age of free enterprise would be denounced by media corporations and by the politicians they support as dangerous violations of free speech and free enterprise. Most citizens would join the press-government choir in rejecting the idea of strengthening public service broadcasting.

THE NEWS ABOUT PUBLIC BROADCASTING

The government regulates the quality of air, food, and water much more actively than it regulates the quality of political information. There is probably more truth in product advertising than in political advertising. People fear government intervention in the area of political information and cannot imagine government regulations that might actually expand the range of ideas in circulation. This hands-off approach to the press has been criticized by communication scholar Robert McChesney as actually limiting the range of ideas in American political debate. Compared to most other advanced democracies, the United States provides little airspace or financial support for public service broadcasting. Repeated government decisions to limit public broadcasting have served up the public airwaves to commercial corporations with little accompanying obligation to serve the public interest.[2]

Despite its bare-bones operation, public broadcasting in this country faces continual attack from members of Congress and from conservative commentators. In many ways, public broadcasting in the United States is not as independent as it could be because it is forced by limited government support to take money from commercial sponsors. As an alternative to this fragile public system, why not shift a tiny portion of the money spent on corporate subsidies or weapons of mass destruction to support an independent media system chartered for the explicit purpose of expanding the range of ideas and experimenting with news formats beyond those found in commercial broadcasts?

All other advanced democratic nations have far more developed public media systems. Sweden even subsidizes local newspapers in areas where there would otherwise be no community voice. The most respected news sources in many countries are the public radio and television news services. Yet Americans generally have trouble imagining how government-funded journalism could avoid being a mouthpiece for the government itself. In thinking about this issue, it may help to remember that the current U.S. press system has not achieved such impressive levels of independence from officials, or set high standards for critical reporting.

There are many ways to insulate journalists from direct government pressure in public service media systems. A common model is to appoint oversight commissions with representatives from different parties and political groups, along with members of major religious, educational, business and labor institutions. These commissions monitor news content and negotiate norms and standards for journalism. The fight between the BBC and the British labor government of Tony Blair concerning the government's grounds for going to war in Iraq suggests that public service systems can be quite independent of the governments they cover.

THE NEWS ABOUT OBJECTIVE JOURNALISM

When combined with a highly commercial and minimally regulated press system, the cultural ideal of neutral or objective journalism may be the greatest limit on the communication of political ideas. No matter how independent they may be, journalists who avoid introducing political perspective in their coverage all end up reporting much the same news. Yet the powerful ideal of a free-but-unbiased press leaves most journalists and citizens unable to imagine another way. It seems that politicians, like the voters who elect them, believe that it is possible to separate the news from politics and arrive at something resembling objective information. So, Americans grudgingly receive a similar replay of the same events and ideas from virtually every mainstream news channel. Political communication scholar Thomas Patterson describes this as the "irony of the free press" in America:

> American journalists have concluded that the marketplace of ideas is enhanced when they are "free" or "independent," in the sense that they are not connected organizationally, editorially, or legally to any political institution or mandate. In this view . . . news decisions should be the free choices of unregulated journalists. . . . [Yet] when journalists are detached from political moorings . . . they tend to generate a form of news that, first, underplays political ideas and, second, is consensual as opposed to competitive in its content.[3]

The myth of a free press persists among journalists, politicians, and citizens, even as it muddles popular understandings about information and democracy. How can we get beyond this state of communication gridlock? A first step is to allow ourselves a more realistic look at the information system behind the myth.

NEWS AND POWER IN AMERICA: IDEAL VERSUS REALITY

In the ideal civics-book version of American democracy, power rests with the people, who are, in effect, the voice of the political system. Leaders are supposed to take cues from the people and express their voice politically. The journalist in this scheme occupies the role of the independent monitor who reports to the people on how well leaders handle the public trust. In simple picture form, this ideal version of power in America looks like Figure 8.1.

It is obvious that the reality of power in America does not look much like this ideal picture. As numerous examples in this book have indicated, leaders and organized interests have usurped enormous amounts of political power and reduced popular control over the political system by using the media to generate support, compliance, and just plain confusion among the public. Grassroots opinion drives various battles over rights and morals such as abortion and religious expression, but on matters affecting economic policy and other sensitive areas of state and corporate concern, the battle for public opinion is waged largely by organized interests and political elites using polling and marketing techniques to deliver images to generally inattentive publics. Which came first, the inattentive public or the blocked communication channels? Either way, the result is not encouraging for public participation.

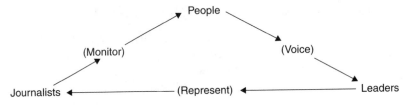

Figure 8.1   Ideal version of power in America

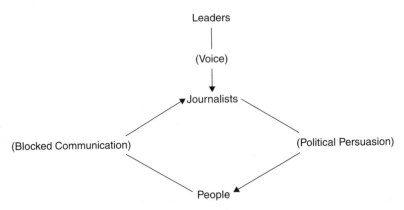

Figure 8.2   Realistic picture of American political power

The media also play a different role in the reality of American politics than the one they play in the ideal version. News organizations are more often political transmission lines to the people than they are monitors or watchdogs of what they are transmitting. The news gates are opened most often to voices from below when government officials or other prominent newsmakers are already in conflict about an issue. Citizen groups seldom get into the news unless they first get on the government agenda. Figure 8.2 provides a more realistic picture of the place of journalism in the American political power system.

There are, of course, a number of obvious reasons why the media do not monitor government actions in an adequate way. To begin with, the news as it currently exists is a successful, profit-making enterprise; news organizations have little incentive to change what they do. Moreover, elite national journalists derive a large measure of professional success and personal satisfaction from their jobs and have few incentives to rock the boat. In addition, critical watchdog reporting often brings social and political pressure to bear on reporters and their organizations. Even routine news reporting is constantly criticized by (largely conservative) media monitoring organizations and by political and economic elites for not being sufficiently objective. Such media criticism has become an important lever in the power system by helping extreme voices gain greater credibility in public discourse.

WHY THE MYTH OF A FREE PRESS PERSISTS

Almost every citizen holds onto some inspiring images of the press. These images are based on the dramatic events and guiding sentiments of American history, as these of Thomas Jefferson: "The people are the only censors of their governors [and they must have full] information of their affairs through the channel of the public papers. . . . [Were] it left to me to decide whether we should have a government without newspapers or newspapers without a government, I should not hesitate a moment to prefer the latter."[4]

Ideas like these have been passed down by every generation of journalists, educators, and politicians throughout American history and have come to represent the spirit of a nation and a people. The real meaning of those sentiments in today's society is hard to imagine, yet ideals that are given such powerful reinforcement and that endow people with such noble purpose often take on a life of their own. They are inspirational, hopeful, ennobling, giving substance to a national history that would otherwise become vague in the minds of new generations. Such are the characteristics of myths. Unfortunately, myths like the free press stand in the way of seeing the realities of power.

The myth of a free press and a free people and its guiding principle of objective reporting would seem to provide different but compelling benefits for different groups. However, there is an irony here: The groups at the top of the power structure gain the material advantages of power and control while the groups at the bottom trade real power (because the myth works in reality to limit their political involvement) for psychological reassurances. Thus the broader the support is for the idea of fair or objective journalism, the more firmly established the inequalities of power become. A brief overview of the interests of politicians, journalists, and the public illustrates the different (and even contradictory) bases of loyalty to the myth.

Politicians and the News Myth

The universal support of political actors for the free press/free people myth is both useful and necessary. It is useful because it is easier to deregulate the owners of media empires (who also sponsor politicians) behind a convincing show of support for truth and popular sovereignty. It is necessary for politicians to endorse the news myth because the American public would never tolerate a leader who lacked the outward appearances of commitment to democratic ideals. Even if interest organizations and the information agencies of government work overtime to influence public opinion, the public demands at least the illusion that their system of government represents their will. It matters little whether politicians are conscious of the contradiction between their public support for the myth and their political efforts to control information. The political benefits accrue as much to those who truly believe the contemporary relevance of the story of the free press and the free people as they redound to the cynical politicians who take the news myth in vain.

Journalists and the News Myth

The benefit of the news myth for the journalist is not power but professional credibility. Without a public commitment to objective or fair reporting, the journalist could not claim professional status and political access. Even if this status is tarnished in the eyes of the public, it is supported by the networks and associations of the journalism profession itself. The news myth provides the reporter, like the politician, with a ready-made role in the ideal picture of American democracy. Because that role is so easily dramatized with the help of the politician, it would be hard to imagine many reporters not embracing the part. Reporters who become frustrated with mass media objectivity and other limits on daily reporting simply leave the major news organizations, perhaps to become freelance writers or reporters outside the mainstream.

Some journalists, like some politicians, may cynically mouth the news myth while harboring a fuller sense of its emptiness. However, many journalists fail to see the contradiction in their pursuit of news objectivity. At some point, most career journalists accept the fact that reporting what officials say and do is really the highest form of professionalism. When Tom Brokaw was questioned about whether the press failed to raise enough questions about the Bush administration's case for the Iraq War, he noted that in the end, "Congress voted overwhelmingly to approve the war—and we had to reflect that."[5] When in doubt, the edge goes to the government. From this assumption, it is a small step from embracing the activities of professional, objective journalism to the assumption that these activities really are the keys to revealing the truth about politics. Telling it like it is can become equated, however erroneously, with telling the truth.

This does not mean that journalists do not worry about objectivity and other elements of the news myth. They do. The problem comes in finding a new journalistic stance that provides more critical distance from the power holders they cover. For example, after the invasion of Iraq, the *Columbia Journalism Review* ran a cover story called "Re-Thinking Objectivity." The story's lead idea was that "In a world of spin, our awkward embrace of an ideal can make us passive recipients of the news."[6] The object lesson was the failure of the mainstream press to challenge the Bush administration's rationale for the war:

> In his March 6 press conference, in which he laid out his reasons for the coming war, President Bush mentioned al Qaeda or the attacks of September 11 fourteen times in fifty-two minutes. No one challenged him on it, despite the fact that the CIA had questioned the Iraq-al Qaeda connection, and that there has never been solid evidence marshaled to support the idea that Iraq was involved in the attacks of 9/11.[7]

The trouble is that the author did not propose a clear alternative to objective journalism other than better investigative reporting. As he pointed out, however, journalists did not need to investigate much beyond the already well-established contradictions in the administration's call to war. All they needed was some new professional guideline that gave them permission to go outside of the officially drawn boundaries of reality.

The People and the News Myth

What can people gain from embracing the news myth? In order to answer this perplexing question, we must return to the two pictures of power in America presented earlier in the chapter. In the second picture (Figure 8.2), which better represents the reality of power in America, the people are locked into a weak power position with their choices structured for them. Their efforts to respond politically are filtered through the gatekeeping rules of news formulas. In such situations, people often develop what psychologists call *learned helplessness,* in which they either withdraw from the source of their distress (in this case, public life), or embrace highly idealized notions about their situation.

Those who seek idealized versions of power in America need look no further than the daily news. Both journalists and politicians continually dramatize the illusory appeal of Figure 8.1, the free press/free people myth, for the benefit of the public. They offer news stories as reports to the people about choices or problems that face them. Leaders appeal in the news for popular support and understanding. If people can suspend their concerns about such nagging questions as where media issues come from, how the proposed solutions are chosen, and what the limits of public involvement really are, then they can escape into an illusory world where democracy is operating just fine.

When the democratic illusion is shattered by the false promises of politicians or by the discovery that news coverage was too little or too late, people may revert to cynicism or withdrawal. However, even those who become disillusioned tend to think that the failings of the system could be fixed with more honest politicians and more neutral journalists. Such mythical solutions, while popular, fail to address the deeper problems with the national information system. The following discussion explores various changes that citizens, journalists, and politicians can make.

PROPOSALS FOR CITIZENS, JOURNALISTS, AND POLITICIANS

It is naive to think that some magic wand of government, journalism, or citizenship can be waved and all will be changed. Yet even small changes within each sphere can make important differences. Above all, it would help to recognize the roots of our communication problems and talk about them differently in public. At this dawning of a new age of electronic democracy, the opportunity exists once again to have a critical national debate about how we should inform ourselves and engage with politics. New information technologies through which citizens can interact with politicians, journalists and each may help us think creatively about striking a new balance of media power.

Proposals for Citizens

Citizens can make a difference by thinking more creatively about how information comes to them. Participating in public life without the illusions of the free press/free people myth is a good start. The next step is to begin thinking freely about alternatives. There is little cost to brainstorming about a more perfect information order. Should we encourage more partisan political reporting? More analysis in news stories? What about government incentives for news organizations that pioneer new formats for covering issues, elections, and chronic social problems? These and other ideas are worth exploring openly and in public forums without concern that they would somehow violate our mythical notions of a free press. Perhaps people should think more about diversity and other qualities on the output side of the communication equation rather than being so preoccupied with the ideal of freedom on the input side.

In addition to thinking more creatively about designing a better national communication system, people would also do well to learn how to better use the one we currently have. The critical analyses contained in this book can be used in decoding the news. If people learn to read between the lines and see beyond the images, they can reduce their frustration and confusion with the news. In short, becoming better informed does not simply mean reading more papers or watching more television. It means decoding the information from these and other sources with a critical eye.

Becoming better informed entails more than just memorizing the who, what, where, when, and how of the isolated events of the day. Understanding the political causes and social consequences of public affairs is also useful for clarifying feelings and deciding how to respond. Armed with the basic introduction provided in this book, it is possible to recognize and decode the most common information biases in the news. The following guidelines should help in becoming a more critical news consumer.

Recognize Stereotypes and Plot Formulas   When new information is translated into old formulas, there is no challenge for people to replace their prejudices with new insights. Yet the easiest stories for politicians to tell and journalists to write are based on familiar images of the world. Unless these warmed-over schemes are detected and discarded, the news remains an unhelpful forum, reinforcing superficial understandings and old ideologies.

It is important to detect and discard loaded descriptions and buzz words. Terms like *leftist, right-winger, big government, freedom,* and even *well-placed* or *informed sources* can set up information for very selective interpretations. For example, "well-placed and informed sources" are often high officials acting irresponsibly by anonymously planting rumor and innuendo in the news. Despite the dubious worth of such leaks and plants, their attribution to an informed, official, or well-placed source can lend them credibility. In general, more weight should be given to the sources who identifying themselves than to those who anonymously spin the news. The exception of course is when sources fear for their lives or livelihoods by blowing the whistle.

The savvy news consumer should recognize that labels such as *liberal* or *religious fundamentalist* are often planted by spin doctors to undermine their opponents. Yet such terms often stick as though they were objective descriptions. This is not to say that there are no leftists or rightists or other "-ists" in the world. However, news audiences often do not want to know more about characters who have been branded with such labels. The point here is not that we would end up agreeing with the statements of criminals, protesters, or terrorists, but we might develop a better understanding of how they think, why they do what they do, and what we should do in turn.

It may be true, for example, that some people really are the crazed, vengeful sociopaths that the word *terrorist* connotes. Surely the dictates and actions of Osama bin Laden and the Taliban were not defensible within the broadest spectrum of American views. However, declaring war on terrorism in general opened up political possibilities that were more questionable. For example, if Saddam Hussein qualified as a target in the War on Terror, aren't there dozens of other really bad regimes out there who qualify for invasion as well? At another level, the blanket declaration of war on terror risks blocking understanding of disenfranchised groups who have resorted to violence as a last desperate measure to make themselves heard and their problems addressed. As political scientist Steven Livingston has shown, the terrorist label is often strategically placed in the news by partisan actors pursuing policy agendas, and that label affects how those policy stories are told.[8]

Look for Information That Doesn't Fit the Plot It is useful to remember the maxim that "There are lies, damn lies, and then there are statistics." Documentary evidence, including statistics and pictures, can be taken out of context to suit the image of the moment. Evidence often seems true or factual simply because it fits so neatly with a powerful image, a familiar plot, or a deeply held belief. An equally useful reminder about reality, by contrast, is that it is never neat and clean. Raw data are always messy and ambiguous. The ambiguity of data is their real advantage—they make us think critically and probe for new patterns. When facts and claims fit too neatly, they provide psychological affirmation, not a reality check. Thus, many Americans were surely prepared to hear that there was some connection between Saddam Hussein and al Qaeda following 9/11, and few stopped to see if there was evidence to challenge this administration claim.

In order to counter this news psychology, the facts must be weighed carefully before accepting them. First, it is important to peer through the rhetorical smoke to see if there are any documented claims or only unsupported charges and assertions. Above all, the news critic should look for loose facts that could become the basis for an entirely different story. Building an interpretation around these loose facts can help illuminate the underlying political issues that are worth paying attention to. It is easier to focus on stray facts and see where they go when one is not trying to fit them into the surrounding news plot. Case in point: if the CIA found no evidence of connections between Iraq and al Qaeda, did it really make sense to link Iraq to 9/11?

Seek Additional Sources of Information to Check Partisan Claims This does not mean consulting *Time* as a reference on *Newsweek*'s presentation of the facts. Rather, it means consulting publications and documentaries that provide richer, more historical accounts that are told, above all, from the standpoint of critics, opposition groups, or disinterested academic observers.

The Internet makes it easy to gather huge volumes of information on almost any subject. The major search engines tap into different domains of news and information. It is important to recognize that not all the results of these searches are reliable, but it is possible to detect patterns of information from known sources that provide solid additions to what may be contained in brief news accounts. It is also a good idea to consult prominent international news organizations such as the BBC when thinking about international developments involving the United States. Moreover, it is easy to set up news tracking and delivery services (for free) with most of the major Internet portals. These tracking requests will deliver new information every day on running stories in the news. Some of these engines also provide user information on the quality and reliability of different information sources. In addition, searching the web on a topic in one of the less commercially biased search engines (**www .google.com** is probably the best) generally produces a good deal of often high-quality information from interest organizations whose political agendas can be deduced and evaluated from their websites. Finally, joining discussions of news reports on Weblogs can be entertaining and thought provoking.

Recognize Spin and News Control in Action   Sometimes there just do not seem to be any loose facts on which alternative interpretations can be built. Successfully controlled news has just the right number of facts to document the image intended by the political script. When politicians present their staged news events, or pseudoevents, successfully, the press tends to report only the documentary facts that were planted to lend credibility to the story. In this case, the critic must learn to recognize the characteristics of pseudoevents and decipher the political messages they convey. The first clue, of course, is that successful pseudoevents do not contain many stray facts.

When a president announces a war on anything, the news consumer should look for signs of staged political drama. Such political staging was plain when Ronald Reagan declared war on crime after nearly two years in office. He announced his support for a complete package of legislation that would make it tougher for criminals to get away with terrorizing law-abiding American citizens. The entire performance was designed to rally the support of a fearful, economically troubled citizenry around a strong leader. It was not incidental that it was staged just two days after Reagan suffered his first major political defeat (Congress overrode his veto of a major federal spending bill). Could the president's media team have prepared a winning scenario and kept it in the wings for just such an occasion? An attentive news critic should be able to detect the signs of scripted political performances and connect them to the political circumstances of the actors who perform them.

Consider in this light one of the stage props used by the senior George Bush in his remake of the Reagan War on Crime, replayed this time as a War on Drugs. The news prop was a bag of crack cocaine that Bush held up the night he declared war in a nationally televised speech. Bush offered the bag—purchased by undercover agents in Lafayette Park, across the street from the White House—as evidence that the drug problem could be found right across the street from his own home at 1600 Pennsylvania Avenue.

In a later investigative report, the *Washington Post* revealed that the dramatic moment was staged by Mr. Bush's media consultants. the *Washington Post* story, which received wide media play, opened this way:

WASHINGTON. White House speech writers thought it was the perfect prop for President George Bush's first prime-time television address to the nation—a dramatic one that would show how the drug trade had spread to the president's own neighborhood.

"This is crack cocaine," Mr. Bush solemnly announced in his Sept. 5 speech on drug policy, holding up a plastic bag filled with a white chunky substance. It was "seized a few days ago in a park across the street from the White House," he said, adding, "It could easily have been heroin or PCP."

But obtaining the crack was no easy feat. To match the words of the speech writers, Drug Enforcement Administration agents lured a suspected Washington drug dealer to Lafayette Park four days before the speech. They made what appears to have been the agency's first undercover crack buy in a park better known for its location across Pennsylvania Avenue from the White House than for illegal drug activity, according to officials familiar with the case.

In fact, the teen-age suspect, when first contacted by an undercover agent posing as a buyer, seemed baffled by the request.

"Where is the White House?" he replied in a conversation that was secretly tape-recorded by the drug agency.

"We had to manipulate him to get him down here," said William Mc-Mullen, assistant special agent in charge of the agency's Washington field office. "It wasn't easy."[9]

Perhaps because the wars on crime and drugs had become too predictable, or perhaps because they were waged more against the poor and minorities than against middle-class drug users or corporate criminals, the press seemed more determined than usual in this instance to point out that the emperor had no clothes. In response to having the cover blown on a staged news event, Bush followed up with a staged reaction. The Bush media team had developed a tactical response to press criticism: From time to time, go ballistic with the press. Bush handlers had discovered that a bit of bristle with the press made the president look tough and committed. Shortly after the earlier *Washington Post* story appeared, the president took an image trip to a Maine tree farm to demonstrate his environmental concern. Rather than dutifully interview the president about his relations with baby trees, the press pack hounded him about the staged drug bust. The president suggested testily that questioning his methods in such a holy crusade made reporters antagonists in the drug war: "I don't understand," he complained. "I mean, has somebody got some advocates here for this drug guy?"[10]

Learn to Become Self-Critical   At this point, you may be concerned that these guidelines will turn you into a cynic rather than a critic. Who or what can be trusted? The goal of news criticism is not to reject everything—it is to think confidently and independently about world events in the face of a lot of pressure to think like everybody else. Nor is the point to distrust all authorities—it is to trust your own judgment.

This brings us to what may be the most important guideline: Recognize the importance of your prior beliefs (and prejudices) in screening and accepting news information, and wherever possible, challenge those beliefs with information that is at odds with them. The point of being self-critical is not to get rid of beliefs altogether or to tear them down as fast as we build them up. The goal is to make sure that our beliefs do not stand as a wall against reality. Beliefs are most useful when they help us engage constructively in the ongoing solution of social problems. When beliefs are proclaimed as absolutes to be defended against all evidence to the contrary, they become the causes of social problems. Because the news contains two sides to most stories, people can simply select the version of reality that comes closest to their prior beliefs and never change their thinking about the world. What if neither side represented in the news provides a useful way to think about an issue? What if both sides have some merit? Where will new solutions come from if we do not actively challenge our beliefs about old problems? Escaping our current political dilemmas requires the will to challenge existing political beliefs, and there is no better way to challenge beliefs than by resisting the daily temptation to look to the news for confirmation of what we already hold to be true about the world.

How can one be open to new information without feeling confused by every new pronouncement? Many people are so open to different views of situations that they just don't know what to believe. Some of the most conscientious citizens, in fact, become paralyzed when they hear conflicting information in the news. The longer they wait for more information to emerge and bring them to an objective understanding, the more confused they become. Clearly, the process of challenging one's beliefs does not mean accepting everything one hears as equally valid. This is where the guidelines for news detectives come into play. Much of the confusion in the news can be sorted out by looking beyond the familiar plot formulas and by discounting the facts that have been produced to support them. These steps will remove much of the distraction from the daily information flow and make it possible to look for new details that are genuinely thought-provoking.

All of this said, the task of becoming an informed citizen would be considerably easier if the news required less decoding and provided more challenging perspectives to begin with. The mass media are unlikely to undergo an "information revolution" and proclaim their independence from formula reporting and the daily pronouncements of government officials. However, journalists can do a lot within the current constraints of the profession to improve the quality of their product.

Proposals for Journalists

Reporters and editors often argue that they would like to do more with the news, but time, space, profit pressures, and fickle audiences just do not permit it. In response to these journalistic laments, consider this challenge: It is the responsibility of the press to prepare the citizenry for participation, and this task can be accomplished within the limitations previously mentioned. Here is how:

Use Personalization and Dramatization Creatively   As suggested in Chapter 2, drama could help rather than hinder in communicating interesting and powerful messages about the world. Current news formats, however, are more melodramatic than seriously dramatic, sacrificing the enduring issues surrounding events for momentary glimpses into the trials and tribulations of political actors. Journalists could easily reduce the melodramatic overtones of the news by developing the historical and institutional contexts in which action is played out. This does not mean eliminating the actors involved—it is hard to tell a story without characters—but rather placing them clearly within the political context where the enduring effects of their actions will be felt. Thus, crime stories could be removed from the realm of the bizarre, grotesque, and sinister and placed in the social world of poverty, loss of community, alienation, group conflict, and psychological disorders. Budget deficits could be removed from the clutches of big-spending politicians and placed in the context of the bureaucratic and social forces that create them. International violence could be taken out of the personalized world of tough talk, belligerence, and mistrust and shown in the context of economic, military, and international institutional structures that sustain many conflicts. Virtually every issue could be thus enriched in favor of more useful social, historical, and institutional analyses. This shift corresponds to Iyengar's recommendations for less episodic and more thematic reporting discussed in Chapters 1 and 2.[11] Such journalistic shifts would make it possible for the general news audience to grasp the larger political implications of events without resorting to so much laborious decoding.

Many reporters and editors believe that more attention to social, institutional, and historical factors would only make the news more complicated and confuse people even further. It is not clear what, other than journalistic superstition, supports this belief. Most people probably could not be any more confused about the world than they are at present. It is also possible that this confusion is the direct result of melodramatic news formats that fail to provide intelligible contexts for developing events. Yet, news professionals opt for ever more simple-minded coverage and wonder what to do with an ever more simple-minded public.

Introduce More of the Journalist's Own Background Knowledge into Stories

This does not mean more cynicism or personal commentary on politicians' games and presumed political strategies. Rather, journalists should learn to use what they, as expert witnesses, have come to know about the workings of the situations they cover.

Current reporting practice leans heavily toward letting the actors tell the story. In these source-driven narratives, the reporter's voice sets the tone of a story. As noted earlier, this tone is often cynical precisely because journalists cannot find ways to say what they really know or think about the situations they are covering. Moving away from actor-centered narrative toward observer-centered narrative would place control over the development of a news story with the journalist, where it properly belongs, not with political actors, whose interest is in manipulating the story to their own advantage. The place where reporters could add most to stories is in the explanation of how different policy proposals were developed, why others were rejected, and what the competing proposals might accomplish if implemented. In her cogent analysis of news coverage of welfare reform, Regina Lawrence noted that during the extended period in which the various proposals were being debated between Congress and the White House, journalists mainly contributed commentary about the games and strategies. However, after the reforms were passed, journalists introduced an impressive review of the substance of the new policies.[12] Such journalistic discussions of political substance simply needed to come earlier in the coverage of welfare and other major issues.

Resist the Standard Plot Formulas

No more horse races in election coverage. No more "Is the president winning or losing?" in his relations with Congress. It is tempting to peg stories to plots that trigger instant recognition from the audience.

However, the more standardized the plot and vocabulary used in a story, the less informative the content. Here is an experiment: Try rewriting a story about a personal defeat or victory of the president or some other prominent politician. Put the personal, dramatic, and authority-disorder themes in the background and emphasize the broader issues, institutional factors, and political consequences involved in the situation.

Define Political Situations in Terms That Appeal to Ordinary People   When reporters clearly define the terms and concepts in a situation, the news audience may begin to see what is going on. New information is hard to assimilate under the best of circumstances. In fragmented, fast-paced news, definition and repetition of new information are essential to comprehension. Pointing out that TV viewers miss the main ideas in two-thirds of all stories, Levy and Robinson urged a revamping of current formats. They concluded that TV news is "produced for people already in the know, it's filled with the jargon of policymakers and riddled with cryptic references to continuing stories. What TV journalists forget is that most viewers need some help in understanding the news, no matter how often the story has been told."[13] The absence of useful definitions is cited as a major reason why people fail to grasp the point of stories:

> One reason TV news fails to inform is that too often it uses language and concepts that are outside the viewer's normal vocabulary. Terms such as Gramm-Rudman, electronic countermeasures, rights of passage, and War Powers Act popped up regularly in three programs we sampled—and just as regularly they went unexplained.
>
> Most viewers need some kind of translation. On one newscast Tom Brokaw showed what can be done by taking the phrase "Contadora observers" and immediately explaining it as "a group of people from Central American and South American countries who go in to make an independent observation of the so-called battle site." Too often though, news might just as well have been written in Tagalog [a language of the Philippines].[14]

Remember to Explain Why the Story Matters   After plot formulas have been banished, background information enhanced, and key terms defined, one important reporting task remains. Although reporters may understand perfectly well why a story is important, the significance may be lost in a condensed presentation to inattentive citizens. A recent Pew Research Center survey of journalists revealed that fewer than half of television news workers felt that "providing an interpretation of the news" was a core journalistic principle.[15] Journalists should be explicit about what matters in a story. Levy and Robinson suggest that reports must pass the "so what?" test:

> It's used implicitly all the time in the newsroom to decide if something is newsworthy. Why, for example, was it important that a space suit had been recovered from the shuttle wreckage . . . ? The TV journalists who covered that news knew the answers; they had to in order to get their stories on the air. But most reports in our . . . sample never explicitly conveyed that "so what?" element of the news. Sometimes it was there—between the lines. But in our experience, information reported between the lines tends to remain there.[16]

Journalists should be explicit about the highest social values and consequences at stake in newsworthy situations. For example, the term *human rights* appears frequently in reports about other nations, particularly those nations that receive U.S. assistance. There is seldom an attempt, however, to explain the relevance of human-rights concerns to U.S. foreign policy. A notable exception has been in reporting human-rights issues in coverage of U.S.-Chinese relations. Since the Tiananmen Square massacre of 1989, Americans have been introduced to the struggle between a hard-line communist regime and those seeking to expand civil liberties and political rights. During the Bush and Clinton administrations, the connection between human rights and trade relations between the two nations became a recurring theme of news coverage. Critics of the Chinese human-rights situation argued that the United States should use favorable trade policies to promote liberal political reforms in the People's Republic. Pragmatists argued that Chinese leaders react badly to such political blackmail and would only turn to other trading partners in Europe and Asia, excluding American business interests from what is potentially the world's largest market. This active debate in the news has opened the foreign policy process to more public scrutiny and grassroots involvement than is commonly the case.[17]

Proposals for Politicians and Government

It is tempting to ask politicians simply to refrain from so much polling, news management, and political marketing in their relations with the public. If politicians did not try to appeal to the emotions and fears of increasingly isolated individuals and instead actually led publics by educating them on complex issues and encouraging them to make the sacrifices required for consensus and change, they might be more popular. Indeed, many politicians would secretly like to shift their public relations strategies in these directions but feel that they would be attacked by opponents.

An unfortunate reality of the contemporary communication system is that politicians who attempt to educate, to discuss complex issues, or to propose new ways of thinking about problems are routinely attacked as unrealistic, or worse, as big-spending, big-government politicians who would rob Americans of more of their freedoms and create more government programs that do not work. As a result, many of the most talented members of Congress from both parties have left government in recent years, frustrated at the inability to speak or act creatively in public. The communication system that has evolved in the United States seems designed to drive out careful, open, thoughtful discussion of public problems in favor of stereotypical and stifling appeals to fear and divisive emotions.

Appealing to politicians individually to change how they communicate may get some sympathetic responses, but few are brave enough to fire their spin doctors and pollsters and step in front of the television cameras to talk openly about complex problems. What, then, is the solution for politicians? One approach is to put public pressure on government to referee the national marketplace of ideas just as it referees every other market to protect consumers from fraud, deception, and safety hazards. Why should citizens have less protection against information "fraud" than against stock market fraud and faulty products? Here are five simple recommendations for government that would greatly improve the quality of political information.

Limit the Flow of Money to Politicians   The news management required to get elected and to serve effectively in public office is extremely expensive. For example, polling and advertising costs amount to roughly half of campaign budgets, and campaign spending has grown alarmingly over the past two decades. No other industrial democracy permits politicians the legal fund-raising channels available to American candidates. Cutting the money supply (e.g., by further limiting campaign contributions and the spending of elected officials on political communication staff) would force politicians to go public with fewer illusions supplied by manufactured images and staged news events. The campaign finance reforms passed in 2003 are a start, but more is needed. Many Americans believe that elected representatives represent their financial backers above their constituents. It is impossible to determine whether this is true, but the perception alone is enough to cloud popular support for public officials and government. The solution is to further limit interest money, lobbying gifts, and to restrict corporate contributions to officials who act on measures affecting those corporations.

Develop Better Formats for Candidate Debates and for Coverage of Legislation   Despite voter enthusiasm for direct candidate debates and citizen-candidate exchanges, the debate system remains ad hoc. Parties, candidates, and news organizations hammer out shaky debate formats according to their various and often conflicting interests. There is no enduring commitment to a format that would require candidates and news organizations to present open and probing issue exchanges to the public.

During the periods between elections, political coverage of government is similar to sports highlight reels. Detailed coverage of legislative activity is limited nationally to C-SPAN, and at state and local levels, to similarly underfunded cable operations. Increased funding for C-SPAN (and state equivalents) along with public school education programs to help citizens tune into these information channels might redress the balance of the currently superficial news coverage of legislative and other government activities.

Control Media Monopolies   The consolidation of ownership of large numbers of print and broadcast outlets is detrimental to the diversity of information reaching the public. Antimonopoly laws are on the books, and news ones could be written with the quality of information expressly in mind. Over the past two decades, government has all but abandoned its regulation of business mergers and has explicitly loosened requirements for corporate media acquisitions. There is a notable absence of public debate about the political and social responsibilities of big business. To the contrary, many corporate opinion leaders promote the idea that the only obligation of business is to make profits for the investors.

A new generation of citizens has come of age, thinking that freedom means no social or economic public responsibilities at all. At the same time, the quality of various aspects of social life has declined, as measured in opinion polls of the very same citizens. It is time to look beyond the myth of press freedom and consider the actual quality of information being produced for public consumption.

A positive development in recent years involves the emergence of a citizen media reform movement (see **www.mediareform.org**) that has put pressure on Congress to consider the public interest when writing media legislation and reviewing FCC activities. In 2003, for example, Congress overturned an FCC ruling that would enable large media companies to control the core media outlets in many communities. This surprising reversal of the FCC followed intense lobbying by citizen activists and many (often conservative) small media companies.

Provide More Funding (and a More Creative Mandate) for Public Broadcasting Current government policies on public broadcasting restrict funding and pressure struggling stations to be less controversial and more like the rest of the media. Instead, the policies should encourage public broadcasters to be what the commercial media are not—that is, to find ways to promote more diversity, more grassroots input, more minority views, and more opposition positions.

If all of this is too much to accomplish under one roof, split the current public broadcasting corporation into multiple organizations under the directorship of different public sectors: political parties and related interest networks (perhaps channels for Republicans, Independents, and Democrats), public interest organizations (e.g., think tanks, citizen watchdog organizations, and foundations), and social groups (churches, educators, arts and culture organizations). Alternately, government—prompted by citizen pressure—can ensure that the current public broadcasting organizations have boards of directors and political firewalls that open them to political viewpoints beyond the congressional factions that currently battle for the soul of public broadcasting. Call it the *Public Citizen Channel.*

Above all, increase funding for public broadcasting so it does not have to resort to corporate sponsorship for much of its programming. If lavish funds are still spent for Voice of America and other broadcasts to other countries, perhaps the value of providing more useful information at home should be considered as well. All other industrial democracies have designed strong public broadcasting systems to meet the public communication requirements of democracy. Continuing debate and scrutiny accompany those systems as they adapt to stronger private competition. By contrast, the United States has not had a serious debate since the 1930s about the ideal balance between public and private media or the possibilities of more useful public information systems.

Strengthen Public Service Requirements for Cable and Broadcast License Holders Many Americans find it difficult to understand that the airwaves that bring them television and the local franchises that bring them cable are sold or granted by the government. Just as we expect transportation companies granted rights to public lands to provide some services to the communities along those right-of-ways, so should we require holders of communication licenses to have obligations other than to commercial advertisers and corporate shareholders.

In the view of communication scholar Robert McChesney, one of the great turning points in the American information system came in the 1930s when Congress granted the great proportion of the radio and television bandwidths to private operators with relatively few responsibilities to create public forums or cover social issues in any depth.[18] Over the years, the FCC, with the encouragement of Congress, imposed some modest public service requirements on licensees. The lobbying efforts of increasingly powerful communication companies, combined with the growing antiregulation mood in the nation, have resulted in rollbacks in operator obligations to run public affairs programs, community forums, and even basic news programming.

Another great turning point in communications technology and business development is now upon us. As governments decide how broadband cable monopolies will be granted, they have increasing leverage over what public service obligations (e.g., C-SPAN and local civic channels) cable operators should have. Local governments can extract subsidies from cable operators for high-quality local arts and politics channels that might promote citizen involvement in local affairs. Perhaps even more importantly, decisions are already being made about how to allocate and regulate the microwave spectrum that will enable the home television to become an interactive communication device. Should the interactive potential of television, personal computers, and other devices be used in the interest of commercial entertainment and home shopping, or should the democratic potential of the new electronic information age be considered seriously? These are just a few of the important issues that will affect civic communication in the next decade.

Stepping back from the focus on government enables us to see other important issues facing all players in the political communication system. This book closes with a case study that explores some of the challenges ahead in this new information age.

Case Study: *Citizen Input from Interactive News to Desktop Democracy*

There are signs that new forms of two-way communication are beginning to emerge in and around the news. A few news organizations, aware of public anger at the press, are beginning to treat people not just as consumers but as citizens as well. For their part, citizens are increasingly equipped with home computers, making it possible for them to join electronic bulletin boards and conferences on important issues, as well as to search huge databases on subjects that interest them. Increasingly, the computer-equipped citizen and the community-conscious news organization are discussing what items should be in the news and how news organizations ought to cover them from the citizen's point of view.

It is not yet clear how this trend will develop, or even if news organizations will be the leaders in bringing citizens into the news frame. However, one thing is clear: the technological potential now exists for useful two-way communication between citizens and journalists. The technology exists for audiences to ask reporters questions, thus shaping what reporters eventually ask their news sources. In addition, news organizations can provide follow-up information packages to people who want to know more about a story than can be told in a brief news format. By monitoring the kinds of questions people ask and the kinds of information they request, news organizations can interact with audiences in the development of particular stories and in the design of broad editorial agendas. The key question is whether this interactive potential will be realized in a deeper sense of educating citizens and guiding journalists, or will it be a superficial public relations tool?

Interactive digital technologies also permit citizens to become reporters and create digital information exchanges that many journalists regard as corruptions of journalistic ideals, and perhaps as threats to the future of the profession. Yet these citizen journalists often post high-quality print and streamed video accounts of situations that journalists would not cover, or at least would not cover in the same ways (see, for example, **www.oneworld.org** and **www.opendemocracy.org**). Social technology developers are creating interesting forums for citizen-driven communication such as Weblogs that can be opened to broad input, and at the same time, edited and rated so that communities of users can regulate the quality and coherence of the communication they create and share (See the *Democracy and Internet Technology* section of *The Center for Communication and Civic Engagement* **www.engagedcitizen.org**). This case study explores developments in these emerging areas of interactive news.

Citizen Input in the Newsroom

Recall the case study from Chapter 3 that reviewed the trend toward marketing the news to appeal to the emotional and sensational aspects of consumer tastes. Also recall that several newspaper chains have taken up the challenge of addressing their responsibilities to citizens. Although citizen-oriented approaches are still greatly outnumbered by consumer-oriented practices, the potential exists to create citizen-friendly news operations.

The idea of involving citizens more centrally in constructing the news agenda began with simple audience response opportunities. Many print, radio, and TV outlets have experimented with citizen forum programs to talk about hot issues or to interact with presidential candidates. Listeners to NPR and many local radio stations can now respond immediately to the stories they have just heard by sending electronic mail messages directly from their computers. Many cable news channels read or scroll e-mail from viewers during their programming. Other citizen-oriented formats include community forums to determine what issues should be covered (and how) both during and between elections. For example, in Seattle, Washington, the local paper and public radio stations joined in an enterprise called "The Front Porch Forum" in which citizens were invited to participate in various ways, from suggesting what the news agenda should be, to evaluating daily coverage.

It is interesting that seemingly simple innovations such as the Seattle "civic journalism" project drew fire from prominent journalists who objected to allowing the public to set the news agenda. They felt that journalists should exercise their professional judgment about what's news. Others condemned the movement toward public journalism as a public relations gimmick designed to fix image problems created by overcommercialized news.

Doug Underwood, a former reporter turned journalism professor at the University of Washington, looked at a model reader-driven newspaper, the Olympia, Washington,

Olympian. The parent corporation, Gannett, saw the *Olympian* as a model for the company's News 2000 program, which aimed at bringing readers onto community advisory boards to comment on how their local papers are doing. The *Olympian* held nine public forums, sent reporters out to conduct surveys at shopping malls, and formed reader advisory panels, all designed "to reconnect newspapers to their communities by involving readers in the entire news production process."[19] For some of the paper's reporters, however, the project was more public relations hype than thoughtful discussion. When citizens simply vent their private opinions and frustrations, their input may be scattered and no more useful than the news they are criticizing. As one reporter put it: "The *Olympian* is the poster child for News 2000. They've taken News 2000 to places where no reporter would want to go."[20]

The growing dissatisfaction with news on the part of citizens and many journalists has converged with new technological developments to begin to redefine the possibilities of news itself. The British Broadcasting Corporation has begun to think about a new mission for news that goes beyond informing and educating citizens to helping them organize and participate effectively in public life. BBC has launched a project called *iCan* which enables citizens to create public campaigns about issues that matter to them; find others who share those interests; and use the interactive features of the *iCan* Web site to find information, create political networks, and draw the attention of BBC journalists to stories that arise from audience concerns.

Part of the BBC project is to encourage citizen-to-citizen dialogue about political issues. According to political scientist James Fishkin, this sort of exchange is precisely what is missing from most current democratic political information systems. The predominant media focus on opinions expressed in polls and instant audience response emphasizes unstable private views that are not really "public opinion" at all, in the sense of being shaped by public dialogue and debate. Before citizens decide what the news ought to look like, perhaps they should be given opportunities to form more "deliberative" judgments.[21] The next section considers this idea of deliberative citizen input in the two-way communication process.

Deliberative Citizen Input in the News

According to Fishkin, what is missing in many current schemes for increasing citizen input into the communication process—such as reporting opinion polls or opening electronic audience discussion forums—is that they generally lack conditions that facilitate new learning about issues. Fishkin proposes that instead of being encouraged to express raw personal opinions about issues, people first need to discuss them in face-to-face settings where they are challenged to consider new information. In Fishkin's forums, people are first exposed to information delivered by experts, and then organized in small groups to discuss what they have heard before coming to any conclusions about the issues.

In a path-breaking trial of this idea in 1994, Fishkin drew a random sample of 300 British citizens and brought them to Manchester, England, under the joint sponsorship of several print and broadcast news organizations. The target issue was crime. After reading various briefing materials, hearing the experts, and debating among themselves, the sample changed its views dramatically about how to approach the crime problem. For example, a preforum survey showed that 57 percent felt that harsher prison sentences were an effective means of fighting crime. After reviewing research and thinking more critically about the relationship between prison and crime, only 38 percent concluded that prison was an effective answer. Fishkin denied that the experience had converted people into liberals, noting that their underlying concerns about the importance of crime and the need to get tough on the problem remained essentially the same after their exposure and discussion. However, their policy views became more realistic and less swayed by the kind of superficial thinking that is commonly heard by politicians and in the news.[22]

Fishkin later ran a similar experiment in deliberation in the United States with a national sample of citizens attending a national issues convention in Austin, Texas. He reported similar dramatic changes in opinion on the issues that were deliberated, along with gains in knowledge and appreciation of the political dilemmas and complexities of major national policy debates. Although it may not make sense to have face-to-face deliberations in place of every opinion poll, it may make sense to assemble a national citizen panel each year and to publicize the results of their deliberations in the news. Communication scholar John Gastil recommends that states assemble citizen panels to deliberate on ballot propositions. Their recommendations and their ratings of the partisan positions on the various ballot issues could be delivered to voters along with their ballots.[23] Fishkin regards such experiments with deliberative forums as helping us learn how to produce "a voice of the people worth listening to."[24]

News That Mobilizes Citizens?

A next step in citizen-oriented news may involve bypassing or retooling conventional media—creating Web sites and in-the-world forums where "issue communities" of citizens find each other and get the news from people who are directly involved with issues. The goal of such communication goes beyond the traditional news goal of informing citizens, to helping people engage more effectively in political activities that address the issues that concern them. These action-oriented networks may combine online forums and offline deliberations to decide upon plans of action.

One mobilization model aims at revitalizing conventional politics—directing citizen responses toward public officials and alerting mainstream news organizations to attract their coverage. An example here is the *iCann* communication model introduced by the BBC in 2003, but there are many other variations. A more spontaneous variant involved the network of Meetups (**www.meetup.com**) and Weblogs (**www.deanforamerica.com**)

that created the remarkable but short-lived mobilization of voters behind the Democratic presidential candidate Howard Dean in 2004. The Dean campaign learned the hard way that the potential of the Internet still must be harnessed somehow to the conventional news media in order to appeal to large audiences.

Another communication mobilization model aims at drawing citizens to less conventional political action such as protest movements that have used the Internet for rapid organization and information exchange in recent years.[25] Newly emerging Web-based media organizations have pioneered interactive formats aimed at using citizen news reports to mobilize activist or protest politics. For example, Indymedia outlets (**www.indymedia.org**) encourage their audiences to "Be the Media." The question is whether these new media outlets can help turn often disembodied audiences of strangers into engaged communities of citizens. If they succeed in this, the potential exists for a profound redefinition of news and information in democracies.

Desktop Democracy?

With the diffusion of personal computers and relatively low-cost online information services, traditional news organizations can offer more depth than ever before. For example, newspapers and magazines can index their articles to follow-up reports available from electronic database services. Such supplementary information could be included as part of the subscription price of the periodical or offered at a small charge attached to each search of the database. The cable television potential is equally great, with the development of software by which a television screen can emulate a computer menu. A tool bar can be brought onto the screen with a simple remote controller, and viewers can both record their reactions to ongoing programming and deliver commands to bring related programming onto other channels or have it sent directly to a taping or storage device.

Not only can citizens fine-tune their information needs with these technologies, but news organizations can monitor use patterns and adjust their information services accordingly. Because the electronic storage and delivery of such information is far cheaper than either printing or video news production, the potential exists for greater diversity of information to be supplied to relatively small numbers of consumers.

To carry this vision one step further, as noted previously, citizens can also network with each other, using information they have gathered to build grassroots communities of interest that are at least somewhat independent of the media images and one-way political propaganda that plague the existing mass information system. Government at all levels can be plugged into these networks through cable coverage of government proceedings (similar to C-SPAN coverage of Washington politics) and e-mail links between citizens and representatives. Indeed, many states have experiments underway with various multichannel communication links between citizens and their representatives. E-mail capabilities have sprouted all the way from the

White House and members of Congress to local governments. One booster of this trend claimed that the interactive television connection to government "can restore for viewers, and voters, the kind of direct connection that people had with their representatives in simpler times."[26]

Another observer of this electronic scene notes that enthusiasts have become so charmed with the possibilities of electronic democracy that they see it as a modern-day Athens on a mass scale:

> . . . a new technocratic version of the participatory dream has emerged. Instead of entering the Athenian assembly, people fulfill their obligations as citizens through new electronic devices that enable all citizens to express themselves on policy issues but also to play a direct role in deciding those issues. . . . Modern citizens sit in the Athenian assembly of their homes armed with laptop computers. . . . Technology overcomes the problems of complexity and size. Technology makes ancient Athens possible today.[27]

Yet critics warn of trouble in this electronic paradise. The warnings strike at the very core of democracy itself. Will great inequalities emerge between technological haves and have-nots? Will the private, personalized world of electronic democracy destroy what is left of the important idea of a public defined by face-to-face accountability and consensus on which stability, legitimacy, and power ultimately depend? In closing, let's consider some of the issues that await this brave new world of—dare we call it?—virtual democracy.

THE PERILS OF VIRTUAL DEMOCRACY

The personalized packaging of news described throughout this book and the computerized citizen just described may converge in the increasing isolation of people from one another. This isolation may be bred by choice, technology, or demographic circumstance. For example, people may choose to subscribe to information services tailored precisely to their needs, tastes, and interests. They may choose to go on-line only with others like themselves, forming virtual communities of people connected only by an electronic thread of hobby, political issue, religion, or other specialized interest.

Other citizens may become isolated because they lack home computers or the discretionary income to purchase specialized information that others can afford. Communication scholars Graham Murdock and Peter Golding warn that a two-class communication society is likely to develop, separating those with full electronic access from those without the means, the education, or the technological support systems to become full participants in the electronic dialogue.[28] This problem has become known as the "digital divide."

Another form of social isolation may emerge simply because of demographics (race, income, zip code, occupation): The magazines or newspapers to which people subscribe may make editorial choices for them, sending some articles to some groups and not to others. On this latter possibility, consider a comment by Patrick Reilly of the *Wall Street Journal:*

> It bothers me that *Time* and *Newsweek* are working furiously on selective bind-
> ing which, they say, will target ads and, more importantly, edit pages to an indi-
> vidual house or a row of houses. It's personally disappointing to read a story and
> sort of slap your head and go, "Wow! That was great!" and then realize that
> there are far fewer people slapping their head at the same time than there were
> last week because you're all getting a different story.[29]

Vibrant grassroots communication or egocentric musings from socially isolated individuals? The future of electronic democracy is wide open to the best and the worst
of possibilities.

The direction of electronic communication will be affected by the kind of public
debate that emerges about what to do with new technologies. An important look at the
prospects and perils of democracy in the Internet age is contained in *democracy.com*,
a book from Harvard's Kennedy School of Government project on "Visions of Governance for the Twenty-First Century."[30] Perhaps the greatest risk for the future of the
citizen's Internet is that many of the most important questions about Internet democracy may be answered before many people are even aware of them. How will the Internet be used? Will it become a vibrant place for citizens to gather, to form communities, and to work out new forms of government, or will the Internet become a virtual
shopping mall, dedicated overwhelmingly to consumption and entertainment, with little space for public life or political communication? These important issues are the
center of lively discussions currently on the Internet among concerned "netizens," but
they have received relatively little attention in the news. Readers may want to tune
into them by checking the listings on the author's Web site under "The Open Source
Movement and Governance of the Internet" (**faculty.washington.edu/bennett/**) and
at *The Center for Communication and Civic Engagement* (**www.engagedcitizen.org**)
in the section on Democracy and Internet Technology.

CORPORATE SOCIAL RESPONSIBILITY: A PLACE TO START

The digital future may lead democracy to new and previously unimagined heights. If
the disorganized forces of markets, politics, and public withdrawal are allowed to
have their way, however, future information systems on the Internet are no more likely
to address the needs of democracy than the current system does. Indeed, the possibility exists that corporate domination of the mass media will drive this digital democracy to the margins of society, to Web sites where virtual huddled masses grumble
about having little public space to gather, or few points of entry to a "shopping mall"
mass media dominated by commercial values. One place to start making room for an
information commons—one that maintains a presence in the commercial media where
larger audiences will continue to gather—is with a political campaign for giant media
corporations to be more socially responsible in their handling of their news divisions.

It is not unreasonable for private corporations to expect news divisions and local papers to turn profits. It is important, however, to urge those companies to settle for reasonable profits that do not drive news that motivates citizens out of the picture. Media companies once branded themselves around the prestige of their news divisions and expected those divisions to make less money than entertainment and sports. A return to the idea that news is a public trust would not seriously harm the bottom lines of giant corporations that do the majority of their business in entertainment programming. The corporate claim that their only responsibility is to their stockholders says that companies do not have to be good citizens. This bold assertion is valid only as long as silent leaders and silent majorities of citizens let it stand. The social and public responsibilities of media corporations today could become major political issues—if citizen engagement in a vibrant democracy is a public value that can be discussed alongside profits. A climate of public opinion that expects good citizenship from corporations would go a long way toward helping companies think about branding themselves around social values beyond profits. Who knows, social responsibility might even be profitable.

Where would such a climate of opinion start? Perhaps it is the time for citizens, public interest organizations, and policy foundations to voice a call for both corporations and government to act more responsibly with the national information system. Citizens who are concerned about the future of democracy are already using the power of personal digital communication media to organize citizen communication campaigns aimed at getting media companies to behave more responsibly. The reader might wish to consider these campaigns at places such as **www.mediareform.org**, **www.adbusters.org**, and **www.mediachannel.org**. Activists concerned about many other social and environmental issues have waged effective campaigns for corporate responsibility with regard to environmental protection, labor abuses, the proliferation of generically modified organisms, and human rights.[31] If critical citizens demand public accountability in the quality of their information environments, it just might be possible to design a communication system with democracy in mind.

NOTES

1. See Erik Asard and W. Lance Bennett, *Democracy and the Marketplace of Ideas: Communication and Government in Sweden and the United States.* (Cambridge University Press, 1997).
2. Robert McChesney, *Telecommunications, Mass Media, & Democracy: The Battle for Control of U.S. Broadcasting, 1928–1935* (New York: Oxford University Press, 1993).
3. Thomas E. Patterson, "Irony of the Free Press: Professional Journalism and News Diversity" (paper presented at the Annual meeting of the American Political Science Association, September 3–6, 1992, Chicago), 2.
4. Quoted from Frank Luther Mott, *The News in America* (Cambridge, MA: Harvard University Press, 1952), 5.
5. "Weighing Anchor: At the Start of His Final Year, Tom Brokaw Takes Stock and Looks Ahead," interview with Jane Hall, *Columbia Journalism Review* (January/February 2004): 19.

6. Brent Cunningham, "Re-Thinking Objectivity," *Columbia Journalism Review* (July/August 2003): 24.

7. Ibid.

8. Steven Livingston, *The Terrorism Spectacle* (Boulder, CO: Westview, 1994).

9. From Michael Isikoff, "A 'Sting' Tailor-Made for Bush," Washington Post News Service, reprinted in the *International Herald Tribune,* Saturday-Sunday edition, September 23–24, 1989, p. 4.

10. Maureen Dowd, "U.S. Presidential Road Show," the *International Herald Tribune,* September 26, 1989, p. 3 (from the *New York Times*).

11. Shanto Iyengar, *Is Anyone Responsible?* (Chicago: University of Chicago Press, 1993).

12. Regina G. Lawrence, "Game-Framing the Issues: Tracking the Strategy Frame in Public Policy News," *Political Communication* 17, no. 2 (April–June 2000): 93–115.

13. Mark R. Levy and John P. Robinson, "The 'Huh?' Factor: Untangling TV News," *Columbia Journalism Review* (July/August 1986): 48.

14. Ibid., 49.

15. Cunningham, "Re-Thinking Objectivity," 27.

16. Ibid., 50.

17. See Leonard Pratt, "The Circuitry of Protest," *Gannett Center Journal* 3 (1989): 105–115 and Donald R. Shanor, "The 'Hundred Flowers' of Tiananmen," *Gannett Center Journal* 3 (1989): 128–136.

18. McChesney, *Telecommunications, Mass Media & Democracy.*

19. Doug Underwood, "The Very Model of the Reader-Driven Newsroom?" *Columbia Journalism Review* (November/December 1993): 42.

20. Ibid.

21. See, for example, Richard Morin, "Thinking Before They Speak," the *Washington Post National Weekly Edition,* May 16–22, 1994, 37.

22. Ibid.

23. John Gastil, *By Popular Demand: Revitalizing Representative Democracy through Deliberative Election* (Berkeley: University of California Press, 2000).

24. Ibid. See also, James Fishkin, *Democracy and Deliberation* (New Haven, CT: Yale University Press, 1991).

25. See W. Lance Bennett, "Communicating Global Activism: Strengths and Vulnerabilities of Networked Politics," *Information, Communication & Society* (June 2003), 6:2, 143–168.

26. Daniel M. Weintraub, "The Technology Connection," *State Legislatures* (June 1993): 44.

27. Thomas W. Simon, "Electronic Inequality," *Bulletin of the Scientific Technology Society* 11 (1991): 144.

28. Graham Murdock and Peter Golding, "Information Poverty and Political Inequality: Citizenship in the Age of Privatized Communications," *Journal of Communication* 39 (Summer 1989): 180–193.

29. Quoted in the "Sound Bite" section, *Columbia Journalism Review* (July/August 1993): 13.

30. Elaine Ciulla Kamarck and Joseph S. Nye, Jr., eds., *democracy.com? Governance in a Networked World* (Hollis, NH: Hollis Publishing Company, 1999).

31. Naomi Klein, *No Logo.* New York: Picador/St.Martin's, 1999.

Index

A&E, 92
ABC, 13, 15, 19, 53, 76, 84, 88, 96, 99, 171
    child molester story, 91
    Cokie Roberts, 54
    crime news and, 24
    executive producer's memo to staff, 52
    KMGH affiliate, 21
    The Koppel Report: News from Earth, 86
    the pap smear story, 66–67
    Politically Incorrect and, 14–15
    PrimeTime, 66–67
    World News Sunday, 91
    *World News Tonight with Peter
        Jennings*, 16
Abortion, 4
Academy Awards, 84
Accuracy in Media (AIM), 28
Acheson, Dean, 114, 122
Action formats, 57
Action news, 57, 61–62
Action, Drama, and Suspense (CD), 93
Actor-centered narratives, 249
Adversarial reporting, 187
Adversarial role of press, 151–152, 188–191
    as ritual, 189–190
    tag team journalism, 190–191
Advertising, 83
    as news coverage, 138

Advertising Age, 93
"Adwatch" coverage, 176
Affect, 129
Affirmative action, 64–65
Afghanistan, 13, 14, 17, 18, 19, 124
Agenda setting, 7, 137
Agendas, 175–176
AIDS, 195
Ailes, Roger, 19, 79, 98–99, 160
AIM. *See* Accuracy in Media
Aircraft carrier landing story, 36–38, 133
    case study, 47–51
Airline bankruptcy story, 224
Al Jazeera, 17
All the President's Men (Woodward and
        Bernstein), 226
al Qaeda, 1–2, 13, 119, 120, 245
Alternative programming, 90
Altheide, David, 123
Amazon.com, 101
America Freaks Out!, 10
America Strikes Back, 10, 18
America's Most Wanted, 94, 106
America's New War, 18
American Newspaper Publishers
        Association, 80
American Society of Newspaper Editors, 82
Ananova, 104

Anderson, Benedict, 228
AOL, 18, 88, 101, 102
AOL Time Warner, 87
Armageddon, 92
Arnet, Peter, 17–18
Arthur Andersen, 115
Asiavision, 96
Associated Press (AP), 63, 97, 186
    civic journalism and, 69–70
Association of Newspaper Editors, 75
Attention deficit disorder case study,
    214–217
Audience trends, 84–85
Audio information, 213
Authenticity, creation of, 97
Authority-disorder bias, 42–44, 64–67,
    95, 152
    political costs of, 66–67
"Axis of Evil," 126

The Bachelor, 94
The Bachelorette, 94
Bagdikian, Ben, 87, 90, 180, 208
Baker, James, 123
Baker, Russell, 61
Balance, 182–183, 184
Baldasty, Gerald, 82, 185
Barnes and Noble, 101
Bartiromo, Maria, 79
Bartlett, Dan, 119
Batten, James, 80
Baum, Matthew, 11
Bay of Pigs (1961), 114, 115, 227
BBC. *See* British Broadcasting Corporation
Beats, 166
Beckham, Victoria, 104
Believability, 203
Belo Corp, 98
Bernstein, Carol, 192, 226
Bertelsmann, 82, 87
Bethell, Tom, 163
Bias, 25–30, 180, 236
    authority-disorder, 42–44, 64–67,
        95, 152
    dramatization, 40–42
    entertainment, 92
    fragmentation, 42
    kinds of, 37–44

as part of the political information
    system, 67
    personalization, 40, 51–55, 248–249
    of reporters, 26–28
    See also News bias
Biden, Joe, 16, 17
Bimber, Bruce, 5
bin Laden, Osama, 1–2, 13, 14, 17, 18,
    120, 244
Blair, Tony, 238
Blumler, Jay, 153
Boca Raton News, 80
Bonner, Ray, 144–145
Boorstin, Daniel, 133, 197
Bormann, Ernest, 230
Brand extensions, 86
Brand-building, 18
Branding, 98–100
British Broadcasting Corporation (BBC), 31,
    75, 82, 256
    News Desk, 63
Broadcast license holders, 253–254
Brokaw, Tom, 86, 242, 250
Brookings Institution, 158
Budget deficits, 249
Buffett, Warren, 78
Buffy the Vampire Slayer, 78
Bulgaria, 114
Bureaus, 167–168
Bush, George H. W., 98, 114–115, 163,
    169, 251
    campaigns of, 221
    news management style, 139
    war on drugs, 246–247
Bush, George W., 2, 10, 13, 15, 16, 26, 27,
    36–37, 47–51, 54, 115, 119–122, 133,
    134, 146, 152, 242
    "Axis of Evil," 126
    Iraq War, 127
    news management style, 140–141
    swagger case study, 47–51
Bush, Laura, 49
Butz, Earl, 194
Buzz words, 244
Byrd, Robert, 17

Cable license holders, 253–254
Campaign finance reforms, 252

Cannon, Lou, 188
Capitol Times, 194
Cappella, Joseph, 68
Card, Andrew, 122
Carey, Mariah, 78
Carpini, Michael Delli, 10, 126, 214
Carter, Hodding, 124
Carter, Jimmy, 55, 124, 137
    Iran hostage crisis, 169, 227
Case studies
    attention deficit disorder, 214–217
    citizen input in the news, 254–255
    demographics, 78–82
    George W. Bush's swagger, 47–51
    Iraq War, 119–122, 156–160
    objective journalism, 185–188
    terrorism, 13–20
Cassidy, John, 78
Castro, Fidel, 114
CBS, 76–77, 84, 88, 93, 97, 122, 138–139,
        176, 230
    crime news and, 24
    60 Minutes, 85, 93, 140, 215
    Viacom and, 76–78
CBS Evening News, 63, 100
Censorship, 17, 18, 19, 92
    corporate news, 90–92
Censorship campaign, 14
Center for Media and Public Affairs, 11,
        24, 176
Central Intelligence Agency (CIA), 1,
        115, 119
Cesno, Frank, 167
Challenger, 13
Chandler, Otis, 101
Cheney, Dick, 2, 120, 122
Chile, 115
China, 91, 114–115
    relations with U.S., 251
Chomsky, Noam, 28
Chung, Connie, 84
Churchill, Winston, 113–114
CIA. *See* Central Intelligence Agency
Citizen information, 7
    news, public opinion, and, 210
Citizen-candidate exchanges, 252
Citizens
    decoding the news, 243–248
    dilemma of, 210–211

discouraged, news bias and, 68–69
information, politics, and, 232–233
input in the news, 255–257
input in the news case study, 254–255
learning to become self-critical, 247–248
looking for information that doesn't fit the
    plot, 245
news myth and, 242–243
partisanship and, 245–246
recognizing spin and news control,
    246–247
recognizing stereotypes and plot formulas,
    244–245
Civic disengagement, 5, 38
Civic (public) journalism, 69, 103, 255
Clarke, Richard, 120
Clift, Eleanor, 171
Clinton, Bill, 27, 40, 52, 88, 142, 190, 251
    feeding frenzy of press, 169, 170–172
    health care reform battle, 220
    impeachment, 12, 93, 225
    Monica Lewinsky sex scandal and, 8, 10,
        12, 45, 115, 126, 128, 172, 193,
        227–228
    New Beginnings, 126
    news management style, 139–140
    personalization bias and, 54
    popularity of, 230–231
    press relations, 143, 144, 163, 191
    Waco, Texas cult, 171
    welfare reform and, 126
Clinton, Hillary, 63, 190
Clooney, George, 86–87
Clusters, 61–62
CNBC, 78, 79, 85
CNBC Asia, 91
CNN, 17, 18, 84–85, 88, 92, 98, 100, 101,
        115, 122, 167
    pollster William Schneider, 12
    "Strike Against Iraq," 92
    "Strike Against Kosovo," 92
CNNfn, 101
CNN Headline News, 98
Coca Cola, 224
Code of professional ethics, 27
Cognitive effects, 129
Collateral damage, 130
Columbia Journalism Review, 76, 87, 242
Comedians, 10

Comedy Central, 10, 76, 78
Comedy monologues, 10
Commercial Press, 82
Commercialized information, 102–103
Communication, evolving form of, 59
Communication mobilization models,
    257–258
Comprehensiveness, 182
Condensational symbols, 129, 130
Congress, 129
    media coverage of, 56–57
Consolidation, 88
Constitution, 21
Consumer-driven news, 79, 102–103
Consumer-driven newsroom, 255–256
Consumer-oriented newspapers, 79–81
Controlling the news, 133–136
    partially controlled situations,
        134–136
    pseudo-events (fully controlled situations),
        133–134
    uncontrolled situations, 136
Cook, Timothy, 11, 57, 161
Cops, 106
Corporate influence, on news, 100–101
Corporate news censorship, 90–92
Corporate profit, news content and,
    76–78
Corporate social responsibility, 260–261
Cosby, Bill, 23
Costas, Bob, 91
Council on Foreign Relations, 16
Countdown, 37
Cranberg, Gilbert, 80
Credibility, of messages, 125, 127–128
Crigler, Ann, 126, 211
Crime and disaster stories, 23
Crime bill coverage, 246
Crime, fear and, 59–60
Crime news, 8, 22
    on-the-scene example of, 43
Crises, 4, 41
Crisis cycle, 41
Critical watchdog journalism, 65
Cronkite, Walter, 77
Cross-branding, 86
Crouse, Timothy, 168
C-SPAN, 87, 90, 252, 254, 258

Cues, 217, 218–219
Curiosity, as reason to follow news, 222,
    223–225
A Current Affair, 98
Cyber-age citizens, 9
Cynicism, in the news, 43

Dahl, Robert, 7
The Daily Show with Jon Stewart, 10, 11, 49,
    78, 119
Damage control, 131–136
Darnton, Robert, 57, 199
Daschle, Tom, 17
Dateline NBC, 53, 215
Dean, Howard, 6, 9, 146, 152, 158, 211, 257
Dean, John, 136
Deaver, Michael, 47, 124, 137
Debates, 252
Decency and good taste standards, 193–196
    morality police, 193–195
    sex, death, and censorship, 195–196
Decoding the news, 243–254
Deep Throat, 192
Defense Department, 124
    budget of, 128
DeGeneres, Ellen, 23
DeLay, Tom, 17, 121
DeLillo, Don, 58–59
Democracy
    desktop, 258
    ideals of, 4
    Internet Web site, 255
    news and, 3, 20
    news that would better serve, 30–31
    personalized information and, 105–107
    political information system and, 1–31
    vs. economics, 83–86
    virtual, 105–107, 259–260
    without citizens, 176–177
Demographics, 77, 87
    case study, 78–82
Dennis, Everette, 28, 103
Des Moines Register, 194
Desktop democracy, 258–259
Detachment, 184
Diamond, Edwin, 61, 202
Diana, Princess of Wales, 23, 40

Didion, Joan, 45
Digital information age, 5, 7
Disillusion, 114
Disney, 76, 87, 88, 91, 92, 96
Disorder, manufactured, 65
Docudramas, 94, 226
Documentary report, 187
Documentary reporting practices, 184,
    196–197
Donaldson, Sam, 138, 171
Dowd, Maureen, 15, 48–49, 172
Dramatic stories, 11
Dramatization bias, 40–42, 55–60,
    248–249
    political costs of, 58–60
    scripts written by journalists and, 57–58
Dramaturgy, 58
Drudge Report, 14
Drudge, Matt, 19
Drug Enforcement Administration, 247
Dukakis, Michael, 221

E!, 11
Economics, 103–105
    vs. democracy, 83–86
Edelman, Murray, 42, 123
Editorial review, 185, 201–202
Eisenhower, Dwight, 114
Eisner, Michael, 91
El Pais, 82
El Salvador, reporting about, 144–145
Election coverage, 46
Elections, personalization bias and, 54
Electronic countermeasures, 250
Elites, 155, 160, 240
Ellsberg, Daniel, 136
Emotionalism, 58
Emotions, 218, 220–221
Enron Corporation, 115, 201
Entertainment, as reason to follow news, 220,
    225–228
Entertainment bias, 92
Entertainment news, 10
Entman, Robert, 64, 127, 176
Ephron, Nora, 36
Episodic news, 46–47
Equal time, 183

ER, 92
Escape, as reason to follow news, 220,
    225–228
Ethics
    code of, 27
    Society of Professional Journalists' code of
        ethics, 182
Ethnocentricity, 55, 158
Eurovision, 96

Face the Nation, 122
Factoids, 218, 219–220
Factual claims, 245–246
Factual misperception, 2
FAIR. *See* Fairness and Accuracy in Reporting
Fairness, 182–183
Fairness and Accuracy in Reporting
    (FAIR), 28
Familiar information, 9
Fantasies, 230
Farah, Barbara, 221
FCC. *See* Federal Communications
    Commission
Fear, crime and, 60
Fear Factor, 94
Federal Communications Commission (FCC),
    21, 88–89, 95, 252–253
Federal Express, 15
The Federalist, 5
Feeding frenzies, 118, 221, 141, 170–172
Feelings, 220–221
First Amendment, 21
Fishkin, James, 105, 256–257
Fishman, Mark, 169
Fleischer, Ari, 15, 141
Focus groups, 79, 128
Foo Fighters, 78
Foote, Joe, 143
Ford Foundation, 102
Ford, Gerald, 114, 136
Formula reporting, 162, 165–166
FOX, 14, 17, 18–19, 27–28, 79, 84, 88, 90,
    93, 94, 98, 99, 100, 142, 216
    Cable News, 215
    entertainment focus of news, 93
    reality TV, 95
    support of Iraq War, 159–160

Fragmentation bias, 42, 49–50, 60–64
  political costs of, 62–64
Fragmented audiences, 82, 84–86
Framing, 37–38, 51, 117, 125, 213–214
  of messages, 125, 128
  See also Message framing
Frankfurter Allgemaine Zeitung, 82
Frasier, 84
Free enterprise, 240
Free press, 76
  irony of, 239
Free press myth, 241–243
  citizens and, 242–243
  journalists and, 241–242
  politicians and, 241
Free speech, 21, 154
  good information and, 20–21
Freedom of the market, 83
Freeway chases, 95
Friendly fire, 130

Gallup, 227
Gamson, William, 4, 212, 232
Gannett Newspaper Group, 81, 88, 100, 256
Gans, Herbert, 153
Gastil, John, 257
Gatekeeping, 8, 11
  defined, 3–4
  new, 10–11, 14
  who and what makes the news, 3–5
General Electric, 76, 83, 86, 88, 91, 92,
    96, 100
Generalists, 185, 199–201
Generational divide, 85
Generic news, 96–98
Gerbner, George, 92, 94
Gergen, David, 135, 137, 140, 143–144
Gingrich, Newt, 27
Ginsberg, Ruth Bader, 190
Gitlin, Todd, 107
Going public, 5, 137, 140
Goldberg, Lucianne, 45
Goldenberg, Edie, 118
Golding, Peter, 236, 259
Goldstein, Steve, 163–164
Good taste standards. *See* Decency and good
    taste standards
Good Will Hunting, 91
Gore, Al, 10, 54, 146, 152

"Gotcha" journalism, 152, 165, 184, 192, 203
Government, 251–254
  newsmaking and, 145–147
  quality of and public information, 1–2
  See also Politicians
Government spending, 43–44
Graber, Doris, 8–9, 126, 212, 213, 214
Gramm-Rudman Act, 250
Grassroots opinion, 239
Grassroots organizations, 118
Gravitas, 158
"The Great Communicator" (Reagan), 27,
    54, 138
Great Society, 126
Greece, 114
Greenberg, Stanley, 220
Greenfield, Jeff, 92
Greenfield, Meg, 140
Greenspan, Alan, 78
Greider, William, 191
Grove, Andrew, 75
Gulf of Tonkin, 115
Gulf War. *See* Persian Gulf War
Gurevitch, Michael, 153

Habermas, Jurgen, 107
Haig, Alexander, 142
Haiti, 167
Haltom, William, 66
Hamilton, James, 214, 215
Hannity, Sean, 99
Hard news, 7, 116, 151
  vs. soft news, 22–25
Hardball, 37, 190
Harper's, 57
HarperCollins Publishers, 88
Harris, Jay, 81–82
Hart, Gary, 169
Hart, Roderick, 208
Harvard, 260
Hastert, Dennis, 16
Hawkins, Taylor, 78
Health care coverage story, 95
Health care debate of 1990s, 62–63, 219–220
Henriques, Diana, 201
Herman, Edward, 28
Hersh, Seymour, 157
Hertsgaard, Mark, 63, 137
Hess, Stephen, 56, 169

Hickey, Neil, 99, 102–103
Hinton, Deane, 144
Historical conflicts, 64–65
"The Home Team," 98
Human-interest stories, 22–25
Human rights, 250–251
Hume, Brit, 17, 99, 142
Hume, Ellen, 163
Hungary, 114
Hunt for Red October, 92
Hussein, Saddam, 1–2, 17, 119–122, 245
Hutchins Commission, 29

iCan, 256
Ideological bias, 39
    of reporters, 26–28
Illusion
    politicians creating, 118
    politics of, 114–116
Imagemaking, 125–131. *See also* Symbols
In Style, 86
Inaugurations, 229–230
Incremental news coverage, 100
Independence, 154
Independent Media Network, 102
Independent Television News (ITN), 96
Indexing, 4, 16, 155, 191
Infinity Broadcasting Corporation, 76, 88
Information
    citizens, politics, and, 232–233
    free speech and, 20–21
    quality of, 3
Information processing, 208–233. *See also*
        Public opinion
Information system, news as democratic, 5–6
Information trends, 89–100
Informed sources, 244
Infotainment, 23, 89, 92–98
    local TV news, 95
    reality TV, 94–95
    TV news magazines, 93–94
Insider syndrome, 163–165
Insiderism, 151, 163, 164
Intel, 75
International news, 8, 23
    decline of, 77
Internet, 3, 85, 216, 245, 257, 260
    democracy web site, 255
    generic news and, 97–98

vs. mass media, 211
Monica Lewinsky–Bill Clinton sex scandal
    and, 8
news on, 101–102, 104
political communication and, 9
September 11 terrorist attacks coverage
    and, 6
See also Web sites; World Wide Web
Internet age, 5–6
Intimidation, 144–145, 156
Inverted pyramid writing style, 184, 185
Investigative reporting, 181
Iran
    "axis of evil," 16
    hostage crisis, 55, 169, 227
Iraq War, 1–2, 19, 38, 147, 155, 242
    "axis of evil," 16
    case study of, 119–122, 156–160
Isikoff, Michael, 45
Iyengar, Shanto, 46–47

Jackson, Andrew, 5
Jackson, Jesse, 152
Jacobs, Lawrence, 132
Jamieson, Kathleen, 62–63, 68
Jefferson, Thomas, 29, 236, 241
Jennings, Peter, 11, 13, 15, 138
Jewel, 23
Jingo-journalism, 159
Johnson, Lyndon, 115, 136, 171
    Great Society, 126
    Gulf of Tonkin and, 115
    Vietnam War and, 169
Jones, Paula, 227
Journalism standards, 184–185
Journalists, 7–8
    decoding the news, 248–251
    defining situations in ordinary terms, 250
    explaining why the story matters, 250–251
    news myth and, 241–242
    resisting standard plot formulas, 249–250
    and their profession, 181
    using knowledge, 249
Just, Marion, 126, 211

KAKE, 175
Kalb, Marvin, 12, 82
Kansas City Star, 80

KARE, 175
Katz, Jon, 84
Keeter, Scott, 214
Kelly, J. Michael, 18
Kempton, Murray, 163
Kennedy School of Government, 260
Kennedy, John F., 114, 115
    Bay of Pigs, 227
    New Frontier, 126
    Vietnam and, 115
Kennedy, John F., Jr., 40, 167
Kennedy, Ted, 121
Kernell, Samuel, 137
Kerry, John, 158
K-EYE, 175
KING-5 TV, 98
Kissinger, Henry, 163
Klein, Ethel, 221
Klite, Paul, 20
KMGH, 21
Knight Ridder, 79, 100
Knowledge, 249
The Koppel Report: News from Earth, 86
Koppel, Ted, 86
Koresh, David, 171
Kovach, Bill, 1
Krauthammer, Charles, 15
Kucinich, Dennis, 158
Kumar, Martha, 141
Kurtz, Howard, 172
Kuwait, 161, 195
KVUE-TV, 174

Labels, 217
Lapham, Lewis, 57, 151
Larry King Live, 84
Late Edition, 122
Lawrence, Regina, 249
Lazare, Daniel, 24
Le Monde, 82
Leaks, 135–136
Learned helplessness, 243
Legislation, 252
Lelyveld, Joseph, 45–46, 97
Leno, Jay, 10, 11
Letterman, David, 26, 164
Lewinsky, Monica, Bill Clinton sex scandal
    and, 8, 10, 12, 45, 115, 126, 128, 172,
    193, 227–228

Liberal press, stereotype of, 25, 28
Life: The Movie, 226
Limbaugh, Rush, 13, 14, 15, 98
Lippmann, Walter, 122, 188, 226
Livingston, Steven, 56, 245
Loaded descriptions, 244
Local report, 43
Local TV news, 88, 95, 174–175
Lockheed Martin Corporation, 132
Logo campaigns, 224
Los Angeles Times, 16, 43–44, 101, 171
Lott, Trent, 17

MacKuen, Michael, 221
Madonna, 86–87
Magazines, 213
Magid, Frank, 57
Maher, Bill, 10, 14–15
Mail (U.S. Postal) system, 5
Maltese, John Anthony, 136
Manheim, Jarol, 128
Marcus, George, 221
Marcus, Ruth, 171
Market research, 128
Marketing, of news, 79–81
Marketplace of ideas, 237
Markets, news and, 173–174
Mass media, 5
    fragmented audience and, 82, 84–86
    Mayhem Index, 20–21
    vs. Internet, 211
Matthews, Chris, 37, 190
The Maury Povich Show, 98
Mayhem Index, 20–21
Mayhem stories, 43, 68, 174
McCann, Michael, 66
McChesney, Robert, 83, 89, 238, 253
McCurry, Mike, 172
McDonald's, 9, 224
    hot coffee case, 66
McHugh, Philip, 51–52
McManus, Doyle, 16
McMullen, William, 247
Media, society and, 105
"Media Buzz," 11–12
Media Channel, 76
Media elite, 163–164
Media logic, 123
Media mall, 82

Media managers, 54
Media mergers, 23, 75, 76–78
Media monopolies, 86–87
    controlling, 252–253
    effects of, 89–100
Media Monopoly (Bagdikian), 87
Media ownership, 237
Media reform, 175–176, 252
Media Research Council, 14, 16, 17
Media Watch, 20–21
Mediated government, 11–13
Meet the Press, 122
Melodramas, 41. *See also* Bias;
    Dramatization
Mergers, 75, 76–78. *See also* Media
    corporations
Mess O'Potamia, 10
Message credibility, 125, 127–128
Message *du jour*, 127
Message framing, 125, 128
Message salience, 125, 126–127
Message shaping, 125, 126
Meta-narrative, 177
Mexico, North-South economic summit
    in, 142
MIA. *See* Missing in action
Micro media, 6
Microsoft, 9
Middle media, 6
Military, as news managers, 124
Mill, John Stewart, 237
Mindich, David, 182, 184, 185–186
Miramax Company, 91
Missing in action (MIA), 130
Monopoly, in media, 87
Monroe, Alan, 132
Monsanto, 9
Morality police, 193–195
Morris, Dick, 113, 176
Moscow meeting of Allied powers,
    113–114
MSNBC, 18, 36–37, 85, 98, 100, 190
MTV, 76, 140
Mudd, Roger, 192
Multimedia Entertainment, 88
Murder, 57
Murdoch, Rupert, 82, 88, 90, 98, 99, 160
Murdock, Graham, 236, 259
Murrow, Edward R., 77
Music, news programs and, 92–93

National Public Radio (NPR), 54, 75, 100,
    215, 255
NBC, 76, 83, 84, 85–86, 88, 92, 96, 98, 122,
    123, 192, 200
    China and, 91
    crime news and, 24
    Today, 52
NBC Asia, 91
NBC Nightly News, 92
Negativity, in the news, 25, 43, 153, 221
Neiman Marcus, 132
Network news, decline in ratings of, 84
Network TV, 23
Neuman, Russell, 126, 211, 221
Neutrality, 17, 19, 45
New Beginnings, 126
New cynicism, 197
New Deal, 126
New Federalism, 126
New Frontier, 126
"New news," 82, 203
New Nixon, 126
New World Communications, 88
New York Daily News, 196
New York Post, 14
The New York Times, 15, 46, 48–49, 50, 53,
    69, 77, 82, 84, 97, 100, 116–117, 122,
    144–145, 152, 158, 168, 172, 194, 196,
    201, 202
The New Yorker, 15, 157
News
    branding, 98–100
    cable TV, 78–79
    changes in, 25–26
    citizen information, public opinion,
        and, 210
    corporate censorship, 90–92
    corporate influence on, 100–101
    definition of, 9
    democracy and, 3, 20
    as democratic information system, 5–6
    episodic vs. thematic, 46–47
    generic, 96–98
    hard, 7
    hard vs. soft, 22–25
    on the Internet, 101–102
    marketing of, 79–81
    markets and, 173–174
    negativity in, 25
    officialized, 118–119

as patriotic drama and as branding process, 18–19
  political economy of, 82
  popular subjects in, 8
  power and, in America, 239–240
  prepackaged, 131–133
  processing, 211–213
  public relations and, 168
  self-advertising as, 90–92
  soft, 22–25, 92–98
  standardization of, 44–45
  trusted sources rankings, 117
  virtual, 104–105
News bias
  discouraged citizens and, 68–69
  ideological bias of reporters, 26–28
  myths about, 25–30
  press-government relations and, 124
  professional practices and, 188
  reporting practices and, 161
  See also Bias
News content
  corporate profit logic and, 76–78
  importance of, 210
News control, 246–247
News Corporation, 82, 87, 88
News cycles, 27
News Desk, 63
News doctors, 57, 173–174
News dramas, 41, 225
News frames, 213–214
News hole, 166
News Hour with Jim Lehrer (PBS), 100, 173, 215, 216
News icons, 13
News images, 122–123
News magazines (TV), 66, 93–94
News management, 115, 128
  expense of, 252
News management styles, 136–141
  Bill Clinton, 139–140
  George H. W. Bush, 139
  George W. Bush, 140–141
  Ronald Reagan, 137–139
News myth. *See* Free press myth
News organizations, 4, 7–8, 165–168
News plots, 198–199
News process, 6

News sources, 116–117
News Watch, 99
News wholesalers, 96–97
"News you can use," 7, 86
Newspaper industry, 75
Newspapers, 23, 100–101, 213
  consumer-oriented, 79–80
  future of, 75–76
  political stories and, 116–117
Newsweek, 10, 23, 45, 158, 171, 259
NGOs. *See* Nongovernmental organizations
Niche media, 82
Niche news, 77
Nickelodeon, 76
Nielsen Media Research, 83, 93, 132
Nike, 9, 98
Nixon, Richard, 28, 113, 171, 224, 227
  death of, 144
  "new Nixon," 126
  pardon of, 114
  press relations and, 163, 191
  pseudo-events and, 134
  Thanksgiving with Vietnam vets, 134
  Vietnam War and, 130, 134
  Watergate and, 136, 137, 169, 191–192, 199
Nongovernmental organizations (NGOs), 102
Nonpartisanship, 184
North Korea, 16–17
  "Axis of Evil," 16
NPR. *See* National Public Radio

O'Neill, Paul, 120, 156
Objective journalism, 239
  case study, 185–188
Objectivity, 19, 45, 99, 154, 180–204
  defining, 182–183
  obstacles to, 182
  origins of, 184–185
  reconsidered, 202–204
  truth and, 30
Observer-centered narratives, 249
Official sources, 244
Officialized news, 118–119
Officials, reporters and, 162, 165–168, 191
Olberman, Keith, 36–37
Oligopoly, 87

Olympian, 81, 256
Online Journalism Review, 87
Oprah, 106
Organizational routines, 153, 173–174
Orr, C. Jack, 189–190
Ownership consolidation, 23
Ozzie and Harriet, 91–92

Pack journalism, 168–170
Packaged information, 7
Packaging the news, 98
Pakistan, 16
Paletz, David, 127
Paley, William S., 77
Palmer, Shelly, 92
Panama invasion, 124
Paramount, 76
Parasocial relationships, 230
Partisanship, 28–30, 245–246
Patriotism campaign, 14–17
Patterson, Thomas, 11, 22, 23, 151, 153, 154, 211–212, 239
Patton, 92
PBS, 84, 100, 173, 215, 216
Pearl Harbor, 115
Pentagon, 13–20
People en Español, 876
People, 49, 86–87
Persian Gulf War, 17, 18, 124, 146–147, 155, 195
Personal news experience, 217–221
    factoids, 218, 219–220
    feelings and emotions, 218, 220–221
    interpretive cues, 218–219
    new information and, 218, 221
Personalization bias, 40, 51–55, 248–249
    political costs of, 55
    the presidency and, 53–54
    welfare reform example, 52–53
Personalized information and, 105–107
Pew Research Center for the People & the Press, 25, 63, 69, 106, 182, 214, 231, 250
Pfizer, 132
Philadelphia Inquirer, 163
Plot formulas, 226, 244–245, 249–250
    importance of, 250–251

Plot outlines, 162
Pocket Books, 76
Poland, 113
Political actors, 7
    press and, 6–7
Political communication
    core elements of, 103–105
    goals of, 125–128
    news images as, 122–123
Political images, 123
    controlling, 125
Political learning, 213–214
Political news, 8
    sources of, 116–119
Political themes, 126
Politically Incorrect, 14–15
Politicians
    controlling media monopolies, 252–253
    debates and legislation, 252
    decoding the news, 251–254
    limiting the flow of money, 252
    news myth and, 241
    press and, 6–9
    press relations and, 164–165
    providing funding for public broadcasting, 253
    strengthening public service requirements for cable and broadcast license holders, 253–254
Politics
    citizens, information, and, 232–233
    generational rejection of, 209
Polling, 128
Polls, 132–133
Popkin, Samuel, 222
Powell, Colin, 17, 124
Powell, Michael, 89
Power, 55, 163
    ideal vs. reality, 239–240
    in the media age, 54
    news and, in America, 239–240
Prepackaged news stories, 131–133
Presidential press conferences study, 189–190
Press, 7–8
    as gatekeeper, 10
    politicians and, 6–9
Press bias, 16
Press conferences, 134–135

Press fairness, 25
Press-government relations, news bias
  and, 124
Press pack, 26
Press police, 14
Press-politics, 12
Press relations, 142–145
PrimeTime, 66–67
Private-affair frame, 128
Private media system, 237–238
Processing the news, 211–213
Professional journalism standards, 184–185
Professional norms, 153–154
Profit-driven press, 7–9. *See also* Media
  corporations
Project for Excellence in Journalism
  (Columbia University), 175
Protective reaction strikes, 129
Pseudo-events, 133, 197
Psychological adjustments, 222, 228–231
Public (civic) journalism, 69
Public agenda, 7
Public broadcasting, 238
  funding for, 253
Public Broadcasting Service, 75
Public Citizen Channel, 253
Public information, affecting quality of
  government, 3
Public information cycle, 68
Public opinion, 122, 208–233
  news, citizen information, and, 210
  See also Information processing
Public relations, 129, 168
Public service, 90
Public service requirements, 253
Public sphere, 107–108
Publics, formation of, 210
Putnam, Robert D., 208, 209

Quality reporting, 154–155

Racism, 194
Radio, 213
Ralph Lauren, 105
Rather, Dan, 26, 63, 74, 77, 93
Ratings, 83–84
  decline of TV network news, 84

  rating point, 83
Ready-made news, 124
Reagan, Ronald, 26–28, 47, 52, 98, 123,
  124, 135
  budget and, 114, 135
  El Salvador and, 144
  favorable press coverage of, 26
  inaugural address, 229–230
  New Federalism, 126
  news management style, 137–139
  North-South economic summit in
    Mexico, 142
  personalizing the presidency, 53–54
  press management style, 142–144
  war on crime, 246
Reaganomics, 114
Realism, 225–226
Reality programs, 24
Reality TV, 94
Rebranding, 77
Referential symbols, 129, 130
Reilly, Patrick, 259
Relax or Die (CD), 93
Reliance on facts, 184
Reno, Janet, 99
Reporters
  bias and, 26–28
  as generalists, 199–201
  officials and, 162, 165–168, 191
  as a pack, 168–170
  Washington, 163–165
Reuters, 97
Rice, Condaleeza, 17, 122
Rights of passage, 250
Roberts, Cokie, 54
Rockefeller Foundation, 102
Rockefeller, Jay, 147
Rocky Mountain Media Watch, 20–21
Rogich, Sid, 139
Rolling Stone, 84, 191, 194
Romania, 114
Roosevelt, Franklin Delano, 113
  attack on Pearl Harbor, 115
  New Deal, 126
Rosenblum, Mort, 63
Rosenstiel, Tom, 1
Rosenthal, Abe, 144
Routines, 153–155, 173–174
  quality reporting and, 154–155